RUSKIN'S LETTERS

FROM VENICE

1851-1852

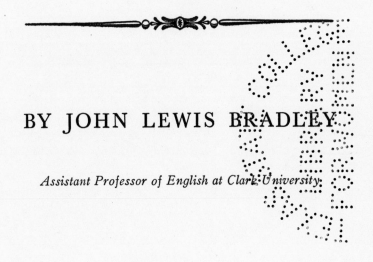

BY JOHN LEWIS BRADLEY

Assistant Professor of English at Clark University

NEW HAVEN: YALE UNIVERSITY PRESS, 1955

London: Geoffrey Cumberlege, Oxford University Press

LIBRARY OF CONGRESS CATALOG CARD NUMBER: 55-9436

YALE STUDIES IN ENGLISH

Benjamin Christie Nangle, Editor

VOLUME 129

Published on the Foundation established
in memory of Philip Hamilton McMillan
of the class of 1894, Yale College

The Philip Hamilton McMillan Memorial Publication Fund

The present volume is the 43d work published by the Yale University Press on the Philip Hamilton McMillan Memorial Publication Fund. This Foundation was established December 12, 1922, by a gift to Yale University in pursuance of a pledge announced on Alumni University Day in February, 1922, of a fund of $100,000 bequeathed to James Thayer McMillan and Alexis Caswell Angell, as Trustees, by Mrs. Elizabeth Anderson McMillan, of Detroit, to be devoted by them to the establishment of a memorial in honor of her husband.

He was born in Detroit, Michigan, December 28, 1872, prepared for college at Phillips Academy, Andover, and was graduated from Yale in the Class of 1894. As an undergraduate he was a leader in many of the college activities of his day, and within a brief period of his graduation was called upon to assume heavy responsibilities in the management and direction of numerous business enterprises in Detroit, where he was also a Trustee of the Young Men's Christian Association and of Grace Hospital. His untimely death, from heart disease, on October 4, 1919, deprived his city of one of its leading citizens and his University of one of its most loyal sons.

To the memory of my Father

CONTENTS

CONTENTS

INTRODUCTION

I

JOHN RUSKIN cannot be counted among the great letter writers of
the English tradition of Gray, Walpole, Lamb, and Byron. He lacks
the restraint and devotion to the letter as a form of literature of the first
three, and he lacks the *élan* and attack that made Byron's letters excellent reading. Rather, he sweeps rapidly from one subject to the next,
seldom pausing to find the perfect word or phrase. His mind teemed
with too many activities to permit hesitation over the niceties of letter
writing. Moreover, his high-strung nature, sensitive to the spiritual and
intellectual ferment of his age, was not prone to calculated reflection.
Ruskin belonged to an era which, in contrast to the eighteenth century,
was groping for a new code of life and conduct in a troubled time. The
nature of his letters reflects the complexities, paradoxes, and uncertain-
ties of nineteenth-century thought.

Although the letters assembled in the present volume do not possess
outstanding literary quality, they do have considerable biographical
interest. They are daily letters from Ruskin to his father, written from
Venice in 1851–52, at the time when the second and third volumes of
The Stones of Venice were in preparation. Indeed, these letters form a
sort of diary of Ruskin's activities and thoughts, sent to his eager parents in London. Cook and Wedderburn consulted them in the preparation of their definitive edition of Ruskin,[1] but most of them have never
been published before, and their full publication is essential to a definitive biography. Because so much of Ruskin's voluminous correspondence has been inaccessible to scholars, the biographies of the great
arbiter of nineteenth-century taste have often been unbalanced studies,
emphasizing one phase or another of his varied life. In most of the
nineteenth-century studies it was Ruskin the aesthete and social reformer who received greatest attention. And because of the impact he
had upon his age the treatment was usually reverential. In twentieth-
century studies Ruskin is frequently treated as a psychological enigma, a
frustrated lover whose sexual life is to be inspected under the merciless
glare of the Freudian spotlight. To do full justice to John Ruskin's life
and character it is imperative that his letters be edited fully and dispas-
sionately as a sound basis for future biography. The purpose of the

1. The Library Edition of *The Works of Ruskin,* ed. E. T. Cook and Alexander
Wedderburn, 39 vols. (London, Allen, 1903–12). Hereafter referred to as *Works.*

present collection is to do that service for Ruskin at a critical period of
his life.

The Ruskin who appears in the letters of this volume is a harassed
and pathetic young man. In 1851 he was thirty-two years old and had
traveled to Venice with his wife. Though separated from his parents, he
is still dependent upon them for sympathy and encouragement in his
work. We see him in the daily compilation of his great work, concerned
with Venetian society and with the tides of the Adriatic, with literary
criticism and with artistic and literary figures of the past and present.
He is deeply troubled about the Italian political situation, the state of
his religion, and the condition of his health, about which he writes at
great length. An event of special significance recorded in these letters
is the news of Turner's death; all Ruskin's veneration for genius is apparent in his feelings on this occasion. The emotional situation between
the older Ruskins and their son and daughter-in-law is evident.

Of considerable interest is the degree of intimacy between Ruskin and
his parents. In 1851–52 there existed still that closeness of contact
which was not to be subjected to great strain until the younger Ruskin
began in the late fifties to develop deeper interests in the political, economic, and social affairs of England. But in these letters disagreements
begin to occur between Ruskin and his father. John James Ruskin,
honest merchant that he was, was often bewildered by his son's opinions
upon current public topics, and we see Ruskin frequently attempting to
allay his father's fears after he has sent his parent a letter that is radical
in tone. Generally, in 1851–52, the son defers to his father's judgment
in economic and political questions, but as the years passed this defer-
ence decreased. The signs of a future breach, faintly evident in the
forties, are painfully apparent in the correspondence of 1851–52.

2

There are approximately 25 volumes of Ruskin's correspondence in
print. Among the significant collections are those edited by Cook and
Wedderburn and incorporated into the *Works; Hortus Inclusus; The
Letters of John Ruskin to Charles Eliot Norton; John Ruskin's Letters
to Francesca and Memoirs of the Alexanders;* and *John Ruskin and
Effie Gray.* Each of these collections is deserving of comment.

By far the greatest number of Ruskin's letters are in the *Works.*
Cook and Wedderburn use correspondence frequently to illustrate various points in their informative introductions; and they quote, either
fully or in part, from individual letters when clarifying problems in the
text of Ruskin's writings. In almost every case, their procedure is helpful in the elucidation and comprehension of Ruskin's work.

Apart from the correspondence dispersed through the *Works,* the editors devote two sturdy volumes [2] completely to Ruskin's letters. These are chronologically arranged and cover the years 1827–93. They form, in broad outline, an "epistolary autobiography." They were selected on the basis of biographical significance, "intrinsic interest," and incidental interest, the last group including casual critical opinions, brief reflections on diverse subjects, and some observations on prominent persons of the time. At the beginning of each volume there is a list of recipients whose friendships with Ruskin are carefully traced by the editors. Of special interest is the treatment accorded Ruskin's relations with his father.

Many of the letters in the two volumes are personal. One frequently sees Ruskin reaching out for friendship here or there. Evident, too, are his didacticism, his hastiness, his solicitude, his affection and generosity, his artistic, literary, economic, and political judgments. The sexual side of Ruskin, as expected, is undisclosed; very little is revealed by the editors about those strange friendships with young women so many years his junior. If mentioned at all, the subject is treated with considerable decorum.

This scrupulously edited work, whose annotations and footnotes are of inestimable value to the Victorian scholar and lay reader, includes, however, no group of letters so detailed, unified, and compact as the 1851–52 correspondence. No brief period is covered intensively so that a reader comes to know intimately the relationship between Ruskin and any one of the people to whom he wrote. Such an undertaking is, of course, not possible within the scope of the *Works;* neither is it intended. Nevertheless, for a full knowledge of Ruskin, his letters need the detailed editing and integrated presentation given during recent years, for example, to Walpole's letters. But the scholarly achievement of Cook and Wedderburn in these two volumes stands as a monument to sound editorial procedure.

Yet another large segment of Ruskin's letters is included in the *Works*. A section in the thirty-fourth volume is devoted to *Arrows of the Chace* [3] which was first published, independently, in 1880 and then revised and enlarged for inclusion in the *Works*. *Arrows* is a collection of Ruskin's letters to the press written, according to the author, "with fully provoked zeal." They contain reflections on nearly all the subjects in which he was most interested; thus their range is vast. This correspondence, as edited by Cook and Wedderburn, includes letters written between 1851 and 1896; but the major portion was composed after 1870. As a result, the volume reveals Ruskin's growing moodiness and irritation; it shows, too, his heavily satirical wit, his adherence to the sweeping statement, and his ease of phrase. But the arresting meta-

2. Vols. 36 and 37.
3. The bibliographical history of *Arrows* is also in this volume, pp. 459–68.

phor and striking word are not so prominent as in earlier writings. For Ruskin, *Arrows of the Chace* is a strangely severe and disciplined work. The letters in *Arrows* are conveniently grouped, both chronologically and under subject matter, enabling the reader to find a particular subject easily; as such, the volume is of great use to the student interpreting the life and work of the later Ruskin.

The scholarly achievement of Cook and Wedderburn is further stressed by the inclusion of a Bibliographical Appendix to the thirty-seventh volume which includes an account of the books, magazines, and pamphlets in which letters from Ruskin have been printed. This appendix, divided into three parts, contains letters to particular correspondents, to various correspondents, and even letters or extracts of letters from sale catalogues. In the first two divisions a full bibliographical apparatus is included, so that the scholar's task in tracing any Ruskinian reference is greatly facilitated. In this, as in other work devoted to Ruskin, Cook and Wedderburn have been accurate, helpful, and considering the enormity of the task, agreeably unpedantic. Their contribution to the explication of Ruskin's correspondence stands in the front rank of scholarly accomplishment.

Hortus Inclusus [4] (1887) is the one part of Ruskin's vast correspondence in which he himself manifested any interest. The letters, not all of which are printed in this collection, are addressed to two sisters, Miss Mary and Miss Susan Beever (with a few from the latter to Ruskin). Both ladies were intimates of the Brantwood circle and close neighbors of Ruskin. The correspondence, as originally published, covers the years 1874–86, the majority of letters being addressed to Miss Susan, who left the MS to a Mr. Albert Fleming to edit upon her death.

Hortus Inclusus, for which Ruskin wrote a charming preface praising the Misses Beever as "loadstones of all good to the village in which they had their homes," is a correspondence of singular attraction. That it has never been edited in its entirety is lamentable. While the subject matter ranges from the trivial to the profound, the letters show Ruskin at his most informal. And in their emphasis upon the value of friendship and their interest in varied subjects, they reveal the range and depth of mind of the cultured nineteenth-century gentleman.

Little editorial effort has been made to assist the reader of this pleasing and intimate correspondence. In many cases the letters are undated, and where dates do occur they are often inaccurate. Neither is there sufficient annotation to identify the many persons and places with which the manuscript abounds. A scholarly edition of *Hortus Inclusus* would aid in elucidating a relatively peaceful interlude in Ruskin's harassed life.

The Letters of John Ruskin to Charles Eliot Norton (1904) consist

4. Its bibliographical history is given in *Works, 37,* 621–3.

of 221 letters which are part of a larger correspondence. This collection, written between October 1855 and March 1887, also includes a few communications by other hands, namely John James Ruskin, Laurence Hilliard (Ruskin's secretary in 1881), and W. G. Collingwood. In addition, there is one letter by Ruskin to James Russell Lowell, and there are four by Ruskin to Mrs. Norton.

Norton's friendship with Ruskin and his family commenced in 1855. That the attachment lasted so many years, mainly through correspondence, is a tribute to the understanding and breadth of ideas of both men. Certainly, the friendship had its ups and downs as the letter to Norton of August 28, 1886, indicates. In it Ruskin criticizes his friend's "niggling and naggling article on Froude's misprints." But their friendship survived such criticisms and continued through the dark period of Ruskin's mental difficulties.

The letters to Norton include discussion of literary criticism, political economy, Ruskin's sensitivity to pain and suffering, the painting of Dante Gabriel Rossetti, and Ruskin's views on American art and civilization. But it is not for these observations that the letters are especially important. Rather, as Norton says: "No other series of his letters extended unbroken over so long a term of years, or was likely to possess so much autobiographical interest—comparatively little, indeed, as a record of events, but much as a record of moods and mental conditions. As a picture of character the letters were as a whole unique." This is a penetrating statement, for in the correspondence one sees Ruskin intimately in the midst of his perplexities. He is seen in the agony of wrestling with his religious convictions and breaking away from his Evangelical background; one sees him, also, in all his loneliness and finds him frequently commenting on the purposelessness of his way of life. And he is pictured expressing his bewilderment over human misery and grieving at the imperfection of his genius. On the other hand, he writes delightfully of the pleasure conveyed by the chirp of a sparrow or the beauty of a sunset; and he even jests about his dreaded brain fever. But the dominating impression is of a tired, lonely, and baffled man ever eager to welcome the friendship so constantly offered him by the less mercurial Norton.

Charles Eliot Norton as editor has discharged his undertaking with distinction. While failing, perhaps, to identify enough persons, places, and incidents, his notes, where they do occur, are full, accurate, and perceptive. Colloquial in form, they often provide a graceful transition from one letter to another; and a running commentary (always brief and succinct) is interspersed between parts of the correspondence. But such commentary at no time becomes so much a part of the text as to intrude upon it. The one serious deterrent to this edition lies in the excision of material which is doubtless of significance. In general, how-

ever, this is one of the most satisfactory and enlightening editions of
Ruskin's letters.

John Ruskin's Letters to Francesca and Memoirs of the Alexanders
(1931) is in two parts, the first consisting of letters exchanged between Ruskin and Mrs. and Miss Alexander. The second section is a
social document faithfully depicting the activities of an elegant, expa-
triate American family. Francesca Alexander (1837–1917), to whom
the majority of these letters is addressed, was the daughter of a Boston
painter who lived many years in Italy. Ruskin was much impressed with
one of her books which he edited and had published. This was *The
Story of Ida.* He also edited and was responsible for the publication of
Miss Alexander's *Roadside Songs of Tuscany* and *Christ's Folk in the
Apennine* which appeared in 1885 and 1887 respectively.

That Ruskin was greatly attracted to the Alexanders can be seen
from his remark made shortly after meeting them in 1882: "I never
knew such vivid goodness and innocence in any living creatures as in
this Mrs. and Miss Alexander." He once remarked of the daughter's
work, in all kindness one trusts, that it was "all 'chiaro' and no 'os-
curo.' " Very shortly after meeting, each of the trio entered into a correspondence to which Ruskin contributed some ninety letters.

Early in the friendship the little band addressed one another by
familiar names. Thus we find Ruskin signing himself "Fratello" or
"Figlio," while Miss Alexander often concludes with "Sorella." Mrs.
Alexander is sometimes referred to as "Mammina" and, on one unfortunate occasion, as "Sweetest Mammie." Behind these effusive names
lurks, one suspects, the Ruskin who wished so earnestly to be loved by
someone, the Ruskin who wrote, "Every word you write—each of you
—is joy and strength to me; and you are the more to me because my
life has been so strangely loveless till now."

Time and again Ruskin turns to Francesca Alexander for the comfort and understanding he believed to have been so long denied him. In
December 1882 her ardent faith prompts this remark from him: "You
have interpreted more of Christianity to me than I had learned of all
my teachers, even of the hills and sky." He also writes to Francesca
with remarkable frankness of the Rose La Touche affair, while Francesca in reply tries to heal the deep wounds it made. The correspondence
is a pathetic account of Ruskin's spiritual and emotional bankruptcy.

Editorially, Lucia Grey Swett has presented a sound text all the more
enhanced by William Clyde DeVane's introduction which places the correspondence in accurate perspective. At no time do the notes interfere
with the letters themselves, and the comment is always revealing and
direct. It is to be regretted, however, that the editorial decision was to
omit certain letters.

John Ruskin and Effie Gray (1947). Admiral Sir William James, in assembling the 633 letters written between 1847 and 1855, published approximately only two-thirds of the available material. The majority of letters in this collection were written by John Ruskin to Effie; some, however, were written by Effie to him and to her father; others were written by Mr. or Mrs. Ruskin to their son, and some by Ruskin senior to Effie's father. In spite of some defects, this correspondence has the virtue of unity, for almost every letter has a bearing on the calamitous relationship between the ill-matched husband and wife.

Admiral James has published a bowdlerized version of the correspondence. Its purpose is to vindicate Effie completely. Excisions, possibly of a most important nature, have been made in this text. The result is, unfortunately, an incomplete account of a marriage which in recent years has caught the attention of literary historians. The text is accompanied by a running commentary which, being indistinctly separated from the letters, makes a judgment of the facts exceedingly difficult. Furthermore, little effort has been made to identify the nineteenth-century figures whose names appear frequently in the text; and the transcription of the letters abounds with trifling errors. If, as has been done with Browning's letters to Isa Blagden, this correspondence could be transcribed and edited afresh with the omitted material included, a study would surely emerge which would lift the veil of secrecy from Ruskin's marriage and put the unhappy union in correct perspective.

From the foregoing, it should be apparent that the editing of Ruskin's letters has not been on as high a plane as is desirable. Because much of his correspondence has been edited in the spirit of prejudice and prudery, we see him today as an obscure and puzzling personality. To a man who influenced his own and subsequent generations so deeply, this does not seem to be entirely just. It is to be hoped that effort will be made by future scholars to edit his correspondence fully and competently, so that the old antipathies and ghosts of Victorian propriety may be finally banished from Ruskin biography.

3

The manuscript of Ruskin's Venetian letters to his father, 1851–52, forms a significant part of the Ruskin Collection in the Sterling Memorial Library at Yale University. The present edition consists of 278 letters written from Venice by John Ruskin to his father, John James Ruskin. The first was sent on September 2, 1851, and the last just as Ruskin and his wife Effie started the return journey to London on June 29, 1852. One hundred and eleven of the letters have been printed in whole or in part in Cook and Wedderburn's Library Edition of Ruskin's works, while a few are to be found in other Ruskin studies.[5] Thus ap-

5. See Appendix for list of letters unpublished and published in whole or in part.

proximately 60 per cent of this correspondence has never before been edited or published.

Not the least important aspect of these letters is the ten-month period they cover—a time span, as already noted, coincident with the accumulation in Venice of material for the second and third volumes of *The Stones of Venice*. The 1851–52 correspondence is, therefore, an epistolary accompaniment to the great prose work which was to appear in 1853 and, as such, becomes a running commentary on Ruskin's work in progress. Indeed, perhaps the most significant aspect of this correspondence is the faithful manner in which it reflects Ruskin's scholarly method. Through the letters one can follow his daily progress as he compiled his monumental work. And, as we have already seen, the minutiae of his daily life are also recorded in detail. Thus the text is packed with events great and small, relevant and insignificant, which made up the life of an individual who is still, as artist and man, an intensely perplexing figure.

The 1851–52 letters occupy a unique place in the Ruskin canon for yet another reason. They are the first collection of his correspondence written entirely in the 1850's to be edited. In fact, the published record of Ruskin's letters during that decade is scant; and since the fifties were the most important years of his career the present manuscript assumes a position of some consequence in any critical or biographical evaluation of him.

While this correspondence tells us much about Ruskin himself, it also reveals facets of the character and personality of his father, John James Ruskin. Although the letters written during 1851–52 by the older man to his son are not accessible, it is possible from what the son wrote to his father to trace their relationship with some clarity. John James, who made a fortune in the sherry business, followed his son's career with painful interest. Doting on the young man, treating him as a genius, and often too indulgent toward him, Ruskin senior may be seen in the letters as a kind and gentle person.[6] While he adhered to his conservative opinions with dignity, he was capable of curbing his son's wild enthusiasms with a gentle firmness that compels our admiration. And it is his fortitude in restraining the younger man that makes the incipient cleavage in their relations all the more moving. One receives from this correspondence, then, contrasting pictures of two nineteenth-century gentlemen: on the one hand, the conservative, self-made businessman, and on the other his liberally inclined, impetuous son, moving each year nearer to his radical position.

The 1851–52 letters have at least the attribute of casting fresh light

6. Consultation of the Bowerswell Papers (especially those pertaining to the years 1851–52) in the Morgan Library reveals another, quite sinister side to John James Ruskin's personality.

on an important time of Ruskin's life. By showing us the man at work and in his moments of leisure, they reveal sides of him hitherto ignored or obscured. They are, therefore, a mine of information for the future biographer and critic of Ruskin. And for the lay reader the correspondence is a document of human interest, rich in the conflict of character and the development of personality. The letters form, in short, a reading of life without which it is not possible to reach a full understanding of Ruskin as a potent influence on the crassly material age in which he lived.

4

While many models exist for editing such letters as these, I have endeavored to evolve an editorial policy based on consistency and respect for the individual problems presented by the text. It is hoped that the extensive footnotes will not irritate readers with facts they already know. But generous annotation was deemed advisable for a correspondence so important in Ruskin's life.

It has been my aim, in preparing this collection of Ruskin's letters to his father, to present a clear and accurate text. Some alterations have therefore been necessary; but these I have reduced to a minimum. I have retained, wherever possible, such irregularities as will convey to the reader a sense of Ruskin's personality. This procedure has also been followed to retain something of the original flavor of the text.

In general my editorial policy has been as follows:

1. I have adhered to Ruskin's erratic punctuation, amending merely for the sake of clarity. It has therefore been necessary to insert apostrophes and interrogation marks with some frequency.

2. The original spelling has been retained and the editorial *sic* inserted only where departure from the normal has been particularly flagrant.

3. By the use of italics and capitalization I have regularized the titles of books, plays, and pictures. Ruskin was notoriously indifferent to such niceties and would often refer, for example, to *The Stones of Venice* merely as "stones." In such cases, in order to facilitate the task of the reader, I have given the name or title sufficient individuality to make it stand out on the printed page.

4. For the ampersand so often used by Ruskin I have given the word in full. Where the ampersand is used with a "c" to indicate "etc." I have adhered to Ruskin's "&c."

5. Ruskin often failed to date his letters fully. Where omissions occur I have supplied the date of the month, the month itself, and in nearly all cases the year. Such dating is based, primarily, upon the postal date on the outside of the letter.

That faults may be found with the editing is more than likely. A few

names and incidents remain untraced either because they seemed relatively insignificant or because it has not been possible to consult the
letters written by Ruskin senior to his son during the latter's ten-month
Venetian sojourn. Certain individuals are referred to in the text as
"John" or "William." Such bare names, without further internal evidence, often leave an editor at a loss, and he is sometimes compelled
to admit defeat. But such cases do not occur in the 1851–52 correspondence with great frequency.

It is hoped that the procedure outlined above will serve to make the
text plainer, more readable, and more informative than the original.
And it is anticipated that the retention, as far as common sense will
permit, of Ruskin's peculiarities as a letter writer will help to clarify
the personality, the mental processes, and the attitude toward life of a
man who left a stamp of individuality on the entire literary, social, and
artistic life of his time.

ACKNOWLEDGMENTS

DURING the preparation of this edition of Ruskin's letters, both for the degree of Doctor of Philosophy at Yale University and for subsequent publication, I have received the assistance of many generous people, who have given unstintingly of their time and erudition. To the following I should like to express my appreciation: Richard L. Purdy, Dwight Culler, and Benjamin Nangle of Yale University; Sir Sidney Cockerell; R. H. Wilenski; Gabriella Bosano; John van Eerde; John Hewitt Mitchell; Karl F. Thompson; Helen Viljoen; the custodians of the Bowerswell Papers in the Morgan Library; and my wife Elizabeth, who labored over the intricacies of manuscript checking, transcription, and textual elucidation. My greatest obligation, however, is to William Clyde DeVane whose patient guidance has been a constant encouragement.

LETTER 1

Venice.[1] 2nd September [1851]

My dearest Father,

We got here yesterday evening, true to our day, and found Mr Brown [2] waiting for us, but no letters; however I suppose you have not calculated on our keeping our time so exactly—but I am certainly now getting a little anxious—though also I hear that letters are very often lost in this post office—not very consolatory information for in general I had much rather wait for a letter than lose one.

Venice is more beautiful than ever, and I am most thankful to be able to finish or retouch my descriptions on the spot. I believe Armytage [3] will by this time be waiting for the enclosed note—I have sent it as soon as I could—and hope that nothing will now delay the publication of the next two numbers [4]—will you be so good as to give the other note to Mr. Smith [5]—it is answer to a packet I got at Verona. I have a great deal to do, so must be short.

Ever your most affe Son, J. Ruskin— Dearest love to my mother.

P.S. I have not been able to get Smith's letter ready—please forward

1. Ruskin very rarely indicates that his letters come from Venice. In subsequent letters, unless otherwise indicated, it is to be understood that they originate in Venice.

2. Rawdon Brown (1803–83), a friend of Ruskin's who resided in Venice from 1833 until his death. Brown, who pursued scholarly interests in the Venetian archives, originally came to Venice to find the tomb of "Banish'd Norfolk" (*Richard II*, IV.i.92). For further information about Brown see Charles Eliot Norton's "Rawdon Brown and the Gravestone of 'Banish'd Norfolk,'" *Atlantic Monthly*, June, 1889. Brown's researches were of inestimable help to Ruskin and are acknowledged in a note to *The Stones of Venice* (*Works*, II, 459).

3. J. C. Armytage, an engraver of many plates for Ruskin.

4. Ruskin is thinking of the second and third parts of his *Examples of the Architecture of Venice* (*Works*, II, 309–50), which appeared on November 1 and November 17, 1851, respectively. The first part had already come out on May 12, 1851. A bibliographical account of this undertaking is in *Works*, II, xxxii ff.

5. George Smith (1824–1901), one of the most eminent of Victorian publishers. Son of the founder of Smith and Elder (from 1824 known as Smith, Elder & Company), George Smith became sole head of the firm in 1846. In addition to publishing many distinguished Victorians, among them Thackeray, Charlotte Brontë, and Matthew Arnold, Smith initiated the *Cornhill Magazine* in 1849, the *Pall Mall Gazette* in 1865, and *The Dictionary of National Biography* in 1882. A friend of both Ruskin and his father, the publisher was a frequent visitor at Denmark Hill. In 1828 Smith, Elder & Co. assumed publication of the annual, *Friendship's Offering*, in which Ruskin's youthful poems appeared. In 1843 Smith published *Modern Painters I*, Ruskin's first extensive prose work; his association with Ruskin continued until 1878 when the author severed relations, which had been deteriorating since 1861 due to the suspension of publication of *Unto This Last* in the *Cornhill Magazine*. Much pertinent information about Smith is to be found in J. W. Robertson Scott's *The Story of the Pall Mall Gazette* (London, Oxford University Press, 1950).

the card to Armytage, 29. Edward's Terrace, Caledonian road, Islington.

LETTER 2

4ᵗʰ September [1851]

My dearest Father,

I was so knocked about yesterday by lodging house keepers that I could not get my letter ready in time for post, and it will be the same today unless I send you this scrap, but we have got very good lodgings at last and I hope shall be quietly settled on the Grand Canal out of reach of all noise and trouble—by the beginning of the week: I am very well—but the weather is miserable—cold—rainy—dark—like England in October. I am beginning to lose all faith in Italy.

No letters yet. I suppose I have quite miscalculated the time it takes to hear from England— Or you have perhaps not got my Vevay letter

Dearest love to my mother.
Ever my dearest Father,
Your most affᵉ Son
J Ruskin.

The quantities of questions about bells and kitchens and beds and things of which I know nothing are inconceivable. But I shall have very comfortable rooms and good fires and quiet, and plenty [of] room, and save some money—as compared with Danieli's.

LETTER 3

Venice 7ᵗʰ September [1851]

My dearest Father,

Thank God I have at last your letter of the 1st. I had not the heart to write yesterday; thinking you must certainly be ill—it seemed hardly possible that both at Milan and Verona the letters should have been lost, and none lying for me here: however, it will be a good lesson not to torment myself again. The especially worrying thing: was my getting *Smith and Elder's* packet, and not yours, at Verona; and then another *Smith* here, looking as if my address was well enough known—but *you* not writing—and I *wrote to* THUN from VEVAY—saying to send letters *here,* so that none coming thence, either, made it fourfold strangeness. I have certainly been intensely uncomfortable, and it will be a day or two before I can get quite right again; but it is all for the best: it makes one feel more as one ought to feel the blessing of being preserved in health for one another—and in the hope of happy meetings, many to come.

I am quite well in health however—only a little nervous and shaky and I hope to be in our own house on Tuesday and to be quietly at my work—with due exercise—&c. by the middle of week— I have been rowing a good deal already—could not do much else.

I wrote to Milan and Verona to make a second inquiry about letters the day before yesterday—and shall write to Brescia, directly. I hope to recover some of your letters at least—though nothing is too disgraceful for Italy in its present state. Dearest love to my Mother. Effie's best love to you both.

> Ever my dearest Father, Your most aff^e Son
> J Ruskin.

LETTER 4

Sunday 7th September [1851]

My dearest Father,

I now sit down to answer more in order: In the first place, you only mention my note from Ivrea; but as you also say you have 21 letters and have had no anxiety I presume you have also mine from Vevay-Martigny and the St Bernard [1] itself: I have for the present nothing but your letters already acknowledged as far as Vevay; and this of the first September, but the others will I doubt not come in in due time. I hope in some of them I may find one of my pamphlets, which I should rather like to see; and should consider on the whole better worth having than this sandy critique of Blackwood's [2]—poor mean people, they shift out of the scrape as well as they can: I will have them up again some day.

We shall enquire for the Madonna della Grazia and the books, but I have no idea what the black case can be—nor do you say anything about the degree of success or of embarrassment which has attended the clearing out of Park St. I quite forget, for one thing whether I gave orders to Foord [3] to take the large picture to Mr Watts's [4] studio—if it has been accommodated in any other way, well and good—let it stand. I forgot to mention also that Boys [5] has a bill against me of 31 pound odd, unpaid—to which must be added a sovereign I one day borrowed of him—if you tell S[mith] and E[lder] to ask him for his bill he will send it in. I suppose also in some of the missing letters I shall hear

1. En route to Venice the Ruskins paused, among other places, in Vevey (August 20), Martigny (August 23), and Gt. St. Bernard (August 23).

2. An unfavorable review of Ruskin's thought in general, and of *Modern Painters II* in particular, appeared in *Blackwood's Magazine,* September, 1851.

3. Messrs. Foord were for some years Ruskin's frame-makers.

4. J. F. Watts (1803–74) painted two portraits of Effie Ruskin, one of which is reproduced in *John Ruskin and Effie Gray,* a correspondence edited by Admiral Sir William James, G.C.B. (New York, Charles Scribner's Sons, 1947).

5. T. S. Boys (1803–74), a water colorist and engraver of plates for Ruskin. A pleasing tribute is paid him in the preface to *Modern Painters (Works, 6, 12).*

what the hesitating gentleman finally determined about Turner's Solway Moss. You never said what you really *gave* for the others? Then I am rather anxious to hear what the Pre-Raphaelites themselves think of the pamphlet [6]—never as yet having heard a word about them—and I want to know whether Mr Moore [7] got comfortably home—and whether Mrs Moore thinks I have taken tolerable care of him—so much for enquiries at home.

Next—I must tell you what we are about here. I was too much hurried and plagued at Verona to write you anything like a proper account of the glorious evening we had there—I told you the empress [8] was staying at the Due Torri: and that the Austrian governor had ordered her some music— Now you recollect that in front of the Due Torri, on the other side of the little square of St Anastasia, there is a straight narrow street going down to the Cathedral— Fortunately the soldiery had been lodged somewhere—(perhaps in the cathedral cloisters) whence they were obliged to come up this street to the piazza—and just as twilight was passing into night, they came in three divisions; composed of the three best bands in the place—with as many soldiers from each of their regiments as could form a circle outside of them, bearing torches: The bright cluster of lights appeared at the end of the street so far away that the trumpets could hardly be heard—the soldiers with their torches marching first and the music following—clanging louder and louder until the troop of torchbearers spread themselves out into one burning line across the square, and behind them the whole three bands at once burst from their march into the Emperor's Hymn. You know what lovely and solemn lines are formed by the porch of St Anastasia and the canopy of the marble tomb above its cemetery gate—all these glorious buildings with the last streaks of twilight behind them, suddenly lighted by the torches into a gloomy crimson—their own red marble flushed by the firelight—and the burst of solemn and simple music from so many instruments—composed together the finest piece of mere *effect* I have ever seen in my life: For there was no pretence—no getting up about it—the buildings were there in a natural way and as a matter of course—not dressed up with rags and tinsel—and yet *such* buildings—for you know that tomb of St Anastasia is the one I have asserted to be the loveliest (to my knowledge) in the world.[9] Of course there was not much sentiment in the idea of the thing—it was but a parcel of Croats playing a tune to a middleaged lady—and so it fell far short in feeling of the religious ceremonies I have seen some-

6. Ruskin's pamphlet, *Pre-Raphaelitism* (*Works, 12,* 337–93), first published on August 13, 1851.

7. Rev. Daniel Moore, incumbent of Camden Church, Camberwell. En route to Venice Effie and John Ruskin passed some time in Paris with Moore.

8. Marianne, whose husband, Ferdinand I of Austria, abdicated the throne in December 1848.

9. In *The Stones of Venice I* (*Works, 9,* 175).

times—but for intensity and completeness of stage effect, I never saw anything to beat it—or equal it.

They are going to have some more spectacles at Verona when the emperor comes. I shall stay here in peace. We have got the Baroness Wetzler's apartments—after a great fight for a room, which we insisted on having: a room for me to write in: we have this, and a kind of hall dining room; a beautiful drawing room; double-bedroom and dressing room—three servant's rooms and kitchen; on the grand canal with south aspect—nearly opposite the Salute; and on first floor; for about 17 pounds a month. We looked at many other lodgings—but they were all either too small or on the unhealthy side of the canal—and were yet priced at 10 to 15 pounds a month. The only apartments I *quite* liked were a long way from St Mark's place and could not have been had for less than 20 francs a day—they asked 30. These we have are however exceedingly good—better than we wanted—but the difficulty is to get rooms with a good light—and yet not too handsome.

I had nearly forgotten to tell you about Mr Block— I met him on the *staircase* at Verona as I was going to railroad, he had before sent his courier to claim my acquaintance but the courier showed me the passport of a Mr T. Pardho [*text mutilated*]— I said I had heard often Mr P.'s name, but had not the pleasure of knowing him. I was going out at the time, and thought the whole thing a mistake—so *went* out; and only came in to start for railroad. I knew Mr Block's face when I saw him—but did not recollect his name till he told me. I hope I was polite—but I was very nervous and in a great hurry.

Monday Morning—I have your nice note of the 3rd with Mr Brown [10] on exhibition, capital, but I must send this at once. Dearest love to my Mother.

Ever my dearest Father,
Your most affᵉ Son
J Ruskin.

Have you heard anything from John Lewis [11] about Pre-Raphaelites?

LETTER 5

Venice 9ᵗʰ Sept. [1851]

My dearest Father,

No letter today, and we are getting into our lodgings so I can only send you a bulletin of health. I am rowing a great deal—and for the

10. Very probably Dr. John Brown (1810–82), author of *Rab and His Friends,* with whom Ruskin corresponded for many years. Brown, though a medical man, was keenly interested in art and literature and acquired some reputation as a critic. Although Ruskin did not meet him until 1853 their correspondence, born of the doctor's admiration of *Modern Painters,* began in 1846.

11. John Frederick Lewis (1805–76), a painter much admired by Ruskin, who

present working little enough—so I ought to be well. Mr Brown troubles himself far more about the matter than I, else I hardly know how we should get on— The Dean of St Paul's [1] and Mrs Milman are here, and the Bp. of Oxford [2] is to be, but I don't go about with them. Am writing in my gondola, by 7 in the morning and cannot sit up at night. Our lodgings look really very nice today, and I hope I shall have a very profitable winter— Winter seems begun—at any rate—I was stopped in my work at Murano yesterday by the coldness of the wind. I can only send this line today—more tomorrow. Dearest love to my mother.

Ever my dearest Father,
Your most aff[e] Son
J Ruskin.

LETTER 6

9th Sept. Evening [1851]

My dearest Father,

I have today your delightful letters, from Verona, of the 24th, 25th, enclosing Lupton's [1] about proofs. I am truly thankful you have them—they are quite inestimable— Lupton's request is of course to be acceded to—as I did not expect to get more than 3 or 4 out of the 7: You have them thoroughly cheap, and I am very very much obliged to Lupton also—and must write to say so— It gives me wonderful peace of mind to think that they are all safe on my shelves.

I have also the reviews Athenaeum [2] and Leader: [3] It is quite true

---

praises him in *Praeterita* (*Works, 35*, 405–6). Lewis, on account of his interest in Spain, was known as "Spanish Lewis." The later years of his life were, however, devoted to Oriental subjects. He was elected A.R.A. in 1859 and R.A. in 1865.

1. Henry Hart Milman (1791–1868), dean of St. Paul's from 1849 until his death. After a distinguished Oxford career Milman gained some reputation for his *Poetical Sketches,* which appeared in 1839. He was also a Sanskrit scholar and a writer of poetic tragedy. A keen student of history who counted among his friends Macaulay, Lockhart, and Hallam, Milman published, in 1855, *The History of Latin Christianity down to the Death of Pope Nicholas V.* Watts has done a portrait of him.

2. Samuel Wilberforce (1805–73), son of the Evangelical layman, William Wilberforce. He served as bishop of Oxford from 1845 until his death. A writer of church histories and familiar of both Gladstone and Disraeli, he earned the sobriquet of "Soapy Sam" for his facile manner of expression and presentation of argument. He is perhaps best remembered for his attack on *The Origin of Species* and his exchange of remarks on evolution with Thomas Henry Huxley.

1. Thomas Goff Lupton (1791–1873) occupied a unique position among nineteenth-century engravers, for he was mainly responsible for the introduction of steel for mezzotint engraving. He engraved many plates after Turner, including, in 1856, *The Harbors of England* with text by Ruskin. Lupton also contributed several plates to *The Stones of Venice.*

2. A most unfavorable review of Ruskin's pamphlet, *Pre-Raphaelitism,* appeared in the *Athenaeum* on August 23, 1851. The critic, apart from taking issue with Ruskin's opinions of certain artists and of Pre-Raphaelitism in general, was especially hard on the preface to the pamphlet. A sample of the criticism will suffice: "Rarely has any oracle's 'Ego' been stretched further in the demand for blind faith and acquiescence than in this pamphlet:—rarely has 'Ego' been more vain-glorious . . ."

that that preface reads haughty enough—but as you say, I cannot write with a modesty I do not feel—in speaking of art I shall never be modest any more. I see more and more every day that all over Europe people are utterly ignorant of its first principles—and more *especially* the upper classes—that the perception of it is limited to a few unheard of artists and amateurs—that it has been the same for three centuries, and that it will need a century more, with hard work from all the men who know anything about the matter, merely to make the people of Europe understand their position, and begin properly. I don't know if the world is to last so long; but I shall work and write as if it were—and I shall probably make some amplification of this discovery of mine, the preface to the second volume of *Stones of Venice*. I am going on writing the text with the things before me—and as soon as the chapters are severally done, I shall make George [4] copy them, and send his copy to be printed as accurately as possible under Mr Harrison's [5] care, whose *gondola,* please tell him with my kind regards, I will not forget this time. When the thing has been got as nearly right as *possible* in London, it will be worth expence of postage to get it thrown off—and one proof will enable me to revise it for press, and have all the letterpress ready by the time I get back—and I daresay I shall be able to send some of the plates by safe private hands, to be got on with also.

We got into our lodgings last night—(this is the 10th—morning) and I am writing with the green water of the grand canal shining through the openings of the golden marble balustrade of the balcony of my very comfortable room— Nothing can be more comfortable than it is all. I would give something if you and my mother could come and see us—I have no doubt your sky was very beautiful; but the warm glow of the ducal palace last night against the white clouds in the moonlight is not to be equalled by anything else in the world.

---

and so on with constant and derisive references to the use of "I" and "my" in the preface.

3. The criticism in the *Leader,* published the same day as that in the *Athenaeum,* while not so harsh, takes Ruskin to task for avoiding the main issue, namely that of the Pre-Raphaelite conception of form in art. Ruskin is also scored for stressing Turner in his discussion, and his pamphlet is dismissed as being "interesting enough as the rambling observations of one who does observe, but carrying forward no high argument."

4. John Hobbs, Ruskin's secretary-valet, who remained with him until 1854. He eventually emigrated to Australia, where he became a justice of the peace, and died there in 1892. Hobbs was called "George" to distinguish him from the Ruskins, father and son. He copied much of the MS of the two concluding volumes of *The Stones of Venice.*

5. William Henry Harrison, who for some 30 years made the final revisions and corrections of Ruskin's works. As editor of the annual, *Friendship's Offering,* a publication "compounded of art, sentiment and fashion," Harrison published some of Ruskin's earlier efforts. Shortly after relinquishing his editorial duties Harrison, in June 1841, entered the Crown Life Insurance Office; but he maintained his artistic interests and was for some time registrar of the Royal Literary Fund. Harrison is the subject of *My First Editor (Works, 34,* 90–104).

Dearest love to my mother. I wish we had some of the heat which used to annoy her here. I was obliged to wear my greatcoat last night. Ever my dearest Father,

Your most aff^e Son J Ruskin

LETTER 7

11th September [1851]

My dearest Father,

I had yesterday yours from *Brescia*—I see I had altogether miscalculated the time of post—and might have saved myself a good deal of anxiety if I had counted days better: This letter says that Mr Smith— to whom will you be kind enough to forward the enclosed note—says that my "lines of illust. plans" [1] are caviare to the general. I don't understand—does he mean the *larger* plates—or what?

We find ourselves excessively comfortable in our lodgings—the evening yesterday after dinner with red moon rising behind Salute, was inexpressibly delightful—and when I have got my books by the next ship I shall be much more at home than ever I was in Park St.

I have just got yours 6th Sept with account of William's Baptismal proceedings—he made it so very seriously a stipulation with me that *no presents* should be made that I should have taken him at his word— but I doubt not he will be much gratified by the silver spoons &c., many thanks to my mother. Pray give William my love, and best wishes for his child.

I am not surprised at effect—or disaffection—of Fielding's [2] sunset —but pray keep it—for two reasons. I would not hurt his feelings by parting with it: and—without dispraising it, it will do to stop the mouths of people who like him better than Turner. I am glad you begin to enjoy the exhibition—but alas, I saw none of the things of which you tell me.

I am very wicked and not at all sorry to hear of Konig's [3] death. A man dies suddenly as easily as slowly—and he was simply a log of wood

1. A reference to the plates of *The Stones of Venice I,* which appeared in March 1851. It was in that volume that Ruskin used engravers for the first time.

2. Antony Vandyke Copley Fielding (1787–1855) devoted his life entirely to painting and was best known for his studies of the English countryside, especially of the Sussex Downs. He was also noted for his paintings of storms at sea. Fielding was president of the Water-Colour Society from 1831 until his death. That Ruskin thought Turner superior to Fielding is seen in *The Art of England, Lecture VI* (*Works, 33,* 371–93), where Turner's *Garden of Hesperides* and *The Building of Carthage* are declared to have put an end to Fielding's work in oil and to have driven him into what Ruskin calls "the quiet presidency of the old Water-Colour Society."

3. Charles Dietrich Eberhard Konig (1774–1851) was born at Brunswick and went to England in 1800. He was a prominent mineralogist who, at the time of his death, was in charge of the mineralogical department of the British Museum.

in the British Museum—nay—an iron fence against any good being done. Something may now be got done in ticketing minerals.

I have also pamphlet from Milan and think it reads excellently.

Dearest love to my mother. Ever my dearest Father,

> Your most affᵉ Son
> J Ruskin.

Effie's best love.

LETTER 8

13ᵗʰ Saturday. [September 1851]

My dearest Father,

I have no letter today, as yet—but read over the one last received— I had not heard of poor Charlotte Withers [1] going in that way, very very strange and grievous: Mr Withers [2] had I believe the misfortune to be a fool—but I don't know whether it is really right to call it a misfortune—people have no right to be fools to such an extent. Solomon always talks of foolish people and wicked people as one and the same.

I quite forgot to advise you before of the coming of Mr Blumenthal, [3] to see exhibition— He will call on you, but I did not give him a letter —though very amiable and obliging he might probably be very troublesome— You have no occasion to do anything for him. We ask *them* to tea sometimes at Venice—not they us: And pray in general do get into the habit of looking on asking people to dinner as a thing *Impossible:* I am sorry to hear business is so bad, but it must not be kept up at expence of health and happiness. Better is a dry morsel and quietness therewith. I am afraid the Denmark Hill house has been somewhat like that described in the latter part of the verse—an house "full of sacrifices," though by the bye I wonder what that means in the Hebrew— what the exact phrase or sense is.

You say there was a *letter* at Milan of date 25th. I have only *got* from Milan the *Pre-Raphaelitism*—no letter. Dearest love to my mother. But why is she so sad? I must write her a letter. Ever my dearest Father,

> Your most affᵉ Son
> J Ruskin.

1. The daughter of neighbors of the Ruskin family. She first met John Ruskin in 1838, and a brief youthful friendship sprang up between them. She was married off by her family to a prosperous Newcastle trader. Ruskin speaks kindly of Charlotte Withers in *Praeterita* (*Works, 35,* 221–2).

2. Charlotte's father, an unsuccessful coal merchant of whom Ruskin remarks in *Praeterita,* "Of him I remember only a reddish and vacant face."

3. Carlo Blumenthal, a Venetian banker, much interested in the tides and lagoons of Venice and therefore of use and assistance to Ruskin.

LETTER 9

Sunday morning. [14 September 1851]

My dearest Father,

I hardly know whether it is Sunday or not—for last night everybody living on the Grand canal received a request from the Podesta that they would hang out carpets at ½ past six to do honour to the emperor [1] who was to pass through Venice at seven—and accordingly we were waked at six by a cannonade which lasted with little intermission till ½ past 7; heavy firing from all the batteries and pontoons off the ducal palace—very pretty to look at—and shaking every pillar of the palace to its foundation— I doubt not more mischief has been done to it by this morning's work than by any five years of "winter and rough weather" it has had to endure— But everybody thought it very fine of course—and the upper balconies of St Mark's were filled with people— (I never saw *one* there to look at the church—or at the bronze horses) and Effie and I went up to the top of the little red marble loggia of the campanile: where we saw all we wanted. The emperor is a well made youth, with rather a thin—ugly—not unpleasant face—he and Radetsky [2] went about together looking just like a great white baboon and a small brown monkey; a barrel organ would have made the thing complete: St Mark's place had a file of soldiers all round it—a large body of men—I imagine about 3000 altogether: and at the door of the church there was a cushion—and the priests came out with the emperor and made him kneel down on it—and all the soldiers kneeled down too— and the chief priest held up his fingers after the manner of Wall in *Midsummer Night*—and then they all got up again—much edified: and a brown dog trotted right into the middle of the Emperor's staff and twice round his cushion—after the manner of Lance's dog—and I thought he was going to proceed to extremities—but he thought better of it, and went into the square and looked all round at the soldiers, and then cocked his tail, and went away home leaving two or three sentries in helmets in a state of indignation impossible to be described. So the soldiers defiled before the emperor, and the mob ran after them—the emperor and Radetsky letting anybody come near them who liked—at last he went away down the grand canal—which was all hung with carpets and tapestries, and looked like a street of old clothes warehouses from one end to another—and there was a great crowd of gondolas, and much splashing and swearing—and now everybody is gone home

1. Francis Joseph of Austria (1830–1916). He came to the throne in 1848, one year before the surrender of Venice to the Austrian empire. At the outbreak of the revolution in 1848 he served with Radetzky in Italy.

2. Marshal Radetzky (1766–1858), one of the most prominent Austrian commanders during the early stages of the Italian wars for unity.

to breakfast—highly satisfied—and I am going to church. Dearest love to my mother. Ever my dearest Father.

                    Your most affect^e Son J Ruskin.

—Effie's best love—I have just read this to her and she asks me to ask you if you would send it to Perth—to Mrs Gray [3]—merely for her to read.

LETTER 10

Sunday Evening. [14 September 1851]

My dearest Father

I have today your nice long letter of the 9th with your pleasant hopes of coming abroad next year with small luggage. I hope—whether with much or little, that you will indeed come and meet us and have much happiness with us: certainly as far as Switzerland is concerned, one's happiness is by no means promoted by much luggage—and I don't think, even in the lovely day we had for it, you would have much envied me my seat in the char on our ascent of St Bernard—for my case with the two Turners I never, during the whole journey, let out of my sight; and in a char, the only way of keeping it in sight was to keep it on my knee—and before we had gone above three miles we saw in one of the villages a wonderful *lock* on a door—which we stopped to examine—bought—and carried off—and it being some foot and a half long by three inches deep, and no room for it but under my feet—I had not the pleasantest posture thence forward as far as Liddes. But our quantity of *packed* luggage is rendered so conspicuous chiefly by the three boxes for which *I* am responsible; namely the box with my drawings and manuscripts, and two others with daguerreotype apparatus— Effie and the maid have three between them—which I do not think very much, because she wanted some winter things here which she could not trust to come by sea—nor could I my daguerreotypes or MS—so that though I never had any intention of staying in Switzerland, I could not diminish my luggage. I always said I *must* D.V. be at Venice by 1st September in order to get some of the summer effects, even as it is I am rather too late—I feared heat—we have only to complain of *cold*.

Before going farther, let me answer your important question. Tyrtaeus was I believe, a Greek poet, who either sang—or wrote poems to be sung, in the front of battle—answering somewhat to our military music: By Tyrtaean I meant therefore, capable of inspiring soldierly ardour.

That is indeed a dreadful account of poor Robt Munro [1]—I suppose

---

3. The mother of Effie Ruskin.

1. Most probably Robert Munro of Busbridge Park, Surrey, who died on April 16, 1852, and whose death is mentioned by Ruskin in Letter 224.

it is of little use to ask what—in his madness, he means; but I always understood that he was allowed to do what he liked, and could not be kept from studying. What does he think ought to have been done?

I am most happy to hear of Newton's [2] being home, and looking so well—I was afraid he would be sadly knocked to pieces by his hard travel home—he looked quite brown when he parted from us at Milan: Mr Harrison also I am glad to hear of—I trust he is better in health than when I bid him goodbye—pray give him my best regards, and thank him for nice notice in Aberdeen journal, but tell him also he must mind what he is about—otherwise if he talks so much about me, the Aberdeen people will find out he is a friend.

Is this Madonna della Grazia the ship by which all the things I left in town were shipped? There was a large case of books, of which I should now be very glad to hear: but I suppose I must allow a fortnight or three weeks for the Madonna. I shall go on with out of door work and writing, and leave reading for winter. I have brought my little volume of Pope's poems with me: which I shall read carefully. I hardly know which is most remarkable—the magnificent power and precision of mind—or the miserable corruption of the entire element in which it is educated—and the flatterings—falsenesses—affectations—and indecencies, which divert the purpose and waste the strength of the writer, while his natural perception of truth, and his carefully acquired knowledge of humanity still render his works of inestimable value— I see he was first educated by a Roman Catholick—and then in *Twickenham* classicism—I am glad to find my term is exactly what I wanted it to be—Pope is the purest example, as well as the highest, of the Cockney classic.

Monday morning—The sun is shining sweetly in at my windows—the chill is gone off—and the weather has become what I hoped it would be— *Effie is gone with a Lady Sorel,[3] to whom Lord Glenelg [4] gave her a letter, to be introduced to the Austrian high Admiral-General*

2. Sir Charles Thomas Newton (1816–94), who had been at Christ Church College with Ruskin. Newton was appointed to an assistantship in the British Museum in 1840 and subsequently served in the consular service in the Near East from 1852 until 1860. During that time he discovered the remains of the mausoleum of Halicarnassus. He later became keeper of the Greek and Roman section of the British Museum, a position he occupied until 1885; he also acquired many sculptures for the museum and did much to further archaeological interests in England. He was the author of several books including *Travels and Discoveries in the Levant*, 2 vols. (London, 1865).

3. Margaret, Countess d'Averton, was the widow of Sir Thomas Stephen Sorrel, once His Majesty's agent and consul-general at Trieste. Lady Sorrel, unkindly termed "the champion bore of English Venetian society," introduced Effie Ruskin to many prominent residents of Venice.

4. Charles Grant (1778–1866) was elevated to the peerage in 1835 as Baron Glenelg. A distinguished civil servant, he was secretary for war from 1835 until 1839.

Wimpffen [5]—*and see a launch*—*I stay at home*—*and am going presently to* Murano to write. Dearest love to my Mother.

Ever my dearest Father. Your most affec. Son
J Ruskin.

Effie is just come in—after having *a walk with*—*whom should you think*—*old Marshal Marmont!* [6] *and giving the signal for the launch of the Artemisia.*

LETTER 11

16th September [1851]

My dearest Father,

I see you have written to Thun—I have written there twice—the last time somewhat impatiently. I had given Interlachen as an address to Perth people, and wrote there for the letters, which have come all right —I doubt not therefore that the Thun ones will follow in due time— only they are now missing, unless there was a letter as well as a pamphlet at Milan. *I showed the Dean of St Paul's over the duomo of Murano yesterday; abusing St Paul's all the time, and making him observe the great superiority of the old church and the abomination [of] its Renaissance additions—and the Dean was much disgusted.* They leave today for Verona—so home by Munich—the Bp. of Oxford was to have been here long ago—but is said to be slightly ill at Milan— overdoing himself in Switzerland—he may come here yet: *Roberts* [1] is coming too—so you will have Venice enough in next academy: not good for anything—I would give anything if John Lewis would come— he is the only man who could draw it. And he would do it *perfectly*. The weather is now lovely and I am quite well and much enjoying myself— Dearest love to my mother.

Ever my dearest Father, Your most affec. Son.
J Ruskin.

5. Count Franz Emil Lorenz Wimpffen (1797–1870) who, after a career in the Austrian army, was appointed in 1849 to the position of Marine-Obercommando in Venice.

6. August Frederic Louis Viesse de Marmont (1774–1852), Duke of Ragusa. Marmont had an erratic career under Napoleon, achieving first eminence and then, at Salamanca, where he was badly wounded, disgrace. An able militarist, Marmont nevertheless failed to put down the Parisian uprisings of 1830; distrusted by his countrymen, he subsequently went into exile.

1. David Roberts, R.A. (1796–1864), worked both in oil and water color and maintained a great interest in architectural composition. He first visited Italy in 1851, from which time many of his subjects were Italianate. In the last years of his life, however, Roberts painted primarily English scenes. He was appointed one of the commissioners for the Great Exhibition of 1851.

LETTER 12

17th September [1851]

My dearest Father,

I had yesterday yours of the 11th with sad account of poor Mr Harrison and Newton. I hope both are by this time better. Mr Harrison was in the habit of eating anything he liked, so that there is room in his case for regimen to do good—he has probably his health in his own power—but must live more like Mr Rogers [1]—poor Newton I am very sorry for; for he has a weak constitution and is always moderate—quite starved himself with us in Italy. But you tell us nothing of what he says of his journey?

You may well wonder at the way the letters went wrong—and think I can have left no orders at post offices, and yet I calculated the matter with some care—except in allowing too little time for letters to get to Milan after I wrote from Vevay: I did not ask at Brescia, because I thought my Vevay letter would have stopped all letters on the old route after Thun; and as I wrote *from Vevay to Thun*—telling the letters to be sent to Venice, I made quite sure of finding whatever letters were there, lying at Venice for me—so that finding none either from Thun— nor following me from Milan for 5 days, was enough to frighten me— it is very curious that *all* the postmasters should have been so tardy. The Thun letters I have not *yet* got and am beginning to give them up. But as you say it is a good lesson not to hurt oneself with fears. I shall not again.

That I had *bed* and *bell* work to do was not Phemy's fault—except as it is her fault that she has learned German instead of Italian. But she reads Italian with me now every morning: I could not leave her to fight it out alone, with the dictionary and bell hanger.

Dean Milman, you will see did not bore me—very discreet— I shall be glad to see Mr Taber—and shall ask him to dinner. I am working very quietly—and have time to spare—though I cannot go out, nor sit up late— Dearest love to my mother.

Ever my dearest Father. Your most affect[e] Son. J Ruskin.

I will look at articles in Times about Bishops [2] &c.—many thanks for naming them. We have Galignani regularly from Paris—which keeps us up with current news, and are everyway most comfortable— It is a great thing to be spared that very unpleasant journal—the *bill* every two days. Though I have had a considerable outlay in getting fairly set up, it is much pleasanter than the gradual process of abstraction.

1. Samuel Rogers (1763–1855) met with an accident in 1850 which besides making him lame for the rest of his life compelled him to live carefully.

2. Articles about the Catholic bishops of Ireland and the National Education question which appeared in the *Times* on September 1 and 8, 1851.

LETTER 13

18th September [1851]

My dearest Father,

I had yesterday your letter of the 12th containing your fears for my disturbance. But I am now settled more quietly than I have ever been since I was at college—and it certainly will be nobody's fault but my own if I do not write well—besides that I have St Mark's library open to me, and Mr Cheney's: [1] who has just at this moment sent his servant through a tremendous thundershower with two books which help me in something I was looking for: I have a lovely view from my windows— and *temptation* to exercise every day: and excellent food—so I think you may make yourself easy about me— You and Mama should have seen the milk this morning—as rich as one can get it in London under the name of cream—and [as] sweet and new as if it had just come from Denmark Hill.

I shall soon be able to send you a very accurate estimate of the expence of living in this way: but at any rate, it is much less than living at an hotel—we save in the first place, about 7 napoleons or 7 nap., 10 francs—a month in rooms; even taking them at the old estimate of 20 francs a day at Danieli's, and now they are much dearer: our eating servants and all—costs us *about* 18 francs: at Danieli's—it was always five each for dinner—four and a half for the rest—giving 19 for us alone—and it would have been nine francs for the servants—so that we save about 10 or eleven francs a day in this—besides waiter's fees: and we have one gondola and two gondoliers for 5 swanzigs a day: which at Danieli's I used to pay for one gondolier alone.

I will be sure and ask Zaccaria for all packages: but I am anxious to know as soon as may be exactly what came by the Madonna della Grazia—for I left a box of *books*—rather large, and very important, to come by some ship or other; and suppose it must be the black case you speak of as containing daguerreotypes—if this was the *grate* my books must either be at Denmark Hill, or have come by some other ship—if the former, I want them sent out as soon as may be.

I am most thankful you like the second volume [2] so much—but I thought you had just read it a year ago? Dearest love to my mother. Ever my dearest father.

Your most aff^e Son J Ruskin.

1. Edward R. Cheney (1803–84), antiquary, collector, and author of the privately printed *Remarks on the Illuminated Manuscripts of the Venetian Republic*, 1868. Ruskin pays Cheney a pleasing tribute in *Works, 24,* 182. An interesting account of Cheney's role as cicerone to Sir Walter Scott during the latter's visit to Rome in the spring of 1832 is given by Lockhart in the *Life of Scott,* 10 vols. (Edinburgh, 1839), *10,* 184–98.
2. Of *Modern Painters.*

LETTER 14

19th Sept. [1851]

My dearest Father,

I have today your two delightful letters from Thun. I would not have missed them for the world; you know they gave an account of all your impatience to get the brown studies for me, for which again and again a thousand thanks: and of all the new arrangements of the pictures at Denmark Hill, which I have been enjoying in imagination all this morning. I should think the Turner and four Prouts [1] must be quite the finest group for general effect we have—it must be so well built and so *airy* at the same time: the little Venice Prout would I should think harmonize in colour deliciously with the oil one: and by the bye, I forgot to tell you what I found out about that Turner: you know Mr Runciman [2] and other perspective rigidians have found fault with the too sharp perspective of the yellow and white palace

instead of ———now as I was examining this palace for the first time a day or two ago, (for being Renaissance I had not paid it particular attention), I found it was *not square,* but that the corner was an acute angle—built of necessity in consequence of the direction of the canal. Turner's perspective is therefore perfectly right. I think my sepias will be much more seen and valued in your room than behind the dining room screen—and I rather congratulate you on having that little upright with the light in the distance out of the study—it used to be rather a favourite of mine—is thickety and wild and good.

The Thun letters also bring directions about letter paper and remonstrances against mosaic of that material. I hope my letters since Vevay have been all right—and I will keep them this size in future— It does not matter their being only on one sheet, does it? I have also Lady

1. Samuel Prout (1783–1852), a neighbor of the Ruskin family both at Herne Hill and Denmark Hill. Although ill much of his life, Prout contributed frequently to the exhibitions of the Water-Colour Society. References to him in Ruskin's work are frequent, perhaps the most significant being an article in the *Art Journal* for March 1849 (*Works, 12,* 305–15).

2. Charles Runciman, Ruskin's first drawing master. A brief account of the virtues and drawbacks of this man is given in *Praeterita* (*Works, 35,* 76–7). Runciman's knowledge of perspective is noted by Ruskin in the preface to *The Elements of Drawing* (*Works, 15,* 18).

Trevelyan's [3] letter—which is delightful. I must answer it and will then send it you. Dearest love to my mother.

Ever my dearest Father. Your most affec[e] Son
J Ruskin.

LETTER 15

20th Sept. [1851]

My dearest Father,

Reading over your letter of the 12th I find this query "is not this Dean—albeit a poet, a little of an ass?" Yes: just a little—yet [not?] so much as to spoil the effect of many very amiable and estimable qualities. He is very fond of hearing himself talk—and very positive—but very good and on the whole sensible: He gave us an interesting and very laboured sermon on Sunday in his rooms at the Europa, on the apparent nonfulfilment of prayer: valuable in matter—somewhat too pompous in language but sensibly and easily read—which was a wonder, for I was sitting behind him, and saw it was marvellously ill written. However I am certainly not the person to make comments on anybody's writing.

You also give a nice account of Mary Monro's [1] dress: which must have been admirable. I am very glad to hear there is at least one comfort in the family. I think we may perhaps bring her some little thing from Venice which may give pleasure, though almost all modern Venetian manufactures and ornaments are as vulgar as they are dear.

All quite well. Dearest love to my mother.

Ever my dearest Father,
Your most aff[e] Son
J Ruskin.

LETTER 16

Sunday. 21st Sept. [1851]

My dearest Father,

I suppose my letters from Venice will now come regularly enough to let you tell me on which day I need not write, in order to allow for Sunday at Denmark Hill, but until I hear from you I shall write every day as usual.

3. Lady Paulina Trevelyan (1816–66), wife of Sir Walter Trevelyan, the botanist. Called by Ruskin his "monitress-friend," she was a woman of literary and artistic tastes as well as a botanist. She died at Neuchâtel while on a tour with her husband, niece, Ruskin, and his cousin Joan.

1. A relative of the Robert Munro mentioned in Letter 10.

I see in your letter of the 21st August to Thun, two queries, Where is Watts, and where is Watts's Effie? Where Watts is I cannot tell—though I hope I may be able to bring him here, but Watts's Effie is lent to her father until we come back—and we hear it is much admired by every body and thought quite perfect—I should have fancied it would have been too fine for them.

I rather wonder at Daily News [1] attacking Pre-Raphaelitism unless they have committed themselves by first attacking the pictures. They talk of my inconsistency because they cannot see two sides at once: all people are apparently inconsistent who have a wide range of thought—and can look alternately from opposite points. The most inconsistent of all books is the Bible, to people who cannot penetrate it: Nevertheless I should have thought the Daily News people had wit enough to get at the thread of the Story in Pre-Raphaelitism. It is not so profound as all that.

Apropos of inconsistency, I was looking for some passages of Bible which might be associated with Job's confidence in his righteousness; and indeed the more I read the Psalms, as well as Job—the more I am struck with the broad distinction asserted always between the Righteous and the wicked—which we are so apt to lose sight of in these days: But in the 7th Psalm: ask my mother to compare the 8th to 11th Verses of the Bible with the 8th to 12th of the Prayerbook. I usually like the Bible best—but here I think the Prayerbook version far the finest—and I should think the truest. It is incomparably the most humble— The "guide" instead of "establish" in the 9th verse makes an enormous difference. The 12th is altogether a different truth, and most beautiful in prayerbook.

Dearest love to my mother.

Ever my dearest Father,
Your most aff[e] Son J Ruskin.

LETTER 17

22nd September [1851]

My dearest Father,

I enclose a letter for Lady Trevelyan which after reading please seal and send— Her letter is enclosed also—which I am sure you will like— You will see she is clever if you knew how good and useful she was also you would be flattered by her signature to me—"your ever dutiful and affectionate Scholar."

1. A review of Ruskin's pamphlet, *Pre-Raphaelitism,* appeared in the *Daily News* on August 13, 1851.

I cannot write any more today. Dearest love to my mother. Ever my dearest Father.

Your most aff^e Son
J Ruskin.

LETTER 18

24th September [1851]

My dearest Father,

I am looking over your last letter for questions— I see Watts's picture still at Foord's—it had better stay there another day or two till I have time to write to Watts about it— You also caution me about rowing—but I never row violently, and never take any one on board with me—except a crab or two, or a sea horse, who though very ill-behaved —and indulging—the latter at least in what might ironically be called horse play—do not put the gondola in any danger of being upset—I am getting on with my chapters; but I cannot send you anything finally ready for press till I have been to Torcello—as the book begins there and the other chapters refer to the first, and I dare not go to Torcello till the frosts begin—as there is a chance of fever just now—at least people say so—and I have always ascribed my little illness at Padua to Torcello at this season but there is no sense or appearance of any danger anywhere—the canals smell much less now than in winter, and the only thing we ever have to complain of is cold or wet—and a mosquito or two less troublesome by their real demands than provoking by the impertinent way in which they make them.

There is nothing else I think about which you need now be anxious— D.V. I look for much happiness and contentment and bettering of health here—if the winter be not too severe, and for a happy spring with you in Switzerland—when I shall be delighted to go to Vevay—or Grindelwald—or Simmerthal, or any place that you and mama choose —as I shall then be resting—not working—or if working at all—not on the Alps. So fix entirely your own line of journey. Dearest love to my mother.

Ever my dearest Father,
Your most aff^e Son
J Ruskin.

LETTER 19

24th September. Evening [1851]

My dearest Father,

I may now as well get into the habit of answering your letters overnight; as I get them about three o'clock afternoon—and cannot send any letter away by that day's post. I have none however today, and therefore only write this by way of beginning at the fixed time— For I have now really a time for everything: and for the first time in my life I feel to be living really in my own house. For I never *lived* at any place that I loved before—and have been either *enduring* the locality, or putting up with somewhat rough habitation—I never found myself settled for six months in any place that I liked.

Effie has had not a little scolding to do—George especially being very restive and grumbling at first at everything—more especially at losing his four francs and a half of boardwages—however we have got our household now into very good order and punctuality—except that Effie cannot succeed in getting her gondoliers to dress well— This is much my fault—unavoidable, as I keep one of them lounging about all day with the boat wherever [I] may happen to want it—and this spoils both his clothes and his habits.

I think I left, in a large portfolio of miscellaneous plates in Park St, Turner's "Grand Canal" engraved from Munro's [1] picture. If you can

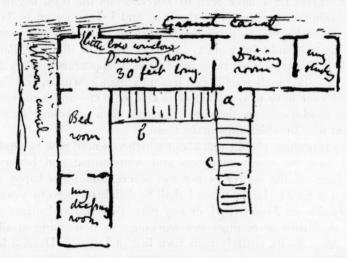

find it, it will give you a perfect idea of the place where we are—our house being just *out* of that picture on the left hand side of it—and looking across the grand canal to the Salute steps. Out of our dining room door, we come on to a landing a. whence about 15 steps go down to the right as at b. under the bedroom, to the door on the narrow canal,

1. Hugh Andrew Johnstone Munro, better known as Munro of Novar, an ardent collector of paintings and close friend of Turner. Munro, the son of a British consul, formed the famous nineteenth-century "Novar Collection." He died in 1868, having lived "a sensuous life." His collection was sold in 1877, at which time Ruskin acquired several Turners. For further information about Munro see Alexander Mackenzie's *History of the Novars* (Inverness, 1897).

and straightforward, as at c. into the courtyard, whence by another door we come out on a little campo, very cheerful and clean—Mama will understand the lie of the rest of the rooms by the plan.

I see you have answered Oxley's [2] note about Roman etchings—so I suppose I need not. Dearest love to my Mother. Ever my dearest Father,

Your most affec. Son
J Ruskin.

LETTER 20

25th September [1851]

My dearest Father,

I have today yours with Dr Croly's [1]—I saw the death two days ago, but was too much shocked to write. The enclosed line—if you think it fit to go, please send. How fearfully some people are chastened—again and again, and yet again— Living in sorrow: I have been trying to understand the meaning of the language of Job [2] lately, and I think I have got at it more than I ever could before— I do not know anything more touching than his always appealing to God as the "Preserver of Men"—"It is thy visitation which has preserved my spirit." Only the hopelessness of his first breaking of silence is very strange. "Let the day perish wherein was I born:" Still—he remembers this afterwards—and calls it "the speeches of one that is desperate, which are as wind." You ask me my opinion of his letter. I think it by far the *most* sensible I ever saw from him—and the most deliberate in style—even in writing. I see no trace of failing mind.

I shall try this letter via Turin—it is very tiresome their going so far round.

Blumenthal is single—about my age I fancy, my banker here, amiable —but commonplace.

Dearest love to my mother. Best regards to Mr Domecq. [3]

Ever my dearest Father. Your most aff^e Son
J Ruskin

2. Perhaps Francis Oxley, wine merchant, whose offices were very close to those of Ruskin senior in the commercial district of London.

1. Rev. Dr. George Croly (1780–1860), a good friend of John James Ruskin. Early in life Dr. Croly enjoyed a limited literary reputation. In 1835, through the assistance of Lord Brougham, he obtained the rectory of St. Stephen's, Walbrook, where he acquired a reputation for impressive rather than persuasive eloquence. The death mentioned by Ruskin was that of Dr. Croly's daughter, Helen-Louisa-Mary, who died on September 8, 1851, at the age of nine.

2. During Ruskin's Venetian residence he wrote a 90-page commentary on the *Book of Job*.

3. Peter Domecq, a partner with John James Ruskin in the sherry firm of Ruskin, Telford, and Domecq. It has been said by W. G. Collingwood in *The Life and Work of John Ruskin,* 2 vols. (Cambridge, Mass., Houghton, Mifflin & Co., 1893), that the partnership consisted of "Domecq contributing the sherry, Mr. Henry Telford the

LETTER 21

26th September [1851]

My dearest Father,

Effie is getting so domestic that we really have no news for you—I have nothing to say now but that I have been writing and rowing and resting—and so an end of the day: I rise at ½ past six: am dressed by seven—take a little bit of bread, and read till nine—then we have breakfast punctually: very orderly served—a little marmalade with a silver leafage spoon on a coloured tile at one corner of the table—butter very fresh—in ice—fresh grapes and figs—which I never touch; on one side —peaches on the other—also for ornament chiefly—(I never take them) —a little hot dish, which the cook is bound to furnish every morning—a roast beccafico—or other little tiny kickshaw—before Effie white bread and coffee: Then I read Pope or play myself till 10—when we have prayers: and Effie reads to me and I draw till eleven: then I write till one when we have lunch: then I go out, and sketch or take notes till three —then row for an hour and a half—come in and dress for dinner at 5, play myself till seven—sometimes out on the water again in an idle way: tea at seven—write or draw till nine—and get ready for bed. I do wish the winter would not come—it is so delightful at present—always cool enough to row—and warm enough to sit still—though the weather has on the whole been bad—much thunder and rain.

Effie thinks at present our household expences altogether will be as much as 800 francs a month—this is rather more than I expected but still much less than it used to be at Danieli's— There my expences were as nearly as possible 53 francs a day: for George with myself and Effie. With our other servant it would have been 4½ more. Still we are living in a very first rate kind of way here—and may economise a little still. It is my bedtime tonight—and I must economise my eyes. Dearest love to my Mother.

Ever my dearest Father,
Your most aff^e Son
J Ruskin.

LETTER 22

Sunday 28th [September 1851]

My dearest Father,

I had yesterday yours of 19, 20, 22nd and direct this Via Chiasso—as you tell me—though it will not be much worth directing anywhere—

capital, and Ruskin the brains." It was one of Domecq's daughters, Clothilde, in whom Ruskin was much interested as a youth. An account of this relationship is given in *Praeterita* (*Works, 35,* 229 ff.).

for we had Lady Sorel to tea last night and so I did not write my letter. She is Lord Glenelg's friend and is very kind and good to Effie—took her yesterday to the Princess Hohenlohe's—and got the "commands" of the Infanta of Spain, who is here just now—that Effie should come and call on her so that I graciously allow of her, Lady S. being asked to tea—provided she go away at 10 o'clock at latest—today there is the highest tide I ever saw in Venice and I am just going out to look at it before I go to church—so I can only send love— Dearest love to my mother. Ever my dearest Father

Your most aff[e]. Son
J Ruskin.

LETTER 23

Sunday Evening 28th [September 1851]

My dearest Father,
I have today, after a very pleasant English service your little note of the 23rd with the one enclosed from Exeter which does indeed give me as much pleasure as any one that I ever received—and I really was rather glad of it as a comfort—for when I read those reviews of *pre-Raphaelitism*,[1] I was so disgusted by their sheer—broadfaced—sheepish —swinish stupidity that I began to feel as I wrote in the morning that I was really rather an ass myself to string pearls for them— It is not the malice of them—that—when it is clever is to be met boldly and with some sense of its being worth conquering. But these poor wretches of reviewers do in their very inmost and most honest heart, Misunderstand every word I write: and I never could teach them any better—and one fancies that nearly everybody else is the same; and gets discouraged. So I was glad of this letter.
I am very much puzzled about Marmont. There is certainly no question but he is the real man— The Austrians ought to know if anybody does—and here he is received—and has been, these twenty years, as *the* Marshal Marmont—but there is nothing the matter with his arm except two fingers shattered— Yet—of all people, Mr Cheney who has been in society these thirty years, making it his study, would be least likely to speak of him as *the* Marshal if he were not. Where is he said to have lost his arm? And to have died?[2]
Effie went to call on the Spanish Infanta today, who was very kind and very graceful—but there was more ceremony in backing out of the room than at our Queen's drawing rooms—and yet she is only a Royal

1. For a full account of the reception of this pamphlet see *Works, 12,* xlix ff.
2. There seems to have been some confusion in England at this time as to whether Marmont was alive or dead. As Ruskin's letter indicates, he was alive and active in Venetian society.

Princess, not a proper queen in any sense; only Don Carlos's [3] son's wife, so I don't see why they make so much fuss about her: I suppose here in Austria they make the most of all the rank they can get.

Villanous [*sic*] weather still—East wind and rain—but quite well.

Dearest love to my mother.

> Ever my dearest Father.
> Your most aff[e] Son
> J Ruskin.   —Over.

I think my illustrations of Venice are in right hand narrow upright recess of lower division of my bookcase in study: If not there, look in the horizontal shelves of lower division.

I am thankful to hear Mama is said to be looking well, and that the little illness was traceable to mulberries—or to anything: I have been trying experiments to see if I can get bad taste out of my mouth in the morning—I cut off vegetables—fruit—pastry—sauces—wine—one after another— No good—then tried how little I could eat—to do with. Went on so for five days—found my pulse get very low—and felt feverish —and Taste in mouth as bad as ever: Put on a glass of wine and dined as usual and am quite well again—but can't get rid of Taste—however it shows that although the stomach does not always do its duty in an agreeable way nor without discomfort—it does not answer always to give it very little to do.

LETTER 24

Monday, 29th September [1851]

My dearest Father,

I am doubly grateful to the American Art Union [1]—both for its own contents—and for procuring me the pleasure of a letter from you three days running—and I am promised one, I see tomorrow also—which however as far as it relates to *Turners* I may at once anticipate by begging you *never* to let *one* out of the house for any purpose whatsoever — I should not have a minute's peace if I thought there was any chance of such a thing.

I have been putting Via Chiasso on my letters—but I will enquire myself tomorrow at what time that post goes—and take care to send your letters by it.

I am much gratified by the Americans' vindication of my consistency,

---

3. Pretender to the Spanish throne and known to his Carlist adherents as Don Carlos VI (1818–61). He was more commonly known as the Count of Montemolin.

1. A long letter from a correspondent appeared in the *Bulletin of the American Art-Union* on August 1, 1851, which purported to clear Ruskin of a charge of inconsistency which had been laid against him. The letter is entitled "Ruskin and the Pre-Raffaelites" and is signed merely "W."

which is very nicely done indeed. I shall say something about it myself in my next preface—but am very glad to find meanwhile that there are really some people who understand me. I should think you must be pleased also. Shall I send you it back?

Effie had a call today from two ladies of high name—Esterhazy [2] and Hohenlohe—the latter she says is singularly graceful and pleasing—the Esterhazy—(Countess) I don't know anything about yet—and have no time to enquire as Effie is busy looking out for old candlesticks to put in the windows—the Emperor is to arrive at eleven o'clock and begs everybody to give him candlelight up the grand canal.

I saw David Roberts today: what you say of him is very true. But Venice has been used to all kinds of libels—and must put up with it— Nobody could draw her but John Lewis. You will be glad to hear however that the first thing Roberts did was to compliment me on my appearance—fine brown colour and so on. I am much in the open air—early to bed—and never working when I feel the least tired.

Dearest love to my mother. Ever my dearest Father.

Your most aff^e Son
J Ruskin.

LETTER 25

30th September [1851]

My dearest Father,

I have today your nice letter with Buchanan's [1] enclosed—and the excellent answer to Scott's request [2] for a Turner—nothing could possibly be better—but I am very sorry you *will* have wine merchants. I think it very wrong of you instead of your duty, as you call it. I am quite sure you might just as well have yourself bled in the arm, as the Venetian ladies do by way of preserving health, regularly once a month or so—or take a limited quantity of prussic acid—or do any other thing partially destructive—by way of doing your duty, as have company.

(1st October. Morning). I asked David Roberts to dine here with a friend, who was travelling with him, and I just feel this morning—

2. Sarah Frederica Caroline Villiers (1821–53), daughter of George Child Villiers, 5th Earl of Jersey. In 1842 she married Nicholas Paul Charles Esterhazy (1817–94).

1. While en route to Venice in August, Ruskin had been in correspondence with a needy Scottish artist, one J. Buchanan of Glasgow. The Buchanan mentioned here would seem to be the same person.

2. Doubtless one of the two men named Scott associated with the art firm of Colnaghi. The first John Scott connected with the firm was a nephew and partner of Dominic Colnaghi (1790–1879), who had been partner to his father, Paul Colnaghi (d. 1833). After Dominic Colnaghi and this first John Scott died, a second John Scott, cousin to the first, carried on the business. It is regrettable that no history of this firm has been written as it occupied a singular position in the annals of nineteenth-century artistic life.

though they went away at 10 o'clock, that half my day's strength is taken out of me—I *cannot* do with anything but perfect quiet, and I am sure after your business, you cannot either.

I have the advertisement of my various Opera—also—which is very cleverly done—and disgusting in the highest degree—I cannot bear using the "Opinions" of these gentlemen as if they were any help to me or good to me. The next advertisement that is to be published I will try and put in a somewhat novel form—I shall copy out some of the choicest bits of abuse I can find—beginning with the Economist—and publish *them* as the "Opinions of the Press." However—I must remember another of the awkward differences I found in the versions of the Psalms the other day: I was reading the 15th and when I came to the 4th verse, (Bible version) "In whose eyes a vile person is contemned" I began to think with myself—"Well—*that* virtue at any rate I am not altogether wanting in." However, I thought I might as well look at the prayer book version—and then I found quite another thing—which did not suit me nearly so well. Dearest love to my mother. I asked myself at Post office about letters, and I believe my late letters must have all come right: the thing is to post them before two o'clock: Tell me after this if any go wrong with the date of aberration. Dearest love to my mother.

Ever my dearest Father Your most aff^e Son
J Ruskin.

LETTER 26

1st October. Evening [1851]

My dearest Father,

Effie is gone out with Lady Sorel to the Countess Esterhazy's—and I stay at home to read Venetian History: interrupted only now and then by a note or two from, I believe Thalberg [1]—who is idling on the piano in the room from which mine is separated only by a thin partition— I say I believe—because I don't know enough of music to recognize a fine touch in two or three notes—but he is staying in the house: and the notes are assuredly not put down by a novice.

Effie had two very pretty cards left for her today, which I have told her to keep for you to look at—the one of a lady of the old Venetian family, Marini—now a Russian princess—but she is prouder of the old Venetian name—and the Née *Marini,* comes bluntly in at the bottom of the card—the other of a Dame d'honneur of the Infanta—sent in the royal way of calling—but what makes the card interesting is the Infanta's own first name upon it—*Beatrix d'Este.*

It is rather curious that while living in lodgings is considerably cheaper

---

1. Sigismond Thalberg (1812–71), a well-known concert pianist. He was the illegitimate son of Prince Moritz Dietrichstein and the Baroness von Wetzler.

than living at an hotel, it is also so much more respectable— Effie is now looked upon as a Venetian lady—before she was merely a traveller: and no one took any notice of her.

I forgot to tell you how much Mr Roberts enjoyed your sherry last night—but I must now; as I shall soon want another dozen or two. The next ship you hear of for Venice, would you be so kind as to send me three dozen—of a *mild* sherry? I find on experiment that I am the better of about a glass and a half each day: neither more nor less. Effie takes a glass: so that a bottle lasts about three days or two bottles a week. But very nearly two went at once last night—for the artists declared it was like the best painting—at once *tender,* and *expressive*— Dearest love to my mother.

> Ever my dearest Father.
> Your most affᵉ Son,
> J Ruskin.

LETTER 27

> 2ⁿᵈ October [1851]

My dearest Father,

I quite forgot to answer that sentence in one of your letters about Mrs Farquharson [1]—pray assure her when you happen to be writing again that there is no coolness between Macdˡ [2] and me, but that when I was in London the only means I had of doing anything was just to see people when I came across them—not otherwise: and that *now* I am more than ever recluse—and shall remain so as long as I live—with every feeling of regard towards my old friends—only a determination to work while I have the light. I can talk when I am old. I shall send you a short letter tonight as I want to finish a little bit of writing before losing the thread of it—so goodbye, till tomorrow. Dearest love to my mother.

> Ever my dearest Father Your most affᵉ Son
> J Ruskin.

LETTER 28

> 3ʳᵈ October [1851]

My dearest Father,

I never have had time to tell you anything about the emperor's visit to us; in fact I was rather upset by it; for I am getting into such quiet ways that sitting up till two that night made me feel very sleepy the

1. A friend or, according to his son, "perhaps flame" of John James Ruskin.

2. William Macdonald Colquhoun Farquharson (1822–93), son of Mrs. Farquharson. In 1841 he changed his name to Macdonald Macdonald as this was one of the conditions under which he came into a large Perthshire estate.

next day—and then we had Roberts to dinner—which tired me the evening after—so that I did not get quite right again till yesterday. For the
Emperor announced himself for 10 o'clock at night—only about 10
o'clock on the previous morning—and there was little enough time to
get ready for him— Everybody on the Grand canal was requested by
the municipality to illuminate their houses *inside:* and the Rialto was
done at the public expense. They spent altogether—in Bengal lights and
other lamps about 300 pounds—a large sum for Venice in these days—
but I never saw the Rialto look so lovely: There were no devices or
letters or nonsense on it—only the lines of its *architecture* traced in chains
of fire—and two lines of bright ruby lamps set along its arch underneath
—so as to light the vault of it; all streaming down in bright reflection
on the canal— We went out a little before 10—and rowed down under
it to the part of the grand canal nearest the railroad station—there are
two churches there, one the Scalzi, the other a small Palladian one—I
forget its name opposite each other, and a great breadth of canal between
them: which was literally as full of boats as it could hold— They were
jammed against each other as tight as they could be—leaving just room
for each boatman to get his oar down into the water at the side—and so
we waited for some half-hour. It was a strange sight in the darkness,
the crowd fixed, yet with a kind of undulation in it which it could not
have had upon land, every gondolier at his stern, balanced, ready for the
slightest movement of the boats at his side—lest they should oust him
out of his place—and the figures standing up on the lower level, in the
open part of the boats—from one side of the canal to the other—one
could not see on what they stood—only here and there the flashing of
the tide beneath, as it flowed fiercely in the torchlight—and beside and
among the figures the innumerable beaks of the Gondolas, reared up with
their strange curving crests like a whole field full of dragons—the black
glittering bodies just traceable close beside one—one would have thought
Cadmus had been sowing the wrong teeth—and grown dragons instead
of men: There was a boat close beside us with some singers—beggarly
fellows enough—but with brown faces and good voices—and another
with a band in it farther on—and presently after there was some report
of the emperor's coming, and they began burning Bengal lights among
the boats, which showed all the fronts of the palaces far down the canal
against the night— And presently the emperor *did* come—in his grey
coat and travelling cap—and they pushed him down the steps into his
boat—and then the whole mass of floating figures and dragons' heads
began to glide after him— He had expressly invited everybody who had
a gondola to come and meet him, and there were no measures taken to
keep them off so it was who should get the closest to him. And one could
not see the water—but the dashing of the oars was like the rushing of
a great waterfall—and there—standing on the black gliding field, were

all the gondoliers writhing and struggling, one could not see what for
—but all in violent and various effort—pushing their utmost to keep
their boats in their places and hold others back—and a great roar of
angry voices besides— We had held on for ten minutes or so to the
singers who had been ordered to precede the emperor up the canal—but
we got pushed away from them, and fell back a few yards into the thick
of the press—and presently came crash up against the bow of the emperor's own boat—and so stuck fast. There was no moving for a minute
or two—Effie and I were standing—I of course with my hat off and
I made signs to my boatman to keep off the emperor if he could— There
was no stirring however for half a minute—when we managed to push
back the gondola on the other side of us—and slip clear of the emperor
—who passed ahead—giving us a touch of his cap. We fell astern of
him—but the next moment were pushed forward on the other side—
until our first boatman was exactly abreast of him— This time it was
not a gondola on our other side, but a barge full of very ill looking fellows,
who I thought might just as well have me between them and the emperor
as not—so I let Beppo [1] keep his place, which for the rest he was anxious
enough to do—and so rowing and fighting with all his might—and
ably seconded by the stern boatsman, he kept guard on the emperor's
flank for a quarter of an hour: the worst of it was that we were continually forced up against his boat—and so shook him and splashed him
not a little—until at last another gondola forced its beak in between us,
and I was glad enough to give way— It took us something like an hour
to get along the whole course of the canal—so impossible was it for the
gondolas to move in the choked breadth of it—and as the emperor did
not arrive till eleven, and after we got to St Mark's place there was
music and showing himself at windows, &c. it was near one before we
could get away towards home—and we left him still at his window. I
lay in bed till eight—but the emperor reviewed the troops at seven in the
morning. He went away for Trieste at 4 afternoon.

I hope you will be able to make out this very ill written letter but I
am getting sleepy and my hand is cramped with rowing.

Dearest love to my mother.

Ever my dearest Father.
Your most aff^e Son,
J Ruskin.

LETTER 29

Sunday, 5th Oct. [1851]

My dearest Father,

I had yesterday your letter of last Sunday, and I see you are to have

1. The Ruskins' gondolier.

mine on Saturday—so we are really quite close to each other. I am going to post this myself and always on Sunday to make sure of it, though I believe George is very punctual on the whole.

There is a great deal to be answered in your letter—first the question about what seems to have given you and mama some uneasiness, what I said about "a house full of sacrifices." I have no doubt the meaning of sacrifices in the verse itself is as mama interprets it. Sacrifices were in most cases offered before rejoicings—and fulness of them implied wealth—so Solomon says that a dry morsel with quietness is better than the fat and sweetness of all sacrifices—with strife—meaning the same thing nearly as Proverbs 15, 17, only perhaps with a farther allusion to the observance of religious formalities.

I forget what I said exactly—but I think I gave a twist to the verse—and meant to make a kind of feeble pun upon it, taking sacrifice in the other common sense; that at Denmark Hill we make a great many sacrifices—we sacrifice a great deal of time—and a great deal of money: and put ourselves about in various ways, and get nothing for it—no peace—only trouble or strife, so that I used *both* the words improperly; if strife in the verse itself means contention. I supposed it to mean only struggle or trouble, as again Ch. xv. 16.

Mama asks what is the essence of the distinction between the wicked and the righteous which is so frequently insisted on in the Psalms. I fancy there are two things to be looked for—Faith and conduct—of which though faith is the most important—conduct is first to be looked for, as that of which the outer world is most cognizant—and which is productive of most good.

Now of the Conduct of one whom God testifies to, as a Righteous and perfect man, we have a *complete* account in the xxxist of Job. We have in it—1st.   Truth. v. 5–7.

2nd.   Chastity. v. 9–12.—(I understand this to include abstinence from other sensual improper pleasures.)

3.   Justice and respect to inferiors. v. 13–15.

4.   Ministry to the poor. v. 16–23.

5.   Contempt of riches. v. 24–25.

6.   Withdrawal from idolatry. v. 26–28.

7.   Freedom from envy. v. 29–30 (N.B. I don't understand the 31st verse.)

8.   General Hospitality. v. 32.

9th.   Open confession of known sins. v. 33.

10th.   Fearlessness of public opinion. v. 34.

I suppose this on the whole to be the most complete and concise account of a man well pleasing to God that we can have—or that exists.

We have however shorter ones from David—1st Psalm, 15th Psalm—24th Psalm—26th—34th—101st—&c. in all which places the first thing is nearly always Truth—e.g. Ps. xv. v. ii. Ps. xxvi. v. 1–3. Ps. xxxiv. v. *12–13:* Ps. ci. v. 7. and the Wicked are nearly always described as persons working deceit and falsehood. David also dwells a great deal upon his indignation against—and refusal to associate with, wicked persons—but I think for the most part—after Truth comes Mercy—as God Himself is called a God of Mercy and truth, and this human mercy is made the test of all men by Christ in the Judgment—not the feeling— but the act. "Ye, *did* it unto the least of these"—so the wicked are described by David not only as lying but as bloodthirsty and cruel. So if I were asked for a short definition of a righteous man, I should say one who was always trying to speak and act truth, and always doing kind- nesses and relieving distresses, and that a wicked man was one who never cared about truth—(and we may be sure that those who do not live in a complete *Atmosphere* of Lies) and who only did what he thought good for himself.

And I believe the world would be infinitely mended, if clergymen preached *this* more and matters of faith less.

But ii. Faith is required as much as conduct, of which I believe the essence to be this—"He that cometh to God must believe that He *is* and that He is a rewarder of them that *diligently Seek* Him."

And that in this respect, the distinction between the wicked and right- eous is that the Wicked man says there is no God, and lives in no hope of another world, and the Righteous man knows there is a God, loves Him—hopes to be with Him—seeks Him—and does all that He does, to serve Him.

And I believe this distinction to be a much wider and stronger one in God's eyes than that into Christian and Pagan: and that in all nations —the men who are trying to serve the Great Spirit, according to what they know of Him, are distinguished as Righteous from those who are living to themselves and to this world.

How far men are punished for their sins by having the true knowledge of God withdrawn from them—and being suffered to serve sticks and stones is a totally different question— We know in general that all ignorance of the true God must have had its origin in sin.

And therefore I say—Conduct is the first thing—though both react one on the other: It is of no use, as far as I see—trying to protestantize these Italians. They are totally incapable of understanding the beauty of Christ's own character. The first thing to be done is to teach them common Decency—Manliness and Truth. They are at present a curious Hybrid between the Fox and the Pig. I may give you one most striking instance of their character—though it is one you cannot well read out to my mother. The four last arches of the Ducal palace next the bridge of sighs having been partially filled up in the Renaissance times, afford a series of corners which—ever since I have known Venice—have been

used by the Italians as those portions of our railroad stations are which
are externally described as being set apart for "Gentlemen." It is nearly
impossible to approach the capitals, though among the most beautiful
of the series; and this is on the broad front of the Palace—in the place
where the Venetian senators used to have their own separate walk—
the most honourable and restricted piece of ground in Venice.

Since the Austrians came back, some order has been attempted with
this abuse and I was delighted to see four large tablets put up in these
arches, with "E vietato di lordare sotto pena di multa." [1] In a week after
they were put up, I saw some marks on these tablets—and on going up
to them—I found them scribbled over with black pencil—with "Morte
all' Austria" written between the words.

This may I think be considered as very nearly typical of the character
of modern Italian republican agitation. They rage against Austria because she will not let them ———— against their own palaces.

I do not at all mean to say everything the Austrians do is right, but
do believe that the officials—Governors and middle men in general, are
as uncorrupt—and as desirous of doing what is right as any man can
be. What the Austrian government may be at headquarters—or what
its views respecting this place, I don't know.

Scott's answer is very nice about Turner. Is it the Scott of Colnaghi's?
Dearest love to my mother.

> Ever my dearest Father
> Your most affᵉ Son
> J Ruskin

LETTER 30

Tuesday 7ᵗʰ October [1851]

My dearest Father,

I did not write yesterday, and have not much to tell you today: a
practical piece of information I have however some time been intending
to give you—when nothing more important came in the way. I suppose
at the Countinghouse you sometimes use Lucifers—and all the Lucifers
I ever tried in England had a sulphurous and highly unpleasant odour—
except the wax ones, which are expensive—and difficult to light without
burning one's fingers—besides that their heads are apt to come off—
and very often—if ill-made, they will explode with a vindictive Crack
—and throw off fiery fragments nearly as high as one's eyes. I therefore
think you ought to be obliged to me for telling you of a Perfect or
Unmatched match—if only you can *get* it. If at any German warehouse
—or through any German correspondents, you can provide yourself with

---

1. "It is forbidden under penalty of fine to befoul the walls."

a box of Wasserdichtes Feuerzeug, (ohne Phosphorgeruch) von *A. M. POLLAK*, in Wien, you will find yourself in possession of a match which lights with a *touch* on the sandpaper: which never fails—which burns with an agreeable odour, and which in all respects fully discharges all imaginable Luciferian functions.

In return for this information can you contrive means of sending me a box of Pills? Mr Brown—one day when he saw me eat little dinner, having inquired the cause—and ferretted out that I was not quite in order in the ulterior of the realm, needs must make me a present of a box of Dr Scott's Pills—requesting me to tell anyone who was coming from London to bring him another. If you hear of anybody fit to undertake so important a trust, please send me a box of Dr Scott's Bilious and Liver Pills—sold by Lambert. No 20. Jermyn St Haymarket.

You have never said a word of whether Newton seemed to have enjoyed his tour with us—or of anything he said? or whether he was much fatigued with his journey home— Ask him to write to us—when you see him. Dearest love to my mother.

Ever my dearest Father. Your most aff^e Son
J Ruskin.

By the bye, did I mention that you had better now direct my letters Casa Wetzler Campo Sta Maria Zobenigo—we shall sometimes get one that might be missed for a day.

LETTER 31

Wednesday, 8th October [1851]

My dearest Father,

I am only going to send you a line today, as it is very fine and mild and I want to make the most of the good weather. I have very pleasant recreation—refreshing after my stony work, in studying the Fish, or rather the aquatic inhabitants of the lagoons, of anomalous and indescribable character; represented mainly by the cuttlefish—with whom I have a species of sympathy on account of his pen and ink—and the Sea-Horse —whom I like much better than a land horse—chiefly because having no legs, there is no chance of his coming down on his knees— It is a pity he is so small—for he is very beautiful in the water—with his crest erect, and a fin on his back, invisible in the dried specimens, with which he propels himself like a screw steamer—revolving it with a velocity like the whirr of an insect's wing. There are also little green long nosed beasts of the same family whom I like for being six sided, like a quartz crystal —and besides—we are great friends with the crabs under the windows, whom I believe to be fellows of infinite jest—as well as ingenuity— In fact they *back* out of any awkward position with a dexterity which her

Majesties [*sic*] ministers might envy. A crab on shore can only be considered as a good fellow at a *pinch*—but a crab in the water is a very different sort of person. I had no idea of their rapidity of motion.

The book is going on very nicely—and I think will be very interesting. Dearest love to my mother.

Ever my dearest Father.

Your most aff^e Son

J. Ruskin

LETTER 32

[10 October 1851]

My dearest Father,

I forget what great man it was who said he had acquired all his knowledge by never being prevented from asking a question by the fear of showing his ignorance. The rule is a very good one in general; but if the knowledge can be acquired without the sacrifice of one's dignity, it is pleasanter—and sometimes I think more prudent. There are a good many things which nearly all schoolboys know—and *I* don't, and when I am among people of the world, I think it better not to ask questions on such subjects—but to have recourse if possible to a dictionary—or a grammar. I happen to have no Latin dictionary nor grammar with me, and I want to know what "Indictionis"—the genitive and other oblique cases of Indictio, mean when used in *dates*. One gets in old inscriptions such expressions as—Die Mercurii octave exeunte Junio *indictione* septima.—Die lunae XI exeunte mense Septembris anno Domini 1189 —*Indic.* VII. Now I should think, if you do not happen to recollect what this means, you may still find some dictionaries or larger grammars among my books, and some morning or evening after you have got rid of all customers, you may ferret it out for me, and spare my blushes— For which I shall be exceedingly grateful.

The weather is getting a little better now—but of course all chance of heat is over until the springtime. It is just such weather that I can open my window—or rather leave it open—for I find it so of course— in my study when I go into it first at seven in the morning, and enjoy the fresh air—but the air *is* fresh—not by any means over soft or dulcet —and there are sometimes gusts of wind from the sea which cover the lagoons with foam, towards the afternoon—and it is not easy to get much foam off a lagoon—for of course the waves cannot rise in the shallow water, and must be very sharply edged indeed to break anywhere but at the edges of the shoals: However I think it must soon settle now into steady weather of some kind—I hope tolerably warm, as I cannot *think* over a place in cold weather. The cold frets me, and I begin to think whether I am safe in standing, and so on—instead of the matter in hand.

Dearest love to my mother.

Ever my dearest Father.
Your most aff^e Son
J Ruskin.

LETTER 33

Friday 10th [October 1851]

My dearest Father,

I have today your note with enclosed Ecclesiologist,[1] which is very satisfactory. I always think the reviews read very well when they quote *me,* and say nothing themselves.

I hope you will miss no more letters—if you do—it will be the post's fault—not ours, as I shall always send George after breakfast with letters—and the Chiasso post leaves at two.

I am not writing quite so well as I ought lately—my hands have got cramped and blistered with the oar—and are not yet quite used to it. I have a letter of Smith's to answer—so must be short tonight—I send the answer on next page, which please forward to him—as well as the enclosed print, to which the note refers: you can look at what I say. Dearest love to my mother.

Ever my dearest Father.
Your most aff^e Son
J Ruskin.

LETTER 34

11th October. [1851]

My dearest Father,

You ask if we see Mr Brown or Mr Cheney often. Very often—when we walked in St Mark's place, three times a week at any rate—now about twice— Their own houses are much more luxurious than ours—so it is a small compliment to ask either of them to come here—but they come to tea sometimes—and we sometimes to them. They are both as good-natured as can be—but of a different Species from me—men of the world—caring very little about anything but Men— Cheney is a kind of Beckford—I am not sure but that there is not some slight affectation of resemblance only he lets people into his house, which I believe Beckford never would.

---

1. A generally favorable review of *The Stones of Venice I* appeared in the *Ecclesiologist* in August 1851.

12th October. That scrawly bit above was written yesterday while waiting for lunch—which was after time—for a wonder, for we go quite by clockwork now—and in fact if the clocks would correct themselves by the motions of our establishment, it would be all the better for them: I say nothing about the *tides,*[1] which appear so entirely to have lost all sense of moral responsibility that they cannot be expected to take example by anybody. I never saw such tides—up and down to all manner of heights at all manner of times— The sea cannot be said to ebb and flow. It shakes up and down. However I shall have an interesting paragraph about the tides in the first chapter of next volume. For it is curious, rather, that the place where Venice was built, was the only place in the world where it *could* have been built. Had the tide been the *least* less than it is—had it been 2½ feet instead of three, the run of water through the streets would not have been enough for their healthy drainage—they would have become slow sewers—and the people would have been compelled to roof them in—and the town would have become pestiferous, like those on the edge of the Pontines. Had the tide been a foot more than it is—had it been *four* feet instead of three—no access could have been had to the gondolas at low water except down slimy steps. The entire system of boat carriage must thus have been put an end to.

No woman—no gaily dressed cavalier—could have been sure of being able to step into the gondola without a complete Brighton pier of planks and other machinery: and the result would have been an extension of the city on higher foundations—and common street carriage —as at any other seaport: But this would have implied also the loss of the aristocratic character in the seamanship—and we should have had *land* nobles as well as Sea nobles—and the whole state would have become like that of Pisa or Genoa.

When people first discover the peculiar adaptations of an animal or plant to its position, they are apt to exclaim—What wonderful preparation for the existence of this little creature—whereas, if they knew more of the Universe, they would begin to understand that everything in existence was put in the place it was fit for, and the mere fact of its existence proved that it was in the right place: And so one might look over Europe and see how each town takes its natural position—and becomes prosperous if it happens to understand that position and take due advantage of it—and one might say—generally, Genoa grows up in the place for Genoa—and Rotterdam in that for Rotterdam, and Venice in that for Venice. But I am almost disposed to admit a sort of special providence for Venice. The tide at this end of the Adriatic is a mystery no philosopher has explained. The structure of the mouths of the Brenta

1. For an extended discussion of tides see *The Stones of Venice II* (*Works, 10,* 12–14) and Appendix Three of the same volume.

and Adige is unexampled in the history of Geology. It seems that—just in the centre of Europe, and at the point where the influences of the East and West—of the old and new world—were to meet, preparation was made for the existence of the city which was to unite the energy of the one with the splendour of the other: and the Sea, which in other countries is an Enemy as well as a Servant—and must be fought with to be enslaved—or else—as to us in England is a severe Tutor as well as a protector—was ordered to minister to Venice like a gentle nurse—and to nourish her power without fretting her peace—to bear her ships —with the strength of our English seas—but to surround her palaces with the quietness of the Arabian sands.

There is a great deal more to be said to strengthen this, about climate—position under mountains &c.—but that is the main point, impressed upon me daily by the degree of ease or difficulty with which my gondola beak runs against the "posts of my door."

It is a lovely Sunday—and Effie is gone to her German church—her knowledge of that very disagreeable dialect enabling her to get a Protestant service from which I am debarred. However—we have prayers in the evening and I have some excellent sermons with me if I want to read any, of d'Aubigné [2]—and a great many excellent sermons around me, as I pass along the streets—of the [text indecipherable] class, besides some lectures by Hamilton,[3] (Miss—what's the name—Effie's friend and dressmaker's man)—on Ecclesiastes, which are *very* interesting. The first sentence—about twenty lines long—is the worst in the book, and for some time kept me from going any further, but now I like it very much.

It is time to post this now—to be quite sure—as far as one can be sure of anything— On Sunday I do it now myself.

Dearest love to my mother.

> Ever my dearest Father.
> Your most affec^e. Son
> J Ruskin.

LETTER 35

Tuesday, 14th October [1851]

My dearest Father,

I had on Sunday your kind letter of the 6th with advices about eating, &c. which I shall attend to— I find them quite in accordance with my

2. Jean Henri Merle d'Aubigné (1794–1872), Swiss historian and Protestant divine.
3. Dr. James Hamilton (1814–67), a Presbyterian minister who, from 1841 until his death, had the living of the National Scottish Church, Regent Square, London. He wrote many religious studies including *The Royal Preacher: Lectures on Ecclesiastes* (New York, 1848), to which Ruskin refers in this letter.

experiments—always excepting cream of Tartar, which I shall try: I find the great thing is Peace of mind—and not doing anything in a hurry—still I am beginning to have sad suspicion, of both Tea and Coffee, and to fancy that if I could live on milk and water, I should in that respect be better. I am not going to try it all at once but to reduce quantity of tea—and take more milk with warm water— The thing I chiefly want to get rid of is the excitable state in which I have been ever since those sleepless nights came on in 1845. I never since then have felt *thoroughly* sleepy: except sometimes in Church.

I am getting on with book—please tell Mr Prout when you happen to see him that I have constant occasion to refer to him—as the only modern parallel of Lombardic Sculptors—that I find my word "Proutism" [1] the most useful [I] have yet coined—and that I enjoy and admire his works more than ever. Only this morning I have been working, all the while I was dressing, at that sketch of the Hotel de Ville at *Ulm* which you must recollect our going hunting for,* ages ago, in the town itself—and I am quite amazed at the skill and science of little bits of drawing which I used to think mere Manner and accident—and that I should be able in time to do like them myself— But I find Prout as inimitable—in his way, as even Turner. And the poor shallow coxcombs of artists that pretend to look down upon him! I wish you would send me the bit cut out of Globe of the 4th, I cannot get it here. I heard the Conde de Montemolin was enquiring for it.

I am rather short for time, though I ought to have a double letter for you today—but my time has been a little trenched upon in the evenings lately, for a gentleman was introduced to us who is going to be Tutor to the Prince of Wales: and I thought I might as well get some hold in that quarter—might do a great deal of good— So I let him be asked to tea, and found him sensible—and have given him several lectures on the Renaissance, which I think he will not forget. He is a lawyer, a Mr Gibbs. [2]

Dearest love to my mother.

> Ever my dearest Father
> Your most affe Son.
> J Ruskin.

* i.e. not the Sketch, but the subject of it.

1. In *The Stones of Venice I* (*Works, 9, 300*) Ruskin writes: "All expedients . . . both of simplification and energy, for the expression of details at a distance where their actual forms would have been invisible, but more especially this linear method, I shall call Proutism; for the greatest master of the art in modern times has been Samuel Prout."

2. Frederick Waymouth Gibbs, a barrister, who was tutor to the Prince of Wales from 1851 until 1858.

LETTER 36

15th October [1851]

My dearest Father,

There may perhaps be a letter for me this morning, but I send George to post office early, and forgot to go to the office myself yesterday afternoon till it was shut—but I left some things unanswered in your last— I am sorry to hear Quarterly is so stupid—and I cannot understand it—for I think Lockhart [1] seems about the best man in London to conduct such a thing. But I suppose he has for some time lost all cheerfulness: and that may prevent him from understanding what it is that other people enjoy: And he is worldly, and gossiping—and likes gossip about 18th century people—which is the dullest in the world— Curiously enough we heard as soon as we came to Venice that he had refused a paper of Mr Brown's, nailed [sic] on some book or other lately out—but in reality all about *Othello*—who was, in reality, the Doge Ludovic Moro [2]—whose shield bore three mulberries—the same as the sign of the Desdemona handkerchief—and who among the various annals of great services done by him for the state—is—just at Shakespeare's time—and before Moro was Doge—described one day as coming from Cyprus, "wearing his beard long, for the death of his wife" and there is a great deal more which Mr Brown has fished out about him, very interesting—but Lockhart wouldn't have it.

The reviews do not annoy me by their malice—but by their stupidity— I am often much more worried in a small way, by people's not understanding me than by their differing with me. So Effie has more difficulty in keeping her temper, sometimes, with Mary than Melina— though Melina was utterly designing and virtueless—and Mary an admirable servant—so soon as she can be made to understand what she has to do. It was impossible for a long time after she came here, to make her receive or believe, as a fact, that the Venetians did *not* understand English: She used to issue directions in pure—quiet English—to the washerwomen—and tradespeople—and come to her mistress next day very angry because they had not been obeyed. Effie assured her that English would *not* do for Italians—but down went Mary to the kitchen and tried more English—a perfect stream of English, at the top of her voice—and Effie went down and found her oratorizing in a great pas-

1. John Gibson Lockhart (1794–1854) edited the *Quarterly Review* from 1825 until 1853. That he should have "lost all cheerfulness" is not surprising, for the closing years of his life were sad indeed. His sight was failing, and he was prematurely old "from excessive abstinence." Furthermore, one daughter had gone over to Rome, and he was estranged from one of his sons.

2. Ruskin has here confused Doge Ludovic Moro with Doge Christopher Moro about whom Rawdon Brown wrote his paper.

sion—and the washerwoman staring at her, and laughing: George tried to interpret—but Mary *would* give her own orders her own way. At last she has given it up—but I believe in a settled conviction that the Italians *Won't* understand English, and that there is a combination among them to insult her; and pretend ignorance: So she is very sulky —or was: for she is beginning to be reconciled to the Great Fact. But it is quite beyond the powers of her brain to understand How it is. So I begin to feel like Mary—that I may talk forever—and no one will Understand me—and I sometimes feel a little disposed to get into a passion about it. It is very odd those Yankees should make me out—the last people from whom I should have expected appreciation.[3]

Bad weather again— Constant sea fog— We have had just one perfect sunny day since we came to Venice.

Dearest love to my mother.

> Ever my dearest Father.
> Your most aff^e Son.
> J Ruskin.

Effie's best love

LETTER 37

16th Octb. [1851]

My dearest Father,

I have today yours with the Edinburgh Review [1]—which is marvellously dull—and I think about the most impertinent—next to the Economist [2]—that has come out. Fancy their coolly saying that my next volume will be much improved—if I engraft their opinions on mine— but that otherwise—for this they imply—it will not be fit to be published. If the man who wrote that could enter into my mind—and see the sort of grasp that these ten years living among stones has given to it! I think they *will* be a little taken aback, at last, when they see the way that the short sentences which they call inconsiderate are fallen back upon again and again in this new volume, and form foundation for all manner of unexpected truth—and when they begin to feel how far I was looking beyond them all when I wrote them. This second volume is to be called "The Sea Stories,"—for what on land we call a ground floor—I always call in speaking of Venetian buildings the *Sea* Story: and this will give the same kind of double meaning to the title

3. Ruskin is thinking of the communication to the *American Art Union* mentioned in Letter 24.

1. A reference to a criticism of *The Seven Lamps of Architecture* and *The Stones of Venice I* contributed to the *Edinburgh Review* of October 1851 by Coventry Patmore.

2. This magazine reviewed Ruskin's pamphlet, *Pre-Raphaelitism,* unfavorably on August 23, 1851.

of the second volume that there is in the first. However there is a good deal of interesting matter in the rest of the review, though I don't think I shall read it. I can't at present, at any rate—having a whole library of delicious Venetian books on my table—all my reading is given to Venetian or Church history—or to *play:* a little Galignani—Pope—or Household Words, but by no means Edinburgh Review.

I have a good many notes to set down tonight, so must say goodbye. Dearest love to my mother.

Ever my dearest Father.

Your most aff^e Son,

J Ruskin

I open this to say on no account to buy the Exhibition lithographs—it would be money thrown into Houndsditch.

LETTER 38

Sunday. 19th October [1851]

My dearest Father,

I am less particular about my Sunday's letter now, as you tell me the post cannot be depended upon. I shall however continue to post it my-self until I hear the result of the postings for the last fortnight. Look-ing over some of the papers you have sent in your last letters, I find the extract from Builder, which you sent, and I glanced at—merely for the use made of my name, to be a very interesting proposal by Mr Garbett [1] for the introduction of a new nomenclature for English Gothic, namely that instead of *descriptive* names, like "Perpendicular" "Lancet"— "Decorated" and the like, it should receive *Historical* names, "Ed-wardian" "Lancastrian," &c. to *fit in* with the now universally received "Norman," "Saxon," "Tudor," and the old classical "Corinthian" "Doric" "Ionic."

This innovation I think admirable—it will make all nomenclature consistent—and will be a great help to people in connecting styles with national character. I therefore mean to send a single line either tomor-row or next day—expressing my entire concurrence in the proposal— for you to send to the Builder [2]—concurrence I mean in the principle of the proposal—whether "Edwardian" or "Lancastrian" be the best terms I do not take on me to decide. But this is only part of the advan-tage of that little extract from the Builder—for in his recommendation

1. Edward Lacy Garbett (1817–87), who contributed this article to the October 4 issue of the *Builder,* was the author of many architectural studies. One of his most im-portant works was a *Rudimentary Treatise on the Principles of Design in Architecture* (London, 1850).

2. Ruskin's letter, expressing agreement with Garbett's ideas, was printed in the *Builder* on November 1, 1851.

of terms, M[r] Garbett divides the architecture of England by the reigns of its Kings in the very way I wanted to have done, and never have had time to do for myself, so that the little two inches square of paper will be of the greatest use to me for rapid reference—and are put aside in the safest corner of my drawer.

I am very glad you like that little drawing of Malvern—there is really a good deal in it—and it has one merit which very few of my works have—it is *finished,* and everywhere with equal care: it being one of the first things which I have done on the *fruits* of former labour. Until now—I have drawn everything with the sole view of learning what things were—the moment I had got all the information I wanted, the sketch was thrown aside—and only preserved as a memorial of certain facts.

I have now arrived at a time of life when I feel that my knowledge must—if it is ever to be so—be expressed in an intelligible form: legibly by others [as well] as myself— The drawings which I now am making here will be brought home not only finished—but *framed*—ready to be sent to the engraver the moment they are unpacked. They will also be much more popular in form and manner—many of them like the little vignettes to Rogers.

The Malvern would have been much better, if I had not been tired at the time—and only doing it as a sort of memorial of the place—besides the subject is a very awkward one, the foreground almost unmanageable.

I did not notice either what you said about Turner's trees and Hobbima's, and finding the latter a take in— Did you refer to the trees in the Bolton [3]—and how do you find the Bolton and waterfall do together? How do you continue to like the Prouts and Grand canal group? [4] And do you at all begin to care for the Black flag at the top of my study chimneypiece? But I forgot you were at Dover, and enjoying—I hope, enjoying real flags and anchors instead— It is curious —but I believe the electric line will be now unbroken to Trieste—and if I were to run over there in the steamer, we might *talk* as long as we liked: only it would be expensive. But I should think conversation would soon become cheap—like Tea—of the fall in the price of which, since Pepys time, I read in Household Words the other day—unless the governments lay a tax on Talk.

I shall write a line tomorrow unless I find at Post office today some positive directions. But I find casting up my accounts a hard business —they are accurate to a farthing—but I can't get them well divided

3. Turner's tree-drawing in *Bolton Abbey* is remarked upon in *Modern Painters I* (*Works, 3,* 586). The same drawing, which was included in the *England and Wales* series, is discussed at length in *Modern Painters IV* (*Works, 6,* 603 ff.).
4. Two studies of the Grand Canal done by Samuel Prout.

into *heads,* the long sums in addition floor me altogether— They can't come till Tuesday.

Dearest love to my mother.

Ever my dearest Father.
Your most aff^e. Son
J Ruskin.

LETTER 39

20th October [1851]

My dearest Father,

I don't know if I shall have time to write my note to the Builder, today, as for a wonder, we have two people coming to dinner—Sir Francis Scott [1] and Lord Dufferin [2]—the former especially recommended by a letter from Mr Fortescue [3] whom I don't want to be rude to because I like his sister [4] excessively; and she also concurs in the recommendation—nor without reason—for when he called yesterday I found him a very eager fellow in my own way, who had spent the time when he ought to have been reading for his class at Oxford in studying architecture, and may be very influential in England. Lord Dufferin called with a gentleman whom we knew in London—whose name— curiously enough, I saw yesterday in Galignani—in an extract from Sir R. Murchison's [5] statement of the geology of Sydney: [6] Count Stralecki [7] was named as the first discoverer of the resemblance between the Australian and Russian gold districts— As Lord Dufferin knew Scott I thought I might as well let him come too. Count Stralecki leaves Venice today—and Scott tomorrow—so the interruption will not be overwhelming.

1. Sir Francis Scott, Bt. (1824–63), who matriculated at Christ Church in May 1842; B.A. 1845; M.A. 1848.

2. Frederick Temple Blackwood, Lord Dufferin (1826–1902), who matriculated at Christ Church in October 1844.

3. Chichester Samuel Fortescue (1823–98), who matriculated at Christ Church in 1841; B.A. 1845; M.A. 1847. His life was devoted to politics and to the Irish question in particular.

4. Harriet Fortescue (1824–89), a woman of wide interests. She married David Urquhart, a diplomat. Her close friendship with John Ruskin and his parents is mentioned in M. C. Bishop's *Memoir of Mrs. Urquhart* (London, 1897).

5. Sir Roderick Impey Murchison (1792–1871), geologist. With two other scientists he published *The Geology of Russia and the Ural Mountains* (London, 1845).

6. An account of Strzelecki's explorations of Australian mountain ranges and their similarity to the Urals, together with the presence of gold therein, is given in the *Memoir of Sir Roderick Impey Murchison* by Archibald Geikie, 2 vols. (London, 1875); see especially *2*, 131 ff.

7. Sir Paul Edmund Strzelecki (1796–1873) was known as Count Strzelecki through his connections with a noble Polish family. He undertook the scientific exploration of part of Australia in 1839 and discovered gold in the Wellington district. He was the author of a geological study entitled *Physical Description of New South Wales and Van Dieman's Land* (London, 1845).

I have half written the line to Builder—but think I had better look at it again tomorrow.

Dearest love to my mother.

Ever my dearest Father.
Your most aff^e. Son
J Ruskin.

LETTER 40

21st October [1851]

My dearest Father,

If you approve of the enclosed note, will you be so kind as to forward it—if not—do not—as it is a matter of no consequence whatever— We had our people to dinner last night and I think they enjoyed themselves exceedingly—and who should arrive—in time to be asked to tea—but Scott the architect [1]—whom you must remember at Denmark Hill— So we had a great architectural séance—and I enjoyed it.

The two Scotts go away today— I shall have Lord Dufferin once more to tea—and then we shall be all quiet again—meantime I must send you only this line.

Dearest love to my mother.

Ever my dearest Father.
Your most affect. Son.
J Ruskin.

LETTER 41

[23 October 1851]

My dearest Father,

Mr Roberts left us last night at ½ past nine to go to Trieste and home by Vienna— He is hurried away from *Venice* to go to paint the *Great Exhibition* for the queen: However, Venice does not lose much. He has been what he calls sketching and brought me his books to look at last night. He sketches the Ducal palace this way—and says it is quite enough. How he is ever to work up his sketches I cannot imagine —however I am rather an unfair judge for I am morbidly accurate— but it just shows what a man comes to, when he draws for the *Exhibi-*

---

1. Sir George Gilbert Scott (1811–78), an outstanding exponent of Gothic architecture. His interest in this style was furthered by a meeting with Pugin, and his first Gothic building of prominence was the church of St. Giles, Camberwell. Scott restored many English cathedrals and also perpetrated two celebrated London architectural atrocities: St. Pancras Station and the Albert Memorial. It has been said that he frequently remodeled rather than restored.

tion only—and then they affect to despise the Pre-Raphaelites. I am the more sorry to see him falling in this way, for he is thoroughly kind,

upright, and good natured—upright at least in all but pretending to draw things when he does not.[1] However he made me lose my evening yesterday—so I must be short this morning. Dearest love to my mother.

Ever my dearest Father.

Your most affec^e. Son

J Ruskin.

LETTER 42

Venice. 24th October. [1851]

My dearest Father,

I have today yours of 17th—18th—with enclosed credit for £300—for which best thanks—and also I have with postmark, Trieste, the invoice of Madonna della Grazia, and the letters which I suppose came by her, Mr Moore, Mr Brown—(two) and Mr Evans. I imagine therefore she must be at Trieste, and that I shall soon hear of my packages. I will leave the credit with Blumenthal tomorrow.

I am ashamed of myself for never having answered your enquiries about the Verona letter. I quite thought I had it—for I had sent *twice* to Verona for letters—and one came, dated 24th—25th August—with Verona on it in your hand—but on referring to it I believe this is the

1. In *Academy Notes* (*Works, 14,* 167–8, 220–1) Ruskin criticizes David Roberts' paintings of *The Ducal Palace* and *The Church of Sta. Maria della Salute*. Ruskin's chief complaint is that the gondoliers in both pictures are in positions in which it is impossible to row.

Milan letter—as it has Milan also in your hand—and it has nothing of finance in it, though it has a great deal of more interesting subjects. So I write to Verona again.

A thousand thanks for the account of indication which I understand perfectly and which is all that I want— It does not appear a system at all likely to make my chronological investigations simpler.

Effie begs me not to allow mama to write to her. I hope she will not, I know what pain it is to her, to write and it makes me shudder to think of it— Effie's best love to her, and we both beg her not.

We have at last, most heavenly weather—quite summer—exquisite for drawing out of doors. I am getting on nicely.

Dearest love to my mother.

Ever my dearest Father,

Your most aff^e. Son

J Ruskin.

LETTER 43

Sunday, 26th Oct [1851]

My dearest Father,

I have today your delightful letter from Dover of the *21st*—but surely you must have made a mistake in the date—the post cannot have brought me your *Tuesday's* letter all the way here, this afternoon— I did not write this morning, not thinking my Sunday's letter was any use, now—but if the post goes at this rate, you ought to have *this* letter on Saturday—at Dover— However I suppose letters are delivered on Sunday everywhere but in London—so I ought to have written to-day : It is of no use taking any measures about posting—for the first month, George posted the letters always between one and two—the post professing to go at two—and the last fortnight or three weeks we have had the letters always posted in the morning before 12, to make sure— but evidently there is no sureness to be had.

I am very glad you liked my account of the position of Venice.[1] I think the whole book will be full of interest of the same kind—though mixed here and there with some architectural matters rather harder in the reading— I am rejoiced to hear also that my mother walks so well—and I look forward to some more happy rambles in Switzerland —only we must go where the roads are not very rough, nor very steep —and above all—you must give orders to have no *Economists* sent after you.

I thought that book of Miss Goldie's [2] looked very nice, but

1. In Letter 34.
2. Perhaps Emma Mary Goldie, authoress of *Poems* (London, 1835).

never had time to read it— I am glad you have found something in it.
Dearest love to my mother.

Ever my dearest Father.

Your most aff^e. Son.

J Ruskin

LETTER 44

30th October [1851]

My dearest Father,

I have today your line from Dover of 23—24th with Mr Harrison's slip—which is very nice. How he enjoys everything he sees—and makes the most of it— I have often thought he would be a delightful travelling companion for this quality only.

Mama asks why Mrs N. is to be pitied—and says there "must be something wrong"— True—but when did one meet with any body who was altogether right: Her husband was almost the only man she was allowed to speak to—and when she first married him, she probably found him not quite in even *comfortable* circumstances—and even now —I think it must require rather a stronger mind than most women have, to see herself in a secondrate circle of people, and obliged to live in the back room of a ruined palace in Venice, when she might have been a leading beauty at the court either of Vienna or Turin without the slightest feeling of regret. I don't, myself, think Mr Nerly [1] at all a person capable of compensating for such a loss.

You are pleased at introduction of Mr Gibbs: He is a very agreeable and clever man—but nothing particular—certainly in *manner* not at all, being rather brisk and captious—and considerably lawyer like. I suppose his function will be chiefly to teach British constitution— which by the bye will be quite a useless piece of teaching, by the time the prince is likely to come to the Throne, if the English go on as they are doing. I am glad to see *some* sensible letters in the Times from "John Bull Slick" and one or two more—stating the case with clearness.

I am very sorry you cannot take tea when you feel it such a refreshment. I am going to try and do without it: I was struck by that account of the water system at Malvern, but I noticed that besides Tea—they forbade "all mental application" which regimen would not suit me just now.

I have also the Spectator extract [2] about Pre-Raphaelites—for which

---

1. Born Nerlich and Italianized to Frederigo Nerly (1807–78). Nerly was a landscape painter who was much assisted by the art dealer and patron, Baron Rumohr. In 1840 Nerly married a pupil related to the rich Marchese Maruzzi.

2. Of October 4, 1851.

many thanks. It is rather prosy, and I think their putting me in a note, that way, very impertinent.

I hope Mr Smith will get an order for *Stones of Venice;* as the Venetian bookseller was here today to beg to be allowed to look at it—so many English having asked for it.

> Dearest love to my mother.
> Ever my dearest Father.
> Your most affec^e. Son
> J Ruskin.

LETTER 45

1st November [1851]

My dearest Father,

You must surely be sending some English November weather over here—and really—I would rather pay carriage for any other article. (By the bye I wonder what the derivation of that word "article" is—and what would be the effect upon the commerce of London—if it were interdicted to the Shopmen. I always fancy that a certain kind of old lady at Swan and Edgar's invariably buys three times as much as she wants—in the excitement of finding that she is buying "articles" and not "things." "Any other article today, Ma'am?")— Today I can hardly at ½ past eight in the morning see to write—and the rain and the rats together made such a clatter all yesterday that I could hardly read. I went and called on a person who sent me a letter the other day—an old Christchurch man—gentlemancommoner—a Mr Russell [1]—whose name perhaps my Mother may remember. I thought he was far away in England at his rectory—his note said he had come to Venice for his wife's health.

I went to call—(remembering a somewhat jovial, sturdy-faced, red-haired young man—) merely out of politeness—intending to have nothing to do with him— I found a thin—broken down man—looking about forty—with a number of children—in a rambling house at the dull end of Venice with a yellow faced and sickly wife—looking about fifty—and speaking exactly with the manner and *voice* of my cousin Margaret, or rather, with more affectation, and of course less heart—but really ill, poor thing—panting for breath at every word. I sat down in some wonderment—and talked about her health. She said she had been very imprudent—the weather was so cold, and she had gone out to mass on Sunday, at St John and Paul. "Mass!" I said, "What were you doing at mass?" "We are Catholics," replied the lady quietly. "Oh," I said, "I beg your pardon. Well—and you caught cold?"

---

1. William Russell, who matriculated at Christ Church College in May 1836—a few months after Ruskin. In 1846 he was rector of Aber-Edw with Llanfarith, Wales,

I staid for half an hour or so—and heard much about marsh air and frosty air—and bad air—and good society—and so forth—and came away in the dripping, melancholy day—to meditate on the shortness and swiftness of life—and on the beneficial effects of Christchurch education.

They are to stay here for the winter and I am very glad of it for through them I shall get a good deal of information which would otherwise have been inaccessible to me, and they are too far off—and too sickly to require any rudeness in keeping them out of my way. Dearest love to my mother.

Ever my dearest Father.
Your most affect^e. Son
J Ruskin

LETTER 46

Sunday, 2nd November [1851]

My dearest Father,

We have had a superb high tide this morning—in all over our courtyard—and over the greater part of St Mark's place—and nothing could be more exquisite than the appearance of the church from the other end, with the reflection of its innumerable pillars white and dark green and purple, thrown down far over the square in bright bars, fading away in confused arrows of colour—with here and there a touch of blue and gold from the mosaics— Had there been sunshine it would have been like a scene in the Arabian nights—but it was gloomy and wet with recent rain—we have now had three days' rain nearly incessant, and strong south westerly [wind] bringing up the tide, with it— and the lagoons yesterday evening were very noble—all wide and green and wild—with sea mists scouring along the horizon and white bands of foam along the channels that led from the Lido beaches. It is one good thing that the strongest wind at Venice is almost always a warm one—when the air is frosty, it is quiet.

By the bye I have been making up my mind that the land of Uz, in which Job lived, must have been close under Lebanon or Caucasus, or in some place at the feet of snowy mountains— All his imagery is that of a mountaineer—but especially the way he dwells on the passing away of the "snow waters" Chap 6. v. 15–18. Chap 24 v. 19. Chap 12. v. 15 and all the imagery of Chap 28th—v. 4–6, 7, 10, 11, and Chap 14. v. 18, 19 is exactly that which would occur to a man living in such a place as the valley of St Martin's—you know how I was disappointed in the autumn when I went to look for my favourite spring at Maglans—that comes out of the limestone strong enough to turn a mill. And there was nothing but the dry stones. It was "snow waters." So even the "great wind from the wilderness" destroying the house when his sons were feasting, was evidently a *mountain* blast—for in the margin you see it is *not* from the wilderness but "from aside"—just the expression which Aristophanes uses of wind coming down the hills.[1]

I think if you will put Job in among the mountains, the whole book will read much more grandly.

I am getting on very nicely with my work, but find myself continually forced to abridge and simplify my designs. Life is not long enough. I shall soon send you a chapter or two to read. Dearest love to my mother.

> Ever my dearest Father.
> Your most affecᵉ. Son
> J Ruskin.

LETTER 47

4ᵗʰ November, Evening, [1851]

My dearest Father,

I had today your nice letter with enclosures out of Builder, which are always very interesting. Garbett writes spiritedly, and I had half a mind to send word back that he might "go ahead" if he liked [1]—but I thought you would not send me any more Builder for fear of disturbing me—so I let it alone. I have often felt the want of an index to my books myself, and there shall be a complete one to this next volume—it will need it for it will be a mixed dish, all manner of subjects in it, and for the index to be useful at all, I must make it myself.

I think Garbett has learned something from my answer to him—the little bit which I enclose back again is quite in my style and a very complete answer to *his* opponent.[2]

I am very glad you have had such weather in England—it was better for you to have it than for me to have it—for in Venice—one can do

---

1. For an amplification of this statement see *Works, 3, 26.*

1. In the *Builder* for October 25, 1851, E. L. Garbett wrote an article, "The Common Sense of Gothic," whose significance lies in a few remarks concerning Ruskin. Garbett wrote: "If Providence spare us our excellent friend Ruskin long enough, and cures him of some few crotchets, he will presently convince more people than you expect, that in all these things the motive of imitation is 'base' and 'unmanly.' . . . Moreover, Mr. Ruskin is showing you, or about to show you, or means to show you,—or if he does not, I will,—that this debasement, and all art debasement, whether here or abroad, in Christian countries, has originated in one source, and that one a source commonly supposed favourable to the fine arts. And I would warn that gentleman, as I know he does not like being forestalled, that if he does not make haste and come to the gist of his argument, I will take a short cut which I see, and tell it before him; which I should be sorry to have to do, because I know he will do it much better."

2. In "The Common Sense of Gothic" Garbett takes issue with several people. His main opponent, however, would appear to be the reviewer in the *Gentleman's Magazine*, June 1850, of his book, *Rudimentary Treatise on the Principles of Design in Architecture*. The critic takes exception to what he terms Garbett's "vaulting fallacy."

with any weather—but not so in London—or even at Dover. Still it is
strange— Nothing here but inundations—the people in misery all along
the borders of the Brenta— Rain again today all day long.

When you have a little spare time, would you kindly tell me what date
Gibbon gives for Attila's destruction of Padua and Aquileia?

Dearest love to my mother.

Ever my dearest Father.

Your most affec^e. Son

J Ruskin

LETTER 48

5th November [1851]

My dearest Father,

I have just finished the enclosed letter—and am ashamed of its ego-
tism now it is done, if you think it too bad keep it for yourself and I
will write Emma another. Meantime it is 10 o'clock and I must go to
bed.

Dearest love to my mother.

Ever my dearest Father.

Your most affec. Son

J Ruskin.

Thursday morning. Excessive cold and continual rain—awful accounts
from the country. They say in Padua the water is up to the first stories
of the houses—and that to the north the people are driven to the hills
and encamped on them in the open air.

LETTER 49

7th November [1851]

My dearest Father,

I had yesterday your nice letter with my mother's regimen—for Effie
I suppose, rather than for me as, I have not been taking malt liquor for
a long time. It was no use telling you that Effie was unwell, as you
would have thought I should be ill next, and I never felt at any time
the slightest feverishness—except when I lived too low for two or three
days as I told you, nor was Effie very unwell—though I thought it best
to let her see a doctor. She could not take exercise as I could—and so
was liable to the effects of the continual changes in temperature and
constant rain. The doctor wanted to put her to bed—but she resisted
that, and by a little quinine and other medicines—especially prepara-
tions of tamarinds, we got her well. I was sorry that I had no port wine
at the time—none is to be had in Venice, so I shall be glad when the

Europe arrives. Please write whether my mother recommends the same dietary for me, though I am doing very well on the whole—the only [thing] that annoys me being want of circulation—which is always, I find increased by study of any kind— I carefully avoid all overwork and hurry or excitement—which I find worst of all, but even in the quietest way—I find that every half hour of mental application is just *so much* of quickened pulse with coldness of hands and feet. The same effect is produced by the least violent exertion in rowing or anything else—but more permanently—so that I am obliged to watch very carefully in both ways— I find that by beginning very slowly and quietly— and never pushing hard—I can row for two or three hours with great comfort and benefit, and so in everything I find quietness the great necessity. I am much better than when I came to Venice—chiefly owing to keeping out of all society. The *frost* has now shown itself in the mornings, and I doubt not that all fear of fever is over. Dearest love to my mother.

Ever my dearest Father.
Your most aff^e. Son.
J Ruskin.

LETTER 50

8th November [1851]

My dearest Father,

I am obliged to send you this shabby sheet of paper, being to my surprise—out of writing paper—and at a very inconvenient moment— the water being just now half a foot deep in the stationers' shops—and all access cut off to St Mark's place except in the lightest boats—and to the shops except on people's backs. The tide is several inches higher than it was on Sunday, and it has been raining all night—so though you have lost your fine weather, we have by no means found it.

I am afraid that by the account of your new waiter—we shall have very different associations with the names of "Joseph and Mary" from those which are in the minds of good Catholics. Mary continues to distinguish herself. Last Sunday when the water was in the streets Effie and I went out before breakfast to St Mark's place in the gondola. Mary—marvelling at this unusual proceeding went to George and enquired "whether the Band was playing?"

It is rather curious that—with all this intense dulness, the natural tendency of her mind is of a higher *tone* than any servants I ever met with. She is very *nearly* the same thing as an oyster—but whatever sensations she has are of the right sort— Just fancy her fixing on the

Great St Bernard as the place, of all she has seen—where she would like to live! And yet there was nothing even of the usual look about the place—it was dirty—doggish—commonplace— Even *I* was not sorry to find myself on the way down. Dearest love to my mother.

Ever my dearest Father.
Your most aff^e. Son
J Ruskin.

LETTER 51

[9 November 1851]

My dearest Father,

I forgot, like a foolish fellow—to lay in a fresh stock of paper yesterday—and am reduced to my measuring paper with some remains of a plan of the Duomo of Murano on it.

If there is any truth in the theory of the transmigration of species, we shall all become webfooted if we stay here for five months more, and this kind of thing goes on. Rain above—all day—and water in our yard—the only access to the kitchen being by a bridge. One envies the long legged birds that are roasted for our dinner every day—not quoad the fact of their being roasted—but quoad their long legs. The tribes of waders and other marsh birds here—answering to our snipes—widgeons—and teal, are very curious—and innumerable—some of them with grand bills like Turkish scymitars—seven inches long—all of them beautiful in shape—and with strange helps to their feet to let them stand comfortably in mud—not webs exactly—but flaps to their spurs—a kind of mud shoes. The fish appear quite infinite in variety—but the most beautiful of them are the nondescripts—things like the seahorses, neither fish nor flesh—and the Cuttlefish. I think the cuttlefish was intended to be a lesson to painters—first to teach them that the best of all colours were as Tintoret said—black and white: or rather brown and white; and secondly to show them what lovely colours might be put into grey: I never saw anything except an opal, so beautiful as the living cuttlefish. They are also very good, boiled; but I think indigestible—somewhat of the lobster and crab family—so I do not touch them, but they are favourites with the commonalty. If I run out of sepia, I intend to try some of the original manufacturer's.

I am impatient to hear what you think of all these Kossuth [1] doings— If the English did but know how all people who are really acquainted with Hungarian matters laugh at them. By all I can gather

1. Louis Kossuth (1802–94), Hungarian patriot and reformer, who fled to England in October 1851 where he received a tumultuous welcome. Kossuth's prominence is attested to by his being the subject of a leading article in the *Times* on October 9, 17, 25, 27, 28, and 31.

—Kossuth is exactly another O'Connell [2]—and has quite as much true patriotism as the agitator himself.

We have prayers every Sunday morning now, more peaceably I fancy at home than when one runs about to the hotels with a quantity of English ladies in their Sunday bonnets staring at each other. Still I shall be glad to hear Mr Moore preach again. Dearest love to my mother.

Ever my dearest Father

Your most affect^e. Son

J Ruskin

LETTER 52

10th November [1851]

My dearest Father,

I have not yet heard of your receiving a letter of mine containing one enclosed to Sir C. Eastlake.[1] I hope this has not miscarried—or I must write another.

A sunny morning at last—very beautiful to behold. It is high time, the distress in the country being very great, but I am very glad to have seen the stormy weather—there were pieces of scenery thoroughly noble—and among them, the way the top of the tower of St Mark's entangled itself among the rainclouds, not the least interesting. It is the Venetian aiguille Dru.[2] The Alps are of course now covered with snow, to within 1500 feet of the plains, and I never saw them look so magnificent, when there opens a gap of clouds to the north over the green rolling of the lagoon.

I have never staid in a day for the weather—took my row, rain or fair—and changed my things when I came in—last Tuesday or Wednesday was a tremendous day for Wind as well [as] rain, and I rowed over to Lido to look at the sea: As I came back I saw Mr Brown's boat at the public garden's steps: His boat is too small for rough weather, and he could not get across to the Lido—and was taking his walk in the gardens. I went in search of him and we had a pleasant walk together in the beating rain and North wind: The Venetians have certainly some reason to think the English odd people. Lord Dufferin was paddling about in the lagoons, all the while he was here, in one of those

2. Daniel O'Connell (1775–1847), Irish political figure known as "the Liberator" and "the Agitator."

1. Sir Charles Lock Eastlake (1793–1865), who was elected P.R.A. in 1850. For a time an art student under Benjamin Haydon, he also studied at the Royal Academy and took drawing lessons from Samuel Prout. He became director of the National Gallery in 1855 and from then on practically ceased painting owing to the necessity of making frequent Continental visits on behalf of the gallery.

2. A peak in the Swiss Alps. For further discussion of the Aiguille Dru see *Works, I*, 195.

indian-rubber boats which you may see hanging up at the door of a shop in Bond St. He took it over to Lido, and rowed some way in the sea with it: when he landed, an Austrian coastguard came to investigate him, and wanted to rip up his boat to see what was inside! I only wonder that he did not take both boat and boatman straight to the police office. Dearest love to my mother.

Ever my dearest Father,
Your most affec^e. Son
J Ruskin.

I hope you admire the hue of this new paper of mine. You see it is a delicate shade of *lagoon green.*

LETTER 53

10th November [1851]

My dearest Father,

I had yesterday your nice letter of the 2nd from Dover with enclosed review of Carlyle—Mr Huggins [1] on Pre-Raphaelites &c. Carlyle must be losing his senses—but what grand madness, too— The Times [2] is excellent, and moderate—and it seems to me just, but the bits of Carlyle are capital, too.

The Archaeological and Architectural Society must be verily what Mr Carlyle calls "Bottled moonshine." [3]

Northcote's advice to his pupils [4] is delicious—and by the bye—defines and marks out the very fact which is the cause of so much mischief.

You ask meaning of "Suonatore," I imagine—street musician—or musician of any kind—probably Mr Butler means the pipers before the Madonna.

Gritstone—or free stone—is I believe a good building sandstone—or general term for it—most *limestones* being on the other hand named from the locality of their quarries—Portland—Caen—Bath—&c., but I am not quite sure what builders mean in all cases by freestone.

There is not much in the critical expressions which you quote about pictures—something of truth—the truth got by listening to what people say or reading what they write instead of feeling for oneself. Titian is much more remarkable for his colour than for his truth or nature except in his portraits—and there is certainly no purity at all—much less

1. Possibly Samuel Huggins (1811–85), president of the Liverpool Architectural Society from 1856 until 1858.

2. A criticism of *The Life of John Sterling* appeared in the *Times* on November 1, 1851.

3. For Carlyle's use of this expression see *The Life of John Sterling* (Boston, 1851), Pt. 1, ch. xiv.

4. "Advice to a Young Artist" by James Northcote (1746–1831), painter, author, and conversationalist, is the concluding chapter of his *Varieties on Art,* which is included in his *Memoirs of Sir Joshua Reynolds* (Philadelphia, 1817).

sovereign purity, in Correggio. I never saw a Caracci in my life anywhere, that I cared to remember—either Annibale or Lodovico [5]—but
I remember *none* of the pictures in the Farnese.

Your letters are not scrawled at all. You see you need not be afraid
of asking questions—as all the answer I can give goes in very small
space, and takes up very little time indeed.

Dearest love to my mother.

> Ever my dearest Father.
> Your most aff[e]. Son
> J Ruskin.

LETTER 54

12th November [1851]

My dearest Father,

In your 30th October letter you say you have got cold, at Dover, you
suppose from disliking the place. I hope as I have been now directing
for some time to Denmark Hill, that the cold is gone—but I certainly
wonder at your going to these seaside places now—where really the
looking at steamers must be very tantalizing—and I thought that sea
air never agreed with you very well. I found our old inland haunt,
Matlock little changed—and very sweet and quiet—and there seem
some beautiful little places about Shropshire and the skirts of Wales—
or why do you not go to one of the country inns in Yorkshire—near an
Abbey—and get fresh trout and Yorkshire cream for breakfast—and
study English architecture—to compare notes with my Venetian, when
I come back? Tunbridge is healthy but must be dreadfully dull. Mr
Cooke [1] tells me that there are more species of fern about it than at any
other place in England. Clayton [2] was at a pretty place near it—but I
forget its name.

I am more and more amazed at the Kossuth doings, and am really
beginning to have a respect for the Times— However, there must be
some root for this great radical feeling in England—which it is our
rich people's fault that they do not get down to and cut away: I was
rather struck, yesterday by three paragraphs in Galignani—in parallel
columns, so that the eyes ranged from one to the other. The first gave
an account of a girl aged 21, being found, after lying exposed all night,
and having given birth to a dead child—on the banks of the canal near

5. Annibale Carracci (1560–1609), a painter born in Bologna. His brother Lodovico
Carracci (1555–1619) is said to have been the founder of the Eclectic school of Bologna.
    1. Edward William Cooke (1811–80), a marine painter who was elected A.R.A. in
1851 and R.A. in 1854.
    2. Rev. Edward Clayton (1817–95), a Christ Church friend of Ruskin and recipient
of significant letters from him. See *Letters to a College Friend* (*Works, 1,* 399–502).

(Maidstone, I think—but some English county town)—the second was the Fashions for November, with an elaborate account of Satin skirts—and the Third—a burning to death of a child—or rather—a dying *after* burning—because the surgeon, without an order from the parish, would neither go to see it, nor send it any medicine. I wonder if this last be really true? [3]

Fine weather is—I verily believe come at last. We have had two fine days—and here is the 3rd.

Dearest love to my mother.

> Ever my dearest Father
> Your most aff^e. Son
> J Ruskin.

LETTER 55

12th November [1851]

My dearest Father,

I have your nice letter of the 6th from the Counting house—with further notes respecting Dowbiggin,[1] &c.— I certainly wrote impatiently—but please consider what a sadly unfavourable place Venice is for the discipline of one's temper. I cannot stir a foot without seeing somebody destroying something—the somebody—not worth one's anger—but the something—worth all one's sorrow—so that bad temper gets accumulated, and is apt to fly out at anything—even small game— Besides, it is provoking [to] find everybody trying to cheat you or squeeze you—even when you are in a strange land—and just when you are getting used to it there, and ready to put up with it—to have a back cut at you in a treacherous way from over the water—where one thought all were friends— However I grant the greater part of the irritability to be produced by consciousness of one's own fault—and yet I *could* not do more than I did before leaving London—the *Pre-Raphaelitism* took me so much more trouble than I expected—and I felt myself in need of rest—and nervous—and could not attend to many things at once—and I had a good deal of trouble in planning exactly what I should want at Venice—and as it was, forgot one important book—Gibbon—which I cannot get here—but I can leave the piece of history work for which I want him to be done when I meet you in Switzerland—so please remember to bring the little Gibbon with you— or at least the volumes on the 4th and 5th centuries.

I am delighted with your sentence about Kossuth—which I shall give to Effie to read at her Austrian parties— It is very difficult to give them

---

3. This entire paragraph indicates Ruskin's interest, which was to occupy him so much in later years, in social and political events.

1. Thomas Dowbiggin, an upholsterer and cabinetmaker of 23, Mount Street, London.

any idea of the independence of our lower classes—or the small importance of our municipalities—no popular expression of opinion of that kind being ever allowed here. Austria is by no means a magnificent power in [this] respect—her small suspicions and small precautions are marvellously contemptible. As I gave you the other day an Italian characteristic in a *little* matter—so in a *little* matter, one may see the characteristic fault of the Austrian government. "William Tell" is a forbidden opera here—this one might excuse, in time of popular excitement. But the *music* of "William Tell" is only allowed to be sold under the title of "William Wallace!" I think the absurdity of this very exquisite and complete. Dearest love to my mother.

Ever my dearest Father. Your most aff^e Son

J Ruskin.

Admire my folding!

LETTER 56

15th November [1851]

My dearest Father,

I do not know if it is the same in Switzerland—but certainly the best views of the Alps, and on the whole the most striking scenery here, of distant effects of every kind, are in the winter: Yesterday was a wonderful day: the breaking up of our week of fine weather—and the whole chain of the Alps were bare and bright, in the strange sharp clearness which one only has before rain, seen along the horizon in a belt of open sky, which the raincloud coming up from the east, gradually gained upon—and at last quenched, and today we have stormy wind and splashing waves and rain. It matters very little to me what the weather is—it neither stays my exercise, nor my writing. Fortunately I find the stove in my study goes admirably, so I am quite set up for the winter. Still I hope we shall have a *little* Italian weather before we leave in the spring—otherwise all my descriptions of Venice will make people shiver.

You will see in the papers that Mr Cooke has been elected A.R.A. I never saw a man so pleased—but he is pleased with everything. A most curious small man. Good—and kind—and pious—but a perpetual buz from one thing to another— I never saw such restlessness—or such activity. You will have the exhibition full of Ducal palaces [1] next year —such as they may be. But Cooke has taken great pains—and though raw and cold and meanlooking—his paintings will be more accurate in detail than any that have yet been taken. I have led him to look into

1. Both David Roberts and Cooke submitted Venetian subjects to the next (i.e. 1852) Royal Academy showing. Roberts offered *Venice;* Cooke also submitted *Venice* and an untitled picture graced by a quotation from *The Two Foscari.*

the detail—and he is as enthusiastic as I am—but his chief failing is that he can never see a dark side—of anything. I see too many: but I see the lights stronger for them.

Dearest love to my mother.

Ever my dearest Father.
Your most affec^e. Son.
J Ruskin.

LETTER 57

Sunday, 16th November. [1851]

My dearest Father,

In Galignani yesterday we had some wonderful additional accounts of Kossuth—and the address to him by the democrats—signed by a whole Man's worth of tailors—and a whole bevy of "proscrits"—with his polite answer thereto—and his *re*consideration" of his resolution to accept no invitations except from municipal bodies. I do not suppose that at any previous period of history there has been more open "Communism" coolly announced in the face of all men— The French Revolution was a phrenzy begun in a necessary reform of vicious government but the principles which that phrenzy reached at its wildest, become now the subjects of the after dinner declamation of our respectable London Citizens. There is assuredly a root for all this—desperate abuses going on in governments, and real ground for movement among the lower classes, which of course they are little likely to guide by any very just or rational principle.

I have just been reading the 62nd Psalm, which has I think a profound reference to the inner feelings of the Great and Small in all time. David had evidently written it in some of his dangers from the revolutionary spirit in his own people—that spirit built upon—and encouraged by Absolom in 2nd Samuel—15. 2, 3, 4; and further—manifested in the great revolt of Israel under Sheba the son of Bichri,[1] and the Psalm opens with the writer's expression of his trust in God for his *own* safety; then comes a rebuke and threat to revolutionists in general—"Ye shall be slain all of you"—in the prayer book the clauses are more accurate, I believe—and they are more general— Mischief against *every* man—imagined by the democrats; Slain all the *sort* of you—generalizing it to all time; then comes a description of them, they consult to *cast down* "from his excellency"—vague in the Bible—much more clear in the prayerbook. To put him out whom God will *exalt* thus teaching them that the inequality of which they complain is indeed a divine institution—then—they give good words with their mouth, but curse with their heart—another great

1. See II Samuel xx.

democratic characteristic, and then a further appeal to God for his defence against them. Thus far the Upper classes have the psalm to themselves. But then David's thoughts pass to the real injuries committed against the poor—and [he] presently addresses these lower classes with a changed tone— Put your *trust* in *Him*—in God—at all times—as he had said elsewhere—put not your trust in princes nor in any child of man; now he says, for the redress of all your real wrongs, look to God— pour out your heart, when it is indeed wounded, before Him, and then he tells them that the whole controversy between high and low is vain— Surely men of *low* degree are vanity—and men of *high* degree are a *lie*. Strong, that—rather, out of a King's mouth, then comes a parenthetical charge to the rich not to trust in oppression—nor set their heart on riches—vide also Job—31. 25 [2]—and then a final charge to the poor who may think or know themselves injured, that they must not rise up against power, for all power finally belongs to God—and that they are to look to Him—for with Him is no abuse of power, and He will assuredly give them what they ask for—"a good day's wages for a good day's work." Understood in this way, one sees the connection of clauses in that last verse—and its entire meaning. If one reads it detached, one does not see how "rendering to every man according to his work," is characteristic of God's *mercy*.

I think that the 9th verse is not often enough quoted nor considered. It is evidently one of the pieces of the Bible which are to *Balance* the passages much more often quoted on the other side, such as Job 34. 18— Proverbs 16, 10—&c. &c.

However, I must mind and not get too sympathizing with the Radicals— Effie says, with some justice—that I am a great conservative in France, because there everybody is radical—and a great radical in Austria, because there everybody is conservative. I suppose that one reason why I am so fond of fish—(as creatures I mean, not as eating) is that they always swim with their heads against the stream. I find it for me, the healthiest position. So that it is just as well that I hear a little of the London radicalism while I live here—for I get very angry every time I pass the guns in St Mark's place, or the pontoons opposite it; and very much provoked—and indeed it *is* sufficiently tiresome—that there is now no "lonely isle" in all the lagoons of Venice— Wherever you go— where once there were quiet little gardens among ruins of island churches, there is now a Sentinel and a powder magazine—and there is no piece of unbroken character to be found anywhere. There is not a single shore —far or near, which has not in some part of it the look of fortification— or violent dismantling or renewing, for military purposes of some kind or another: and there is hardly an old convent window out of which you

2. "If I rejoiced because my wealth was great, and because mine hand had gotten much."

will not see a Croat's face peeping—or his pipeclayed swordbelt hanging. It reads curiously enough, over the Gothic doors, "Caserma, de Jesuiti." [3] However, better the Croats than the Jesuits.

The Grand duke Constantine has come here—they say for the winter —for the sake of his wife's health— I am afraid—if that be the reason— he will have to go farther south. I should be very sorry to stay here if I were in a consumption. We had another gale from the east yesterday, which searched out every corner of Venice—like a great, solid—inevitable broom: I think Venice must have been *blown* clean—if it had not been previously washed clean, by two months' rain.

Dearest love to my mother.

Ever my dearest Father.
Your most affectionate Son
J Ruskin.

LETTER 58

Monday 17th November [1851]

My dearest Father,
I am afraid I shall never be able any more to associate Venice with fine weather. I look upon storm and cold as quite natural to it— Still— as I was dressing this morning with pinched fingers; and vainly endeavouring to shave with frosty water—it *did* occur to me as rather strange that here in Venice in the middle of November, the weather should be what we should consider in London, very creditable to the general character of the middle of January. I hope at least we shall have some revanche in the Spring. Are you not beginning to lay any plans for your journey, or fix any places which you should like to go to? I hope you still are fixed to come by Lyons, as I want much to show you the carving of Cathedral front there, and the approach to the mountains is sublime —going down towards the Chartreuse though poor towards Geneva. I think it would be nice for you to see Bourges on the way, and just call on M. des Roys [1] as you pass Moulins and then you are at Lyons next day, and I would meet you there—but what places you would like to go to after the Grande Chartreuse, I do not know.

Effie is reading to me the history of the Crusades,[2] in the evenings: there are many valuable things in it for me; but I was especially delighted with the report given by his servants of Godfrey of Bouillon when there was scrutiny made into every man's private character in order to choose a King of Jerusalem. Godfrey's servants said he had no fault but one

3. "Jesuit barracks."
1. The husband of Elise Domecq; she was the daughter of one of John James Ruskin's business partners.
2. *Histoire des Croisades* by J. F. Michaud, 6 vols. (Paris, 1841).

—"that whenever he got into a church he would stand looking about him at everything and asking what the pictures meant, for hours together, *till they were all tired,* and that he would often—on such occasions, keep the dinner waiting till the dishes were quite spoiled; and that it was a shame." [3]

We have got a French history—very good for Effie to read, but with a nasty sneering Gibbonish way with it. There is unfortunately enough in the Crusades to provoke into such a temper. Dearest love to my mother.

> Ever my dearest Father.
> Your most affec^e. Son.
> J Ruskin.

LETTER 59

19th November [1851]

My dearest Father,

I have your nice Salmagundi letter of the 9-10th and yesterday I had your 8th with Smith's: about fairy tale [1] which you answered of course quite rightly. I will not have my name to it, but they may publish it in any form they like.

You ask if Russell is an Oxford made Roman— No—only "prepared" at Oxford—the finishing touches given after he had taken duty at some English rectory. But I have not yet been able to enquire more particularly about this—for his poor wife is already gone where she will find out which is the right side. It is now about a week or ten days ago. She was attacked by a fever—gastric, I believe—or in some way serious—but apparently chronic in its character. She was speaking of getting out when the weather got finer to call on Effie. We had sent to ask for her at 3 in the afternoon, she was said to be better—and died at seven in the evening. I went to see Russell the next morning, the moment I heard of it— Happily his wife's sister had come to see her, having heard of her illness, and reached there four hours before she died—so there was some person to help him at first and take charge of the children— I saw him there, and have been to enquire for him since, and shall go again today. I don't know if he means to stay in Venice or not.

I am very glad to hear of Monro's scholarship [2]—pray offer his father my sincere congratulations.

---

3. A tale about Godfrey, to be found in Michaud's *Histoire, 2, 5,* is used by Ruskin in *The Stones of Venice III (Works, 11, 77).* The anecdote concerning Godfrey in the above letter also comes from the *Histoire, 1, 353.*

1. *The King of the Golden River (Works, 1, 305–54),* written for Effie Ruskin in 1841 and first published a decade later without Ruskin's name on the title page.

2. An academic distinction awarded Hugh Andrew Johnstone Munro (1819–85), illegitimate son of Munro of Novar. This young man was to become one of England's foremost classical scholars. Between 1849 and 1851 he collated the Lucretian MSS in the Vatican and Laurentian libraries.

I have the two bits upon Helicon which I like very much, but if you can get the old Times and cut out the review of Jones' Chantrey [3] I should much like to see it— You speak of Quarterly showing its own ignorance— There is a passage in Blackwood which I could not have believed without seeing, could have got into a periodical of this date. It is in an article on Paris [4]—talking of the Artesian Wells—it says the digging of that at Paris "entirely overthrows the geological theory of superimposition of beds, according to their weight—*all kinds* of *beds being found* at *different depths!*"

Now just fancy that printed in 1851, year of Great exhibition—when for twenty years back—geologists have been able to give a section of nearly every spot in Europe—and to describe the microscopic character of every shell in every bed of sand—from the North cape to Gibraltar.

I will answer the rest of your nice letter tomorrow.

Dearest love to my mother.

> Ever my dearest father. Your most affec^e. Son.
> J Ruskin.

LETTER 60

Wednesday Evening, 19th [November 1851]

My dearest Father,

I see you say that the Builder has a long letter of advice "from a Father to a Son, with Seven Lamps"—is this with a present of the Seven Lamps—or what? If so—I should like it cut out and sent. [1]

Sterling's criticism of Dent du Midi [2] is much worse than Newton's—it is not so witty—and quite as degrading—even untrue—affectedly untrue: Sergeant Talfourd's [3] "iced plumcake" is genuine—the same thing had struck me a dozen times—though I did not like the resemblance—and therefore never expressed it— But snow is not like silver in the form of *plate,* much less in that of a teapot— Who ever saw a teapot with a peak at the top? I have been thinking a little more over the way my money went in London—and—if it will be any relief to you—I can assure you that I do *not* consider myself *economical*—neither do I think myself extravagant. I placed no severe check on my expences on the one hand—but I never bought anything idly—or that I did not want, on

3. In the *Times,* August 20, 1850, appeared a scathing criticism of *Sir Francis Chantrey, R.A.; Recollections of His Life, Practice and Opinions* by George Jones, R.A. Jones's biography is also castigated in the *Times,* November 8, 1851, when another study, *Memorials of Sir Francis Chantrey, R.A., Sculptor in Hallamshire and Elsewhere* by John Holland, was reviewed.

4. "Paris in 1851," an article which appeared in *Blackwood's Magazine,* September 1851. See especially pp. 317–18.

1. The article referred to appeared in the *Builder,* November 8, 1851.

2. See *The Life of John Sterling* (Boston, 1851), p. 212.

3. Sir Thomas Noon Talfourd (1795–1854), judge and author, more commonly known by his legal title of Sergeant Talfourd.

the other—unless sometimes a number of Punch. For a large portion of
the sum—for whatever indeed I spent on myself—except as aforesaid—
something in Punch—and a pound or two in buns and ices, I have value
to show. Those books which load the timber of Denmark Hill are well
worth what they cost me—and I have [a] good £140 worth in Liber
Studiorum [4] and Albert Durers—as well as my instruments and enormous collection of Daguerreotypes : besides some valuable minerals. I did
indeed once begin to save all I could, with a motive—whenever I could
do without lunch—or save an omnibus—or do without a purchase—I
put what I thought I had a right to consider as saved, aside ; in what
I called the "Turner" fund hoping in time to get a Turner with it. It
rose—in a year to about twenty-eight pounds—and then one day a bill
came in which I had no money to pay—and I said to myself—"What is
the use of my going to my father for money when I have money lying
by me ? If I had *in reality* saved this out of my income—it would be
properly mine—but I may just as well ask my father for money for the
Turner hereafter—as keep this now—and ask now for more :" So I paid
my bill with it, and gave up, and you see when I wanted the Lupton
Turners, I did not fail to ask for it and more. On the whole, I can very conscientiously say that I believe while Effie and I can by no means congratulate ourselves on our good management—and while I have been much
to blame for carelessness in account keeping yet—since our marriage—
I do not think we have *wilfully* spent more than 100 pounds above what
we ought to have done—that 100 being diffused not over London life
—but over certain really extravagant Hotel Bills—which by a little care
and self denial—we might have kept down.

Dearest love to my mother.

Ever my dearest Father.
Your most aff[e]. Son.
J Ruskin.

LETTER 61

20th November [1851]

My dearest Father,

I have not much of interest to communicate to you of my own adventures—but Effie sometimes sees a little of what is going on in the world.
She was out last night at one of her best friends—a young Italian Countess—or rather German, married to an Italian : Countess Palavicini—
a very amiable creature—only strong Austrian—which as her husband

---

4. A series of Turner drawings etched on copper. The first part of the *Liber Studiorum*
appeared in 1807. A full account of this work is given in A. J. Finberg's *Life of J. M. W.
Turner* (Oxford, Oxford University Press, 1939), p. 128 ff.

is Italian—is unfortunate—but he is very fond of her, and lives here, instead of at Bologna—where his palace is, that she may see more of the Austrians. She asked Effie last night to come and meet the Arch Duke Albert [1]—the son of the great Archduke Charles. He came to tea —in the quietest English domestic way, or rather in the German way which is still quieter than the English. Mad^me Palavicini remembers playing at battledore and shuttlecock with him 18 years ago—when she was a little girl and he a little boy, at Vienna—now he is Governor of Hungary—and came to see her, just before going away in the steamer to Trieste—on his way to his place of duty. Everyone rose when he entered—the officers saluting * or as Effie says somewhat vaguely— "doing something" with their swords; but after that—all was as easy as at any family fireside. [He] attacked Effie playfully about the Kossuth doings—she pleaded that she was not to answer for them—being Scotch — "Nay" he said, "if Kossuth goes to Glasgow, you will see he will be received quite as well as he is at Birmingham." He was speaking of the reception which—on the other hand, the Emperor had received in parts of his late journies in Gallicia—more especially at Cherrevitz—where the people came out of the town and put a man with a torch on each side of the road *at every ten paces* for *twenty miles* (Italian—about the same as our English) and illuminated the town besides. There is something very grand and wild in this idea of an avenue of Torchmen—twenty miles long. Very Highland—only on a grander scale even than the Highlands. It was the peasants who had done it of themselves—without any preparation.

He is a great admirer of Palladio at Vicenza—so it was just as well it was Effie there, and not me. She gets on very nicely, Lady Sorel says, with the foreigners—not being stiff or shy like most English.

At last—we hear that the Boxes by Madonna are at St Giorgio Maggiore. St George—tomorrow being a festa—will certainly not do anything so improper as sending me my boxes; so I must wait till Saturday.

Dearest love to my mother.

Ever my dearest Father. Your most aff^e. Son
J Ruskin.

* Being asked for further information—Effie avers "it was a very shabby thing whatever it was, a sort of backhanded scrape."

1. The Archduke Albert (1817–95) was from 1851 until 1860 in command of the Austrian army in Hungary. He had also served with Radetzky in the Italian campaign of 1848–49.

LETTER 62

22nd Nov. [1851]

My dearest Father,

I have your nice letter of the 13th from Tunbridge with enclosed Miss Rathbone [1]—and pieces of Builder—all very droll— I hardly know what to say to the lady: I can hardly leave her note unanswered, and still less can I compliment her on her success as a writer of fiction. She and her family must be very liberal—to like the *Stones of Venice*—Catholics though they be. I wish I could see Blackwood. But alas, there is now no reading room here—as far as I know, and if there ever was, it must now be closed—for there are no more to be seen the groups in St Mark's place with Murrays [2] under arm, and commissionaire in attendance which indicate the Venetian Season—or Season for foreigners at least. Still I may be able to get a glance of it at Mr Cheney's or somewhere.

I am very glad to hear Mama enjoys Tunbridge so much, and all I have to beg is, that whatever likenesses she may find at Tunbridge to France or Switzerland, she will be so kind as, when she is next in Switzerland to discover none to Tunbridge.

You say the Sea is cold "like a Fishmonger's shop." It is rather characteristic of Venice that going down stairs just now to look at the state of the tide, I find George *fishing for flounders out of the hall door.* He has caught two good big ones too.

I note all you say about large and small illustrations—which is very good and true— All the illustrations for text will be size of book, and I am not going to trouble myself about large plates at present—but I think after third volume of *Modern Painters* I shall finish my 12 numbers [3] as I intended—only at my leisure, and perhaps putting better plates in altogether and raising price except to the present subscribers. Dearest love to my mother.

> Ever my dearest Father.
> Your most affe Son
> J Ruskin

LETTER 63

23rd November [1851]

My dearest Father,

You enquire in your last letter about bad taste in mouth. I do not

1. Perhaps Hannah Mary Rathbone (1798–1878), novelist.
2. A popular guidebook for travelers.
3. Of *The Examples of the Architecture of Venice*, three numbers of which had already appeared on May 12, 1851, November 1, 1851, and November 17, 1851, respectively.

think now it is of any consequence—for I find I am getting into good health again—getting rid of the nervousness and quickness of pulse which was what chiefly annoyed me. It was merely the consequence of being so often up till past midnight last season—and it seems to be a fixed law that the time taken in recovering from mischief, shall be, *at the least* equal to the time taken in doing it: One may indeed do oneself any amount of mischief one pleases in any space of time—and that irrecoverable: but the best that can ever be hoped is, that in about the time taken for the harm—will be the recovery, if recovery is possible. The rest of a month will not recruit a frame overworked for six. So as I had been sitting up late—&c.—for six months—I do not expect to be quite right again until six months from the time I came here—for I had not much rest in travelling. But I am now making steady progress, and hope that it will be quicker every day, as I have perfect quiet. Effie did not even ask me to [go] to the great fete of the Salute with her, when they made a bridge over the grand canal. I staid at home writing—she went with Lady Sorel and was very uncomfortable all the time in the crowd, while Mr Cooke—who must see everything—got fixed in a draught from an open door, and has had a rheumatism on one side of his head ever since.

Preparatory to my chapter on the situation of Venice, I have begun to study the tides carefully, as I found it was hopeless to arrive at any result by mere watching— I have got a tide book—and am putting down the hours of turning very carefully, the first curious result being that we have had high water at the same hour for three days running in the morning—and low water twenty minutes *later* in the afternoon of the second day—what it will be today remains to be seen.

I am delighted to say the Madonna boxes have at last arrived from Trieste—all safe, and I have been rejoicing this morning in a bit of Wordsworth, and some Milton. Pope is very wonderful—but turns sour on the stomach. We have got Tennyson also—and *The Antiquary,* and I was reading some of my own *Seven Lamps* last night with great satisfaction. It is a fine book. The seven *other* lamps [1] will hardly do. The man is sensible enough, but has not a logical head, and cannot divide his subject.

Dearest love to my mother. I *shall* be glad to hear more of her sayings and doings.

Ever my dearest Father.
Your most aff^{e.} Son
J Ruskin.

1. A reference to the *Builder* article mentioned in Letter 60.

LETTER 64

24th November [1851]

My dearest Father,

When you have nothing particular to do, I should be grateful if you would look what the word Turquoise [1] comes from; whether it means Turk's stone, or whether blue was called Turk's colour: I find blue was called *Venetian* colour, but it was a particular kind of blue called Turchi*no*. The turquoise is called Turchi*na*, and I don't know if the stone was called from the colour—or colour from the stone.

The Venetian women used always to wear—in the very early ages— a flowing robe of this colour down to the ground—it must have been very beautiful—and the Madonna is represented in the early mosaics in this, the usual dress of the women of the period. Would you also enquire at any old bookshop you are passing—mine—Willis's in Covent garden, will perhaps be as good as any, what is the likely price of the folio edition of the works of St Gregory—Gregory 1st—Pope: I rather want to refer to his commentary on Job [2]—but find the book costs about £2-18 or £3, here—and with heavy carriage, this might be much more than I could get it for in London. I want also the epistles of Ignatius and Polycarp. Milnes [3] says they were first published by Usher. I should like to know what editions there are—whether the earliest is to be had, and at what price.

Bulwer's part of Blackwood [4] is always so far interesting: he seems to be holding on to the Caxtons [5] as Dickens did to Pickwick.

I must be short today, for it is very fine, and I want to make the most of it— Dearest love to my mother.

Ever my dearest Father
Your most aff^e. Son
J Ruskin

1. For further information concerning turquoise see Apps. 7 and 8 in *Works, 10,* 447–8.

2. The commentary of Pope Gregory on Job is to be found in Vols. *18, 21, 23,* and *31* of *A Library of Fathers of the Holy Catholic Church* (Oxford, 1844, 1845, 1847, 1850).

3. Perhaps Monckton Milnes (1809–85), whose acquaintance Ruskin made a few years before this time.

4. *My Novel* by Bulwer-Lytton (1803–73) ran serially in *Blackwood's Magazine* from September 1850 until January 1853. This book was written under the pseudonym of Pisistratus Caxton.

5. This name appears in several of Bulwer-Lytton's novels, one of which, *The Caxtons,* ran serially in *Blackwood's Magazine* from April 1848 until October 1849.

LETTER 65

24th November [1851]

My dearest Father,

I have today your nice letter of the 14th-15th from Tunbridge wells, with notices of Mezzotint &c. I quite agree with you in all you say about keeping illustrations small—in fact—now that I *know* the architecture, it is easier for me to give its character small than large—but I could not when I was last here because it took me all the 5 months to learn it thoroughly: Now that I have all the parts large, I find great pleasure in making vignettes and Turnerizing a little, but this would have been quite impossible without the previous study. I am very glad to hear that Lupton's plate satisfies you—and I daresay I may at my leisure do some fine things in this way, but I will keep all small at present: I shall probably do [*text mutilated*] and rest after *Modern Painters* are finished— if I am permitted to finish them—which I trust—for I have much to say.

The passages you quote from Mrs Piozzi [1] are delightful—she must be very clever and very just in feeling— I did not know there was such a book—and I must see it as soon as I get home, and put in bits of it among my notes. In case—in press of matter I should forget—please take care and put me in mind of it.

I think she is quite right about floor being to *imitate* waves in St Mark's: [2] There is no reason for its settling when there is no weight. If it had settled so much under plain pavement—what would it have done under the piers? I think it a very beautiful intention and that it was partly intended to be marked for such by the very curious mosaic of the Fat Lion on the Sea—and the Lean Lion on the Land—which in another manner—warned Venice always to keep upon the waves.

What she says about the long robes [3] denoting peaceful *professions* would hardly have been accurate in old times—for Sansovino [4] says of the dress of everybody "And because their mind was bent upon giving

1. John James Ruskin has evidently written his son praising Mrs. Hester Lynch Piozzi's *Observations and Reflections Made in the Course of a Journey through France, Italy, and Germany*, 2 vols. (London, 1789).

2. See *Observations, I*, 152, where Mrs. Piozzi, in describing St. Mark's, speaks of its floor as one "on which you place your feet without remorse, but not without a very odd sensation, when you find the ground undulated beneath them, to represent the waves of the sea, and perpetuate marine ideas, which prevail in everything at Venice." For additional comment by Ruskin see *The Stones of Venice II* (*Works, 10, 62*).

3. In *Observations, I*, 159, Mrs. Piozzi remarks, "It is observable that all long robes denote peaceful occupations, and that the short cut coat is the emblem of a military profession, once the disgrace of humanity, now unfortunately becomes its false and cruel pride."

4. Francesco Sansovino (1521–86), whose monumental history of Venice entitled *Venetia Citta nobilissima et singolare, Descritta in XIII Libri* (Venice, 1658) was a valuable source for Ruskin's researches.

no offense to anyone, and living quietly as far as it might be permitted them they thought good to show to everyone, by external signs this their endeavour, by wearing a *long dress,* which would have been in no wise convenient for persons of a gay temperament or of eager and fierce spirits."

Red was a frequent colour in the dress, but Prout's figure is I think a Greek or Turk, not a Venetian.

Dearest love to my mother.

> Ever my dearest Father.
> Your most aff^e. Son.
> J Ruskin.

LETTER 66

25th November. [1851]

My dearest Father,

The grate is up, and we had a coal fire yesterday, all owing to Mr Brown's kindness, for the coal merchants told us that unless we wanted a *shipload*—it was not worth their while. Under which circumstances —as it was at Mr Brown's suggestion that we sent the grate, we applied to him to tell us how to fill it—and on his personal application to the coalmerchant's feelings, we were allowed to have a couple of tons— There were still Tongs, poker—and shovel wanting to our establishment which Mr Brown raked up out of his stores—and sent us, and we had a nice scene at the first lighting of the fire—for our Gondolier servant Beppo had never seen one, and did not believe that coals would burn; and Bastian, Mr Brown's servant—who came with the fire irons, thought it necessary to instruct George that the poker "was to break the coals with"—on which George immediately asked him in a humble manner —the use of the tongs; which Bastian having also explained with great gravity—George proceeded to enquire that of the shovel; but then Bastian found him out—and appeared for a moment disposed to let him feel the weight of all the three. It was quite a little bit of Molière.

I am quite puzzled what to answer to Miss Rathbone's very polite and complimentary note—I fancy it must be just a polite acknowledgment for I certainly cannot compliment her on the talent displayed in her story—nor on the "love of truth" apparent in her representation of the possibility of finding a portion of the "Vera Crux" "in the neighbour-hood of Mount Calvary." [1]

I am *very* glad to hear that Dr Croly appeared in health and spirits. Poor thing—he probably suffered more from seeing the child's illness

---

1. Ruskin may here be speaking of Hannah Mary Rathbone's novel, *Life's Sunshine,* 2 vols. (London, 1850).

than he will from her actual loss.[2] I have seen my friend Russell again
—who bears up, also, better than I expected— He is an instance of the
want of teaching at our Universities in two ways. He has gone over to
Rome—and destroyed his constitution by *overwalking himself one day*
in Norway. Now if instead of so much Sophocles, he had been taught a
little *surgery*—he would not have broken the muscles of his leg by trying
to outwalk a Norway guide—and if instead of the Thirty nine Articles
—he had been taught a little Christianity, he would not now have been
consoling himself for his wife's death by the help of a copper image of
the Virgin. Dearest love to my mother.

Ever my dearest Father.
Your most aff^e. Son
J Ruskin.

LETTER 67

27th November [1851]

My dearest Father,

I wish that you were here, now, very often—for more things than
one—but chiefly that you might see the Alps in their winter snows. The
Sunset views beyond Murano would be the very things to please you—
and the time is just coming when they are most perfect. Yesterday there
was one blue-grey mass of dark cloud upon the plains running along the
whole horizon—not a *bit* of the bases visible—but their tops out, so—in
glowing rose light.

You never saw anything so fine—even the Bernese Alps are hardly so
grand—there is so broad an extent of them here—and they rise from the
dead level of the sea—contrasting so suddenly with the waste of lagoon
and sand island. One cannot see them in summer, it is too misty.

There cannot be any district in the world so fine as this from Venice
to Milan—with its Alps and architecture and historical interest united,
and climate never unhealthily hot—and when cold—as it is sometimes
very thoroughly—paying for it in marvellous scenery— I don't care how
many bad days I have—when the clouds go and wrap themselves afterwards into such robes about the Alps as they did yesterday.

2. The death of Dr. Croly's daughter is mentioned in Letter 20.

Effie had some of her friends to tea last night—but I only conde-
scended to go in for half an hour at the end of the evening—merely to
show that I wasn't a *myth:* I would tell you who they were—if I could
spell their names—but there were Count and Countess Palavicini—and
a Princess—and another couple of Counts—one a Knight of Malta—
and an English gentleman—Mr Hope Johnston. They enjoyed themselves in their quiet German way—chatting and laughing till eleven
o'clock—and went away like decent people. Dearest love to my mother.

Ever my dearest Father
Your most aff^{e.} Son
J Ruskin.

I have enclosed this—as I don't like any names to be seen through thin
paper—and I should put the sealing wax in among the Alps.

LETTER 68

28th November [1851]

My dearest Father,
   I find that as to printing any of the volume till it is finished, it will
be impossible for almost everything I read gives me some little notes to
add—and there are perpetual gaps left which cannot be filled up till the
book nears the close. So I must just send you a detached bit to read here
and there as it comes into form. I shall give George a little to copy today,
and send it you in a day or two.
   I enjoy my life in Venice exceedingly—now that I am not working
hard—but the sad *little* that I do every day vexes me sometimes. Still—
I believe it on the whole to be more profitable and that I shall think and
write better by just working as I find it pleasant—and resting thoroughly
each day: mixing other subjects with my architecture. I have got Lyell's
Geology with me—and five or six volumes of Scott [1]—and these change
the subject considerably. What a curious simplicity there is, running
through all Scott's knowledge of human nature, so infantile a sense of
the romantic— The more I read of him the more I feel that he is only
strong like almost every other great painter—when he paints from life.
The Master of Ravenswood with his Montero cap and feather, is a lay
figure, with Academy cast of drapery: but the Paul Playdells—the
Dinmonts—the Oldbucks—the Fair Services—the Nicol Jarvies—
Nanty Ewarts—and the *Women* everywhere—are the glorious pieces
of his handiwork.
   I find a good deal of weakness in the Bride of Lammermuir—of which
I have the opening bit only—the scene with old Alice and the Lord

---

1. Ruskin's interest in Scott was considerable. Throughout his works references to
Sir Walter are frequent, and Letters 31–3 of *Fors Clavigera* (*Works, 27,* 562–621) are
devoted almost entirely to him.

Keeper is eminently—to my mind—unnatural and forced. Old women —however highbred, never speak in that fashion. Was this one of his last works? I have bought *The Antiquary,* which is all beaten gold,* and inexhaustible.

Dearest love to my mother.

Ever my dearest Father
Your most aff^{e.} Son
J Ruskin

* I see people getting "two pounds of gold *before dinner"* at Sydney.[2] I expect to hear next that they will continue to get the gold—but not *the dinner,* and they will find the latter in the long run, the most important of the two.

LETTER 69

29th November [1851]

My dearest Father,

I have your delightful letter of the 17th from Tunbridge with extracts from Mrs Piozzi, which I will note in order—as I can—first however confessing my total inability to translate the epitaph on the skeleton lady: I never could read an epitaph—either in Latin or Greek—in my life, for it is made a point of honour to contract every expression into its lowest possible terms and I can hardly read Latin when it is opened out—but when it is squeezed into a mould, and doubled up in all manner of intricate convolutions to get it into less space, I give it up.

Those must be most interesting travels every way: full of valuable bye notes—and most right in feeling—except by the bye in admiration of Sta Giustina—Padua—which you may well forget. It is a large Renaissance church, which you may remember as a kind of Second Show place after St Antonio—a great way off at the other side of the town at the side of a large circus or oval surrounded by posts and a kind of moat. It has domes like St Antonio—but a great blank whitewashed interior.

I see nothing of the way the upper Venetians give their alms and I do [not] think Effie, who is more with them has had much experience of that kind— But she went to see the Padre at the Lazaretto who was her physician when she was here last, yesterday, and Beppo—our gondolier —was hailed by some of his comrades who had got laid up there—not in the diseased ward—but in the accident ward. Beppo went to one and then to another—and Effie saw him put his hand in his pocket and give a penny here and a penny there—it was only about sixpence in all—still

2. See the *Times,* November 15, 1851, for the account of gold-seeking in Australia and of the man who "took out of his pocket a bag containing 2 lb. of gold, which he had procured before dinner."

it was out of his sixteen pence day's wages, and more than many a fine lady would have given.

I doubt if Mrs Piozzi is right in saying *fraud* is a characteristic of northern climates: Surely the Greeks, Italians—Arabs—and Jews—have been quite as fraudful as the Saxons—Danes—or Normans. What she says about freedom and ease in society is still quite true.[1] They enjoy themselves with as little affectation as children. Thank you for date of Attila.

By the bye—what *does* Fenelon say of the isle of Cyprus?[2] I want this for a special paragraph.

We are going to have a terrific winter, I fear, though the frost seems harder with you than with us; still, "we have it, and soundly too."[3] Dearest love to my mother.

> Ever my dearest Father
> Your most aff[e.] Son.
> J Ruskin.

I have Mr Harrison's scraps—very nice. It was Effie's fault putting the initials—not his. He asked us for some news that he might *use*—and I thought Effie understood this in writing—as *I* certainly did.

LETTER 70

30th November [1851]

My dearest Father,

We have a fine day for Advent Sunday and I hope the cold may have relaxed a little with you, as it seems generally to have come and gone over the whole of the North of Europe at the same time— I go back to points in your two last letters. Guido's [1] Massacre of Innocents is very likely to have been borrowed from Tintoret's [2]—I forget the exact date of Guido, but imagine him to have "flourished" as the guidebooks say—50 or 80 years later than Tintoret, and he certainly lived at a time when people did not think it necessary to *"cross the Alps* to steal" but stole from every body round them. If he did not steal it—it is quite possible that the same idea might have occurred to him—there is nothing strange or very original in the thought. As for Tintoret's stealing from Guido—that is quite out of the question. Tintoret was literally incapable of stealing, from his own over abundance. If you fill a man's arms—and hands—and pockets, with gold plate—and put a basket of it on his head

---

1. Ruskin's interest in Mrs. Piozzi's *Observations* is also evident in Letter 65.
2. Fénelon's account of Cyprus is contained in the fourth chapter of his work, *The Adventures of Telemachus, Son of Ulysses.*
3. *Romeo and Juliet* III.i.110–11. Read "I" for "we."
1. Guido Reni (1575-1642), the painter, who was born near Bologna.
2. Jacopo Robusti (1518-94), more commonly known as Tintoret.

—till he staggers under it—how is he to steal—if he were even so disposed? Tintoret is always in the position of a man throwing things away in a hurry—never of a man picking anything up. I should not think Mrs Piozzi had mistaken her picture.[3]

Crossing to Lido in a *storm* in a Gondola, sounds very grand: and indeed there *is* some sublimity in it—but not the sublimity of danger. The lagoon—as you know—is only covered two feet deep with water at high tide—therefore to have a wave four feet high—the sand must be laid dry between each surge, which is impossible—therefore the waves never can rise—in the wildest gale more than a couple of feet—and this is of course a mere trifle when your boat is thirty feet long. In the deep canals the waves are something larger and stronger—but constantly broken at their turns—so that unless one could get out of the port, (which the Austrians do not allow—even if one wanted) it would be a matter of great difficulty and ingenuity to get upset. But the great green foaming waste of water is thoroughly magnificent—though it cannot rise like the sea.

I enclose you today, four pages of *nearly* the beginning of the chapter on St Mark's [4]—if you keep the pages in order—I will send you them in a regular sequence as they are finished—or as George can write them, for you may suppose he has a good deal to do—the house depending on his stewardship. The real beginning of the Chapter is something about St Mark and St Barnabas [5]—for which I want to know what Fenelon says of the isle of Cyprus.

I hope the enclosed will not hurt your eyes—if you would like it better only on one side of the sheet, you can soon tell me.

Taylor's P. von A.[6] I have never read. I heard he took 10 years to write it—and I thought the man himself a coxcomb—so never troubled myself about it. He is however looked up to with great respect by his set.

Dearest love to my mother.

Ever my dearest Father
Your most affecᵉ. Son
J Ruskin

3. In her *Observations* (2, 275–6) Mrs. Piozzi first compares the *Murder of the Innocents* by Rubens with the same subject executed by Guido Reni. Later in her book (2, 374–5) she ponders the question of imitation in Rubens' *General Judgment* and Tintoret's *Virgin in Paradise*.

4. This became the fourth chapter of *The Stones of Venice II*.

5. The opening sentence of the fourth chapter of *The Stones of Venice II* (*Works*, 10, 69) reads, "And so Barnabas took Mark and sailed unto Cyprus."

6. Henry Taylor (1800–86), minor government official and lesser man of letters whose best-known work is perhaps *Philip Van Artevelde*. His plays are discussed at some length in *Blackwood's Magazine* for November 1851.

LETTER 71

30th November [1851]

My dearest Father,

This Marmont double entendre is becoming the most complete farce I
ever knew, off the stage—*The Comedy of Errors* was nothing to it.
I always had maintained to Effie that there was great oddness in your
thinking him dead—and that I had never knew [*sic*] you make any
mistake of the kind before—and was therefore rather inclined to doubt
her Marmont: at which she was very indignant: Mr Harrison's insurance evidence today I considered conclusive—but Effie would not give
in to it. I suppose a woman has no capability of weighing Evidence in
general. I was on the point of going and calling on Mr Cheney, to get to
the bottom of the matter at once, but I got into the public gardens instead
—and thought my Sunday afternoon would be much better spent in
walking quietly among the sycamore trees—and watching the lines of
their branches on the blue sky, and the setting of the sun over the quiet
flowing of the tide, than in bringing the Marmont evidence into [*text
mutilated*]: So I stayed there till ½ past four—and on walking home,
I found the Governor of Vicenza—Count Festetiks, in the drawingroom
—paying Effie a visit on one of his runs to Venice and back: I ought
to have said that it was only by a stupid slip of the pen that Effie wrote
Istria for Ragusa—as the Marmont here is always called duke of Ragusa.
But now comes the cream of the jest—Effie asked the Count whether
he knew who the Marmont here was—as they said in England the
Salamanca Marmont was dead— The Governor stared; and said "that
could hardly be"—as he had himself known Marmont since he, Festetiks
—was five years old and that in Marmont's "Travels in Hungary and
the Crimea," there is an account of a visit paid by said Marmont to his
(F's) father—which had made him not a little angry, as the old F. was
mentioned in these very disparaging terms—"The Count F. is not so
mad as people say." After this, the Governor went away to dine with the
resuscitated Marmont himself—and Effie went after dinner to spend an
hour or two with a poor sick lady—the British consul's wife, who is
at present forced to keep to her sofa, and whose husband was also dining
with the Myth of a Marshal, at M[me] Esterhazy's: The consul came in at
the close of the evening, and said the old Marshal had been in a terrible
rage about Kossuth—that there never had been two Marmonts, and
being questioned respecting his authenticity, that he had himself heard
this Marmont apologize for the loss of the Battle of Salamanca—saying
he had been struck down at the beginning of the action by the *wound*
in his arm, so that there was no one to command.

After all this—the only hypothesis that seems to me still tenable as
reconciling the two accounts is one founded upon the character of John

Bull as a "gullible" individual—on which you were lately expatiating.
As however it would be very awkward if in consequence of our letters,
the Marshal had to refund to the Insurance company, I must beg you not
to say anything of this to Mr Harrison—as I suppose it would instantly
become his duty to make the facts known in other quarters— Not that
I suppose the Crown Life office can undertake a siege of Venice in the
pursuit of the commander of Salamanca—but at any rate it will be as
well not to speak too much about it. But I wish you could make some
further enquiries as to the facts of the Insurance evidence. It is infinite
jest.

Mr Domecq's letter is very pretty: it is curious how much tact he has
in writing—and how little comparatively in speaking, at least inasmuch
as he does not perceive when he is tiresome.

You will think us marvellously obstinate about Marshals and Tea-
trays—but—I must just ask one question more— Did either you or my
mother *see* the Tray in question?

Mr Harrison's slips are very nice, above all, his account of the wed-
ding, when the bridegroom "tried to look as if nothing had happened
to him." But I am very sorry to see that his old friend Major Johns is
dead. He looked so strong and healthy that I could hardly have been
more surprised; or grieved for a person whom I had only seen once in
my life. Mr Harrison will also lose many a pleasant day. But he is always
making friends here and there.

That must be a very graphic account of earthquake in Mrs Piozzi's
quotation [1]— They must be unpleasant for nervous people. George, as I
think I told you, was waked by a slight shock at Aosta, and so frightened
that he looked quite pale and grave the whole morning afterwards—
though the worst it had done to him was to shake his window shutters.

What do you think about the great earthquake which the French
promise to oblige us with in 1852? I do not trouble myself much about
it—for I think anything the French promise is pretty sure not to take
place.

Dearest love to my mother.

Ever my dearest Father.
Your most aff^{e.} Son
J Ruskin.

LETTER 72

2nd December [1851]

My dearest Father,

I send you another two pages of St Marks, rather too closely written—I will make George write the rest, larger—still it is perhaps more

1. In *Observations*, 2, 52 ff., Mrs. Piozzi gives a vivid account of the Messina earthquake of 1783.

legible in his hand than mine—only he is like the prologue in the Mid.S. Night, and "doth not stand upon Stops." [1]

Some weeks ago I got a letter from Boys with an enclosed etching which I wanted some time to look over as it required care. I mentioned it to you at the time. The letter was in Boys's usual style—a nasty mixture of flattery with request for more work—I saw—as I thought what it was made of, and threw it aside—only noticing the important point, the price of the plate. I got a second letter the day before yesterday which refers to the first, in which I now find a little bit I had missed— saying he wants the price of it "to meet a bill the first week in December." As it is now too late to send it him—and as his letters have rather a serious begging tone about them—it is just possible there may be an execution in his house, in which case you must of course not pay for the plate till you *get* it. I should be obliged to you to call on Boys, 18. Albany St. Regent's Park and get out of him how the matter stands: if his house is his own, you may at your proper judgment—pay him the money £33-10-0, or still withhold it until he has executed certain alterations which I want made in the plate, he has directions in my letter to him of today, which latter would of course be safest—and then pay him as soon as the plate is sent to Lupton, otherwise there is a chance of the plates being seized after the money is paid. I think Lupton may as well be going on with this mezzotint as it is a fine one, and will take long time. I am very sorry to give you all this trouble—and still more to have to draw on you for money for unprofitable work—but this plate is the last I shall have done till I see my way clearly: and it is so beautiful and cost me so much trouble that I don't like leaving it unfinished.

Dearest love to my mother.

> Ever my dearest Father
> Your most aff[e.] Son
> J Ruskin.

LETTER 73

3rd December [1851]

My dearest Father,

I did not know you thought so highly of French tragedy as you say in your letter of the 21st—you never read us any of it. I never looked at it just because I thought it was written rather by *critics* than poets, not because any Hallams [1] or Hegels [2] had abused it. In fact I thought the

---

1. v.i.118.
1. French tragedy is criticized by Henry Hallam (1777–1859) in his *Introduction to the Literature of Europe,* 4 vols. (London, 1837–39). See especially *3,* 291 ff., and *4,* 257 ff.
2. See Hegel, *Werke,* 18 vols. (Berlin, 1842), *10, Pt.* 1, 302 and 306 especially.

critics held up French tragedy as a model of "the Unities" and considered Shakespeare barbarous—but there was considerable power and life in what I heard repeated the other night. What does Hallam say of Don Quixote,[3] which annoyed you so? I think when I read it next—for it is long now since I looked at it, I may perhaps be a little doubtful about the main scope of the book—and purpose of it—things which in old times I troubled myself little about. That is to say, I believe there is by no means enough *Knight* Errantry in the world—a good deal of Errantry without the Knighthood, but little of that Spirit which Cervantes has at once raised and ridiculed in his marvellous portraiture—and—in nine minds out of 10—Quixote is merely ridiculous—so that I imagine the book—in the long run to have done great harm: Knighting a man for building a Greenhouse [4] is not the way to restore the world to a just feeling on this head—however it is better than Knighting one for bringing up an address. The fact is, Knighthood never ought to be considered so much a reward as a Sacrament: It is not—or was not, when it was *any*thing so much receiving a dignity as taking a vow: and the votive part of the ceremony is now lost sight of—how it would make some modern Knights stare to be put in mind of it. However—every man may be a Knight if he likes, in that best sense—which is the lasting one.

Dearest love to my mother.

> Ever my dearest Father
> Your most aff[e.] Son
> J Ruskin

LETTER 74

3rd December [1851]

My dearest Father,

I have today your letter of the 25th—you did quite right to tell me my mother was grieved—but either I must have written very carelessly—or you interpreted rather hastily—for surely my mother does not want me to go to a service which I cannot understand a word of— At least such an observance of form, for form's sake, is more than the Minister himself—who lunched here last week—and who I should think attaches as much importance to his own sermons as most people—expects of one— Surely I said very distinctly that Effie went to her *German* protestant service? There is no other church in Venice but this—and the Mass—to which last I go as often as need be, I believe—but [as] for hearing a German sermon of an hour long every Sunday by way of going

3. Hallam's discussion of *Don Quixote* is in his *Introduction, 3,* 379 ff.

4. A reference to the knighting of Joseph Paxton (1801–65), architect and gardener who designed the Crystal Palace.

to church—I don't think my character—in the public estimation—is
likely to be much injured by my declining such a piece of martyrdom:
There was service one or two Sundays at Danieli's, and other Inns—to
which I always went—though there was little good in them and danger
of being fastened upon by people afterwards—but I never missed once. I
am very sorry my mother has been crying about my depravity, but I don't
know that I am much worse than I always have been— I have written
a commentary of 90 pages on Job, since I came here—merely in my
morning scripture reading—I have had prayers every day—and prayers
for the servants—the whole English service—on Sunday—because they
do not understand German any more than I, so I hope my mother will
make herself comfortable again— I only wish that going to church—
or not going—were as really important a matter in my case as she seems
to think it—and that my tolerably decent observance of outward ceremonies and proprieties had any effect upon my character, but I am
somewhat hard, by this time; and as I hear the service read—I often
wonder whether the people in their best bonnets and Sunday breeches—
who profess to be crying for mercy and calling themselves "miserable"
and "contrite" feel any more miserable or contrite than I do? I never
can command my contrition at the right places. However if it will afford
my mother any satisfaction, she may rest assured that as long as I live,
while I have my health—I shall go to church once at least every Sunday
—whenever there is a Protestant service which I can understand.

There is something about the effect of church going in the enclosed
continuation of St Mark's Chapter—you have now I think 8 consecutive
pages of it— There will be a more detailed consideration of the effect
of such architecture upon religion in the end of the chapter.

Dearest love to my mother. Ever my dearest Father

Your most affec^e. Son

J Ruskin.

I am afraid this reads rather pettishly—but I was really very much
vexed at my mother using her poor eyes to cry with, for no cause whatsoever. But it would be better for me to stop away from church altogether
and be good and meek, than to go there punctually and be pettish when
I am found fault with—my mother should know by this time pretty
well what I am, and am *not,* but it was most fortunate you told me—
Openness always best.

LETTER 75

5th December [1851]

My dearest Father,

In case any accident should happen to my yesterday's letter—as an
accident often does happen just with what is of more importance than

things that have gone safely—I may repeat in this, for my mother's comfort that there is no Protestant church in Venice but one in which the service is in German, to which Effie goes, but which would be of no use to me—and that I have never missed my English service.

All Venice is astir with news from Paris,[1] which we hardly know if to credit or not. The Austrians seem very well pleased—so shall I be—if it puts a stop to all chance of disturbance in the spring, and gets whatever explosions are necessary to French existence, well over in the winter, while we are here under the Austrian guns.

I got [a] letter from Mr Smith yesterday—very polite and kind as usual, but containing the somewhat unpleasant information that neither the *Stones* nor *Pre-Raphaelitism* are selling [2]— I am always "going to write something that is to carry off the dead weight with it"—and never doing it—I must really make this second volume as popular as I can and put few plates in it and pretty ones— There is no use in writing fine books, if nobody will read them. But I do very much wonder that the *Pre-Raphaelitism* don't sell—for I don't often read my own books, after the first look through them when they come out—but that pamphlet tempts me to read it, as if it were a stranger's work—and it seems to me full of interest, and rather amusing too, and I can't imagine why it doesn't sell— As for my having any *reputation*—if people won't pay 18 pence for so much of my writing—it is mere humbug.

Dearest love to my mother.

Ever my dearest Father
Your most aff[e.] Son
J Ruskin.

LETTER 76

6th December [1851]

My dearest Father,

I send you pages 9 and 10 of St Marks. I would send more but George has a good deal to do and can only write scraps at a time.

Mr Blumenthal arrived on Thursday, sent me the pills and white all right—but has left the *sealed letter* behind him—a good instance of the risk of private hands—he says he has written for it and hopes to recover

1. The Republican-Royalist controversy was raging in Paris at this time. It centered largely on Louis Napoleon, who sought a *coup d'état*. During the night of December 1, 1851, a proclamation was printed which concerned the restoration of universal suffrage and the possibility of a revision of the constitution. It is to these events that Ruskin refers.

2. The slow sale of *The Stones of Venice I* and the pamphlet, *Pre-Raphaelitism*, caused both Ruskin and his father, who was his son's literary agent, some irritation. The elder Ruskin was doubtless disappointed by the small return upon his investment. And Ruskin himself felt he had been dealt with harshly and perhaps unfairly.

it, but if there was anything that you recollect in it of important information perhaps you may as well keep a note of it in case the letter be
finally lost.

I am enjoying my mother's Ham at breakfast—in an indescribable
manner—nothing of the kind being obtainable at Venice. It is quite
delicious, our Italian cook having with much difficulty and pains been
at last instructed in the mystery of broiling it. His first preparation of
the slices or segments thereof was in a Copper saucepan—with butter!

By the bye—you say Harding [1] has more heart than Roberts— No,
indeed—and ten times no—Harding was with us—*travelling* altogether
at my expense—and living altogether with me for six weeks. Roberts
dined with me twice: but if you will go and call upon him and ask about
us you will find him delighted to see you and very grateful for the
nothing I did for him. Just say I sent you to ask for a peep at his sketches
of Venice.

Dearest love to my mother.

Ever my dearest Father.
Your most aff[e.] Son
J Ruskin.

LETTER 77

7th December. [1851]

My dearest Father,

I got yesterday your nice letter with enclosed Blackwood [1] and critique
on Tennyson,[2] and am very glad indeed you like the Contarini mezzotint.[3]
You will also find I believe what I thought rather a nice bit in the text
about it. I do not know if I gave Smith and Elder a note of the persons
to whom plain copies should be sent. Boxall [4] ought to have one, and
Henry Acland,[5] and one of the Richmonds [6] but I forget which—and
Mr Runciman.

1. James Duffield Harding (1798–1863), landscape painter and pupil of Samuel
Prout. He did much teaching and also wrote extensively about painting. Ruskin
traveled on the Continent with Harding in 1845.
1. For August 1851.
2. A review of the fourth edition of *In Memoriam,* which appeared in the *Times,*
November 28, 1851. The article was entitled "The Poetry of Sorrow."
3. Reproduced in *Works, 11,* 340.
4. William Boxall (1800–79), a painter who was elected R.A. in 1864. He succeeded
Eastlake as director of the National Gallery the following year and was knighted in
1871.
5. Sir Henry Wentworth Acland (1815–1900), who attended Christ Church with
Ruskin and became his lifelong friend. Acland had a distinguished career as a teacher
at Oxford, culminating in his appointment as Regius Professor of Medicine in 1858.
While retaining an active interest in cultural subjects, Acland did much to advance
the cause of public health in England. Ruskin has left a charming portrait of him in
Praeterita (Works, 35, 206–8).
6. Either Thomas Richmond (1802–74), the miniature painter, or his brother George
Richmond (1809–96), portrait painter and R.A. Both met Ruskin first in 1840.

The Blackwood on Millais[7] is abominable. Unlucky magazine, its writers neither understand one kind of art nor another.

I have not yet read the story—it seems an imitation of *Tristram Shandy,* but many thanks for it.

The Critique in Times is excellent—I wonder who wrote it. I have not read anything so nice for a long time. I agree with it in every word but a sentence or two which I will note presently—but the best of it all is that speech of Johnson's to the pompous man coming out of church, who said—"Sir—we have had an excellent discourse—" *"That may be, Sir; But it is impossible you should know it."* I have so often felt that— with different people—but could not express it.

I dissent from the Times in I think only four points. First, of course in their commonplace about the "Pencil of Claude,"[8] which as a passing sentence—may be dismissed with a mere bad mark: Secondly, in their dislike of the little bit of Church controversy in *Lycidas,*[9] which is in fact the only passage in the poem that gives importance to Mr King's death, except as it affected Milton himself—and which considering the poem as a work of art, is of use in its harshness and rigidity as a stake is to the vine—to hang its lusciousness on— Thirdly: I dissent in the passages they have chosen as examples of Tennyson's obscurity: of which one, "the Shadow waiting with the Keys"[10] is obscure to them only because they had not read the previous poem, which introduces said shadow. What they say about the Bar of M. Angelo is however capital —I wish they had *not* "kept the secret."[11] Fourthly—I *entirely* and in a most serious manner dissent from their recommendation to *abridge.*[12] If a man has matter in him, and thorough power—his natural and easy

7. In the review of *England und Schottland: Reisetagebuch* by Fanny Lewald (London, 1851) which appeared in *Blackwood's Magazine,* August 1851, the critic quotes a cutting condemnation of Millais' *Christ in the House of His Parents.* The reviewer regards the words he quotes as "An unprejudiced piece of criticism, which we recommend to the notice of Mr Ruskin and the other supporters of a small and conceited clique of pretentious innovators in art." In the July 1850 edition of *Blackwood's* this same painting had also been viciously attacked.

8. In the *Times* criticism (see n.2 above) the reviewer, discussing *Lycidas,* said, "We admire the poem not so much because, as in despite of, its plan. The pencil of Claude turns a crook into a sceptre and makes it kingly."

9. The critic remarks that "His [Milton's] anti-church invective reads like an interpolation by Mr. W. J. Fox, or a stray note from Mr. Binney's sermon."

10. Of this line and the stanza preceding it the reviewer says, "He [Tennyson] is not difficult from excess, but want of meaning."

11. See the concluding line of Section *87* of *In Memoriam.* Of it the critic says, "We shall not say if we comprehend the closing line. We can keep a secret." In Hallam Tennyson's *Memoir, 1,* 38, Tennyson is quoted as saying of these two lines, "These lines I wrote from what Arthur Hallam said after reading of the prominent ridge of bone over the eyes of Michael Angelo: 'Alfred, look over my eyes; surely I have the bar of Michael Angelo.' "

12. Of abridgement the *Times'* critic remarks, "Compression is indispensable to a modern versifier. The circulation of his blood is too languid for a large body and scarcely reaches the extremities. His chances of fame in the future may be calculated by the thickness of his volume. Posterity will only preserve the choicest metal."

expression is his best, he will never say anything altogether empty—
and it will be as impossible to compress him as to compress a flowing
fountain—the utmost you can do is to freeze it: Where a man can be
compressed at all I believe even in the end you will find him Spongy.
Heaven forbid that we should lose a single sentence of what any truly
great man has ever done or said—except his errors: in that sense a
man's works may sometimes need amputation—but not compression.
People are so apt to forget that what is not necessary for strength or
weight—is often useful for lubrication—and that fresh meat when they
can get it is better than potted Soup hard for India— At this rate—one
might say, the world would soon be too full of food—a good fault—but
that is only because at present everybody is expected to eat everything
—we do not understand that one man ought to be fed by another man—
but not by *all* other men—*I* feed on Turner—Newton feeds on Phidias
—Richmond feeds on Raphael—none of us can quite relish the other's
dinner; but we all acknowledge the said dinners to be equally wholesome
for those who eat them—and we should be wonderfully in the wrong
to try and boil down Turner and Phidias—and make them up into
"concentrated" pills—that each of us might take a pill of all three. As
if indeed it were possible to make them more concentrated than they are!
Wherefore finally I throw the recommendation of the Times in their
teeth—and I profess to them that if there is anything in the world I hate
in its way—it is, "an abridgement,"—more especially an abridgement
of my pleasures, or profits. Fancy their offering to take a pruning hook
to Dante—of all men in the world—whose couplets carry as much as
other men's cantos.

I have always forgotten to ask you to call at Matthew's, Charing Cross,
the Indian Rubber place, and to inquire for us whether they would send
one of their indian rubber baths here—or whether they merely sell in
London—it is for Mad^me Palavicini, who wants one like Effie's. Perhaps
by the bye better wait till tomorrow—when Effie will tell me what she
wants done if the people won't send the bath.

What was the early drawing by Turner which T. Richmond speaks of
as picked up for a pound or two in the city?

I miss today at my morning prayers Mr Cooke—who used to make the
responses in a most serious and earnest manner. The smallest clever man
I ever knew—a man who could be best defined—just as I said above of
a truly great man that he could not be abridged—so Mr Cooke is so
truly small that nothing could ever enlarge him, and yet full of affection
—most unselfish—ready to help all the world, and full of accurate and
valuable knowledge in natural history—with which he is always overflowing at wrong times, flying perpetually from one thing to another:
and yet—if you ask him a plain question about something which you
really want to know—you get no answer: He knows a thousand things

apropos of it—but not *It:* If you would like to see some very curious and laborious oil sketches of the Ducal Palace—and will just send a line to the Ferns, Victoria road, Kensington—to know when he would be at home, he would be delighted to see you, and will tell you a great deal about us. He is the most curious mixture of conceit with humility I ever met with. They have just made him an associate R.A. Now he has as good a right to be R.A. as anybody—far better than Lee [13]— Creswick [14]—or Roberts: but he felt it such a high honour that it quite threw him into a fever of excitement, which I in vain endeavoured to allay by assuring him it was no honour at all—unless to the Academy: But his tiny self importance and affectionateness came out, in his telling us the next day that, "all the artists in London had been quite in a state of excitement about it!" (his election) and that their sympathy was most gratifying!

Dearest love to my mother.

> Ever my dearest Father
> Your most aff[e.] Son
> J Ruskin.

LETTER 78

7th December. [1851]

My dearest Father,

I have just got your letter with the announcement of our poor friend's death. Looking back on my London life—of—I suppose some 18 or twenty months altogether, I recollect only ten or twelve pleasant evenings passed in society—and those were with Mr George: [1] Burlington St is the only street in London with which I had happy associations —now *all* are cut off.

On Friday evening—the 28th November, both Effie and I, were singularly depressed—Effie—like most exciteable persons—is liable to fits of depression sometimes—but I am by no means so—and on that evening I mentioned the feeling to her with some surprise—saying my stomach must be out of order, for I did not feel inclined to do anything— She said she had exactly the same feeling—and even asked me to mark the day—"to see if anything had happened to us." I laughed and said that we both wanted some blue pill: it would be rather curious if you are right in naming Friday as the day of his death: If it was, I

13. Frederick Richard Lee (1799–1879), landscape painter. He was elected A.R.A. in 1834 and R.A. in 1838.
14. Thomas Creswick (1811–69), landscape painter, elected A.R.A. in 1842 and R.A. in 1851.
1. John Durance George, friend of Ruskin and his father, is also mentioned in a letter of January 1849 (*Works, 36*, 92–3), where Ruskin gives an interesting account of a dinner party at Mr. George's attended by Jenny Lind.

shall be a little more careful in noting feelings of this kind: I have not many friends, and this is the first person, whom I really cared for, whom I have lost for many years: for though I admired Paulizza [2] and pitied him, I was not attached to him—for the simple reason that we never could get through two consecutive sentences on any subject—he and I knowing equally little of Italian. I had certainly no presentiment of Paulizza's death— He died the night that you and my mother and I slept at Leamington on our way to Malvern, and I was very happy that evening.

Thank you for the extract from Times which is very interesting— and gives a most just estimate of Chantrey. The Times is really getting to be a valuable critical paper—a thing heretofore quite unheard of.

Thank you for notes and trouble about Turquoise—but you do not seem yet to have got at the real point—the origin of the name— I know what the stone is; it is a phosphate of alumine, coloured with copper. I believe its resemblance to or occurrence in bones to be altogether accidental: But the question is—*why*—and *when* was it first called Turquoise— Turque—is French for Turk, and Turquoise is the regular derivative—Turkish: So Turchi is Italian for Turks, and *Turchino* regular derivative—Turkish. But why do *they* call *blue* Turchino: and why do the French or anybody else—call the *blue stone*—turquoise?

The poetry which you quote from Cumming [3] is Longfellow's "Psalm of Life" which of all modern poetry, has had most practical influence on men's minds, since it was written. It is now known by heart by nearly all the modern reformers and agitators—good and bad—but *does good* to all of them. I question whether all Byron's works put together, have had so much real influence, with all their popularity, as this single poem, because Byron's influence is for the most part on young and comparatively unformed minds. L's of a reversed kind and on the strongest minds of the day. It has been a kind of trumpet note to the present generation. You may perhaps recollect that on the strength of it I bought a small volume of Longfellow's earlier poems on our Malvern trip—in which there was a good deal of stuff—but I read the first stanzas to you—and you at once pronounced the man a poet on the strength of them. The character of Longfellow's poems in general is peculiarly Motive to action: other poetry soothes or comforts —Longfellow's strengthens—knits up—and makes resolute: there is no

2. Paulizza is a peculiarly elusive figure. He was an Austrian who settled in Italy and who, according to Effie Ruskin's letter of October 27, 1851 (see the Bowerswell Correspondence in the Morgan Library), to her parents, had recently died in Venice. James, in his *John Ruskin and Effie Gray* (p. 170), notes that Paulizza had been "very pressing in his attentions" to Effie.

3. Dr. John Cumming (1807–81), an ecclesiastic. Some stanzas of *A Psalm of Life* are printed at the conclusion of Lecture XXVII of Cumming's "Lectures on the Seven Churches of Asia Minor," which form part of his *Apocalyptic Sketches* (London, 1848–50).

Marseillaise stuff in it—neither—it is all good and true, though a great many men who are moving too fast, like it. For my own part, I had rather have written that single stanza—"Art is long," &c., than all that I ever did in verse put together; though—by the bye—I do not deny the Scythian pieces to be spirited.[4]

Your question of "what was in the boxes" comes rather apropos of this—for one of the books which I expected to find in them and did not, was Effie's copy of Longfellow's poems—given her by an American— Mr Brown—who visited us in London: It is not worth sending now— as I have "In Memoriam" which I did *not* expect, but I name it because you *may* find it among my books—a *square* book—about seven inches each way—and many things in it besides the *Psalm of Life* well worth reading.*

You know that we used to have Shakespeare readings with poor George. He always read in Knight's Shakespeare—and I found the notes so good that I went to Willis's and got the same edition for myself. Two volumes of it I have here—the other six should be among my books; large octavo in green: I name it because I almost wonder you have not mentioned meeting with them as I should have thought you would have taken them up and found them interesting: If you have not done so—you might as well look them out—your Shakespeare is a pleasant text to read, but its notes are execrable. If you read your text and my *notes*—you will find it perfect. This book by the bye was an expensive one—the edition is getting scarce and not likely to be reprinted, and I count it among my *money's worths*.

What else there was in the boxes I hardly know, chiefly I believe preserves, and the ham mentioned in my yesterday's letter. I will ask George what was in them tomorrow. But we miss nothing except said Longfellow.

If the people won't send bath from Charing Cross, it might come in a box with Gibbon, by sea— We shall not want any more port wine I believe: Time goes very fast.

Dearest love to my mother.

Ever my Dearest Father
Your most aff[e] Son
J Ruskin.

* Effie now thinks she wrapped up Longfellow and put him into one of her boxes—so he is uncomeatable [*sic*].

4. For further comment by Ruskin on Longfellow see *Works*, 4, 355, 5, 229, and 6, 394.

LETTER 79

9th December. [1851]

My dearest Father,

I send you pages 11, 12 of St Marks. I have read the Blackwood with much pleasure—still I quite agree with you that 8/6 is much too large a tax to pay for anything of the kind—after this, if you please, I will wait till I come home. The descriptive part is excellent, considering how often a bull fight *has been* described. I was surprised at the freshness and vigour of that bit. "My grandfather" is I think wonderfully like *me*—except that—in *ordinary* circumstances, I *can* think—and in *extra*ordinary circumstances cannot. With him it was the reverse. But his quiet and humane disposition—his regret at cutting the green lizard in two, and his amiable sensuality—the Shakespeare—mullet—and figs at breakfast—are very like me—vide account of our breakfast in one of my former letters.[1] Still, I am afraid I am not quite so goodnatured— It would have been a long while before any speeches from young ensigns would have got *me* to ride to a bullfight.

There is no excuse for the cut at Millais—but I don't think it is done in spite at me—I am not so important a personage. It is I believe merely written in calculation on the sympathies of a large portion of the public. There will always be—in all magazines, pieces expressive of any sentiment of the Manyheaded. To make a redfaced citizen, over his muffin— laugh—and say—"very good—just what *I* said"—is the aim and scope of most of magazine writing. He buys the next number.

Dearest love to my mother. Ever my dearest Father

Your most aff[e.] Son.
J Ruskin.

LETTER 80

10th December [1851]

My dearest Father,

If a box is being made up with bath and Gibbon, I wish you would put into it also two copies of each of the three numbers of my prints (common prints) of Venice— I think after all Mr Brown has done for us, keeping us for a week in his house &c., I can hardly but give him a

---

1. The similarity between Ruskin and "my grandfather" can be seen by turning to Letter 21. "My grandfather" is the central figure in some reminiscences printed in *Blackwood's Magazine* in November and December 1851. The qualities attributed to him are seen especially clearly in the first chapter of the reflections entitled "A Legend of Gibralter." The account of the bullfight occurs in the third chapter where an ensign, Frank Owen, accompanies "my grandfather," John Flinders, to a bullfight in Cadiz. The author of these memoirs has maintained a discreet anonymity.

copy—not that he will care about the thing itself, but he will like it as a compliment; and another copy ought to be in the library of St Marks.

When you have a little time to spare, I wish you would kindly get Lyell's "Principles of Geology," the last edition, and look through it to see if there is anything said about the delta of the Po, or lagoons of Venice. There may be some useful hints for me, and at any rate I should not like in what I am writing about them, to show ignorance of what Lyell had said. I should think there would be an index referring at once to any places of the kind. Mind it is the *Principles* of Geology—not the *Manual of Elementary Geology*. This latter I have with me.

I send you another sheet of St Marks.

Dearest love to my mother.

Ever my dearest Father
Your most aff^{e.} Son.
J Ruskin.

If you find anything perhaps Ritchie [1] would be so good as to copy it and send it me. Unless there be possibility of treating the geology as I don't like to treat poetry and you can send me an *abridgement*.

LETTER 81

11th December [1851]

My dearest Father,

Yesterday arrived the Europa, or at least the letters by her, and invoice of wine—I have no doubt I shall have the cases today— The packet of paper consisted of a curious assemblage of sermons, reports, and a letter or two—one about the Cathedral of Coutances with no beginning or end—another from a stupid person, Allen, wondering why I do not answer the letter I never got, and a whole and a half one from T. Richmond, very flattering—perhaps *rather* too much so. I am particularly obliged for the two sermons of Mr Melville's. [1] They will be much more useful to me here than in London—but what were the *reports* sent for? I never read anything of the kind— I see a letter of F. Close with one of them—but it begins Dear Sir—and has no address, so I don't know what to make of it. And where did the slip about cathedral of Coutances come from? I [enclose] some more St Marks: George writes close—there are three of my foolscap pages, and about $3\frac{1}{2}$ of the letterpress of Vol 1. in his two.

1. Henry Ritchie, a clerk in Ruskin's father's office. He is rather unkindly characterized in *Praeterita* (*Works, 35,* 228) as "a portly gentleman with gooseberry eyes, of the Irvingite persuasion."

1. Rev. Henry Melvill (1798–1871), incumbent of Camden Chapel, Camberwell, from 1829 until 1843 and later canon of St. Paul's. Volumes of his sermons were published in London in 1853, 1872, and 1880. Melvill is also mentioned in *Praeterita* (*Works, 35,* 386).

As the tides were inordinately high a month ago—now they run out altogether— There was twenty feet wide, of mud in front of the houses on the Grand Canal yesterday: It affords me a fine opportunity of studying the structure of the lagoons.

Dearest love to my mother.

> Ever my dearest Father.
> Your most aff^e· Son
> J Ruskin.

LETTER 82

12th December [1851]

My dearest Father,

These French proceedings appear to be satisfactory thus far—if Bonaparte can hold his own now, I hope there will be no stir in 1852 and that we shall have our Swiss journey in peace. Have you as yet formed no guess about the time you would like to start? I am afraid that perforce it must be somewhat late—for if the winter holds as it has begun, no pass of the Alps will be safe till the middle of May, so that I fear it will be impossible to meet you as I hoped on your birth day. But it will be so far necessary for you to tell me what time it will be most convenient for you to come, that I may agree for my lodgings for the proper period. I have them only till March 9th, and it would be awkward to be turned out near the close of my stay by someone taking them over my head, so that I must speak to Mme Wetzlar soon about a proroga-tion.

I enclose another sheet of St Marks—not particularly interesting I fear, this time. Somehow—it always seems to read ill in George's hand —he gives it a foolish look.

Dearest love to my mother.

> Ever my dearest Father.
> Your most aff^e· Son.
> J Ruskin.

LETTER 83

(13th December) [1851]

My dearest Father,

I have today your nice letter with Mr Domecq's from Paris enclosed and very valuable notes on Turquoise which Effie translated for me. I don't think the derivation from the helmet crest sounds plausible— I shall be glad to hear Dr Richardson's [1] account— I don't recollect Mr

1. Ruskin's cousin, Dr. William Richardson. A brief account of him is given in *Praeterita* (*Works, 35*, 410–12).

Brayley's [2] name—in connection with clouds—or any other subject—
but have no doubt he is right, as my memory is very little trustworthy
except for things that interest me excessively— Mr Grundy [3] is capital
—you did quite right not to let him have Turner—I never would let
a Turner be exhibited for sale—if anyone will take it at once, well and
good.

Please tell Tom [*text mutilated*] when you next see him that whatever change there is in the plate, is my fault—not Lupton's. Lupton
wanted excessively to go on with it farther, and I stopped him—he
wrote two letters about it and sent me my own drawing to compose with
the plate—being very anxious to make the plate lighter and more refined. I set the two, side by side in my Park St Study, and deliberately
preferring the *plate*—refused to let it be further touched. I allowed
however—as in mezzotint one must allow—for some wear and tear—
it is best always to err on the dark side.

I am glad you have paid Boys as it may have averted the catastrophe
—but very sorry you have not found Humphreys,[4] who is a very poor
and deserving man— Surely 6. Southampton St, Fitzroy Sq. will find
him? There is another name on the door—he lived in third flat.

I am quite sure you need not fear Gold for a long time to come—
But I begin to think that people in general know as little of the true
principles of commerce as they do of those of art. The *first principle*
of a metal currency is that it represents a certain *fixed* quantity of the
reward of labour, by a quantity of metal *variable* according to the pre-
ciousness of the metal. Within certain limits—a metal currency like
our copper and this Austrian silver may be taken for more than its real
value. But the necessary operation of any *great* change in the quantity
of a metal in the world, will always be in commerce, the enlargement
of the coinage of that metal a greater weight of it being needed to express the same value: and the only bad effect upon commerce will be the
loss upon each coin to the holders of the coinage at the period or periods
of change—a loss trivial in itself—but which might indeed produce
grave effects upon commerce by the fear of it—and which therefore
every *rational* nation—(not that I ever heard of a rational nation
yet—) ought long ago to have provided against—by agreeing to bear
such loss conjointly—that is to say, that the Government ought to undertake at all times, to keep the coinage *up* to the commercial value of

2. Edward Brayley (1802–70), who devoted his life to scientific investigation. He
wrote much concerning chemistry, geology, and zoology.

3. John Clowes Grundy (1806–70), print-seller and art patron. He was well known
as a competent judge of engravings and was one of the first to appreciate Samuel
Prout.

4. William Humphreys (1794–1856), a line engraver, who spent some years in
America. He later returned to England and finally died at Genoa where he had gone
for his health.

the metals, and should be answerable for the same: a shilling being always a shilling's *worth* of silver—and a sovereign twenty shillings' worth of gold, and whatever change took place in value of metals, the Government—i.e. the Nation—should always undertake to furnish the enlarged coinage in exchange for the old coinage—without loss to the holders of such older coinage—coin being given for coin—and the loss thus borne by the nation universally: There ought to [be] a change in the dies every ten years; as *well* as at the accession of a new monarch: and at every change of the die—the government should be answerable for the value of the coinage issued. 10 years would be quite frequent enough to ensure a safe return to any *possible* changes in value of metals. All this is so simple that a child ought to know it by instinct. Our financiers ought to be ashamed of themselves for even talking about metal currencies: they ought to have been settled ages ago, all over Europe— *Paper* currency is a very difficult question.

Dearest love to my mother.

Ever my dearest Father. Your most aff. Son.

J Ruskin

LETTER 84

14th December. [1851]

My dearest Father,

I am very glad to have the sermons of Mr Melville for today and next Sunday, if the box with the bath is not yet sent off I wish you could put half a dozen or a dozen into it—if it is gone however never mind as I have plenty of religious book[s]—Young [1]—George Herbert—Vinet [2]—d'Aubigné—Milton—Wordsworth and Milner [3]—only there is something very refreshing in Mr Melville. I class Wordsworth as a thoroughly religious book—in fact I believe for all practical use— he is much more so than Milton— It is almost impossible that anything can be more noble or *useful* than the entire passage beginning about 60 lines into the 4th book with "And what are things eternal" and going on to the end of the speech of the Wanderer—some hundred and 70 or 80 lines, but more especially the passage beginning "Here then we rest not fearing for our creed." [4] This passage—and the whole of the poem called the "Happy Warrior," and Young's very correspondent descrip-

1. Probably the five sermons in letter form entitled *The Centaur Not Fabulous* by Edward Young (1683–1765), better known as the author of *Night Thoughts*.

2. Alexandre Rodolphe Vinet (1797–1847), a French theologian and literary critic.

3. Joseph Milner (1744–97), an Evangelical whose chef-d'oeuvre was a *History of the Church of Christ* (Cambridge, England, 1800–03); this work was continued and revised by his brother Isaac. Many of his other religious writings were posthumously published.

4. *The Excursion*, Bk. IV, ll. 197 ff.

tion—far in the poem but I forget in which book—of "the man on earth devoted to the skies" [5]—are as far as I know—the best things that profane poetry has yet done for the help and guidance of mankind—Dante being prevented from having his full effect by his imaginative wildness and Romanism, and George Herbert being the expression in *detail* of that which these passages sum up in the most comprehensive and philosophical manner.

I have just got the letter which Mr Blumenthal left behind—the poor fellow is very ill of a pleurisy, I hear by the servant—and I must go and ask for him, and see if anything can be done for him. The letter seems all right—several Harrisonian slips, and one or two letters—one from a clergyman [6] at Matlock which I am very glad to have—as I thought he had forgotten my commission to search for a poor Scotchman whom I met in the Via Gellia [7]—but I hear he has been unsuccessful. I am glad to know that he tried.

Dearest love to my mother.

Ever my dearest Father,
Your most aff^{e.} Son.
J Ruskin.

LETTER 85

15th December [1851]

My dearest Father,

One of the letters which I got yesterday in the Blumenthal packet was from a clergyman at Matlock saying he had not been able to find a poor Scotchman whom I begged him to look after—and of whom I *think* I wrote you some account from Matlockbath last spring. I left word with Mr Barker that if the old man was in distress he might supply him weekly with what would keep him from starving—and in case anything should be heard of him, I have now written to Mr Barker to send word to you: saying that you will send him any such small sums as he may expend or have expended. Please recollect Rev. W. Gibbs Barker, Matlock Bath.[1]

We read Mr Melville on Joshua yesterday—"Choose ye this day whom Ye will serve" [2]—on which he founds the position that it was impossible for a *nation* to become atheistical. This is rather a bold position—all that the verse really proves is that Joshua thought it impossible for the *Israelites* to become atheists: it does not follow that the

5. *Night Thoughts,* Night VIII, l. 1081.
6. Rev. W. Gibbs Barker.
7. Ruskin's meeting with the "poor Scotchman" is noted, in some detail, in *Modern Painters V (Works,* 7, 269–70).
1. In Derbyshire.
2. Joshua XXIV.15.

French may not. Still I suppose that the great body of the nation still serve the Madonna, and that it would be very difficult to turn the peasantry from all divine service whatsoever—I see a paragraph in Galignani, saying that Louis Phillipe had allowed some blasphemous frescoes to be put up in the church of St Genevieve and that the building has been restored to its sacred office by the President.

By the bye—how can he be a *President* if there is no assembly? He is now in Handel's position—"I am de gompany." But they must surely call him something else—Consul the best. Dearest love to my mother.

Ever my dearest Father.

Your most affect. Son.

J Ruskin

LETTER 86

16th December [1851]

My dearest Father,

In the packet brought by Blumenthal was a letter from Mr Lendrick —whom you may recollect my speaking of at Rossie in '48. He is the last of a large family—and his father begged me with tears in his eyes to take some care of him and if I could, interest his mind so as to keep it from dwelling on his health. As the letter which was in other respects very deserving of answer, bore date October, I thought it my duty to answer it directly and so must be short today—but enclose you the letter to read—as there is a little *criticism* in it. Only as in the case of yesterday's letter—I have still to beg of you to take some trouble for me with this—for Lendrick gives me his English address, (now on the back of the letter) and his Irish one, (in the inside of it) without saying whether he is to be in London or Dublin. I would therefore beg of you—any time when you are passing Jermyn St to enquire if he be there, and if so, to leave [this] letter, but if not—then to solve by the assistance of any Irish friend the question proposed in the inside of the letter respecting the Irish address—and putting the right address, to dispatch the epistle by the careful hands of the Post.

Would you also be so very kind as any time when you are passing Tennant's in the Strand to obtain from him what information he professes on the following points?

1. Is *Greek* alabaster now used in the fine arts?

2. What is the appearance, and where are the quarries, of the most valued alabasters now used, and what is their price at the quarry, and in London—per cubic foot?

3. What is the locality especially of *veined* and zoned alabasters—

yellow and white—white and grey—and white and deep purple : like flux spar, and what is their price per cubic foot?

4.   What is "Verd antique" understood generally to mean by miner- alogists and where is it found, and what is its price per foot?

6th. [*sic*] Finest deep red porphyry—Its locality and price per foot.

There is a troublesome commission for you, it is apropos of what you are just reading about Jewel shafts. After I had *written* this, I took an Italian sculptor with me to St Marks, in order to get his estimate of the value of the shafts—but he can give me none—says nothing of that size is now to be had for money—that they are "inestimable," and "come un giojello." [1] I hope however, to get some more definite in- formation than this from Mr Tennant— And by the bye, ask how the price rises for *large* pieces—for instance a St Marks shaft of alabaster is 15 ft high, and 5½ round; or say 6 at base—and 4½ at top—includ- ing I think about 45 cubic feet—but this must be much more valuable than 45 detached cubic feet.

Dearest love to my mother.

Ever my dearest Father
Your most aff[e.] Son.
J Ruskin

LETTER 87

17th December [1851]

My dearest Father,

I have your nice letter of the 9th and am very glad you like so much of the MS—for the part which you do not like I shall be able to judge better when I come to it with a fresh ear, or in print, with a fresh *eye:* but as it is not in the beginning of the book—for this St Marks is the 5th chapter, (I believe it is marked Chap. 3rd—by mistake, in some of the leaves) I think it possible the passage will not jar on you so much when you see it in its proper adjustment with the rest. The order of chapters is,

Chap	1.	The Lagoons.
——	2.	Early History.
——	3.	Torcello.
——	4.	Murano.
——	5.	St Marks.[1]

---

1. "Like a jewel."

1. In the final draft of *The Stones of Venice II* Ruskin's arrangement of chapters in the First, or Byzantine, Period was as follows: 1. The Throne; 2. Torcello; 3. Murano; 4. St. Mark's; 5. Byzantine Palaces.

But there will probably be many alterations made before it is finally printed, from the state in which I now send it you—which is merely George's copy of my rough draught; once looked over.

I am very sorry you thought my letter about Marmont *Indignant*—there was not the *least* feeling of the kind—I said that *Effie* was indignant—*I* thought the whole affair a capital jest. I was, and am still, indignant about blinds and teaboards, but I wish my mother would not use her eyes to write—the matter cannot be mended now. I must be short today also, having to go out this morning for light at eleven o'clock in a particular chapel. Dearest love to my mother. Ever my dearest Father.

Your most affec^e· Son
J Ruskin.

LETTER 88

18th December [1851]

My dearest Father,

The enclosed page finishes the introduction to St Marks: The historical part is not yet finished. The architectural description which follows, though I think very interesting, would be quite unintelligible to you without the plates, which I cannot at present send: so I think I shall next send you a piece of the opening of the *fourth* chapter, on *Murano*.[1] I am much hindered in finishing bits of stray chapters by the cold weather—I can always find work to do in the gondola—or indoors, but almost every chapter requires at the end of this page or that —some little bit of out of doors investigation—and though the weather is fine—the cold is steady—and not a dry cold either—but a damp sea mist which gives hoarfrost in the morning; and in the middle of the day makes everything drip: and towards the evening lies down again upon the sea in broad banks of purple haze towards the west—and draws itself like a dark folded crape veil over the bases of the Alps— their summits glowing like a golden chain in irregular links all round the horizon. I *can work* out of doors, because when I am at work the cold does not hurt me, but I cannot *think* when I am exposed to the cold—I am disturbed by the feeling that the sooner I have done the better, and so I cannot finish the bits requiring out of doors investigation—and this is a great hindrance—for one cannot divide one's chapters into paragraphs nor number one's plates till all is done: and the mere care required to keep one's papers in perfect order, without which

1. For publication "Murano" became the third chapter. See note to preceding letter for Ruskin's ultimate arrangement of chapters.

the confusion would in the course of a week become quite inextricable—
loses not a little time. Dearest love to my mother.

Ever my dearest Father.

Your most affec^{e.} Son

J Ruskin

I quite forgot—and cut my paper small just now seeing I had an awkward size to fold—I won't do it again.

LETTER 89

19th December [1851]

My dearest Father,

I had yesterday your two delightful letters of 11th, 12th, 13th—indeed
it was no wonder you thought we didn't go to church—from the way
in which I had written. My letters like my MS of other kinds want a
fresh eye—but I am very glad Mama is now at ease of mind— I am
comforted also by your liking MS last sent and very glad that Mr Smith
does not think I am quite losing my reputation. There is a great deal of
truth in people's waiting for the second volume [1]—somebody said to me
very plainly in London that they would not look at the first till they had
the second. I am getting on with it—but alas—anything but fast— I
find I cannot write well for a long time together without tiring myself
—and as I was very absolutely in need of rest when I left London—I
am just doing what I find I can do easily—nothing more—and as you
see—reading Waverley novels, and some geology, enjoying Punchiana
in Galignani—and not a little the delicious bit enclosed in your letter.
I gave it to George at once even before I saw reference to him—by
which he was highly flattered— He laughed—I thought he would never
have done.

I am much appalled by the idea of the December account for my unfortunate folio publication.[2] I must really mind very seriously what I am
about. Still—I do not think I shall lose by it in the long run—at all
events—the public shall not have it cheap, however long they hold off—
there may be something also in the printsellers hoping to get it into
their own hands: and so not pushing it. I am sorry I have not a sheet
for you today—but I found some bits in Murano which wanted a little
fitting— Dearest love to my mother.

Ever my dearest Father

Your most aff^{e.} Son

J Ruskin

1. Of *The Stones of Venice.*
2. The slow sale of *The Examples of the Architecture of Venice*—a most expensive
publication—worried both Ruskin and his father considerably.

LETTER 90

20th December [1851]

My dearest Father,

I now enclose you the beginning of the fourth chapter,[1] with which I shall go on—through architecture and all—leaving you to miss those pieces which must necessarily be unintelligible for want of the plates: but it will give you an idea of the general make of the book. I am afraid I am too late to wish mama and you a happy Christmas—but I shall wish it you on the day: If we can get rid of the Red Republicans and other sources of disturbance we may have electric telegraph all over Europe—and be able to talk at our ease. That, by the bye, is one of the things which I hope in these days of cheapness—will gradually come down to a more moderate price—electric communication. It can never come quite down to a penny postage—but by having more lines of wires laid down —and more men to attend to them—giving the said men some other employment—from which—if of a very abstract nature—they might always be roused by an electric shock—when one wanted to be attended to; we may get our conversation cheap, though not for nothing: Indeed it would be rather desirable that words in general should cost something more than they do, than that the tax should be taken off telegraphs. Dearest love to my mother.

Ever my dearest Father
Your most aff^{e.} Son
J Ruskin.

LETTER 91

21st December [1851]

My dearest Father,

I begin to wonder what weather you have in England—ours is so thoroughly settled, it is difficult to fancy it changing elsewhere. We have at present every day cloudless, with about two or three degrees of frost in the night—so that there is always hoar frost on the pavement in the shade when it is not trodden away— It is warm in the sun in the middle of the day: but steadily chilly in all shady places—the Alps are open from morning to night, but never *brilliant*—a slight frost mist always making the light dim upon them. I am very glad—at once—and very sorry to have arrived at the shortest day, for I do not get much work done in the morning now—I don't know if one may depend upon what "Household Words" assert to be facts, but in a paper in one of the

1. "Murano," which when published became the third chapter of *The Stones of Venice II.*

late numbers on early rising [1]—while that wholesome practice was in the main, recommended to all persons desiring health or longevity, it was stated to have been ascertained that in winter, it was more wholesome to use candlelight—whatever candlelight was to be used—in the evening than the morning, and that to get up in the dark and work by candlelight was worse than to sit up in the evening. I know for my own part, that I always feel exhausted if I get up very early: and that I am very sorry for it—for I like getting up early, and would always see the sunrise, even in summer—if my strength allowed it— But it seems to me a certain quantity of effort is always required which takes the nervous energy out of one—and I don't get up at present till it is light—and as I always pack up my work at 10 o'clock, I get a very reasonable quantity of sleep.

Effie—looking over my shoulder at my yesterday's letter, declared it to be a very stupid and unsatisfactory letter—having "no news" in it. As she has been out to several parties lately, I shall tell her to write a "model letter" herself, the present sheet being—I am afraid open to a similar charge. She was paying a visit yesterday to her old doctor— padre Prosdocimo, at the convent of the "Do good" brethren—on these occasions she collects most of the monks, and the Prior—and has a chat with the whole of them— Yesterday they complimented her on her better health and looks—"but"—said the Prior—"you will do yourself a great deal of harm at the Carnival"—"How so?" said Effie—"Why," said the Prior—"there are so many balls at the Carnival—and *we all know what a dancer you are.*" Fancy Effie's fame as a dancer having extended to the brethren in the Island Convent! Dearest love to my mother.

Ever my dearest Father.
Your most aff[e.] Son
J Ruskin.

LETTER 92

22nd December [1851]

My dearest Father,

In two of your late letters there have been some enigmatical references to Mrs Acland, as connected with some large family coming either to Denmark Hill or Tunbridge—I am not sure which: I should like to have some elucidatory remarks on these points, and to know how Acland [1] is— I have been almost afraid to write to him any length of letter—

1. An article entitled "Sleep," which appeared in *Household Words,* February 8, 1851.

1. That Acland was given to overworking and making himself ill is evident from J. B. Atlay's *Henry Acland, a Memoir* (London, 1903), pp. 167 ff.

lest he should be ill—and one does not like to send mere notes of inquiry so far. And do you know whether they lost much by the fire at Holnicote? [2]

And would you kindly also look over the letters for me which you have put aside as not of a pressing nature—and just—at your leisure—tell me the dates—signatures—and main *points* of the communications? For as it happened, this much despised Blumenthal packet contained two letters which I should have been particularly sorry to have missed—and one of which—even as it was, remained considerably too long unanswered.

We read Mr Melville's sermon on the Fish—tribute money—last night with much satisfaction, and after prayers, I had a long quiet walk on the quay which is described in the last sheet sent you, commanding the view of Murano and the Alps.[3] Though it has a north exposure yet the buildings are in so unbroken a line that the wind is *stopped* by them altogether—you must have noticed that when it is blowing a gale steadily in the direction of the arrow against a line of building ab. it is often calmer and more *dead* air on the side A than on the lee side B, when the current is apt to turn back with a swirl: So though there was a fresh north wind, it was quite calm on the quay: and quite lonely—all the Venetians being drawn to the other side of the city, like the damp, by the sunshine: and the hoar-frost—untrodden— lay thick upon the pavement—and the Alps without a cloud— 150 miles of them—in the clear winter air; and the sea blue and cheerful with a full-bent sail glittering here and there upon its deeper channels. I wish you had been with me, instead of taking Mungo down to Dulwich —though those Dulwich hills are not despicable things in the curves of their woods and meadows on a frosty day. Still—on the whole you would have preferred the Alps—though you might have made some objections to the dead wall beside you, and the other—of the cemetery—across the water— Indeed I am not sure whether I could have kept you there—if you had known what a fine band was playing all the time in St Mark's Place.

Dearest love to my mother.

> Ever my dearest Father
> Your most affectionate Son
> J Ruskin.

2. Acland's house at Holnicote was burned to the ground August 30, 1851.

3. For an interesting parallel between this passage and one in *The Stones of Venice* see *Works, 10,* 38.

LETTER 93

23rd December [1851]

My dearest Father,

One of the extravagances which, when I found how much it cost, I exceedingly regretted in my journey here, was subscribing for Galignani at Paris; but as it has turned out I am glad I did—for the English papers are not to be had—and the paper after dinner keeps my head from running in the usual furrow of the day's work—the French events are very interesting, and we have the cream of Punch, "Mrs Baker's Pet," [1] weekly. I quite agree with you in rejoicing at L. Napoleon's piece of despotism [2]—and am only sorry he let Thiers [3] go—the greatest mischief maker of the set. The Republicans have been showing themselves in fair colours: I don't know that even in the Reign of Terror, they identified themselves so completely with the Pickpocket and footpad: In that first time, one had various forms of the human tiger and viper—blood thirsty and venomous creatures—but this sneaking assassination—this sacking a town and chopping up its gendarmerie, and running away the moment there is any danger, with pockets full, this I believe—there was not in anything like the present form of degradation. It is even worse than the common burglar: *at his worst.* Take your great antipathy—*Sykes* in *Oliver Twist:* even he, when it comes to the push, stands by the boy—fires his pistol at the footman—and drags the child away though wounded: [4] But these French Republicans do not so much as fire at a footman—unless he be unarmed. I am surprised to hear the Austrians here expressing fear of "war with France in three months." They seem to think Napoleon cannot keep his place except by war. I begin however to pay little attention to anybody's anticipations—and never to expect anything that *is expected.* Dearest love to my mother.

Ever my dearest Father.
Your most aff^{e.} Son
J Ruskin.

1. A series of four separate scenes, in dramatic form, concerning a little dog. They appeared serially in *Punch* in 1851 and are to be found in Vols. *20* and *21.*
2. Louis Napoleon was elected president of France in December 1848. The "despotism" mentioned by Ruskin refers to the mass arrests in France which were made at Louis' order in December 1851. Royalist and Republican alike were thrown into prison "in order to make the Republic more sure," as Louis said.
3. Louis-Adolphe Thiers (1798–1877) was arrested during the *coup d'état* of December 1851 and escorted out of France.
4. For this incident see *Oliver Twist,* chap. xxii.

LETTER 94

Christmas day [25 December 1851]

My dearest Father,

It is a lovely morning—I trust you have it as bright at Denmark Hill, and will have a happy Christmas—this is one of the days on which one really must regret being on the Continent: for there is no Christmas feeling like that in England—and one misses the sight of friends and dependants: One need not however be of less use, for the distress here is more universal than that in England, and there are fewer to relieve it.

I had yesterday your nice letter of 16th, 17th as you say you have then received my 10th, I hope this will reach you in time to wish you and Mama many happy new Years, and especially a happy one in 1852, in Switzerland—which thanks to Napoleon 2nd [1] we may now I trust look forward to with some confidence. You say indeed truly that these Socialists want to be hunted down like wolves—I don't know whether till the world ends, it will be understood that those words, "Seek ye *first* the Kingdom of God" [2] are addressed to nations as much as individuals; and that Europe, seeking nothing but political aggrandizement in each of her national divisions, and content to accept a thousand different forms of Christianity within herself, and content also to leave the rest of the world to Paganism, so long as it supplies her with sugar and tobacco—must receive an intestine punishment, and be perpetually tormented and vexed by a Devil, which is continually requiring and continually breaking its chains—and raging into places of tombs.

I don't know what one is to do with these Red Republicans, when one catches them. With all wicked men—but most of all with these—one feels the weight of that question of Job, "Who shall repay him what he hath done?" xxi. 31. and there is no answer—but "Vengeance is Mine."

Nevertheless, I think I should be disposed to choose out one or two of the more conspicuous among the monsters: and instead of hanging them: I would put them in a cage—within glass, in the Jardin des Plantes —labelling them, "Hyaena Humaniformis, (Hyène Rouge)—South France," and feeding them once a day, all their lives.

I think you are a little unfair upon Longfellow: The Ars longa vita brevis [3] is *intended* to be remembered—and though as you say there is a touch of this and that, in it, yet I think the true test of a good cook is

1. Ruskin means Louis Napoleon, who became Napoleon III in December 1852.
2. Matthew vi:33.
3. A reference to Longfellow's poem, *A Psalm of Life:*

> Art is long, and Time is fleeting,
> And our hearts, though stout and brave,
> Still, like muffled drums, are beating
> Funeral marches to the grave.

the way he can serve up a second day's dinner. The piece about the heart is besides his own altogether.

Those are magnificent words you quote—but whose are they? The name is, it seems to me, plainly written Mullet Dupan.[4] But I never heard of him?

Many thanks for notes from Lyell [5]—however little, it will be very valuable.

Effie's Bath is a circular one about four feet over, folding up into small space for carriage. I should think the people could not make much mistake—any size would do—from 3 ft over to 5. It blows up: and springs into position.

The enclosed little scrap of plan refers to the sixth line of the 10th page —enclosed—in case you should happen to take a fancy for a puzzle—for those two pages cannot be considered as anything else— I wish I had a more interesting leaf to begin the year with, but you must consider it as commencing our proceedings on a stern basis of fact!

The *numbers* on the plan, 1 to 13, refer to the measures on page 9, the letters to page 10.

Effie joins in best love and wishes to you both—now and ever. Dearest love to my mother and many happy years.

> Ever my dearest Father
> Your most affec[e.] Son
> J Ruskin.

LETTER 95

26th December [1851]

My dearest Father,

I am sorry that at my party last night I saw and heard nothing worth reporting— Nobody there of any particular interest merely formal dinner —but the largest dinner I ever saw in my life, I thought it would never have done. At last it finished however in an abrupt manner—sooner than I expected—for the gentlemen rose and went to the drawingroom with the ladies. This sounds very polite—but as in Paris, I find the real meaning of it is that the gentlemen mean to have their part of the eve-

---

4. Jacques Mallet du Pan (1749–1800), French political journalist and disciple of Voltaire who, during the years of the French Revolution, was exiled for his political views. In 1798 he founded the *Mercure Britannique* in London.

5. Some information which Ruskin senior had culled for his son from the *Principles of Geology*.

ning later—for after coffee, they went away to whist in another room
—as the French people did to smoke. I shall not go out any more.

The enclosed paper is interesting and worth keeping—the announcement of the death of the last male of the noblest house in Venice— The
daughter is old—and has no children. The nephews are by the female
side. All are going the same way : One of Effie's oldest and feeblest
friends is the last—even of the female branch—of the Mocenigos—and
—where we dined yesterday, in the Ca' Barbaro—five or six stranger
families—the English consul's one—inhabit the lower floors and state
rooms of the palace—while its possessors—two old men, brothers, the
last of the Barbaros, live in one of the garrets on the fourth storey. There
is reason enough for all this, as I shall show in my book.[1]

In the little square at the side of our house—there is a church—Sta
Maria Zobenigo—and in front of it—instead of saints—or sacred sculptures, there are four large niches in the most conspicuous divisions of
the architecture—filled by *four Statues of the Barbaros,* and a fifth
over the door.

So they have been brought to their garrets, justly.

The bells are ringing merrily today, for it is another fete, St Stephen's :
The Italians are feting themselves into starvation—and that not slowly.

I have not a sheet for you today George having been variously occupied
yesterday, but hope to have one tomorrow.

Dearest love to my mother.

Ever my dearest Father
Your most aff[e.] Son
J Ruskin.

LETTER 96

December 27th [1851]

My dearest Father,

I had a sheet for you today : but it being of quality like the last, may
well wait till I answer your two interesting—but very melancholy letters,
received yesterday together, of the 18th and 19th–20th : enclosing the
pieces of Lyell [1] most legibly and accurately copied by poor Caroline
Powell—to whom pray return my best thanks. She must have had hard
and careful work in copying all the scientific words without a mistake.

The letters mention also my mother's sadness at not seeing me for so
long, but surely the time is now shortening very fast—it seems so at
least to me to whom every day is worth gold. But it must indeed be
different in the lonely rooms at Denmark Hill.

1. See *Works, II,* 149–50.
1. Some information requested by Ruskin in Letter 80.

There is also the sad news about Andrew [2]—you named the thing before, but I did not speak of it—having little to say of what seems entirely unfortunate and irremediably so; my Mother at least has often impressed upon me the utter hopelessness of the case of a man given to drinking. I think that Andrew has much more cause to complain of—or regret— his own *ir*religion, than his landlord's rigidity: After going out and buying a horse on Sunday at Carlisle—borrowing the price from you—and never paying it, I do not think his contact with persons over-rigidly righteous can with justice be alleged as likely to have done him much harm. On the other hand, were I in MacDonald's [3] place, I should not, when Andrew's affair is settled—and his creditors have left him satisfactorily penniless, keep his Mother's plate and linen. I should hold that very nearly equivalent to "taking the widow's ox for a pledge" but we must remember that Macd. did not know his Mother: And, before condemning him at all, we must consider how subtle and inevitable—in all men, is the self deception which cloaks a weakness under a virtue—so that conscience itself may advise the wrong: M. is *naturally* fond of money: and how easy for him to argue with himself touching the impiety of letting it go into undeserving hands—and the propriety of getting all he can, lawfully, out of a drunkard's fortune, that he may be able to help the more deserving. It would take I believe, a much stronger head than MacDonald's, to discover exactly how much of this logic had been arranged by the Tempter.

As to what is now to be done, you know best—and always do right in such matters.

The question respecting my plans is not a little difficult—I am at present living from hand to mouth—thinking the evil and good of each day sufficient for it. But I am very sure that I ought not to live far from you and my mother: [4] and therefore wherever it is necessary that you should be, I will henceforward live somewhere near you. Not in the same house—that would cause dispeace between Effie and my mother—if not

2. One of Ruskin's Perth cousins, Andrew Richardson, who is fleetingly mentioned in *Praeterita* (*Works, 35,* 66, 410). In his letter of December 10, 1851 (see Bowerswell Papers), John James Ruskin also speaks of this unfortunate man: "Andrew Richardson has left . . . having lost the £600 I gave him and all his own money and sold all his clothes plate and linen and such is the course of a Drunkard and a fool."

3. Macdonald held large estates in Perth, so that his connection with Andrew Richardson was more than tenuous.

4. The question of where the younger Ruskins should live upon their return to London from their Venetian sojourn was complicated in the extreme. Proximity to the parents was desired by the son—but not by the daughter-in-law! In the autumn of 1842 John James Ruskin moved from 28 Herne Hill to a residence on nearby Denmark Hill while retaining the lease on the Herne Hill house. After endless epistolary discussion the matter was resolved by Effie and John Ruskin occupying 30 Herne Hill, a house taken and furnished for them by the father. A full and authoritative account of Ruskin's various domiciles is given in E. T. Cook's engaging *Homes and Haunts of John Ruskin* (New York, Macmillan Co., 1912).

between Effie and me: Not next door, for then whenever we dined by ourselves—you and I should both be thinking—why in the world dine with a partition between us? About ½ a mile to ¾, away, is the proper distance. After I have been in Switzerland this summer—or if you and my mother change your minds and do not come, when I come home in June, I shall have six months' work with engravers and printers before I issue 2ⁿᵈ Vol Stones: I then—God willing shall do *Modern Painters,* which will require a year, and a tour through England in search of Turners; on which if you and my mother could accompany me it would give me infinite pleasure: I must therefore, for my work, be two years at least in England after I come home. And I must live verily economically—that is, by no means *in style:* I am obliged to spend—even here —twice what I intended, merely by being in too large a house, and being on visiting terms with the upper classes. All this money has I trust been spent not unreasonably: I have seen what I could not have written generally of the world without seeing: but it does not in the least add to happiness, and I must now positively put an end to it. The sort of home that I should think proper for me and that I should best like is one like that just beyond the turnpike on the quiet road going past Mungo's little pond; where the parrot is, with the little sloping field behind it—if that house were to be had for three years and you were going to stay where you are, I should ask you to take it at once: As to your leaving Denmark Hill—if you have no pleasure in it—but fatigue I should do so at once. If you do so—or think of doing so—please note that it is a matter of *entire indifference* to me where I live in the neighbourhood of London—so that I have a green field or two about me and that the country be not absolutely flat—I mean, I should not like to live in the bottom of Dulwich—although in a larger house—half so well as on that little knoll at the turnpike: But even in this, I am very nearly indifferent—and should not mind living in the Walworth road—so that I could keep people out of the house—but in order to do that, one must be at least 3 or 4 miles in the country.

I am thus indifferent because I shall be living altogether in Turner; and shall consider any prosaic character of scenery—or disagreeableness of neighbourhood, as so much more increase of my pleasure when I am able again to journey to the Alps: But *quiet,* and therefore, *not London* itself—and economy—veritable economy—are *both absolutely* necessary.

I do not speak of Effie in this arrangement—as it is a necessary one— and therefore I can give her no choice. She will be unhappy—that is her fault—not mine—the only real regret I have, however is on her account —as I have pride in seeing her shining as she does in society—and pain in seeing her deprived, in her youth and beauty, of that which 10 years hence she cannot have— The Alps will not wrinkle—so *my* pleasure is always in store—but her cheeks will: and the loss of life from 24 to 27 in a cottage at Norwood is not a pleasant thing for a woman of her temper— But this cannot be helped.

I shall write something more of this tomorrow.

Respecting Turners—you did quite right. The Carisbrook [5] at 50 would have been well—at 80, ill—it is a drawing I care very little for: My list includes all that I should be grieved to lose—if they came in my way: Still, in case you should be struck by any one in future—please note, that *any* Turner—of the middle size—or average—i.e. from 10 inches by 15 to 12 by 18—and *past* the Girtin period [6]—*is a bargain under* 70 guineas: and is *nearly always* worth 80. The Carisbrook ranks in my mind with the Kenilworth [7]—and these are both drawings which I should never buy—unless they came such complete bargains as Carisbrook would have been at 50: About the St Mawes I am puzzled—there are two—one about 9 inches by 5—the other, England size, 16 by 11. [8] If this latter—with a *black ship* on the left—went at 40 guineas—it was certainly a great miss— Of mere English subjects, it is a great favourite of mine, it has a bad name with the picture dealers because it has so *much of Turner* in it, and so little of *anyone else.* I rank it with Winchelsea and Gosport [9]—and should always think it a bargain under 70 guineas.

The other small one—a "court series" drawing is much esteemed—and may have well brought 40 guineas— I should be glad to give *30* for it as it has points of great interest—but should think it dear even then. It ought to go for about 25, but will probably be kept up by the dealers—and is never worth enquiring about. Dearest love to my mother.

Ever my dearest Father.

Your most aff[e.] Son

J Ruskin.

5. A Turner drawing executed for his *England and Wales* series. A short history of this work is given in *Works, 13,* 599.

6. In their earlier years Turner and Thomas Girtin (1775–1802) were closely associated. Both executed drawings in the house of Dr. Thomas Monro (1759–1833), a man who enjoyed a wide circle of artistic friends. An account of the relationship between Girtin and Turner is given in A. J. Finberg's *Life of J. M. W. Turner* (Oxford, Oxford University Press, 1939), pp. 35 ff. Why Ruskin wanted works done "past the Girtin period" is perhaps to be deduced from Finberg's statement (p. 36) that "There is good evidence to show that Turner's drawings were all, or nearly all, joint productions."

7. A Turner drawing which Ruskin first saw when introduced to the artist at the house of Thomas Griffith, the art dealer, in 1840. Ruskin's account of this meeting is recorded in *Praeterita* (*Works, 35,* 304–5). *Kenilworth* was engraved for the *England and Wales* series.

8. The two water colors of St. Mawes, Cornwall, are 5¼" by 8½" and 12" by 16½" respectively. Both are described in Sir Walter Armstrong's *Turner* (London, Thos. Agnew & Sons, 1902), p. 266.

9. Both *Winchelsea* and *Gosport* were once in Ruskin's possession. The *Winchelsea* was a twenty-first birthday present of John James Ruskin to his son. Both are described in *Works, 13,* 437–40.

1. Oxford.[10] 2. Windsor from Eton— 3. Eton College. 4. Bedford.[11]
5. Malvern Abbey.[12] 6. Carisbrook. 7. Kenilworth. 8. Stonyhurst.[13]
9. Bamborough (large) [14] are drawings which I should be sorry to have
—even under 50. I know no others which would not be cheap under 70,
except the Girtin Time—which I care not at all for. But especially
Yorkshire,[15] valuable, next to those named in my list.
I am glad you saw poor Humphries. I don't think he can do more to the
plates—the angel is much too fat as you say—but can't be thinned—
Get plates (properly greased) and send him his money.

LETTER 97 [1]

28th December [1851]

My dearest Father,

Yesterday's subject could not be discussed in a single letter—but before I go on with it, please tell me *what* you feel in my writing different
when I am far away—from when I am near. Is it in my MS or in my
letters? Perhaps, if you will tell me what *Kind* of difference you mean
I may be partly able to account for it. There may perhaps be something in the mere sense that it will be a week before a letter can be
read.

Touching the houses—the question is especially difficult with me—
because I never was so doubtful as to what my remainder of life would
probably be devoted to: I always, before, had some faint idea of becoming a clergyman either abroad or at home: but after the experiences I
have had of the effects of my intercourse in a casual way with society
for the last three years, I have given up all thoughts of it. I can do nothing
right but when I am quiet and alone: But still I cannot settle my mind,
because I always feel that though I am not fit to be a clergyman, it is

10. One of approximately a dozen studies of Oxford done by Turner.

11. *Windsor from Eton, Eton College,* and *Bedford* are three drawings criticized in
Modern Painters I (Works, 3, 235) for "their coarseness and conventionality." All are
included in the *England and Wales* series.

12. One of four water-color studies of Malvern Abbey.

13. Included in the *England and Wales* series. Turner also painted Stonyhurst in
water color.

14. A water color discussed briefly, and unfavorably, in *Modern Painters I (Works,
3,* 248).

15. Forty Turner drawings, commonly known as the "Yorkshire series," which first
appeared in T. D. Whitaker's *History of Richmondshire,* 2 vols. (London, 1823).
Ruskin considered this work to be "the chief tutor of Turner's mind"; further significant criticism on the series is to be found in *Works, 3,* 233–4.

1. This letter and part of the preceding one throw considerable light on the strange
relationship existing between the older Ruskins, their son, and daughter-in-law. For
Effie Ruskin's side of the question the reader should consult the Bowerswell Papers.

my own fault that I am not: i.e. though I don't love people, and am made ill by being disturbed, and am over excited in discussion and so on—I ought to love people more—and ought to like to see them—and to do them good—and I can never tell but some change might come over my religious feelings which would make What is now my poison become my food: I can see that my natural quiet disposition and highly nervous temperament and exciteable circulation are exaggerated the one by selfishness—the other by pride and vanity, and if I could conquer the evil principles, the natural temper and habit of body would be much modified also. So that I have been putting off all thoughts about my future life until the works I have undertaken are done—but then this renders the question of taking a house still more awkward as every house I live in can only be looked upon as *lodgings*—and this is bad for Effie —uncomfortable for me—I have never the heart to arrange my room as I should like it—(and there is something for a studious person in the arrangement of his room)—because I have never thought of staying in it long, and have never cared to work in the garden, or attach myself to anything—because all was soon to be left. And for a man who has no attachments to living things—to have none to material things—leaves him very anchorless indeed: I love certain rocks in the valley of Chamouni: but that is the only limpet feeling I have.

I believe the *proper* thing would be for me and Effie to live at Denmark Hill as long as you stay there—while I am working on my two books —only I am afraid Effie would succeed in making my mother and you both so uncomfortable—if she chose—that you could not bear it. You would both get angry, and I fear the thing is impossible. But I have not been thinking of it lately—and hardly know: *I* could do perfectly well—and if you and my mother could treat Effie with perfect coolness —if she was late for dinner, let her have it cold—without comment or care—and if she chose to be out late at night—let her own maid sit up for her—content—so long as she did not set the house on fire—that she was either out or in, I believe all might go perfectly well. Effie would not be more uncomfortable than in the cottage at Norwood—and I should save money. You may say this would not be altogether as it should be— No—but nothing in this world, that ever I have seen, is or can be— altogether as it should be—and the more I see of it, the more I find that people commit two errors in judging of others. First, they are not careful enough to determine what *is* wrong and right: secondly in what they believe or know to be wrong, they judge too harshly—without allowing for the weakness or temptations which they do not themselves feel— I say—first they are not careful enough to determine what *is* wrong—this is all the world's first error—there is actually no fixed code by which they test conduct—but they endure willingly in one what they

abuse violently in another: and then—when they once make up their
mind that there *is* a wrong—they do not allow enough for different
natures. There is indeed no question but that Effie is wrong—but—for
want of the Fixed and understood code of right and wrong—it is impossible in the present state of her conscience—to convince her of it.
Her duty is not determinable by an established law—and probably the
world is nearly equally divided in its opinion respecting us—one half of
it blaming *me* for neglecting *her*—the other half blaming *her* for neglecting *you*. Then in the second place, we are always too little disposed to
allow for different nature and education. It may literally be as impossible
for Effie to *live solitary* without injury, as for me to *go into company*
without injury: *I* feel—because I am older, that there is Wrong in *my*
case— She does not yet feel that there is wrong in hers: I, at 21 was just
as self-willed as she is—fretted myself nearly to death—tormented both
you and my mother into grey hairs—yet never would allow that I was
wrong— Allow for difference of education and Effie's 23 may well be
rated as correspondent to my 21; And I recollect perfectly well that no
good was ever done me by any scolding, however well deserved: Scolding only does good to good people—or people in a good state. Bad people
—or people in a bad state—can only be benefited by Kindness—or letting
alone—(unless they come to that pitch of badness that they must be
punished for the sake of society—I don't mean that Red Republicans
are to be won by kindness—or mended by letting alone). Therefore I
am always either kind or indifferent to Effie—I never scold—simply
take *my own way* and let her have hers—love her, as it is easy to do—
and never vex myself— If she did anything definitely wrong—gambled
—or spent money—or lost her character—it would be another affair—
but as she is very good and prudent in her general conduct—the only
way is to let her do as she likes—so long as she does not interfere with
me: and that, she has long ago learned—won't do— So that—really, I
believe the question of whether we could live with you at Denmark Hill
or not—is much more for your consideration than mine—if my mother
could let things go on without troubling her head about them—and above
all, without bringing Miss Edgeworth's principles [2] to bear on Effie's
ways of life—and could be content as long as she saw me happy and
busy—all might be as well as it *can* be in any other way— Effie will
mope wherever we are as long as we are quiet—but mope she must: I
told her fairly what sort of a person I was before I married her—and she
must do as well as she can with her bargain.

  If however you have no more pleasure in your morning garden walk,
and really are tired of the worry of Denmark Hill—you can always be

  2. Ruskin is thinking of the adherence to the socially conventional which informs
much of Maria Edgeworth's work.

on the look out for such a house as you would like—and a cottage to let
for two years for us: anywhere near London. But I should be sorry to
feel that my expensive habits had driven you out of a place where you
were comfortable.

Dearest love to my mother.

Ever my dearest Father
Your most affec^{e.} Son.
J Ruskin.

LETTER 98

Venice, Sunday. 28th December, [1851]

My dearest Father,

I received your letter some hours ago—telling me of the death of my
earthly Master.[1] I was quite prepared for it, and am perhaps more relieved than distressed by it—though saddened. It will not affect my
health, nor alter my arrangements: The sorrow which did me harm was
past when I first saw that his mind had entirely failed—but I hope I
shall have another letter from you soon: for I cannot tell by this whether
it has yet been ascertained that his portfolio is safe—or whether, of
which I lived in continual dread—he has destroyed anything.

I shall not enter into any particulars about pictures tonight—being
Sunday, but merely sit down to acknowledge your letter: For *one* thing
I was not altogether prepared—the difference of feeling with which one
now looks at the paper touched by his hand—The sort of affection which
it obtains as that on which something of his Life remains— I have the
Farnley [2]—as you the *Rigi* [3]—beside me—perhaps the most touching
picture of the two *now*—I think it more beautiful than I ever did before.

The last sentence of my postscript to the last edition of *Modern
Painters* [4] will come true indeed.

Monday morning. I slept very well—only waking early. I feel it a

1. J. M. W. Turner, who died December 19, 1851.

2. *Farnley Hall,* which is briefly discussed in *Works, 13,* 431–2.

3. Turner's *Rigi at Sunset,* often spoken of by Ruskin as *The Red Rigi.* The history
of this drawing is given in *Works, 13,* 604.

4. The postscript to the fifth edition (1851) of *Modern Painters* is to be found in
Works, 3, 631. It concerns the absence of Turners from the Academy Exhibition of
1851, the final sentence reading: "The populace of England rolls by to weary itself
in the great bazaar of Kensington, little thinking that a day will come when those
veiled vestals and prancing amazons, and goodly merchandize of precious stones and
gold, will all be forgotten as though they had not been, but that the light which is faded
from the walls of the Academy is one which a million of Koh-i-Noors could not re-
kindle, and that the year 1851 will, in the far future, be remembered less from what it
has displayed than for what it has withdrawn."

little more than I thought I should however—every thing in the sunshine and the sky so talks of him. Their Great witness lost.

I have been working among tombs, curiously enough, for this last three weeks—and I was thinking of adding to that a passage about the cemetery of Murano—saying that Turner had been struck with it—and had made its long purple wall the subject of the second most lovely picture he ever painted of Venice.[5] But I shall come back to it some day, at evening—and speak of Turner then—and perhaps also name Paulizza —who is buried there: and has no tomb.

Touching pictures—the first and most important of all are the original sketches of my St Gothard [6] and Goldau: [7] and if possible the original sketches of all the Swiss drawings we have—Mr Griffith knows which they are—but especially—after the St Gothard and Goldau—the one of your *Schwytz*.[8] You speak of sketches in *Bodycolour*—but I never named any in my list. These sketches are in such *pure* thin watercolour that you may crumple them like banknotes, without harm— There are, I know—unless he has destroyed them—a vast quantity—for which the *public* won't care a farthing— It is just possible that for five or six hundred pounds you might secure the whole mass of them—getting them for from three to four guineas each—or even less. I don't mean all his sketches—but *all his Swiss sketches since 1841,*[9] and if you can do this—I should like my whole remainder £600 spent in this way—*if necessary:* But if you find that these sketches fetch a price, and you cannot get *them all,* then spend 300 pounds in them—doing the best you can with that sum: but securing, at all events—St Gothard—Goldau—and Schwytz and if they can be found—the parcel which was first shown us in 1841: containing a Laus-
anne, something in that way
in purple and blue sunset—
very misty: and a bright col-
oured group of Swiss cot-
tages— I hope Mr Griffith
may recollect the parcel—if
not—you must choose those you think best out of the lot. But spend 300 in them for this reason. I can get *more* of Turner at a cheaper rate thus, than any other way— I understand the meaning of these sketches—and I can work them up into pictures in my head—and reason out a great

5. The *Campo Santo,* whose history is to be found in *Works, 3,* 251 n. 1.
6. This work was executed for Ruskin by Turner in 1843 (*Works, 13,* 456); it is the subject of close analysis in *Modern Painters IV* (*Works, 6,* 354 ff.).
7. Also painted for Ruskin in 1843 as indicated in *Works, 13,* 455–6.
8. According to Cook and Wedderburn (*Works, 13,* xxiii), this "must be one of the drawings of the Lake of Lucerne."
9. Which are significantly mentioned both in *Pre-Raphaelitism* (*Works, 12,* 390–1) and in *Works, 13,* 475 ff.

deal of the man from them which I cannot from the drawings. Besides
—no one else will value them—and I should like to show what they are.
By the Bye—Griffith mentioned some of Fribourg—which I have never
seen, very fine—please try to see these, and do try to get some of those
above mentioned—I have been so often disappointed about these sketches
that I feel as if there were some fatality in them— Then—the remaining
three hundred pounds, in case you cannot get all the sketches—please
invest in *Mountain* drawings of any sort you like best yourself—as I
cannot give you any specific directions—further than these.

   1. Please do not buy—for *me,* any very highly laboured or popular
drawing, especially if large: The popular drawings are *nearly* always
bad—though our Coblentz [10] and Llanthony [11] for instance are both
firstrates—especially the first—and would be popular also—but in general—a drawing much run after will be bad.

   2. Any drawing which has a bad name among picture dealers is *sure
to be worth having at the price it will go for*—and very nearly sure to
be a firstrate in its way—as for instance our Winchelsea, and Gosport.
So if you see any *odd* drawings with ugly figures—*spoiling* them, as the
picture dealers call it—going very cheap—pick them up.

   3. But the chief thing is to get mountains. A mountain drawing is
always to me, worth just three times one of any other subject—and I
have not enough, yet: the only two *thorough* ones that I have are the
St Gothard and the Lake Lucerne [12] last got from Monro—the Rigi is
divine as an evening thought—but the mountain form is heavy. The
other Lake Lucerne [13] feeble, the Harlech [14] a little slight, and distant.
I want drawings as like the St Gothard as possible—and—if it may be—
in Switzerland or *North* Italy if not—in Cumberland—Wales or Scotland—but *don't buy on any account* any in South Italy—Rome—Florence or Naples—nor *none* in the east—Greece—India—or Holy Land.
Nor none on the Rhine—unless you should see something especially
delighting you.

   I now recollect two more sketches I especially want— One was part
of the Goldau batch with a little bridge at foot of a great overhanging
rock—so, the other a great arched single bridge between two walls of

10. This painting is described fully in *Works, 13,* 454.

11. *Llanthony Abbey,* purchased by Ruskin and subsequently sold because, as he ex-
plains in *Works, 13,* 590, it "possessed none of Turner's distinctive qualities, but was
merely an effect of Copley Fielding's better executed." It is reproduced in *Modern
Painters I (Works, 3,* 402).

12. In all probability the *Fluelen,* a drawing executed in 1845 for Munro of Novar
who subsequently exchanged it with Ruskin for other Turners. It is reproduced as
Plate XXIV in *Works, 13,* 459, where it is also analyzed by Ruskin.

13. One of several scenes of Lake Lucerne owned by Ruskin and enumerated in
Praeterita (Works, 35, 380).

14. The fourth Turner purchased by Ruskin senior; its acquisition is amusingly related in *Praeterita (Works, 35,* 257–8).

rock. Mr Griffith may perhaps recollect his saying to me—"What would Turner make of it?"— It is very blue in colour.

So now I must leave you to do the best you can for me—remembering that I would always rather have *two* slight or worn drawings than one highly finished one. The thought is the thing. Buy *mountains,* and *buy cheap* and you cannot do wrong. I am just as glad I am not in England— I should be coveting too much—and too much excited—and get ill. I must now go to my work and keep my thoughts away from these things.

Dearest love to my mother. Ever my dearest Father

Your most affec. Son

J Ruskin.

other sketch something like this.

If there are any touched proofs of Liber Studiorum please try and get them.

Don't buy any steel or copper line engraving of any sort or kind.

LETTER 99

Tuesday 30ᵗʰ [December 1851]

My dearest Father,

I must be short today, having been writing you rather lengthy epistles lately: I would send you some Murano, but you will have little heart for such dry work for a day or two— You will probably feel our loss more than I do [1]—as you did not so completely lose pleasure in his later works. I am very anxious for your next letter, as surely the executors will at once have gone to the gallery and put the pictures in a safer place and got out the contents of the *cellar,* and Griffith will let you know what there is.

We have the advantage of you in weather. It is the most lovely sunshine—but the sunshine reminds me of him more than the shade—and every turn of the canals where the water is bright—and the Salute always opposite my windows: By the bye you never said whether you found the engraving in my portfolios—of Grand Canal.

By the bye—also—I am aghast at the loss of my beautiful Shakespeare. It was certainly left on the shelves of my study—open—with all my other books—I hope it will turn up—packed away somewhere. Nobody was in the house before my books were packed? Dearest love to my mother.

Ever my dearest Father
Your most aff^{e.} Son
J Ruskin.

LETTER 100

30th December [1851]

My dearest Father,

I am very thankful to God for giving me some power over that which above all things in the world, I should desire to have power over—as well as for the feeling that though Turner would do me no favour, he had some trust in my feeling towards him. Before, however talking more of this, let me beg you not to part—as I hope you have not parted, with the Carisbrook in the vexation of receiving my letter of the day before yesterday. If you like it, keep it—I shall always be glad to have the opportunity of examining it—and it will always change for another (if my unfavourable estimate of it continues)—or increase in value as long as we hold it. I always admired the soft sky, and undulating ground, in distance—as well as the bushes and figures of foreground—my objection being the *rubbed* and ugly warm colour of the stonework, and the uninteresting forms—and absence of colour: in most of the composition— the figures being if I recollect right—put in with common *ink,* but the rubbing was the great fault. I am exceedingly grateful to you, all the same.

You ask about Teignmouth.[1] If you mean a drawing with a skeleton of a ship in front on the right, it is a small one—well worth 20 guineas,

---

1. The death of Turner.
1. Reproduced in A. J. Finberg's *Turner's Sketches and Drawings* (London, Methuen & Co. Ltd., 1910), p. 113.

but likely to fetch 50. I would not give more than 20 for it. If you wrote *Teign* for *Tyne*mouth—and mean an England and Wales drawing with a black sky and black ship ashore and yellow mast in front, cast ashore by a stormy sea—it is one I have long desired to possess if it could be had cheap— It would be a bargain at 60—it is worth 70—I believe, in the market I would not give more than 75 for it. Do you know what has become of the *Arundel* [2]—*That* is a fine drawing—worth 120, but *not* more to *me*— It had come down to 150 when I heard last. Still I would rather reserve all payments for hope of getting something after the main sale, as I cannot now be a purchaser at the sale itself.

Touching coming home I shall of course wait till I hear farther from you, but Effie could easily—as she has an English maid and a kind of Chaperon in Lady Sorel—stay here, if the business could be settled by my coming home for a month. I would bring some drawings with me and set engravers to work, but it would interrupt me considerably by taking all my thoughts out of my head as the sight of new Turners would. What I should best like myself if it were possible would be to come home early in April—leaving Effie here—settle business—come abroad again —with you—spend a month or two months in Switzerland, and then August and September again in Venice—coming home before the October Snows fell.

Wednesday morning. Effie says this would not do—in fact it would *not* be right to leave her so long by herself— After sleeping upon it, I think the best thing would be to come home at once provided you can ascertain that if I did so, *all* business requiring my *presence* could be *immediately* settled: and that I could see all the pictures and drawings. The Mont Cenis is safe in the mid winter—but not safe in very early spring: I would be ready to start on receiving your answer to this— would get home, I hope in about 10 days: settle business and set engravers to work on ten or twelve plates—get all done—say in three weeks—back here by middle of February—March—April. I would start again with Effie 20th May, meet you at Grenoble—as before planned, spend whatever time you could spare, with you in Switzerland—and if it was necessary—take another month or couple of months at Venice afterwards and return in October to England for good. I should send home another packet of plates by you from Switzerland—and some text—so when I came home in October I should only have one or two more plates to do and press to correct. I think if you consider this well—you will agree with me—provided it be ascertainable that the business *can be done* if I come home now. The interruption would not injure the book—but only throw it back—as I should be a week or two before I got into the course

2. Either a water color of Arundel Castle or the *Arundel* in the *England and Wales* series.

of it again—after my head had been full of Turner. In fact I am—as you may suppose—a little off the rails as it is.

I have just recollected two other drawings which I should warn you *against*—Flint Castle [3]—which has been knocking about the world a great deal, and Great Yarmouth [4]—now belonging to Mr Kingsley [5]— but which might perhaps come into the market, and though a valuable drawing—is not one of my likings.

I can give [you] one test—in case any drawings should come before you—quite infallible— Wherever the colours are vivid—and laid on in many patches of sharp *blotty* colour—not rubbed—you may be sure the drawing is valuable— For Turner never left his colours fresh in this way unless he was satisfied—and when *he* was satisfied—I am.

All drawings with black skies—without exception—are fine like our Winchelsea, and nearly all in which the clouds are worked into *dark blue* as a *storm* colour, are bad, like the Bamborough which you may recollect had an indigo sky. The Land's End [6]—though to me unsatisfactory—is assuredly a fine drawing. Its sky is black—but too laboured. Windus [7] has a black picture of *Fowey Harbour* [8]—this is also fine—but I should not like it—because people are being drowned in the forewater and we have enough of that in Slaver.[9] Compare—taking them down from the wall—first, Schwytz and Richmond, Surrey; [10] you will see the Schwytz is throughout *rubbed*—no colour has an edge, nor any purity— Look at the way the blue is dashed on in the woman's shawl and the light distant sky in the Richmond—and the edges of the trees—look at the *thin* fresh colour in them— *Whenever* you see the colour thus laid on—the drawing is fine.

Look again, at the way it goes on behind the tower and trees in the Winchelsea—and all over that sky—and look how the distant castle is

3. Reproduced in *Works, 22,* 62, and described by Ruskin in *Works, 13,* 442–3.

4. From the *England and Wales* series.

5. Rev. William Kingsley, sometime of Sidney Sussex College, Cambridge University, a friend of Ruskin and authority on Turner.

6. A water color which drew favorable comment in the *Examiner,* February 3, 1852, when it was displayed at W. B. Cooke's.

7. B. G. Windus, a retired coach-maker and Turner collector. He was also among the earliest buyers of Pre-Raphaelite paintings.

8. A water color described in Sir Walter Armstrong's *Turner,* p. 254. It was also engraved for the *England and Wales* series.

9. *The Slavers,* one of Turner's best-known oil paintings, which was purchased by John James Ruskin in 1843 and later sold by his son. It is now in the Museum of Fine Arts, Boston, Mass. Also known as *The Slave Ship,* it is glowingly described by Ruskin in *Modern Painters I* (*Works, 3,* 571–2). Ruskin senior gave it to his son in gratitude for the success of *Modern Painters I.* See also, concerning this picture, *Praeterita* (*Works, 35,* 318–19).

10. *Richmond Bridge, Surrey,* the first Turner Ruskin ever received from his father. It is analyzed in *Works, 13,* 436–7. An account of this acquisition is given in *Praeterita* (*Works, 35,* 254).

painted in the Dudley,[11] and the mountain distance on the left in the St
Gothard—all *blots*. Wherever the colour is so left—it is a sure sign that
Turner was satisfied— When he was not—he worked on, and stippled
or rubbed— Not but that—in his very finest drawings our Constance [12]
and Rigi for instance—he stippled up his first thoughts with exquisite
care—but you cannot be *sure* of the universally rubbed and stippled
drawings— They *may* be elaborations of a fine thought—or corrections
of a blunder. The Fresh drawings are *sure*. I only name *these* tests in case
of any drawings going cheap—for the great thing is to get *mountains*.
They are almost always sure to be invaluable, and of other subjects—
the brighter the colours the better. Dearest love to my mother.

Ever my dearest Father. Your most affectionate Son.

J Ruskin

Renewed thanks for your kindness about Carisbrook.

Please add to list of *superfine* drawings—in case Munro should be exchanging—his High Force of Tees [13] with birds in nest in foreground—
It is invaluable. I don't mean that I ever hope or wish to get all the firstrates I name—but it is well you should know which I *think first rate*—
in case one or other should come in the way.

Observe, the remarks on Turner's execution, on last page—refer only
to the drawings of his middle period [14]—noticed in *Pre-Raphaelitism* as
that in which he most erred—and to the failing drawings of his last Swiss
series. In buying early drawings in the colourless Yorkshire manner—
like our Richmond Yorkshire [15]—you *cannot err*. They are all faultless,
though none of them rise to such achievement as he purchased afterwards by occasional error, and his first Swiss series—Ours—Bicknell's [16]
—and Munro's—are quite priceless.

LETTER 101

January 1st. 1852.

My dearest Father,

Many many happy new years to you and Mama both—and a pleasant
house—with me near you and whatever else you would like. And good
hope of better things to come.

11. *Dudley Castle,* a Turner drawing once in Ruskin's possession and reproduced in
Works, 22, 60.

12. Acquired by Ruskin in 1842, this Turner is reproduced and discussed in *Works,
13,* 454–5.

13. *High Force, Fall of the Tees,* used by Ruskin to illustrate certain points in
Modern Painters I (Works, 3, 486 ff.).

14. In *Pre-Raphaelitism* Ruskin divides Turner's artistic periods roughly into three
parts: 1. 1800–20; 2. 1820–40; 3. the years following 1840.

15. Turner did several studies of Richmond, Yorkshire.

16. A Herne Hill neighbor of Ruskin, whose collection of Turner is catalogued in
Thornbury's *Life of Turner* (New York, 1877), p. 599.

I send you half a sheet—merely by way of beginning the New Year with a piece of work; and partly also because by glancing at the part of it which is not scratched out, you will see how my present work will bind all my past on architecture into one, and confirm and recapitulate all. I have run a line through the parts—which must of course be perfectly unintelligible to you—but which I send merely to connect all together.

You say you are glad the history—&c.—is to come first. I believe in this book, every chapter will contain some opening and closing passages of interest, and the dryer or bony parts, in which the strength of the book consists, will never be so long as to be unmanageable— Such pieces, even, as I now send, will not be altogether uninteresting when the plates are at the side, and I think as I read them over that I shall be able to abridge them considerably when the book is quite done. They are written *at length* in consequence of hurry, and that I may be sure I have all I want.

Tell my mother that I have been reading the Psalms through in little bits each day—and that—coming in this way to the 119th I *do* find it nicer than the others—much more serviceable—but only taken a little bit at a time. I have been pained however in going through them by the continual cursing of enemies, and partly also by the quantity of repetition, and by the ambiguousness—one never knows whether David is speaking of himself or of Christ. I cannot help often taking that Pharisaical speech into my heart, if not into my lips—"If thou be the Christ, tell us plainly." [1]

I am sorry to send you only half a sheet—but I want to call on some people today to wish them good new Year, and I have some Charities to see about, and I want to get some work finished for bringing home, in case any letters come requiring me soon.

So Goodby with dearest love to you both.

Ever your most affectionate Son
J Ruskin.

LETTER 102

1st January. Evening. [1852]

My dearest Father,

I got your kind letter and mama's note today, as you so nicely planned it—and my best thanks for the precious letter, as well as for the sermons —and all the trouble you have had respecting Carisbrook—&c. I have passed a very happy New Year's day—it has been lovely, and I have been getting on with my work: and though at first a little pained at all the sketches being thus forever out of my reach—yet I am so thoroughly satisfied and thankful for the general tenor of the will [1] that I can well

1. John x.24.
1. Of Turner, which is reproduced in Thornbury's *Life of Turner*, pp. 620 ff. Its clarity

put up with my own loss. Indeed I shall gain as much as I lose—in the power of always seeing all his works in London, free of private drawing-rooms. If the rest of the executors would only make me curator of the gallery [2] I should be perfectly happy.

I am thankful also that I need not be interrupted in my work, nor take the bitter cold winter's journey.

As for the life,[3] I will think about it. I should like to know a little what kind of materials are to be had— There might be much that would be painful to tell and dishonest to conceal—and on the other hand— apart from all criticism of his works, probably little to interest—and all criticism I shall keep for *Modern Painters*. But I should like to have a shy at Sir George Beaumont,[4] and the owls too, and the materials for the life would include I doubt not—a few good—available, brickbats. If I were not going to write *Modern Painters* I should undertake it at once, but I will make *that* so complete a monument of him, D.V. that there will be nothing left for the life but when he was born—and where he lived—and whom he dined with on this or that occasion. All which may be stated by anybody. I am anxious however at present about the locale of the paintings and drawings. They ought not, by rights, to be kept in London at all—but if in London—only at the British museum—and yet that can't be neither until they are really national property. The danger of fire is so great in any private house and in Queen Anne St [5]—of damp also—in fact they can hardly light a fire there till the house has been repaired—*and* fancy bricklayers in a house with Turner drawings— and paintings already cracking off the canvass. I wish I were in London. By the bye—for any favour, write to Mr Griffith and tell him that if I have any power in the matter—not a single drawing is to be *mounted* or touched—but that the pictures, some of them ought to be *lined* and if they want my concurrence to do it, I will sign anything they send me here—to the effect that any oil pictures may be lined, but *not cleaned* if they don't want lining.

has been variously debated. Suffice to say that from it, through intervention of relatives, much confused litigation arose. Until 1856 the dispensation of his property remained in abeyance.

2. As one of Turner's executors, Ruskin is here expressing the hope of becoming curator of the Turner Gallery, a room or rooms attached to the National Gallery which Turner in his will hoped might be erected. The plans for this gallery, which Ruskin makes in the following paragraphs, came to nothing.

3. John James Ruskin was anxious for his son to write a life of Turner. Ruskin considered the idea but abandoned it; he gave considerable assistance to Thornbury, however. For Ruskin's relations with the latter, see *Works, 13*, 554–5.

4. Sir George Beaumont, Bt. (1753–1827), amateur painter and friend of Sir Joshua Reynolds. Ruskin's desire to "have a shy" at the baronet is understandable if one reads a note to the preface of the second edition of *Modern Painters I* (*Works, 3*, 145) where, because of his theories, Beaumont's "prostration of intellect" is considered both "ludicrous" and "lamentable." Beaumont was also in violent artistic opposition to Turner.

5. One of Turner's residences to which a gallery was attached.

I don't think there is much fear of the relations oversetting the will—first—because the interest of the nation is so concerned that the entire public feeling will be against them—and secondly because—if what is reported be true, the only near relations he has have no legal claim upon him. I hope—and believe that the National Gallery people *won't* build a new wing—but will leave us to do it : and that it will be a year or two before it is begun, and that then I shall have the management of it—(this between you and me)—for I would build such a gallery as should set an example for all future picture galleries. I have had it in my mind for years. I would build it in the form of a labyrinth—all on ground story—but with ventilation between floor and ground—in form of labyrinth, that in a small space I might have the gallery as long as I chose—lighted from above—opening into larger rooms like beads upon a chain—in which larger pictures should be seen at their right distance—but *all on the line,* never one picture above another. Each picture with its light properly disposed for it alone—in its little recess or chamber. Each drawing with its own golden case and closing doors, with guardians in every room to see that they were always closed when no one was looking at *that* picture. In the middle of the room—glass cases, with the sketches—if any—for the drawing or picture—and proofs of all engravings of it. Thus the mass of diffused interest would be so great that there would never be a crowd any where : no people jostling each other to see two pictures hung close together. Room for everybody to see everything. The roof of double plate glass of the finest kind—sloping as in crystal palace—but very differently put together— No *drip*.

50,000, would do it all—splendidly—and leave 30—for interest for repairs, and servants' salaries.

I am very thankful you have got Carisbrook. Keep all you have and get all you can— Keep red [*sic*] last picture as you say : it is now valuable. I wonder if he has destroyed the other eight—which he began for me.

Dearest love to my mother.

> Ever my dearest Father
> Your most affect. Son.
> J Ruskin.

LETTER 103

3rd January [1852]

My dearest Father,

I am very thankful to God for giving me so honest a father, which is better than any quantity of pictures—but at the same time—I think it rather too bad that the only result of all I have done for Turner should be that I have *not the same chances* of getting pictures as anybody else—

and that my having all the trouble of the executorship [1] should only be rewarded by my losing the last hope of ever getting anything— Surely the difficulty about the Wallis [2] drawing was easily enough settled— Could you not have secured it—and then—when the truth of the will came out—asked him what he would give you to have the drawing back —and either restored him the drawing—or given him the difference? But now you do *him* no good—for of course Monro and others will now search all London and get all they can, and you do yourself and me injustice— I am in a state of mystification about this drawing—was it the St Catherines Hill [3]—with—"Try the Red Lion—N.B. No better under the Sun?" If so—that is a drawing I have been wanting all my life—and only did not put it on my list of highest rank because I thought you had an insuperable dislike to it— Of all drawings that I know, *not* of mountain scenery, it is one of the most precious—the rolling and sublime sky mixed with the strange expression of humour and the over-coming of marvellous difficulties in the arrangement of the tents— I live in hope you may have thought better of it and gone back and secured it.

There is *one* more drawing which I may add to the list of those that I would *not* have—even now—*Blenheim:* [4] I would not have it at *any* price, disliking both drawing and subject. I think, as things now stand—that any other drawing coming into the market, except those named as bad in the list I sent you the other day, would be well bought at any price up to 150. The Yorkshire—Swiss—and fine mountain drawings are without price.

Miss Mitford's [5] letter very nice—but I cannot be sure of the two words: "actual marvel," I *think;* but this does not make very good sense.

Effie is going to write you some account of her late doings.

Dearest love to my mother.

> Ever my dearest Father
> Your most aff^e. Son
> J Ruskin.

1. Of Turner's estate.

2. Robert Wallis (1794–1878), engraver, whose renditions of Turner were notable in their day.

3. A Turner drawing from the *England and Wales* series for some years in Ruskin's possession. It is reproduced as Plate LIII in Bell and Daldy's edition of *Turner's Picturesque Views in England and Wales* (London, 1873).

4. From the *England and Wales* series.

5. Mary Russell Mitford (1787–1855), who was a close friend of Ruskin's. Their acquaintance is sketched briefly in *Works, 36,* xxix–xxx.

LETTER 104

Sunday. 4ᵗʰ January [1852]

My dearest Father,

I did not yesterday thank you for the notes of Tennant's somewhat negative information.[1] It is always however satisfactory to know how little is known—this being in general the conclusion of prolonged investigations.

You also ask for some of my personal doings. Mine are confined to staying at home. I made a round of visits on New Year's day however—to Mr Brown—Lady Sorel, and the English Consul's—and everybody was highly flattered. But on other days I am either in my study ashore —or my floating study, the gondola, all day: and am I believe, by many people supposed a Myth.

The Oldfield [2] criticism on Carisbrook is excellent: very characteristic of the man.

What you say of Turner's death at Chelsea is very sad—and it is a striking monument of the evil ways of this century that its greatest mind should have been left thus neglected. But the longer I live, the more the world and all that it inherits becomes a mystery to me. When I read the Bible—especially the New Testament—the standard it fixes appears so high that it is impossible for any creature to come near it; the great mass of the world therefore seems to give it up at once, and live as they list, in a sort of tacit despair: and we are worse in this respect than if we had no Bible. While the few who try to live by God's word find so much to dwell upon in themselves and to conquer that they are all intent upon their own battles—experiences—and dangers—and never seem able to look round with a practical glance upon the outside world.

Have you still any of those feelings of religious despondency which came upon you so severely some time ago—or were they merely one of the forms of the disease? You have not said in any of your letters lately how you sleep, &c. I was sorry to hear your account of poor Griffiths— he was sadly thin when he left his London room. I have an affection for him, having passed many happy hours in his Norwood house and having got, through him, all that I most value in the world. Other picturedealers, while they were quite as far from the rigid line of plaindealing—were always acting not only for their own interest—but for other people's

1. In an earlier letter Ruskin asked his father to ascertain some information from Tennant's concerning alabaster.
2. Edmund Oldfield (1817–1902), Assistant Keeper of the Antiquities at the British Museum and close friend and former schoolfellow of Ruskin. He was an authority on stained glass and Gothic architecture; he also designed a window for the Camberwell Church. His talents as an art critic are noted in his obituary in the *Times*, April 15, 1902.

rather than mine—and showing what they had to Munro—Stokes [3]—
Windus—or anybody else—*before* me. But Griffith always gave me first
sight—first offer—first choice. Many a golden offer he put in my way
—such as I shall never have more—and you know we always had the
first choice in the Turner sketches. Give him my best regards.

Dearest love to my mother.

Ever my dearest Father,
Your most affec^e. Son
J Ruskin.

LETTER 105

5th January [1852]

My dearest Father,

I am not sending you any more architectural text at present—as your
thoughts must be otherwise taken up, but I shall make George copy on,
and have it ready to send when you would like to have it. I am sorry to
see in one of your later letters that you have so much more correspondence
and hard work for so little profit. I would not do it, if I were you, but
just work as much as you had comfortable leisure for—and take what
profit came.

I have been thinking about writing Turner's life,[1] but have nearly
made up my mind to let it alone, merely working in such bits of it as
please me with *Modern Painters*. Biography is not in my way. Besides
I should be too long about it—there will be a dozen lives of him out before mine would be ready. It would be curious if I got the whole collection of his works to illustrate and explain and build the gallery for—and
so take the position of his Interpreter to future generations. Perhaps this
was what I was meant to do. A curious thing happened to me on Saturday afternoon. I was rowing back from Fusina ; and exactly at the very
spot—and very time—five minutes before sunset—of Turner's picture,
my old favourite—"San Benedetto looking towards Fusina" [2] to my
great surprise, there was—in the very place where he had put it, in that
picture, the very boat—one of a kind I had not seen before in Venice—a
sort of covered waggon with a great curved rudder—(I tried to draw
it but did it so badly that I was ashamed, and cut it off)— I asked my
boatman directly whether it went regularly to Fusina—"It used to do"
—he said—it was the cheap passage boat to Padua before the railroad,
but was now of course no more used, except sometimes in luggage. So
it was by mere accident—a most lucky one that I got this little illustration

---

3. Charles Stokes of Gray's Inn, a friend of Turner with whom Ruskin had exchanged some drawings.

1. This matter has already been broached in Letter 102.

2. An oil painting fully described in *Notes on the Turner Gallery at Marlborough
House, 1856* (*Works, 13,* 164-6).

of Turner's putting everything in its own place: For it was only in that picture, with its especial reference to Fusina, that that boat could have been used. It never would have been seen in any other part of Venice.

Most likely Turner had come by it and you by it—the *cheap* passage boat.

We read the sermon on advent, Yesterday— It must have been very impressive when delivered—but is a little loose in arrangement for reading. Still most valuable. I never understood the verse before. I mean the "who is this that cometh from Edom?" [3]

Dearest love to my mother.

Ever my dearest Father
Your most aff^e. Son
J Ruskin.

LETTER 106

Twelfth day. [6 January 1852]

My dearest Father,

The bells are ringing merrily, for the Epiphany is a great Festa here— and I do think the Catholicks have in this respect—some advantage over us protestants: When I was a child, I not only had never heard of the "Epiphany" but had no other idea whatever connected with Twelfth day except that of cake and a private Pantomime, and it must be so with multitudes more: I think this ought to be altered—Cake and Pantomime are good things—but not proper memorials of the Star that Stood over where the Young Child was— I think these religious feasts should be much better kept, and more solemnly, and the festivities ought to be shifted to mark the epochs of some great profane historical event of good fortune. For instance I would have a great feast on St Crispin's day, and another on the day of the discomfiture of the Armada—and I would have cakes with fleets on the tops of them—and French Kings and Spanish admirals—as many as you please. And a great feast on May day. And at Harvest home and the Apple Harvest— I am sure the children would not be worse off—under my rule, and new calendar.

I had yesterday your kind and interesting letter, with pleasant accounts of Miss Mitford—and many other agreeable matters—among which I should first thank you for your gift of £500—but indeed I look on all that I spend as your gift—at all times: what you have put entirely in my power just as much as what you are continually giving me, and, I must say, the sense of Debt never oppresses me in any way as to hurt my digestion—so long as it is only to you, and the sum known, but I am

3. Isaiah lxiii.1.

sorry to have spent so much, and will try to spend less—whether you consider me out of debt, or in.

By way of beginning to economize—I wish you could get the Salt Ash,[1] if its price is at all reasonable— It is an invaluable picture— I would not bid for it before—because I had hopes of better things—but now must take what we can get—and that is almost unique in its human character— Do not annoy yourself about it however, if either it should be gone—or you do not yourself like it. It is rather one of my *esteemed* than beloved—but most precious. Don't buy the mill [2]—on any account.

The shopkeeper's wife on radicals excellent.

I have no doubt that Turner has sufficiently provided for his unknown relations—or he would have left more money. I understand now his continual and curious hesitation in parting with a picture—he was always doubtful if he had money enough for his great purpose and yet wanting to keep as many pictures together as possible.

Dearest love to my mother.

Ever my dearest Father
Your most affec. Son. J Ruskin.

By the bye—if Saltash is gone—or if you do not like it—keep your eye on Allnutt's [3] *two uprights—St Gothard:* rock subject—in case they should come into market—they are very fine, but I don't care about his Bonneville.[4] Bicknells *Ivy Bridge* [5] is a noble picture: I merely name things as they occur to me—in case you should be struck by anything in the market. There is a large drawing of Grenoble somewhere at Hampstead [6]—not likely to be ever sold, I fancy—but full of the most noble mountains he ever did in his middle period.[7]

---

1. Turner did several studies of Saltash, Devon. Two are water colors, and two are oils. Yet another study is to be found in the *England and Wales* series; this last-mentioned drawing is unfavorably discussed in *The Harbours of England (Works, 13,* 48).

2. Possibly one of two Turner sketches entitled *Mill and Stream.*

3. Abel Allnutt of Clapham, a Turner collector.

4. For a short time in the possession of Ruskin, *Bonneville, Savoy,* is analyzed in *Works, 13,* 419.

5. *Ivy Bridge, Devonshire,* an oil painting described in Armstrong's *Turner,* p. 223.

6. Once in the possession of a Mrs. Holford, this Turner was said by Ruskin to be "exquisitely realised" (*Works, 13,* 266).

7. Ruskin's divisions of Turner's artistic life are numerous. There are, first, the periods already mentioned in Letter 100 n. 14. In the *Notes on the Turner Gallery at Marlborough House (Works, 13,* 91–181) Ruskin (p. 99) divides Turner's artistic life as follows: 1. 1800–20; 2. 1820–35; 3. 1835–45; 4. 1845–51. Another classification appears in the *Catalogue of ·the Sketches and Drawings by J. M. W. Turner, R.A., Exhibited at Marlborough House, 1857–58 (Works, 13,* 250 ff.). Yet another category appears in *Works, 13,* 407 ff. But as these came later in Ruskin's studies of Turner it would seem more likely that he is here referring to the classification given in *Pre-Raphaelitism.*

LETTER 107

7th January [1852]

My dearest Father,

I hope I have not been annoying you very much by my ramblings about *so many* pictures of Turner: but I wished you to be able to act with decision in case of any one that you liked coming in the way—and indeed you will not wonder at me when you consider how I have always been losing by too much prudence. When you offered me the beautiful little oil Venice in the Academy you know I would not have it—because I wanted to make Turner work. Then he remained two years without working—and did me at last the three bad pictures [1]— Then when Griffith had the beautiful Lake Lucerne, now Munro's—at 80 guineas —still I would not have it because I wanted to make Turner do more— which he never did— Only eight months ago, Griffith had a series of river scenery drawing which we might have had for 50 each—but I would not touch them that I might have something to spend in Turner sketches— Now I have lost all these opportunities—and find prices likely to double on me—so it is no wonder that I write you word of anything that comes into my head. But do not be annoyed at this for as I told you —I am now content with my collection—the only things I had set my heart upon were the small sketches—and I have been now for these five years so accustomed to disappointment that it does not much affect me. Don't give a long price for Saltash. I thought it might be got perhaps for 250, and meant to have written so in my yesterday's letter—don't go beyond 300 for it. I am very thankful you got those Liber Studiorum from Lupton; they are precious beyond all expression. I am glad Watson [2] liked the ropes of the flag: [3] I don't understand why you feel that drawing so little—for you used to draw a great deal in Indian ink yourself— and you know how difficult it is to lay it on—and to see the unerring rightness of every touch in that most difficult work of drawing folds of drapery with a pattern undulating over them would I should have thought have given you pleasure in that drawing even without the colour. To me, it is now one of the inestimables. I have got my mind settled

1. Turner did little work, after his health collapsed in 1845, until 1847. The "three bad pictures" may be *Undine, The Angel Standing in the Sun,* and *The Hero of a Hundred Fights,* which are adversely criticized in *Works, 13,* 167, by Ruskin.

2. Possibly Henry Watson, a clerk in the service of John James Ruskin. Watson and his family, whose tastes were above those ordinarily ascribed to men of his profession, were on visiting terms with the Ruskins. A brief account of Watson and his relatives is given in *Praeterita (Works, 35,* 171 ff.).

3. Most probably a reference to a Turner drawing done for the wrapper of his intended serial publication in association with Lupton entitled *The Ports of England.* The flag is reproduced in *Works, 13,* 6. An account of the aforementioned work and Ruskin's connection with it is given in *Works, 13,* 5.

again; peacefully, and am getting on very nicely with my work. It is coming together.

Dearest love to my mother.

> Ever my dearest Father. Your most aff^e. Son
> J Ruskin.

I am afraid the scattered notices of pictures in my letters may confuse you. I will send you a complete list of all I know—and their relative values in order.[4]

LETTER 108

8th Jany [1852]

My dearest Father,

I am ashamed to say I cannot answer your question about the Music in Shakespeare. I thought it was in *Romeo and Juliet*—but find on looking at the passage that it is different—and I am quite confused as to the other. So you see your questions to me get much less satisfaction than mine to you. I am getting on again with my work very nicely and hope to send you some nice bits as soon as you have got through Murano —but you may as well know the *worst* of the book at once. I shall send another sheet tomorrow. The weather is a little milder and the sense of lengthening days very delightful. It was most fortunate that I was enabled to return to Venice this winter, for I am shocked at finding the number of rents and gaps there were in my former work from over hurry: now it will all be nicely filled in.

I don't think the Ducal palace will stand 5 years more [1]—its capitals are so rent and worn. I am having some of its sculpture cast—there is a poor sculptor here whom it is a charity to employ—and for a few shillings I can get the most accurate facsimiles of pieces of sculpture which will soon be lost forever—and then freight home will be very little. They talk of taking down Tintoret's Paradise and "retouching [2] it." The world is such a heap of idiots that if it were not for the Turner gallery—I believe I should go and live in a cave in a cliff—among crows: Dearest love to my mother.

> Ever my dearest Father
> Your most affec^e. Son
> J Ruskin.

I intended not to have sent the enclosed, which is unreadable, but as it is only half a sheet—and completes connection it may as well come.

---

4. See Letter 123.

1. For an informative note on Ruskin's concern for the Ducal Palace see *Works, 10*, App. 15.

2. Ruskin's attitude toward the retouching of old masters is seen in *The Stones of Venice II* (*Works, 10*, 435-7).

LETTER 109

9th January [1852]

My dearest Father,

I had yesterday your very interesting letter with enclosures—(Mrs Buckland [1]—&c.) of the 3rd: The "talking over" your character between Mrs Buckland and me is to some extent a facon de parler—it having been—as far as I recollect confined on *her* part, to the simple—but energetic statement that she was "in love with you"—and on mine to the consolatory assurance that you were "worthy of her love." We did not dissect you—took you as you are, and said it was not easy to find such another. If we went beyond this, it was in some explanation on my part of your obstinacy in not dining out—saying that you would offend friends of forty years' standing if you did such a thing now—and I think also some pictorial comments on your forehead. You say you [are] sick of the folly of mankind—I have been so a long time—but the great mystery to me is that so much is *mere* folly—that so much grievous harm is done in mere ignorance and stupidity—evermore to be regretted as much as [the] consequences of actual crime. You say Turner kept his treasures to rot—not knowing or understanding the good it would be to give me some [2]— Yes—but in the same way, I myself through sheer ignorance of the mighty power of those Swiss drawings—suffered the opportunity of his chief energy to pass by—and only got the two—St Gothard and Goldau. Had I had the least idea at the time of the real power of those sketches—I should have gone down on my knees to you night after night—till I had prevailed on you to let me have all that Turner would do. But I *knew it not*—I thought them beautiful—but sketchy and imperfect compared with his former works. This was not *my fault*. It was the necessary condition of my mind in its progress to perfect judgment, and yet it had this irrevocably fatal effect—leaving in my heart through my whole life the feeling of irremediable loss—such as would—if I were not to turn my thoughts away from it—become "in my memory a *rooted* sorrow." [3] I am thankful indeed for what I have got, but it is the kind of thankfulness of a man who has saved the fourth or fifth of his dearest treasures from a great shipwreck—it needs some philosophy not to think of what he has lost. And this you see is a consequence of innocent ignorance—one does not see the use of it—one does not see what good this gnawing feeling of regret is intended to do

1. The wife of William Buckland (1784-1856), geologist and ecclesiastic. An account of the Buckland family, whom Ruskin knew well as a Christ Church undergraduate, is given in *Praeterita* (*Works, 35,* 204-5).

2. Ruskin senior was, to say the least, irritated at the manner in which he considered his son had been slighted by Turner's will.

3. Cf. *Macbeth* v.iii.41.

—or why one was not allowed to see what was right in time. The more I watch the world—the more I feel that all men are blind and wandering —I am more indulgent to their sins—but more hopeless—I feel that braying in a mortar with a pestle [4] will not make the foolishness depart out of the world. I have been rather low these two days—for I have heard there is a project to take down the Paradise of Tintoret—and "re-touch" it and put it up—well varnished. I went up to look at it: and though miserably injured it is *now* as *pure* as if he had left it yesterday —and all California and Botany bay together could not express its value, if men did but know what God had given them—and what he leaves it to their own hands to Take away. Dearest love to my mother.

Ever my dearest Father. Your most aff^e. Son

J Ruskin.

(I wish I could have sent you this drawing home—it is almost the most beautiful I have).

LETTER 110

10th Jan. [1852]

My dearest Father,

I forgot—my head being full of Turner and Tintoret yesterday to thank you for your kindness both to Hunt [1] and me in buying the Ring-dove [2]—no subject could possibly be better fitted to show his powers— I would—if I had given him a commission—which he says I oughtn't [3]— have commissioned him just for that. You must come some day to visit Mr Fawkes [4] with me and see Turner's Ringdove,[5] a rainbow made of down, but I doubt not Hunt's will be *very nearly* equal to it. I am sorry to hear he is aging. Hunt, Lewis—and Prout are the only men now living whose work I care a straw for.

That is a fine price, truly, for the little Vignette of the dead-house.[6] I know the drawing: there is about ten minutes work of Turner in it, but

4. Proverbs xxvii.22.

1. William Henry Hunt (1790–1864), who was elected a full member of the Water-Colour Society in 1826. His artistic career was both prolific and financially profitable. Ruskin's criticism of him is in the *Notes on Prout and Hunt* (*Works, 14*, 365–448).

2. A study by Hunt mentioned briefly by Ruskin in *Works, 13*, 443–4.

3. Ruskin senior had written his son: "I got a piece of advice from Hunt,—never to commission a picture." (*Works, 14*, 444 n. 1.)

4. Francis Hawksworth Fawkes, owner of Farnley Hall, Yorkshire, whose father was one of Turner's close friends as well as a collector of his paintings. Ruskin, who visited Farnley Hall with his wife in April 1851, dedicated *Pre-Raphaelitism* to Fawkes.

5. *Ringdove at Farnley*, favorably mentioned by Ruskin in *Works, 13*, 274, 370.

6. *The Dead-house of St. Bernard*, one of many vignettes executed by Turner for Samuel Rogers' *Italy*.

I suppose the dogs by Landseer [7] and figures by Stothard [8] are thought to enhance the value. To a collector I suppose they would, and I daresay he will get the money for it.

What you tell me of Hunt's and the Dutch flowers [9] is very interesting— I never thought, before—why his flowers were always so roughly painted— Sometimes there is a freshness in his roses, and a dewy scent, very valuable—but the Ringdove will be worth a million of them.

I wish I could send you the plates illustrative of the enclosed, but this scrawl may give you some idea of the central series with its black

centre—first spoken of in p. 17. here, in the last sheet I sent, and tomorrow I will send a scrawl of the *upper* series spoken of in p. 17— *This* one is the *6ᵗʰ Centre* of p. 18.

Dearest love to my mother.

Ever my dearest Father
Your most affᵉ. Son
J Ruskin

P.S. If the scrawl had got wet it would have been quite spoiled—so I enclose this today, and the p. 17. 18. will come tomorrow.

LETTER III

10ᵗʰ Saturday Evening [January 1852]

My dearest Father,

Before putting away your late letters I see there are several things

7. Sir Edwin Henry Landseer (1802–73), best known for his animal paintings. Son of an engraver, Landseer was elected A.R.A. in 1826 and R.A. in 1831. He worked with Turner on *The Dead-house of St. Bernard;* their collaboration is discussed by Ruskin in *Works, 13,* 514, and is also mentioned briefly in M. F. Sweetser's *Landseer* (Boston, 1879), p. 51.

8. Thomas Stothard (1755–1834), engraver and painter. He made many illustrations for books but after 1791 worked chiefly in oil. He was elected A.R.A. in 1791 and R.A. in 1794. For his connection with the *Dead-house* see *Works, 13,* 376 n.

9. In *Notes on Prout and Hunt* (*Works, 14,* 380) there is an echo of this sentiment in Ruskin's comparison between the methods of flower-painting employed by the Dutch and by Hunt: "The Dutchman never got a wet flower to paint from. He had his . . . poppy or tulip brought in from the market . . . and put on its dew-drops for it as a lady's dressing-maid puts on her diamonds, merely for state. But Hunt saw the flowers in his little garden really bright in the baptismal dawn, or drenched with the rain of noontide, and knew that no mortal could paint any real likeness of that heaven-shed light;—and never once attempted it: you will find nothing in any of his pictures merely put on that you may try to wipe it off."

I have not noticed—the fortunate getting of sketch by C^t D'Orsay [1] who must be a clever fellow—with this and my most valuable young one in the study, we shall do capitally. I shall look out for the Izio, and all that is to come by her with many thanks. I shall be very cautious according to Rutter's [2] advice—and sign nothing as executor.[3] I shall be anxious to hear more of what was found in the gallery—I wish I had been at home, but it would have been absurd to have taken the long miserable journey and interrupted all my work, besides they would not have waited for me. I am sorry to hear we are to have no more Harrison slips—but I was a little afraid that would not last, it was too trifling—yet very amusing— Perhaps they will find they have made a mistake and come back to Mr Harrison again.

You speak of a little Plymouth at Wallis's— All those drawings are good—but Plymouth is an uninteresting subject. You speak of a Sun in middle of picture which you cannot regard as a Turner. It is not—I should think, very likely to be one.

Sunday. I scrawled in the enclosed scrap by candlelight, last night— it ought to have had its grey triangles a little darker and greener. It is the *upper* series referred to in the sheet sent yesterday, I think, and today, in the lettered list of the kinds of triangles—I have put the *letters* in the drawing to their respective triangles.

Effie has written you a nice long model letter, so I hope you will have a nice packet altogether, today. She seems to be getting a worse opinion of the Austrians than of the french—as far as religion goes— The worst of them is that they all think they do perfectly right. But I was considerably surprised the other day to find that one of them actually did not know what the Bible was.

I have been reading *Paradise Regained* lately. It seems to me an exact parallel to Turner's latest pictures—the mind failing altogether—but with irregular intervals and returns of power—exquisite momentary passages and lines,

> To warm him wet returned from field at eve . . .[4]

> He added not—and Satan—*bowing low*
> *His gray dissimulation,* disappeared.[5]

By the bye—when merchants speak of "indorsing" a thing—have they any idea how finely the word has been used, .

1. Gédeon Gaspard Alfred de Grimaud, Count d'Orsay (1801–52), celebrated dandy. For an account of this man as artist see *D'Orsay, or The Complete Dandy*, by W. Teignmouth Shore (London, J. Long Ltd., 1911).
2. Either J. C. Rutter, senior partner in the law firm of that name, or his son, Henry Rutter, who was Ruskin's solicitor. J. C. Rutter was executor to John James Ruskin.
3. Of Turner's estate.
4. *Paradise Regained, 1,* 318.
5. *Ibid., 1,* 497–8.

> The field, all iron, cast a gleaming brown,
> Nor wanted clouds of foot—now on each horn
> Chariots—or elephants *indorsed* with Towers . . .[6]

I must quote his description of the temple in my chapter on St Marks.

> And higher yet the glorious temple reared
> Her pile, far off appearing, like a mount
> Of Alabaster, topt with golden spires.[7]

Exactly what St Mark's is—It was all gilded at top [8]—in old time.
Dearest love to my mother.

Ever my dearest Father
Your most aff^e. Son
J Ruskin.

Letter 112

Monday. 12th [January 1852]

My dearest Father,

I had yesterday your interesting letter of the 5th about houses, &c. It is quite true that those lonely Norwood [1] houses are not very desirable —I have seen in Galignani lately, two stories of robberies and assaults at Norwood—and one it was said—between Denmark Hill and Camberwell. But neither would Tunbridge do—Railroad is at once costly— fatiguing—and dangerous. I could not run up whenever I wanted to see a touch in a picture. What sort of houses are there of Mr Sharp's row,[2] looking out on triangular field—I always liked that place. As for visits from London I shall soon put an end to them : I don't care whom I displease—I shall see the Richmonds, or Eastlake—or John Lewis—if they choose to come so far, whenever they like. No one else.

I am sorry that you are going travelling—both for your sake—and mama's and mine, as my letter about the Fair will come just when you

---

6. *Ibid., 3,* 326–7, 329.

7. *Ibid., 4,* 546–8.

8. In *The Stones of Venice II* (*Works, 10,* 112) Ruskin likens St. Mark's to a *Book of Common Prayer,* speaking of it as "a vast illuminated missal, bound with alabaster instead of parchment, studded with porphyry pillars instead of jewels, and written within and without in letters of enamel and gold." And, again, Milton is echoed in *Deucalion* (*Works, 26,* 192) where Ruskin remarks that St. Mark's was "once itself a sea-borne vase of alabaster full of incense of prayers ; and a purple manuscript,—floor, walls, and roof blazoned with the scrolls of the gospel."

1. Norwood was one of the districts considered by the elder Ruskins when they were thinking of moving. It is on the Surrey side of the Thames and more agreeable then than now.

2. Samuel Sharpe (1799–1881), Egyptologist and nephew of the poet, Samuel Rogers. Sharpe was living, at this time, in Highbury Place in north London. That district was, of course, more rural in Ruskin's day than at present.

are at Liverpool. I don't understand either about contradictory reports of Turner's will—I thought the will had been thoroughly read—and all its main points stated to you unmistakeably? As for his £19-19-6: I will be indebted to him for no such matter: I will wear some sign of mourning for him, though.[3]

I wonder if it be true that he ever said I knew more about his pictures than he did. I hardly think so—but there seem some genuine anecdotes in the papers you have sent.

I am sorry to hear about Harrison's uncomfortablenesses at Bridge St. It would be more serious, his losing that, than his Aberdeen affair.

Dearest love to my mother.

> Ever my dearest Father
> Your most aff^e. Son
> J Ruskin.

LETTER 113

13th Jan. [1852]

My dearest Father,

Making such scrawls as the enclosed,[1] with 10 minutes' work in each— would have been no great sacrifice of time—seeing that they must I should think make all the difference between you reading my late sheets with pleasure, or with none, or not being able to read them at all— But as it happens—it is very lucky I have made them, for this last I have drawn with fresh colours while my study was made on the spot from the time stained ruin of 600 years—and I had no idea till I put them down, how pretty the fresh colours would look. So in my book I shall give it restored—instead of in its present state.

I don't know if you happen ever to have met with the following note [2] to Shakespeare in Steevens. If not—it will give you such a laugh as is not to be had everyday.

> There's a divinity that shapes our ends,
> Rough hew them how we will.

"Dr Farmer informs me that these words are merely technical. A butcher and dealer in skewers lately observed to him that his nephew— an idle lad, could only *assist* him in making them—*he* could *rough hew* them—but *I* was obliged to *shape their ends*. Whoever recollects the profession of Shakespeare's father will admit that his son might be no

3. As one of Turner's executors, Ruskin was left nineteen guineas for a mourning ring. As this was the only legacy left him, it is not surprising that John James Ruskin wrote his son that "Nobody can say you were paid to praise."

1. The enclosure mentioned has been separated from the original letter. This is also the case concerning the enclosures referred to in Letters 116 and 129.

2. See Steevens' edition of *Shakespeare*, 15 vols. (London, 1793), *15*, 324.

stranger to such terms. I have frequently seen packages of wool pinned up with Skewers."

Dearest love to my mother.

Ever my dearest Father
Your most aff^e. Son
J Ruskin

LETTER 114

14th January [1852]

My dearest Father,

There is so much in your kind letter of the 6th-7th that I cannot answer it all today. The main point which you tell me to answer directly is about Mr Boucher's house. I should like such a house as that you describe very much, and the situation would be excellent—but the [£]1000 for furnishing is a very serious consideration. I shall of course have to furnish any house that I settle in permanently, but if I settled in York-shire or Switzerland I should have no need of expensive London furni-ture, and the savings would be enormous— Furnishing a house for two years' residence is serious work— On the other hand there might be some good in getting at once a few of the things that I am likely to need during my life—if I live—I might always be accustomed to my furniture if not to my house. I don't want the two acres of land—but this might be useful in case of your going into the house if you left Denmark Hill —this is a great consideration— I must leave you to do as you think best—you will of course see that there is a comfortable room for me to escape into if people come whom I don't want—and Effie does—it would not do always to have to cross over to my study on the other side of the road. And see that the chimnies [*sic*] don't smoke—I would make no bargain for a house without trying its chimnies in all the four winds. I should like the position very much.

Touching my writing—I hope the difference you feel depends chiefly on your getting the sheets as I write them—before they get any retouch-ing or cutting out. When I get into a thorough writing humour I can do a good deal nearly in correct hand, but when I write only for two hours each morning—and that partly with the desire only to *secure* facts rather than to set them in the best light—the result needs a great deal of squeez-ing and lopping before it comes right. I have no doubt as I go over the sheets you are now receiving, that at least one third of their bulk will be evaporated—and the remaining two thirds rearranged and enriched, but I cannot do this till the whole matter of the book is either before me, or in my head. Much of the *Seven Lamps* was written three times over —some of it five times. Besides this—which is enough to account for considerable inferiority—the very contents of this book are by no means the same—they are in great part mere accounts of buildings in the most complete terms I can use—seeing that they are soon likely to be destroyed, and the facts that columns are so high—and so far apart—and that a triangle is not a square—cannot be made very piquant—though some time hence, people will thank me more for them than for all the fine writing in the world. You may say that other people than *I* could do this—Yes, but other people *won't* with the requisite care— Even *I* find myself now more accurate than I was two years ago and yet not so accurate as I want to be. It will also make a further difference when you see all in clean print—and with the diagrams: There may also be some definite inferiority in what I write at present—for I am in a sort resting, and never work hard at anything—and perhaps writing like other things —though not to be done by *laborious* effort—is still only to be done by getting well into the heat of it.

It is very vexatious about Turner's will—but I hope I shall have the sketches after all— As you had this account a week ago—you will not have acted hastily on my request to make an offer for the Saltash: I shall be very glad if you have got the *Fair;* [1] but for anything else we had better wait. If you see good—I wish you would ask for a copy of the will, in my name. Cannot this be had? Or is it unsafe? And please tell me in whose care are all the pictures at present?

Dearest love to my mother.

> Ever my dearest Father
> Your most aff^e. Son
> J Ruskin.

Scotsman very nice, I will keep it carefully.

LETTER 115

15 January [1852]

My dearest Father,

I have not a sheet for you today, mislaid George's writing yesterday. I hope to have one tomorrow— I was thrown into astonishment and confusion by hearing of Newton's appointment—Consul of Mitylene. I don't know what to think—good or bad for him—Excellent for Brit museum and England—delightful for me to have him here in Venice for a little while—but very sad to have him playing Robinson Crusoe in the Egean sea. On the whole, I think he ought not to have gone without a better appointment. He can't do much with £250 a year—and there is always risk of fever and such things— But I am so pleased at the idea

1. This may possibly be *Louth, The Horse Fair,* although in *Works, 13,* 602, it is asserted that this picture did not come into Ruskin's possession until 1877. But see also Letter 128.

of having him in Venice to tell me the things I can't find out: and be astonished as he will be by the first sight of Byzantine architecture— that I can hardly feel angry with him yet. How would mama and you do—if you were *his* father and mother instead of mine, having seen him for about a fortnight once a year, since he was at college—and now having to let him go to the Troad? However—if other such men would take the same fancy—and we had an intelligent consul in every Greek city —what treasures would yet be saved, and how soon a *Kind* of Christian and civilizing influence might be extended over the Mahometan coun- tries.

I am rather puzzled about coming home before Switzerland—I don't think Effie will stay in Scotland this time—she did not find it so pleasant before [1]—and besides people made so many impertinent remarks to her, and talked so much scandal that I don't much wonder at her not choosing to do it a second time. And the *travelling* with Effie is just what I wanted to save you by your meeting us, for she is slow and must stop to lunches and cannot rise early—and in fact—would not fit with our ways of doing the thing. But we will think over this. I want to get at the clear facts about Turner's will first—and then we can plan. Dearest love to my mother.

Ever my dearest Father Your most aff^e. Son
J Ruskin.

Letter 116

16th January [1852]

My dearest Father,

I did the enclosed scrawl too fast and made the middle arch too narrow —still, it may serve to show you what I am talking about. It is the upper story of the extremity of one of the aisles.

I think I may manage to get home by 10th May if the mountains are open. I have a plan in my head, which I will disclose in full when I have time to sit down to a nice long letter but I overslept myself this morning, and must be short. Dearest love to my mother.

Ever my dearest Father
Your most affec^e. Son
J Ruskin.

We have lost pages of Murano. This follows the last you got—we begin 1. 2. again.

---

1. One year after his marriage Ruskin toured the Continent, from April until September 1849, with his parents while his wife remained in Scotland with her family.

LETTER 117

16ᵗʰ January [1852]

My dearest Father,

I had yesterday your kind note with account of Ann's [1] mission to poor old housekeeper [2] at Qu. Anne St, of which I am glad to hear—and of her readiness to let me in whenever I like—and of Turner's wise and just bequest to her. She has more sense—respecting the gallery, than he had himself. I am doubtful about it now, too seeing that only the finished pictures are to compose it—the rags left on his walls by way of pictures are now hardly worth the nation's having.

There was with this pleasant news the somewhat disagreeable account from Colnaghi's—mortifying in other ways as well as disappointing in a money point of view. When I have done these two books,[3] D.V. I shall give up being an author altogether. Dr Croly is quite right, it is a vexatious life: the pleasures of it not worth the labour—and the pains all into the bargain. I shall live in study of nature—go back to my old geology and mineralogy, and leave the world to darkness—*not* to *me*. I am really very sorry—and getting somewhat uncomfortable—one may be very sorry without being fidgetty—but I am getting fidgetty too—at the continual drain I am making upon your purse—giving you no return. Tomorrow I must draw the last 50 of the three hundred credit you sent me two months ago—making £800 spent on this journey already—or at least—before the end of February; you know I had to pay my other three months in advance—so the lodgings are paid till 9ᵗʰ March: but I am taken quite by surprise at the sums which go in candles and fuel and house expences. I have spent also about £25 in casts—of which I am packing up today 21 pieces of Ducal palace capitals &c., which are both invaluable in themselves—if I can get them sent safe home—and have saved me for the present some laborious drawing: as I can work out what refinements I want better from these than from the original pieces which are so high as to be out of convenient sight.

However—I can this time show you *how* the money has gone to the last fraction. I have given a great deal in charity [4]— There is not, I

1. Ruskin's Scotch nurse, Ann Ker, a loyal servant of the family. She is pictured in *Praeterita* (*Works, 35*, 30–2). She died in 1871, having been in the service of the Ruskins all her life.

2. Hannah Danby, housekeeper to Turner. In a codicil to his will the painter left her £150 a year—possibly for services over and above those generally demanded of a housekeeper. Disfigured by disease, slatternly, and grasping, Hannah Danby did not, ultimately, receive her legacy. Neither was she employed, as directed in the painter's will, as custodian in the projected Queen Anne Street gallery.

3. *The Stones of Venice II* and *III*.

4. Both Ruskin and his wife were very active in charitable affairs and gave generously to the poor in time and money. Ruskin senior dispensed his son's charities in

think—one man of the lower classes whom I ever have known in Venice who does not come begging: and with as much justness of claim as habitual improvidence can give to anyone. They spend all they earn in the summer—and beg or half starve all the winter.

I assure you I will mind better what I am about in future—but I thought "living in lodgings" in Venice would be so delightfully cheap that I need not mind paying a good rent for the rooms— It turns out much the same as Park St. I am especially puzzled because it seems to cost nearly as much as when we had Miss Ker [5] with us and two carriages and lived at an hotel.

I shall certainly keep all my illustrations small size— I think the better way with the large ones would be to withdraw them [6] at once from the market and bear the present loss, and keep them in a heap—like Mr Turner—till people would be thankful for them.

Dearest love to mother.

Ever my dearest Father
Your most affec^e. Son.
J Ruskin.

LETTER 118

Venice. 18th January [1852]

My dearest Father,

I must really have sickened you with these details at Murano—I will after this sheet, miss one or two—and give you the conclusion of Murano —and then some more interesting reading.

The only plan I can devise for making our spring journey comfortable is to do as I should have been obliged to have done had I been called home just now—leave Effie here—run home as fast as I can, settle such affairs as can be settled—see Turner gallery—Royal Academy—Watercolour —and start with you again immediately.

You would come with me as far as the lago Maggiore, where you have always wanted to stay for a day or two— I will leave you at Arona—and fetch Effie from Venice in five days—unless you found it cool enough, and were disposed to take a look at the Ducal Palace again yourself. I see no other means of managing the thing than this: if I come home before the Swiss journey: For if I bring Effie home—I cannot calculate on

---

England during his absence; the older man, too, was constantly assisting poor and deserving artists on behalf of his son.

5. Who, with Mary Richardson (one of Ruskin's cousins) and the elder Ruskins, formed the party that constantly toured the British Isles and the Continent during Ruskin's youth.

6. Ruskin is thinking of *The Examples of the Architecture of Venice;* they were not withdrawn and later proved to be a most profitable investment to those who bought them.

much less than three weeks for the journey—especially in cold weather
on the Alps—to be home by 10th May I should have to start in middle
of April, losing what little fine weather I hope for in the Spring to neutralize my cold and frosty impressions of Venice—then Effie would be
seized upon by people in London, knocked up altogether, and keep us
perhaps at some place on the road back—we might not get into Switzerland till near July: As it is—she has her maid here—and the Venetians
will see nothing in the least surprising in my being called away for six
weeks: I shall simply say what is true that I have important business in
London, and that Effie could not bear the journey—there are plenty of
wives here without their husbands—some of the nicest people in Venice.
I am not able now to work as I once could—if I overdo it in the least—I
pass a sleepless night—and three days at present are not worth—for
effective result—more than one was when I was seven and twenty: so
that this six months in Venice has been little enough for what I desired
to do: Take all the time that I have had here—about 12 months in all—
in which I have had to examine piece by piece—buildings covering five
square miles of ground—to read—or glance at—some forty volumes of
history and chronicles—to make elaborate drawings—as many as most
artists would have made in the time—and to compose my own book—
what of it is done—(for I do not count the first volume anything) and
you will not I think wonder that I grudge the losing of a single day— It
is not now as once, when I could say "I will work fiercely for three months
and then rest." If I were to work fiercely for two days, I should break
down. I am recovering strength as it is—but only by letting each day
have its own measure of *un*hurried labour—and equivalent rest. I did
not think of leaving Venice to meet you in Switzerland till 15th or 20th
May—to get home by the 10th I must start 26th April—but to leave with
Effie, and do all *packing up* necessitated by quitting the whole establishment, would nearly involve the loss of the whole of April—and a very
serious injury to my work. Coming by myself—I shall bring the drawings, to set engravers at work upon, under my arm—a few papers and
memoranda in my trunk—my MS I shall leave in Effie's care, locked
up here— She will manage to pack and settle everything and be ready
to come with me early in June. She is satisfied with this plan herself.
Dearest love to my mother.

> Ever my dearest Father,
> Your most affec^e. Son
> J Ruskin.

I see I must send another half sheet after this to finish passage.

LETTER 119

18th January [1852]

My dearest Father,

I was reading over some passages of the *Seven Lamps* this evening, and I certainly do not wonder at your finding considerable inferiority in the text I am now sending you. I took great pains with most of the *Seven Lamps,* and I recollect—as I read the passages, the labour they cost me —some of them being as highly finished as it is I believe—possible for me to finish prose. I remember for instance that the last half page of the Lamp of Beauty cost me a whole forenoon—from 10 to two—and that then I went out to walk, quite tired, and yet not satisfied with the last sentence—and turned and returned it all the way to Dulwich: *Now*—as I told you, I do not like to tire myself—and I still less like to give the time— If half a page takes me an hour, I get angry—and say to myself —this will never do—I shall never be done; and run it off any way it will come—and if I go out to walk—I see something the first step I take, which brings a new subject into my head—and it is all over with the difficult sentence. The feeling of Time running away from me operates very unfortunately on writing—for I am firmly persuaded that neither writing nor drawing can be well done against time. There is also something burdensome in the vast breadth of the subject at present— It is all weighing on my brains at once, and I cannot devote my full mind to any part of it. As soon as I have it all down on paper—out of *danger* as it were—and well in sight, I can take up any part and finish it as highly as I like, but as soon as I begin to dwell on any bit carefully, thoughts come into my head about other parts—unfinished—which I am afraid of losing and then I go away and touch upon them. I don't think my powers are diminished—the only passages in the whole of the *Stones of Venice* [*I*] which I finished as highly as I could are the opening page— the little bits about the Matterhorn in the 5th chapter—and the 17th paragraph of the 21st. and I think they will bear comparison with anything in the *Seven Lamps,* though they do not treat of such high matters. There may however be a little want of spirit in me at present owing partly to the watching my health and partly to the various little mortifications and anxieties which while they do not disturb me in any straightforward work of inquiry or examination, may perhaps without my knowing it, deaden the tone, and render lax the spring, of a written sentence —just as they might a little deaden the eye—or lower the voice. But I trust when you see the whole book together, with such retouching as I may be able to give it at home, that you will not think my twelve months in Venice have been misspent; I should say that I have great confidence in producing an impression with it—but my confidence has been now too often disappointed— I thought all the *Seven Lamps* would have sold within a year after the book was published [1]—and though I did not suppose myself to have as many friends as the hare [2]—I thought there were more than fifteen people in London who would have given a guinea for five drawings with which I had taken all the pains I could. So I will be confident no more, but finish what has cost me thus much labour as well as I can—and then trouble myself as little as I can about it. Dearest love to my mother.

Ever my dearest Father
Your most aff[e]. Son
J Ruskin.

LETTER 120

19th January. [1852]

My dearest Father,

I got yesterday a letter from McCracken of Belfast [1]—saying that he hoped in a week to have Hunt's Proteus and Valentine [2]—for which he has given 100 guineas and a picture of *young Danby's*.[3] I pity poor Hunt [4] for the bargain, but there was enclosed in the letter a very interesting critique on Hunt's picture from a Liverpool paper—and an extract of a letter from himself, all excellent: One thing struck me as curious. Before I left London, McCracken told me he had long ago ordered my folio illustrations [5] from his bookseller—and asked when they were to be out. I told him the first number had been three months out— He writes me now—dating, 9th January—that he has *just got* the first number. Is this Irish business—or whose fault is it? I am sorry I cannot send you the

---

1. *The Seven Lamps of Architecture* first appeared in 1849; the second edition did not come out until 1855. And from that date until 1880 there was no further edition of this book.

2. See John Gay's *Fables: First Series*, No. 50.

1. Francis McCracken, shipping agent and picture collector. He is the subject of an amusing and informative sonnet by William Allingham reproduced in George Birkbeck Hill's edition of *Letters of Dante Gabriel Rossetti to William Allingham, 1854-70* (New York, 1897), p. 31.

2. A painting by William Holman Hunt (1827-1910), one of the leaders of the Pre-Raphaelite Brotherhood whose cause Ruskin was espousing at this time. *Proteus and Valentine* was more commonly known as *Valentine and Sylvia*. This painting was adversely criticized by the London papers and subsequently awarded a £50 prize by the Liverpool Academy, whereupon McCracken purchased it. A reproduction of the work is to be found in Sir George Williamson's *Holman Hunt* (London, 1902), p. 24. Its full title is *Valentine Rescuing Sylvia from Proteus*.

3. Either James Danby (1816-75), marine painter, or his brother Thomas Danby (1817?-86), landscape painter.

4. In his own words, Hunt was so poor at this time that, upon writing a letter, he did not know "where to find a penny for the stamp."

5. *Examples of the Architecture of Venice.*

plate to which enclosed sheet refers—but I am now so near the end of Murano that I thought it no use to break the text for a leaf or two.

I have had a letter to write to Sir C. Eastlake about colour, nothing interesting in it—or I would have enclosed it to you—so I must be short— Dearest love to my mother.

Ever my dearest Father
Your most aff^e. Son
J Ruskin.

LETTER 121

19th January [1852]

My dearest Father,

I wish when you get back to town, any time you are passing Winsor and Newton's in Rathbone place, you would be so kind as to ask them what they have been doing with their Chinese white. I used to be able to do *every*thing with it—now I can do *nothing*— Every touch I put of it I have had in a drawing I am just now making, to put twice over—and that not always enough. It is good for nothing. I find these sheets read watery myself—as I look them over. They will need a great deal of evaporation—but I assure you they are not bad sherry.

I have not had a letter now for some days. It has just struck me that you may perhaps think I do not care for your letters because I do not always express the pleasure I have in receiving them: I do not do this generally, partly because I suppose it understood as a matter of course, partly for fear of pressing you, when you have many other things to do. But I assure you I look for your letter as the best thing the days bring me. I must be short tonight—for I have been doing rather a tiresome piece of drawing and my eyes are tired.

Dearest love to my mother.

Ever my dearest Father
Your most aff^e. Son
J Ruskin.

LETTER 122

Venice 23 Jany 1852

My dearest Father,

We are really coming to the end of Murano at last, and then you shall have something more interesting. There is a passage missed in the enclosed page, about the pavement, which I have not yet done. You will see the importance of the conclusion which I get at by the balustrade, worth considerable pains.

All my chapters won't be so long as this. The three longest in the book will be St Marks, the Ducal Palace, and the general chapter on the tombs,[1] of which I shall send you some fragments as soon as Murano is done.

I hope my mother will not try to make out any of the sheets while you are away from home: but will put them all aside for you: I suppose they cost less sent in this fragmentary way than if I made a packet of them, or I would not send any while you were travelling.

Dearest love to my mother.

Ever my dearest Father
Your most aff^e. Son
J Ruskin.

LETTER 123

23rd January. [1852]

My dearest Father,

I had today your most kind and interesting letter from Liverpool of the 15th—with account of your correspondent's son—who of all the people I have heard speak of my books, seems to me to understand them best when he says he reads them like "Euclid." I have always tried to get one step to follow from another in true geometrical series, and yet people in general call me a bad reasoner—begging their pardon, because my reasoning is a little too consistent for them to follow without some pains—and because if they lose a link—they cannot recover it.

What you say of your former motives for not buying Turners is very just—and indeed it is curious, the way in which I forget at one time the motives which actuated me at another, and only see the motives which *ought* to have actuated me. Were my life to come over again for these last 10 years—I would devote myself altogether to Turner—the man, I mean, recording every sentence that he spoke—and collecting every picture that came in my way. But I cannot recollect the kind of feelings I had, when I had not a single Turner—or thought Richmond perhaps the only one I should ever have.

I am however now likely to be perhaps more quiet than you suppose. I never liked travelling—my hope was at one time to *live* in Switzerland, but not to travel much—and now I am not so careful where I live: I do not think I shall ever be able to be a strong climber on the hills—and without that power, the sight of them would sometimes be less pleasure

---

1. A "general chapter on the tombs" never materialized. In *The Stones of Venice III* Ruskin, in the second chapter, gives an account of some Venetian tombs; but the whole subject was planned on a far more elaborate scale than the remarks there indicate. For further discussion of tombs see the appendix to *The Stones of Venice III* (*Works, 11*, 289–307).

than pain. I rather fancy I may have partly brought on the feebleness of circulation which now makes me nervous and unfit for work, by my long walks as well as my mental labour, and I do not intend to take any more hard climbs for several years—and when a man is 33, and likely to lie by for several years—it is very possible he may not care to scramble much more. This Spring—in Switzerland with mama and you—I shall walk *with you* only—or Effie—and be with you all day, going on a little with my book—and looking on the Alps as inaccessible.

And as for travelling in Italy—it is now really too painful— Everything is being destroyed—and I should become a misanthrope of the bitterest temper if I were to live or travel much here. Wherever *my home is,* I shall stay much more quietly than you might think. Indeed I never was a rambler in the common sense— My delight was always to *stay* in places that I loved; and I am sure that neither my mother or you ever recollect my wishing to leave *any* place when I was comfortably settled among hills.

Be this as it may, I should certainly hope now and then to be able to buy a Turner—for some years to come; if I do not succeed in getting them at the sale—for they are to me Nature and art in one—all that I best love in nature with all that I most revere in art: I am *content* with my collection *now,* as I said—but the exquisite pleasure that every new one gives me is like a year added to my life; and a permanent extension of the sphere of life.

However I can talk of this afterwards—it is too broad a subject for a letter : I will begin my catalogue raisonnée tonight and go on with it bit by bit.

I should divide all Turners into four classes.

1. Those which I would give *any* price for if I *had* it to give.
2. Those which I would give anything in reason for.
3. Those which I would give something for—if they went cheap.
4. Those which I would not buy at all at any price they are ever likely to go for.

Class 1st.   1. Monro's   Lake Lucerne, morning.[1]
             2. Monro's   Pass of Splugen.[2]
             3. Fawkes's   Vignettes from History of Cromwell—or
                            Commonwealth.[3]

1. Also known as *The Dark Rigi*, this picture is termed "exemplary" in *Works, 13,* 477.
2. A Turner drawing much coveted by Ruskin. How he came to acquire it is related in *Works, 13,* 487–8.
3. Ruskin never acquired any of these. The closest he came to getting anything Cromwellian by Turner was the acquisition of the frontispiece to *Fairfaxiana,* which is discussed in *Works, 13,* 600.

4. Fawkes's   4 studies of Birds:[4] Ringdove, Kingfisher, Heron, Peacock.

For these above, if at any time they come into the market I should think no price I could afford too dear.

Class 2nd. 1. Monro's   Lake of Zug.[5]
         2. Monro's   Lucerne, by moonlight—from the river.[6]
         3. Bicknell's   Lake Lucerne.[7]
         4th. Windus's   Lake Lucerne.[8]
         5. Monro's   Kussnacht.[9]
         6. Windus's   Arona, Lago Maggiore.[10]
         7. Fawkes's   Mont Cenis [11]—and Sallenche.[12]
         8. ———   Such sketches as may be found of mountain subjects—especially Swiss—among Turner's stores: The three of ours, St Gothard, Goldau, and Schwytz, should have gone into first class.
         9. Grenoble—mentioned in one of my late letters—at Hampstead.
        10. Weathercote Cove,[13] Yorkshire series.
        11. Ivy Bridge.[14]

I have named them as they came into my head rather than in order of value. The sketches should have been first, and then 1, 2, 3, 5–9.

Class III.

The drawings above named are those which I *want,* and which some time in my life—if I can, I hope to possess at all events a few of— I cannot hope that I can get them all, but they are my *mark,* highwater mark. Those which I next name are the ones which in case any of them

4. In a book of drawings of birds' feathers at Farnley Hall some dozen were in Turner's hand. For further information about this book see Edith Mary Fawkes's "Mr. Ruskin at Farnley," *Nineteenth Century Magazine,* April 1900, pp. 617–23.

5. An 1843 Turner which later came into Ruskin's possession; its history is given in *Works, 13,* 606.

6. Perhaps the Lucerne study of 1845 mentioned in *Works, 3,* 552.

7. A few words on this drawing are to be found in *Works, 13,* 483.

8. Ruskin gives a brief account of this drawing in *Works, 13,* 204. In the same volume, p. 369 n., it is compared with Turner's *Loch Fyne.*

9. Executed in 1843 for Munro of Novar, this drawing is mentioned in *Works, 13,* 202; a note on the same page gives a short history of the drawing.

10. For a time in Ruskin's possession, this drawing is analyzed in *Works, 13,* 456–7.

11. Plate XVII in *Works, 12,* 374. Selected by Ruskin as representative of Turner's "second period," this drawing is described in detail in *Works, 12,* 374–5.

12. Turner executed several studies of Sallenches.

13. One of the drawings done by Turner for Whitaker's *History of Richmondshire.*

14. Briefly described in *Works, 13,* 269. It is also favorably noted by Ruskin in *The Queen of the Air (Works, 19,* 411–12).

came in your way at a reasonable price—I should be sorry to let go—
but not vexed about—while I should certainly be grieved if any of the
1st or 2nd class escaped me. So do not be alarmed at the largeness of the
III class: I shall here put opposite to each the price which I should think
cheap for them.

1.	Any *Yorkshire* drawing.	80 to 100
2.	Llanberis,[15] (now Windus's).	120
3.	Lower Force of Tees,[16] (Monro's).	150
4.	Coventry,[17] Monro's.	120
5.	Carnarvon,[18] Monro's.	120
6.	Ulleswater,[19] Monro's.	120
7.	Fawkes's Coliseum, Rome.[20]	120
8.	Schaffhausen fall [21] (Windus's).	100

These are the best I know; but I shall better and more shortly describe this list by giving you the negatives—i.e. those which I never
should think of buying. For I don't mean you to add up all the above
list—and say—"It will be so much—does John think of spending all
that?" No; of the drawings named probably not one fourth will come
into my reach. Fawkes's are very unlikely *ever* to come into the market
—and especially the Cromwell vignettes. I merely name those of which
if any occurred—I should think it desirable to obtain them, in prefer-
ence to others—if I could afford it.

I should never buy these:

1. Any vignettes.
2. Eastern or Italian drawings—the Coliseum above named
   is a rare exception.
3. Any "southern coast" [22] drawings—a set highly valued by
   dealers.
4. Any Rhine drawings.

15. A drawing from the *England and Wales* series, a portion of which is analyzed
in *Works, 7,* 417 ff.
16. There was evidently some confusion in Ruskin's mind over the various drawings
of the Tees done by Turner, as a glance at *Works, 3,* 424, will indicate. It would seem
extremely probable that the *Lower Fall of the Tees* mentioned by Ruskin in *Works, 3,*
489, and, more fully, later in the same volume, pp. 554-6, is the drawing he is speaking
of in this letter.
17. Discussed in *Works, 3,* 405, this work is notable for its fine cloud formation and
is also mentioned in *Pre-Raphaelitism (Works, 12,* 376).
18. *Carnarvon Castle,* purchased for Ruskin at the Novar sale of 1877. One of the
England and Wales series, it is eloquently described in *Works, 13,* 442.
19. From the *England and Wales* series; it is praised in *Works, 3,* 489-90.
20. This drawing is eulogized in *Works, 22,* 37, for the effect of its masonry.
21. The *Falls of Schaffhausen* was for a time in Ruskin's collection; it is discussed
in *Works, 7,* 221-3.
22. Forty drawings executed by Turner between 1814 and 1826. References to them
in the *Works* are surprisingly scarce.

5. Oberwesel; [23] Heidelberg; [24] Virginia Water; [25] Hampton Court; [26] Blenheim; Windsor; Bedford; Stoneyhurst; Yarmouth—Bamborough: Fowey Harbour, (Windus's), Malvern Abbey, Holy Island [27]—Folkestone.[28]

6. Oils—of any description whatsoever—except only Bicknell's Ivy Bridge—which if it ever went cheap—is very beautiful, and I am much obliged to you for offering 300 for the Saltash, which is a highly curious and interesting picture, but not worth more.

I send you the end of Murano—at last.
Dearest love to my mother.

Ever my dearest Father
Your most affec. Son
J Ruskin

LETTER 124

Sunday. 25th January [1852]

My dearest Father,

When I said that I could not answer hurriedly to your letter respecting religious despondency,[1] I was almost doubtful if I ought, in my own state of mind, to speak further on the subject at all. But as I believe that you may at some future time fall again into the same state, and that you may at present sometimes suffer in various ways from a conscientious reserve, fearing to speak out lest you should do me harm— it is just as well that you should know there is no danger of doing this, and therefore, in what state my own mind is, with regard to religion.

I have never had much difficulty in accepting any Scriptural statement—in consequence of those *abstract* reasonings which seem always to have disturbed you. That the doctrine of the Trinity is incomprehensible—or the scheme of redemption marvellous, never seemed to me any objection against one or the other. I cannot understand what sort of unity there is between my fingers that move this pen, and the brain that moves *them:* so it is no trouble to me that I cannot understand the Trinity, and for the scheme of Redemption—I feel that I cannot reason

23. This drawing is briefly mentioned in *Works, 3,* 250, 552.
24. One of several studies of Heidelberg done by Turner.
25. This drawing was ruined by exposure to damp and sunlight in 1857 at the Manchester Exhibition. *Virginia Water,* according to Ruskin (*Works, 13,* 592), suffered more than other drawings similarly exposed, and "the rose colour in the sky literally disappeared."
26. For Ruskin's comment on this drawing see *Works, 3,* 308.
27. From the *England and Wales* series.
28. A drawing briefly noted in *Works, 3,* 390.
1. See Letter 104.

respecting that unless I had the power of understanding God's nature—and all His plans. I am perfectly willing to take both on trust: Neither is the meanness and baseness of man any trouble to me—that is rather a confirmation of Revelation, neither is God's choice of this contemptible creature, to raise above angels [2]—for that also I feel is God's affair, not mine: and until I understood all His ways and works, I could not expect to understand that. Nothing of mysterious or strange—so that it be plainly revealed—is any trouble to me.

But on the other hand—while I am ready to receive any amount of mystery in *What* is revealed, I don't at all like mystery in the *manner* of revealing it: The *doctrine* is God's affair. But the revelation is *mine,* and it seems to me that from a God of Light and Truth, His creatures have a right to expect plain and clear revelation touching all that concerns their immortal interests. And this is the great question with me —whether indeed the Revelation *be* clear, and Men are blind; according to that "He hath blinded their eyes and hardened their hearts;" [3] or whether there be not also some strange darkness in the manner of Revelation itself.

When I was a boy—I used to read the poetry of the prophecies with great admiration—as I used to read other poetry: But now their poetry torments me: It seems to me trifling with what is all important, and wasting words. I don't want poetry *there:* I want plain truth, and I would give all the poetry in Isaiah and Ezekiel willingly, for one or two clearer dates.

This is my first trouble: But the answer to this is very ready at hand. Although, from the peculiar life I have led, poetry happens to be useless to *me,* to ninety nine out of a hundred, it makes those prophecies more impressive. To *me* it has a suspicious look—a Delphi oracle tone in it —savouring of tripods and hot air from below. But to the mass of mankind it assuredly makes those prophecies more impressive—to *them* poetry appears the proper form of divine language, and I have no right to expect revelation to be made fit for my particular taste. Then as to the obscurity of it, the answer commonly given is that it is just as clear as it can possibly be so as to leave human action free. It could not be prophesied that Louis Napoleon was to send the Assembly to prison on 2nd December 1851, or the Assembly would have taken care of itself.

This answer is good to a certain extent: but it does not seem to me perfectly good. Though prophecy could not be thoroughly literal and clear, it might yet have been so definite, within certain limits, that at the close of these 2000 years after Christ, we should be able *indisputably* to attach a meaning to a considerable portion—and to show, to the con-

2. Hebrews i.4.
3. John xii.40.

viction of every thinking man, that such and such events were foreshown
—and none others. Now respecting this—there are two questions (A)
How far it is so? (B) How far we have a right to expect it to have
been so?

A How far is it so? The prophecies respecting Babylon—Nineveh—
Alexander—and the Jews, are accomplished visibly, in great part, and
this is a strong sheet anchor. On the other hand, the book which is especially called the *Revelation of Jesus Christ,* and is said to be a Revelation of things which must *shortly* come to pass, remains altogether sealed
—and the most important parts of the prophecies of Daniel and Ezekiel
—and *all* our Saviour's prophecies except those respecting Jerusalem,
remain subjects of continual dispute. Now observe the main question is
—how far these disputes are the result of man's pride and not of God's
secresy. Elliott [4] and Cumming [5] published a plausible view of the Revelations. Dr Wordsworth [6] presently publishes a book with a totally contrary view. Is this because the Revelations are obscure—or because D^r
Wordsworth is a university man, and determined not to be led by D^r
Cumming! It is one of the works which I am chiefly desirous to undertake, to ascertain how far the prophecies have been accomplished clearly,
and how far the obscurity of their accomplishment has been increased
by man's pride and folly.

B Then: How far have we a right to expect it to be so? Is it indeed
before hand to be expected that a mathematical proof—such as must
convince every thinking man, was to be certainly attainable of the truth
of revelation? Or would not even this have been interfering with human
free will, more than in this dispensation it seems even to be intended to
do: Is it not rather apparent that God's purpose is to leave every man
dependent upon his own conduct and choice for the discovery of truth,
shutting it up in greater mystery as men depart from His ways, and revealing it more and more to each man's conscience, as they obey Him—
and would not this purpose have been utterly defeated, by a Revelation
which was intellectually and externally satisfactory?

Having got thus far, I believe I must send off my letter this morning,
this first difficulty being pretty thoroughly set at rest. I will go on however writing this subject out—for tomorrow's letter: meantime I enclose
you a fragment of a chapter—much later in the book. I cannot number it

4. Edward Bishop Elliott (1793–1875), an ecclesiastic interested in the study of
prophecy. His main work was the *Horae Apocalypticae, or a Commentary on the
Apocalypse Critical and Historical* (London, 1844).

5. John Cumming (1807–81), a Scottish divine and author of *Apocalyptic Sketches;
or, Lectures on the Book of Revelation,* 3 ser. Each series consists of lectures, and
each lecture has as its text a quotation from *Revelation.*

6. Christopher Wordsworth (1807–85), scholar and divine, to whose *Lectures on
the Apocalypse* (London, 1849) Ruskin is here referring. Wordsworth, who first gave
these lectures at Cambridge in 1848, was a nephew of the poet, public orator of the
university, and a fellow of Trinity College.

at present—it is the chapter on the Tombs of Venice: I shall send you as they are ready a bit of it here and there—it is a chapter I have worked upon at intervals for some tombs are in draughts where I cannot stand just now—and others are in dark places and require fine weather—and others are here and there out of the way, so the chapter is in a very *un*consecutive condition at present—but it will read in bits.

Dearest love to my mother.

Ever my dearest Father
Your most affec^e. Son
J Ruskin.

I shall page each tomb separately—(you can set the several groups of pages in order hereafter) heading each page with the name of the person to whom the monument was erected.

LETTER 125

Sunday. 25th January. [1852]

My dearest Father,

In the letter I have just sent off [1]—I had got to a tolerably satisfactory solution of doubts derived from the *mystery* of Scripture; in prophecies and statements of doctrine— Much more serious difficulty appears to me to belong to the consideration of the mystery of Scripture as a practical guide. For here it seems to me that we have indeed a right to expect perfect clearness.

And up to a certain point, we have it.

> Love God, and love your neighbour. Watch and Pray.
> Do as you would be done unto
> Oh, dark instructions! even as dark as day!
> Who can these Gordian knots undo?

So far—all is very clear: but How to show either our love to God—or love to our neighbours; and how they *would* be done unto, are matters on which all men are not agreed: For instance, an old Christian would have thought it sometimes love to his neighbour to cast him out of the church, or sentence him to a six years' penance: and a modern Christian sometimes thinks he shows his love to his neighbour by letting him alone. And when we look for definite instructions upon such matters we find none—and finding none, we dispute with each other upon trivialities and neglect judgment—mercy and truth.

Now, if indeed the Bible said *nothing* about such matters, there would be little difficulty—no man could conscientiously contend for them. But The Bible says a great deal about them, complicated with allusions to a state of things evidently now obsolete—and yet of whose future obso-

1. Letter 124.

leteness there is no prophecy—and for its consequences, no provision. If on any disputed point, we appeal to some plain text, desiring to act on it literally, as for instance such an all important passage as 1st Corinthians Ch. XII. v. 28 to 32, we find a distinction instantly implied between the church and *the world,* in the 32nd verse: and when we go on to enquire what constituted this separation, we find in the next chapter —concerning spiritual gifts—that the body of the Church had in it Apostles—Prophets—teachers—miracles—gifts of healings—governments—diversities of tongues, of all which, now, nothing but the teachers is left. And there is not a single passage in the epistle, which if I now press upon anyone as an authority—he may not turn upon me, and say—Where are your miracles—where are your healings—where are your tongues, and I cannot find any intimation that the apostle expected these tongues and prophecies to cease, until that which was *perfect* was come, Ch. XIII. 10. Now this is indeed a very grievous difficulty. It seems to me that everything would induce us to expect the Bible to give us clear guidance at all times, and, if a period was coming when miraculous power were to cease to have foretold and provided for such ceasing— But no such provision is made—and the chief saints and fathers of the church continue to lay claim to miraculous power and to bear witness to miracles—for many subsequent ages, so that no man can say where or when the miraculous power ceased in the Church—or why there was not a grievous outcry when it did cease.

And two terrible errors have been made in consequence of this. Your thorough Protestant denies all miracles after Apostolic times: not seeing, that, to do so, he must suppose every eminent Christian of the three first centuries a wilful liar. And the other—that your high Churchman— unable to fix the point of cessation—determines that the miraculous power must be there still—and goes over to see St Januarius' blood liquefy.

Now there seems to me but one way of explaining this, namely That the church has lost her miraculous powers as a sedentary person loses the use of his limbs: and does not know it is lost: Christians were meant to devote themselves to Christianizing the world—and in so doing were to receive increase both of their spiritual gifts and temporal blessings: They have not done so, and the Holy Spirit ceases to bear witness to their being Christians at all.

Why wiser and better people than I do not think this, or discover this —is a mystery to me—the greatest of all. How clergymen can preach Sunday after Sunday from the parts of the Bible which they profess to understand—quietly skipping chapter after chapter which now has no meaning, as if it had never been intended to have any, is very marvellous to me.

Most of my main difficulties and doubts are traceable in the end to this source. I am ready to believe everything that Christ tells me—however mysterious—His word I will take—(however contrary to my own feelings respecting the Divine nature)—that "He that believeth shall be saved—he that believeth not, shall be condemned." Mark 16. 16. But if I believe the 16th verse—I must also believe the 17th. Now the 17th is for the present—not true—and how can I have confidence in the 16th? It is not said—these signs shall follow *you*, the apostles: But as generally as it is stated that salvation depends on belief—so generally is miraculous witness promised to the belief. And I take refuge at last in that verse, "When the Son of Man cometh—Shall he find faith on the earth." [2]

I have often also felt what you speak of—the desire to know more respecting the future state, but I am conscious in this of much that is "carnally minded." The one thing that we know of it is that we are to be with Christ—and this if we loved Christ—would be all we should care to know. I do not—but love mountains—and pictures, and gratification of my vanity—and many other things which must be left behind on this side the ferry: And it is not so much my complaint that I do not know enough, as that what I know is not to my taste.

And now—as I would not write hurriedly of these things, I must fold up this letter, for it is late—and I am going to Verona tomorrow to see Marshal Radetzky, whom all describe as one of the kindest and best of men— What his religion may be is another question. I shall send you a line from Verona tomorrow, but leave this to be posted here—as the Verona office is the worst in Italy.

Dearest love to my mother.

Ever my dearest Father,
Your most affe. Son
J Ruskin.

LETTER 126

Verona. 26[th.] January [1852]

My dearest Father,

We arrived here very comfortably at two o'clock—and one of the Marshal's aid-de-camps, Count Thun, was at the station with the enclosed letter for us, which I think worth keeping, and therefore for fear I should lose it, enclose it to you forthwith. I have to finish a drawing here, and the days are so short that I believe I must stay all tomorrow and return to Venice by the Wednesday *day* train. We had a lovely day to come here and I never saw the mountains look more heavenly; about Vicenza especially, and the Euganeans in the soft wintry haze on the other side. I did not lose my day either—having read [1] through the opinions of 15 architects in the year 1577 as to whether the ducal palace

---

2. Luke xviii.8.

1. In the Abbate Giuseppi Cadorin's *Pareri di XV Architetti, con illustrazioni* (Venice, 1838). This book is frequently mentioned in *The Stones of Venice II*.

could be saved after the fire, with much edification, and as the Marshal opens his doors at eight—and likes people to come early, I don't expect to be kept up very late tonight. However I must go and dress, for I have been drawing a little—and had to call on the Minischalchis,[2] which took up time.

Dearest love to my mother.

Ever my dearest Father.
Your most affᵉ. Son
J Ruskin.

LETTER 127

Verona. 27ᵗʰ January [1852]

My dearest Father,

I have been as busy as I could be, all day—in this heavenly city—and so could only send you the line I wrote last night. I will make Effie write you an account of the Marshal's ball—one of the chief points about it was that there was entertainment for *every* body—there were musicians for the dancers—cards for the whistplayers—sofas for the loungers—and a library for the readers, with all manner of valuable books laid open, so that instead of having to stand with my back to the wall in a hot room the whole time, I got a quiet seat—and a book of natural history. Effie was well dressed—and allowed by everyone to be the reine du bal: the old Marshal took her up the room himself to present her to the Mareschale—and then to the Archduke Charles Ferdinand—another of the sons of the Archduke Charles. The dancing was very much more spirited than ours: till twelve o'clock, when all the ladies were taken down to supper: There had meantime been tea, for all who liked it—in a room beyond the library—not tea handed over a counter by confectioners' girls, as it is in London, making the people's houses look like railway stations, but tea made at a large comfortable table where people sat down and talked—and in large cups, the teamaker being one of the Marshal's aid-de-camps, the Count Thun—the same who met us at the railroad. But at the ladies' supper—the old Marshal was head waiter himself—he went down and stood at the end of the room, just behind Princess Esterhazy's chair—seeing that they all had enough—and not only so—but kept running into the Kitchen to order things for them—and at last brought out a bowl of soup himself—keeping his aid-de-camps not less busy the whole time—nor that a short one—for the ladies were exceedingly comfortable and sat at their supper full three-quarters of an hour. This—we hear from the said Count Thun—was as much in politeness to the Marshal as in kindness to themselves—for he is exactly like my mother—nothing annoys him so much as the idea

2. A Verona family appearing briefly in *Praeterita* (*Works, 35,* 480).

that people have gone away without having been made comfortable—
but especially without having enough to eat. "Il a toujours peur," says
his aid-de-camp—"qu'on meurt de faim." With this substantial attention to all his guests, there was great simplicity. The supper looked as
if it were meant to be eaten—not to be looked at. There was not a single
showy dish nor piece of finery on the table.

The Mareschale is a very old lady—like most other old ladies— The
gentlemen—of course chiefly soldiers—looked all of them like gentlemen—*and* soldiers— I cannot say much for the women. The Countess
Minischalchi was there—and looking very beautiful—but she and Effie
were, I thought, the only pretty women in the room—and the appearance of the assembly in general did not at all assist the endeavour to
suppose oneself in the palace of the Capulets.

But the exquisite beauty of every scene in the city gains upon me
each time that I return to it. We go back to Venice tomorrow—but I
hope to wait on the old Marshal once more, when the weather is finer.

Dearest love to my mother. Ever my dearest Father. Your most
affec⁸. Son

J Ruskin.

LETTER 128

Venice 28ᵗʰ January [1852]

My dearest Father,

Returning today from Verona I found your most kind letter of
19/21: with happy assurances of the acquisition of the Fair which is
a great comfort to me: for it was not only a drawing that I always liked
—but its sky is of a kind excessively characteristic of Turner—and yet
of which—wonderful to say—we had *no* specimen. That rolling cloud—
solid above and breaking into rain below. Our skies are for the most
part—less forward—more diffused or fragmentary. The finest sky we
have on the whole is that of the Gosport: the Goldau though full of
power is full of faults— The Winchelsea is very fine—but hasty; my St
Gothard storm is quite subordinate to the mountains: on the whole I
should say our collection was curiously weak in skies: and this Fair will
be a magnificent addition—best thanks for it.

I have also the circular which is excellent on one side and pleasant
on the other. If I were a wine merchant, it would make me order directly, for fear you should raise your prices, but I am rather nervous
about raising of prices on account of Turners. You do quite right to
scold me about being sad—but it is not possible beyond a certain point—
to conquer these feelings. I believe the way they tell on me is not that
the original depression remains upon me for days—but that anything

that excessively pains me turns my stomach, and then the stomach depresses me. I mean in cases like that of threatened retouching of Tintoret, as for the regrets about Turner I think I said only that they *would*
become hurtful if I did not turn my mind away from them; they do not
interfere with my health, or work, which always takes up my entire
mind when I once get into it, and their only effect is taking away from
me a little of the animal spirit which must go, sooner or later—and
leaves one less exposed to variations of temper afterwards. But I could
not make myself merrier by thinking of the general evanescence of all
things human. Men are more evanescent than pictures yet one sorrows
for lost friends—and pictures *are* my friends. I have none others. I am
never long enough with men to attach myself to them—and whatever
feelings of attachment I have are to material things. If the great Tintoret here were to be destroyed, it would be precisely to me what the
death of Hallam was to Tennyson—as far as *this* world is concerned—
with an addition of bitterness and indignation—for *my* friend would
perish murdered—*his* by a natural death. Hearing of plans for its restoration is just the same to me as, to another man—hearing talk behind
an Irish hedge of shooting his brother. He does not go home to dinner
with the same appetite, and that is all I believe—of mischief that is done
to me—for the present. But I could not—or should not work at all—if
I thought these things trifling. All my labour and all my writing are
done under the conviction of pictures being of enormous importance,
and of our neglect of them being Sin. So that, needs must be—if I am
ardent at one time I am despondent at another, and in exact proportion
to the pleasure I have in getting a Turner—or saving some record of a
piece of architecture is the pain I have in losing a Tintoret—or seeing a
palace destroyed. Nothing can make a man permanently cheerful in this
world—but steady progress, or religious hope. No man—with his heart
set on any earthly treasure—can be cheerful the day he loses it.

In the short catalogue that I sent you the other day [1] of desirable
Turner pictures, you would be surprised at the high prices I attached
to those which I *called* cheap. But I of course estimated them as they
are *now* likely to go—and I never expect to see a truly fine Turner
drawing under 120, anymore: and the list I sent is as I hope you understood—one merely for *reference* in case any drawings should come in
your way. I never expect to get all that are *named*—much less all that
are *not excepted* in my list of exceptions: if I were allowed at this time
to choose all the drawings that I was ever to have, I should be content
with my class first and 2nd and, four or five of the Yorkshires; as it is, I
would only buy the less valuable drawings because I cannot get the
others at what I consider low prices—and that only now and then: The
Fair which you have just got I should have put in the second class. I

1. Letter 123.

think it, now, very cheap at what you have given for it: but when it was last in the market, it was offered for 70: so you see what a rise one must allow for, in now talking of cheap drawings. In saying my collection of *skies* is weak, I am thinking also of another class of skies, beside those rolling ones; very characteristic of Turner—the sunsets and sunrises with the sky *covered* with *light* clouds (like those in our Venice) —represented in our collection only by Constance and Goldau: the masses of cloud in the Constance are few, and very simple, and in the Goldau—wild and stormy instead of serene. There is one drawing—and only one that I recollect, which I should in all respects like, of this kind of sky—and it may possibly occur in the market—I don't know where it is—it is *Castle Upnor:* [2] I think I should almost put this drawing into my second class. Fond as Turner was of those skies, there are very few drawings containing them which I should care for, they are almost always vignettes—or small annual drawings—or else too glaring and yellow. Windus has a very fine one but of a totally uninteresting subject, whiting fishing at Margate [3]—and of an enormous size—so that I never should think of buying it. Castle Upnor is the only satisfactory representative I know.

Dearest love to my mother.

Ever my dearest Father
Your most affect. Son.
[*No signature*]

LETTER 129

30th January [1852]

My dearest Father,

I had yesterday your kind letter of 24th with account of house opposite and enclosing £300, with Miss Mitford and Mr Gray,[1] &c., but of which the most important point is your change of mind about coming abroad—for which I am exceedingly sorry— I wait however to see what you will answer to my succeeding letter—which may alter your feelings—but how is it that you have thus given up a plan which you said when I left England would be something for you to look forward to, all the Winter? In one of your letters you spoke of alterations in

2. *Upnor Castle: Mouth of Medway.* This water color, which was also engraved in the *England and Wales* series, was never in Ruskin's possession.

3. A study characterized by Ruskin as "an elaborate drawing on a large scale, with a beautiful sunrise" (*Works, 13,* 60).

1. A letter from Effie's father to John James Ruskin. From the end of 1851 there had been a domestic battle raging between the elder Ruskins and the Grays concerning the extravagance of the young couple in Venice. Ruskin's irritation, indicated a little later in this letter, arose from a communication in which Mr. Gray told the older Ruskin that his son was spending too much on pictures. For an elaboration of this matter see James, *John Ruskin and Effie Gray,* pp. 185 ff.

Inns, &c., but we may go to new Inns, and perhaps be happier than old memories would allow us to be in the old ones—or if not to new inns—to new places. In any case, the more I think of it, the more it seems to me that it will be necessary that I should leave Effie here and run home, whether you come abroad with me again or not—for the sales [2] are sure to take place in May: and how to get home with Effie by early May I do not well see. However I shall wait till I hear next from you.

The Bills sent in to Park St are I suppose right—Lambert's is; certainly, they would not send it in twice. I told Effie and George to get in all the bills—while I was at Malvern, and supposed it was done. I neither knew what bills they had to get in, nor had time to see their being got. For the other about the glass—Mr McDougal may send in claims for anything—for what I know or can help; the next bills may be for a new stair carpet—or a new chimney piece—or for a new house—for anything I can see to the contrary. The next point is about Mr Gray's letter—I certainly should *not* like it published. It reads to me very insipid and even foolish, and as all of it is second hand—there is little value in it. I am glad to see that I write better nowadays, at least to my mind. I may be dull—or dry—but I don't drivel. There is variation from Paxarete to Amontillado, but I don't send Manzanilla.

Respecting the house—even supposing we could get it, I fear it is much too large. We should need a great many servants—at least unless we only furnished the rooms we lived in—which indeed would be what I had best do—otherwise—people would be coming and staying with us. But this is always an awkward arrangement. I think you had much better look for a smaller house.

Best thanks for the offer of the Turners, but how came you to name the Red Righi [3] among those which might go? I thought you liked it very much.

I should have liked to have written at more length—but I have been finding out some important things about Ducal Palace [4]—and my head is full of them. Dearest love to my mother, and thanks for sermon.

Ever my dearest Father
Your most aff^e. Son
J Ruskin.

Pull off the thin paper, put to keep it from rubbing. I did the little vignette enclosed for part of the chapter on tombs—there was to have been others beside them. I found the scale a little too small and am doing them large, so the enclosed is waste paper and may amuse you. The

2. Of Turner's work.
3. *Rigi at Sunset,* which was for some time in Ruskin's possession. For its history see *Works, 13,* 604.
4. For the eighth chapter of *The Stones of Venice II.*

lowest and richest is the tomb of two Doges Tiepolos,[5] of whom you hear.

31st January [1852]

My dearest Father,

George has written the enclosed much too close—I hope it will not hurt your eyes—if you find it troublesome throw it aside and I will make him write it over again. You will observe that the ‾ strokes in the Latin inscription always mean n. or m. Tremēdus is tremendus dū is dum. I can't tell what they meant by unio—unless what I have supposed in the translation. The pieces of evidence referred to in the text will be intelligible only when you see all put together—and the notes at the bottom are reference to passages which I can expand afterwards if I have time. In fact the whole sheet—chiefly written on the spot to secure the necessary points, may be much concentrated and better expressed. But what a dream this human life is and how fast it goes—I am getting rather jealous of time spent in turning sentences musically.

I see that though George writes better than I do—his printing is not distinguished—and he had drawn the lines round the inscriptions in such a staggery way that I cannot touch them into any resemblance of stone.

I have found out some most important things about the ducal palace. The reason the Venetian chroniclers say so little about it is that it was the first movement of their *aristocracy after its confirmation in 1297.* I find the first stone of the present palace laid in 1301.[1] I shall soon be able to send you some text about ducal palace.

Dearest love to my mother.

Ever my dearest Father,
Your most aff[e]. Son
J Ruskin.

Sunday. February 1st. [1852]

My dearest Father,

I am afraid the details on the other side will still read very remainder —biscuitish—unless you have the plates—and understand exactly the terms—leaf plinth—panel moulding—&c. They must do so—all then

5. The tombs of the Doges Jacopo and Lorenzo Tiepolo are discussed in *The Stones of Venice II* (*Works, 10,* 85–6).
1. See *The Stones of Venice II* (*Works, 10,* 340).

will be explained in the beginning of the chapter in a general sketch of
mediaeval forms of sarcophagi—which I cannot yet finish because I
have not yet got all the exceptional cases. Sending you the sheets in
this state is a good deal like sending you the blue ground, of a picture
afterwards to be glazed with warm colours.

I am happy to say however the book is now coming well together. I
see both ends of it in one view which is comfortable, and I am very
happy to find that my farther investigations confirm and fit in delightfully with my first chapter.[1] You will see that that first chapter promises
three divisions of the main subject: The Greek or Byzantine period,
the Transitional period, and the Gothic period—the last mainly represented by the Ducal palace: Now I said at page 4. of Vol 1.[2] that the
second period of the career of Venice opened with 120 years—the *central struggle of her life,* beginning in 1300, finishing in 1418—or—in
the next sentence—five years later, i.e. 1423. Now I knew when I wrote
this that the Ducal palace was fourteenth century work—but I did *not*
know what I know now that the first stone of it was laid in *1301,* the
last, in *1423!* [3] Observe the *third* division of my second volume is the
opening of the *second* period of the Venetian Career. The two periods—
one of 900—the second of 500 years p. 3. § IV. vol I [4]—are each divided into two styles.

1st period.	{ Greek Style.	§ XXXI.	Chap. 1. 1st section of IInd volume
	{ Transition Style.	§ XXXII.	Chap. 1. 2nd ——— — — ———
2nd period.	{ Gothic Style.	§ XXXIV.	Chap. 1. 3rd ——— — — ———
	{ Renaissance Style.	§ XXXVII.	Chap. 1. 4th ——— — — ———

I said in § XXXIX. that I should not devote a fourth section to Palladio [5]
—but I have made interesting observations now on the Renaissance,
and the book will be more symmetrical in having its four sections complete, so it is so planned [6]—and I am especially delighted to find my 3rd
or Gothic period limited to the *very years* which in the first chapter I
gave for the central struggle of Venetian life. I think this will interest
you and make you happy, so I don't mind writing it on Sunday.[7] Dearest love to my mother.

Ever my dearest Father. Your most affectionate Son
J Ruskin

1. Of *The Stones of Venice I.*
2. See *Works, 9,* 20–1.
3. *Ibid., 10,* 346.
4. *Ibid., 9,* 19, para. 4.
5. *Ibid., 9,* 47.
6. The plan outlined here, which culminates in the Renaissance observations, does not
represent the final arrangement of the last two volumes of *The Stones of Venice.* Ruskin
treated the Transitional and Gothic styles together so that the divisions, as published,
are as follows: First, or Byzantine, Period (*Works, 10,* 3–179); Second, or Gothic,
Period (*Works, 10,* 180–439); Third, or Renaissance, Period (*Works, 11,* 3–245).
7. Ruskin's Sabbatarianism is recorded in *Praeterita* (*Works, 35,* 346).

LETTER 132

2nd Feb. [1852]

My dearest Father,

I read yesterday Mr Melville's sermon on the shutting up by the law
—but, do you know, I begin to fear Mr Melville is either falling off—or
I am changing my taste— There is always a good idea somewhere in the
sermon—and commonly at the foundation of it, but it is so repeated and
turned over and over that I get tired—and there is a great deal, it seems
to me, which requires oratorical delivery to make it forcible. Instead of
Mr Melville's delivery being *really* bad, I believe it to be highly studied
—and that many a sentence which is nothing in print, becomes a great
deal when spoken—partly because really rendered more impressive by
his vital energy—and partly because what fault there may be in it—is
laid on *the score* of the delivery. However, I am very glad of them—one
good idea is always worth reading a couple of pages for.

Do you see that the Protestant missionaries are sent out of Pesth? I
did not know Palmerston was identified at all with Protestantism—
what a pity it is that we cannot get Protestants and Radicals separated.
I don't know a cleverer trick of the Devil, since the world began—than
getting Protestant energy, at this moment—confounded, in Austria and
Italy with red republicanism, and Popery identified with peace, a clever
dropping of the dead fly into the apothecary's alabaster—and fitting the
sheepskin on the wolf. I must be short today for it is fine and mild and
I want to do a great deal. Dearest love to my mother.

Ever my dearest Father
Your most affe. Son
J Ruskin.

LETTER 133

III. Feb [1852]

My dearest Father,

I send you the first page of the chapter on tombs which however, still
wants its introductory sentence: after laying before the reader the difficulties in ascertaining the precise date of the ducal palace—which is the
main object of the essay—I show him how he must seek for evidence
among *dated* monuments of the same style, and then the chapter begins.

There is such a quantity of it that a great deal is left merely blocked
out in notes and memoranda—which however I shall let George copy
straight on—as it will give you some idea of the kind of work I have to
get at my broad generalizations.

They are getting on with their gold, I see, at Sydney. Read the 7ᵗʰ of Ezekiel, v. 19.20. It is worth observing that the constant desireableness and *beauty* of Gold is represented as appointed by God in the opening of the 20ᵗʰ verse. It will hold its own, I believe, though we have indeed made the images of abominations therein, and it may be set far from us.

Another lovely day which I must make the most of.

Dearest love to my mother.

Ever my dearest Father
Your most affec. Son
J Ruskin.

LETTER 134

4ᵗʰ February. [1852]

My dearest Father,

I had yesterday your kind letter of the 26ᵗʰ· 28ᵗʰ· enclosing Griffith's and architect's to which latter I will send answer tomorrow. I hardly know what to say about your altering your mind and staying at home this year. I trust that my mother may retain her sight and present powers for many years to come, but I cannot in much comfort calculate on its being so—and she will be able to hear my books or my praise read to her, when she can no longer walk in the green fields of Lucerne: Looking back to my past journeys with you—I am apt to ask whether my work or any of its fruits was worth the separation from you that it cost, and whether—in after years, if I let you pass by this spring—I may not in like manner ask whether any book or work was worth the loss of some more mountain walks with you and my mother. We should be happier now than even last time—for last time I had not done my work at the Matterhorn [1]—and that was hanging over your heads— and making me restless—now I have no work to do in Switzerland— and should merely rest and enjoy myself. I never pass by the quay beyond Danieli's—the quay of San Zaccaria—without thinking of the way your eyes brightened one day when I offered to go and show you the John Bellini [2] in that church—when I had left you alone all the morning for my own work, and I would willingly give twenty such sketches as that I made in those Venetian mornings, to get back the opportunity of walking in the public gardens with my mother and you— I do not see neither why the Swiss journey should hinder my book—and I don't think at your time of life, that your business should hinder *it:* The only

1. Ruskin is thinking of the summer of 1849 when he went abroad with his parents and left his wife in Scotland with her family. On that trip he studied the Matterhorn closely, and the results are to be found in *Modern Painters IV* (*Works, 6,* 224–7).

2. *The Virgin, with Four Saints* by Giovanni Bellini (1426–1516), which is in the Church of Sta. Zaccaria.

loss of time would be the ten or twelve days occupied in going and re-turning— I can bring all my MS and materials home with me—and can surely go on writing as well in some pleasant rooms looking out on the lake of Geneva, as at Denmark Hill. You need not fear my being tempted to the mountains—I have them in sight here—and could be among them any day in four hours, but I do not want to go—my head and heart are altogether in my book, but I would rather when I go out for exercise—be able to ramble in a pine forest or mountain pasture, than walk up and down Herne Hill. Think over it a little, again.

I am sorry my sentence about anxieties troubled you—but you know it can hardly but be so to some little extent at some period of a man's life. Christ says the "cares of this world" choke the word—in a general way, and there is no avoiding them altogether—except by caring only for the next. As a man passes 30—his hopes get damped—and his dis-appointments more frequent. The steady sense of progress is the thing that causes so many men to attach themselves only to making money. I am not, I assure you—at all over tormented by solicitudes—only I have less to look forward to than I had—the feelings of a youth free among mountains—and the sort of hope with which I looked to Tur-ner's fresh pictures can never now come back to me again—and so any little thing which formerly would have been shaken off at once—be it the hearing that people withdraw their names from my books—or the finding a hundred francs gone for firewood—or the failure in a drawing with which I have taken great pains, may certainly tell so far as to diminish the *opening* of a sentence— But I hope it may add to the *wisdom* thereof. The anxieties about which I spoke, however—were chiefly those about Turner's death.

You speak of a letter of the 14th—which you say you are glad I did not get— I don't think I have got it yet—I have one of the 15th only. *Cuff's*[3] bill is I believe right—but Please look on my file in study if there is no receipt for the first four pounds which I thought I had paid. You see I had so little fear of the St Catherine's Hill being false that I forgot to speak of it. You are much more likely to suspect a real Turner than to buy a false one.

Dearest love to my mother. Ever my dearest Father.

Your most aff[e]. Son.

J Ruskin

3. R. P. Cuff, an engraver who did work for Ruskin on *The Seven Lamps of Archi-tecture, The Stones of Venice,* and *Modern Painters.*

LETTER 135

5th Feb. [1852]

My dearest Father,

I did not in my line yesterday answer what you said about my health
—and the harm which might be done by travelling: I ought not to complain of my health—nor ought you to cast reflections on the salubrity
of Venice— I have now been here 5 entire months—at the worst season,
and I have never had so much as a tendency to cold in my head—or the
slightest cough or even roughness of throat: though out in the most
stormy days, rowing for at least two hours against the wind and rain;
and coming home dripping—and on the frosty days often standing for
half an hour together drawing—sometimes kneeling on the pavement
beside the ice, and passing hours in the fireless churches: so that I ought
not to think myself weak— But the thing that I have to watch is the
tendency to excitement and sleeplessness—the aggravation of that ex-
citeability of pulse which my mother used so often to notice when I was
a boy: the least overwork any day causing a restless feeling all over—
and exhaustion afterwards. All my work, nearly, excites or interests me
too much—it is not like natural history—soothing—but stimulating;
and therefore it is that I find it so necessary to watch constantly, and
that I can do so little each day. I have made some curious moral observations on the effect of the evil passions upon the heart— I find that
there is nothing so harmful as any feeling of pique—jealousy—or envy:
nothing which quickens the pulse and weakens the body so much—hence
that verse in the Proverbs—"Envy is the rottenness of the bones." [1]
Anxiety—hurry of any kind, and anger, are the next worst things—and
any *exceeding* delight and interest are not over and above good for one,
though the excitement is of a more healthy kind. All feelings of Rever-
ence and affection soothe the heart—and *strengthen the body* and gentle
sorrow is very good also. Trust—and peacefulness of acquiescence in
God's will—and a gentle and continual hope, are the best medicines for
humanity, the best kind of morphine.

This by the way: As to travelling, there is no doubt the playing
courier was very bad for me. But to take my own place in a diligence,
and stay in it having nothing to do with changing horses, will I believe
be rather good for me than bad, so that you need not fear the coming
home for me—much less the travelling again with you. I wish you and
my mother to do exactly in this matter as you think will be most pleas-
urable for yourselves: and I should really find it difficult—if you were

1. Proverbs xiv.30.

to consult only my good or my pleasure—to tell you how to decide— I shall be just as happy hearing my mother read a little to me in the study —and going with you to exhibitions as I should be walking at Vevay or Lucerne: but I want you to consider whether in other years, we may not be happy at home, while my mother's strength for travelling may be considerably diminished.

Would you be kind enough to enclose the little note to Hillyer [2]—and send it to 4. Lind St. Ryde. Isle of Wight.

Dearest love to my mother.

> Ever my dearest Father
> Your most aff[e]. Son
> J Ruskin.

LETTER 136

6th Feb. [1852]

My dearest Father,

I send you the enclosed rather to show you the kind of reading I have to do—than with any hope of its being interesting to you without the plates. The Tomb here spoken of is the lowest of the two on the little scrap of paper I sent two or three days ago [1] but I found it necessary to do it larger, owing to its great curiosity and importance. The places where short references are made are left unfinished—because, if I were to go thoroughly into each thing that interests me—I might chase a single doge through all the shelves of St Mark's library. When the book is all in form and place, I shall see which points require salience and then my side references will enable me to add whatever I want—and the useless ones will be given in the notes for the reader's benefit who likes to work them out himself.

Did you see in the papers lately the seaman Forster of the Amazon [2] —returning the sovereign he had got from the poor box saying he had got enough for himself—till he found another ship? A rare instance this—of true charity— I have a notion our national defences are not very weak, while we have such men before the mast—whatever the lords of the Admiralty may be. But I am provoked at our English press. When the French were cutting each others' throats in the streets, they said—the nation had a right to do as it liked—now—that they are

2. George Hillier (1815–66), antiquary, who lived most of his life on the Isle of Wight and who died at Ryde.

1. In Letter 129.

2. One W. Foster, able-bodied seaman, is noted in the *Times*, January 7, 1852, as the survivor of a fire at sea of the Royal Mail Steam Packet Company's ship *Amazon*.

showing commonsense—and taking order with their ruffians, we call them "slaves," and "under the yoke of despotism" [3] and what not.

Dearest love to my mother.

Ever my dearest Father
Your most aff[e]. Son
J Ruskin.

If this paging is not right—7. 8. alter it—it should be consecutive with last sheet.

LETTER 137

7th Feb. [1852]

My dearest Father,

I had yesterday your delightful letter from Colchester with account of reading correspondent at Ipswich, and Dr Allison [1] in Park St. I had not heard of him—but what he says of society is all true—and truer in England, I think, than here; that is to say—when people meet in crowds in England, they drop their good qualities and show their worst —here it is the reverse—people who are utterly immoral in private life being graceful and agreeable in society: Of whatever good material a crowd is composed in England, whenever you enter a drawingroom, you may be sure that everyone in it will, if they can without hurting their own character for politeness—say a disagreeable thing to you: and that their main object is to make each other uncomfortable: many of them being *at home* well disposed people enough. Here—and I suppose on the continent generally—people who would be unbearable in private life, set themselves, in society to make everybody as happy as possible—and are therefore easy and happy themselves. In both cases, society is a mere thing of surface. Here—it is the apples of Sodom dust inside; with us cocoanuts—milk inside—and a monkey face and rough shell outside. But I don't intend to live on the shell any more. Your correspondent at Ipswich must be a capital fellow—I like him for considering everything rotten. You must have an enormous advantage with men of this kind, in your own literary tastes and knowledge—I don't suppose that the commercial gents who leave their boots waiting at the door in the morning—are likely to elicit such confidences from their literary customers. But why in the world does such a man *Ride?*

I was reading at Breakfast this morning some of Schlegel's criti-

<hr />

3. Ruskin is thinking of such editorials as appeared in the *Times*, January 23, 1851, where the French middle classes, as a result of recent political upheavals, are described as being "terrified and silent."

1. William Pulteney Alison (1790–1859), sometime professor of medicine at Edinburgh University.

cisms on Shakespeare [2]—very good and complimentary—but treating the plays much more as elaborate pieces of art than as deep and natural expressions of a great man's mind. This is shallow—I believe Shakespeare wrote with the most perfect ease—but had in each play—a simple and very grand purpose—which gives to it that consistency that the common critics think the result of laborious composition. I don't think this purpose has been at all noticed—on the contrary—people have found fault with *Romeo and Juliet* because the catastrophe turned on an *accident*—as if Shakespeare had merely brought the accident that he might *get* a catastrophe. It was not without a meaning that in *Romeo* and *Othello*—both catastrophes are brought on by mistakes—in *Hamlet* by inactivity—and in *King Lear* by an old man's weakness and hastiness. I see that Shakespeare knew long ago what I am just beginning to find out—that the sorrow of the whole world is *all* the consequence of *Mistake;* and its chief miseries are brought about by small errors and misconceptions—trifles apparently—which our own evil passions leave us to be the prey of. Thus the whole of *Romeo and Juliet* is evidently written to show the effect of Heedless and unbridled passion— exposing men to infinite calamity from *accident only*— Every thing concurs to give this lesson—Mercutio fights in a jest—Tybalt in a fury —both are slain—Romeo and Juliet fall in love at first sight—and at the first sight of sorrow—kill themselves—Capulet and Montague are *first* introduced calling for swords—and are *last* seen reconciled by the loss of all that is dear to them, the whole being a most profound teaching of the character of human passion—and its folly—and its punishment wrought out *by* its folly: In order that this lesson may be more true and inevitable the passion of the lovers is invested with all the charms of poetry that human passion ever can profess.

In *Othello*—two of the greatest of human souls are seen by one weakness—becoming the prey of the vilest, another awful lesson. Hamlet is exactly opposed to Mercutio—abuse of the intellectual faculties being the sin in both. *King Lear*—the most highly wrought of all—is written to show the evil of irregular passion—in Gloster and Edmund, and of hasty judgment in the King, but the evil passion to which these follies then expose them is the blackest of all—ingratitude, and therefore Shakespeare seems to have taken more pains to work out the whole.

Dearest love to my Mother.

> Ever my dearest Father
> Your most aff^e. Son
> J Ruskin.

2. August Wilhelm Schlegel's *A Course of Lectures on Dramatic Art and Literature* (London, 1846). See especially Lectures XXII–XXVI for Shakespearean commentary.

LETTER 138

Sunday, 8ᵗʰ Feb. 1852

My dearest Father,

I had yesterday afternoon your kind letter intended for today, assuring me that you will be on watch for Turners—and containing also my mother's little notes in pencil—that—she says—I may rub them out—What does she think would be in my fingers, if I rubbed out any of my mother's writing, much more her prayers on my birthday—it is very provoking they are not in ink.

You ask for a full and particular account of my health—which I shall proceed to give you though I wish I had some better way of thanking you for your promise about the Turners, but first let me say a word for poor Munro: Suppose I had not promised Turner to keep the drawings I liked, of which I sent him a list, and that some one were now to come and make me an offer—suppose for Ehrenbreitstein [1]—I should say, no: They—suppose—rose in their offer—200—No—300—No—400—No—500—No—1000—Well—I should begin to think about it at 1000 —and perhaps—if I saw three or four fine mountain drawings accessible for 200 each—I might let them have Ehrenbreitstein at 1200—Now—would they have a right to abuse me because having only paid 80 for it—I *took* 1200—which was its actual worth to me? Just in the same way, Munro liked Schaffhausen [2]—didn't want to part with it. It was worth 200 to him—when I came up to that value—he let me have it—I can see no villainy in this. Munro is richer than I, and had I been in *his* place—I think I should have either kept the drawing altogether—or given it for 80— But I have no right to abuse him because he—with his fortune—perhaps no whit larger than mine in proportion to his habits—does exactly as I would do with mine— Only I should be more extortionate.

Well—now about my health. I have two things to watch—my stomach and my circulation—neither of which are so well as they were in 1844. I should fix on the time I was in Chamouni, in that year, as the healthiest period of my life—though I was not so strong, muscularly, as afterwards. I had recovered from the affection of the chest, and was every way well. The first sign I had of a change in constitution was some discomfort of stomach in climbing hills at Macugnaga— Till I was six and twenty—I was always better and better in spirit and general sensations, the higher I got, but in 1845, at Macugnaga, I noticed that, if my stomach was *at all* out of order, I was apt to feel feverish and

1. This was painted for Ruskin in 1842 and is minutely analyzed in *Works, 15,* 167 ff. It is also briefly alluded to in *Works, 13,* 454, in which volume it is reproduced as Plate XXII.
2. *Schaffhausen: Town,* which was originally executed for Munro of Novar in 1845. Its history is given in *Works, 13,* 476 n., 604.

headachy in the high air, and once, at 9000 ft, on the top of the Moro—
I was totally unable to move for an hour, with sick headache—lying on
the rocks with a northwind and frosty snow beating in my face—after
that I used almost always to take a Seidlitz powder in the morning before my long walks—and then found myself very comfortable. Coutet [3]
said it was so with many people; headache coming on in the high air—
still—it had never till then been so with *me*. I then went to Venice with
Harding—and decidedly overworked myself, sitting up late at night—
Coutet used to look at my eyes in the morning and say, "C'a ne va pas.
Vous le sentirez *après*."

I then came home—annoyed a good deal in my journey—slight illness at Padua—short of money at Verona—and, chiefly—John Richardson's death—announced to me at Vevay,[4] and I came home weakened and far from right. That winter—1845–6, I wrote IInd vol of
Modern Painters—the greatest exertion of thought I ever made— The
last sheet of it was written at Calais, and I had then a general feeling of
weight all over the head—and the veins swelled in the left temple—and
my eyesight dim. I rested till I got into Italy—but with a constant feeling of quickened pulse and over excitement: and nights *entirely* sleepless, then for the first time, perhaps once in a fortnight or so. At Verona
I began to work again. Then came the correction of press of *Modern
Painters* first vol: the feeling of weight in the head remaining constantly—at last just before I left Switzerland, the new black serpent
appeared in my left eye, on which I gave up all work and lay back in
the carriage in great despondency and prostration all the way home.
The feeling of quickness and hardness of pulse much increased; and
especially a feeling of the pulse beating violently in my *back*—on the
left side of the spine under the shoulder. I then went and paid Acland
a visit [and] told him what I felt. He examined my heart—said there
was no disease—but I had been "dreadfully overworked" and gave me
some Prussic acid, which did me good.

I was in no humour for work—that winter [5]—but was ass enough to
go into society—and to write two quarterly reviews [6] in the spring
which not only cost me much reading—but were done against the grain.

3. Joseph Marie Couttet (d. 1875), for thirty years the guide for Ruskin and his
parents on their Continental travels. An account of this man is given in E. T. Cook's
Life of John Ruskin, 2 vols. (London, G. Allen & Co., 1911), *1*, 169–71.

4. There is no record of Ruskin being in Vevey on his 1845 travels. He was, however,
in nearby Martigny on October 23 and at Nyon on October 25. In the *Gentleman's
Magazine*, November 1845, the death is announced as of October 1 in Upper Berkeley
Street, London, of a John Richardson "late of Sydney."

5. The winter of 1846–47.

6. These two reviews appeared together in the *Quarterly Review* for June 1847, pp.
1–57. They are criticisms of *Progression by Antagonism: a Theory Involving Consideration Touching on the Present Position, Duties, and Destiny of Great Britain* (London,
1846) and *Sketches of the History of Christian Art*, 3 vols. (London, 1847). Both books
were written by Lord Lindsay.

In the summer I went to Jephson [7] who did me some good—and to the Highlands; [8] which were too cold for me—and did me none: when I came back I was still unwell—and Keel's sudden death—I having never seen a man on his deathbed before—put my nerves and stomach all wrong again. I went away to Folkestone [9] and then resting entirely for six weeks came back much revived. I then made steady progress during 1848; and though the terrible disappointment at not going abroad threw me back a little and made me catch that terrible cold which I had not spirit enough to throw off, at Dover and Salisbury,[10] still, I was resting and quiet, and the pulse got better—and I was very well on my Norman tour [11] in the Autumn—though working steadily. The winter of 1848–9 I wrote the *Seven Lamps,* being in very good health and my journey in Switzerland with you, 1849,[12] did me great good—though I noticed my stomach was precisely in the same state. I was obliged to watch it very carefully if I intended to go into the high air.

Much recovered in general tone, I went to Venice—1849–1850— I had grown wiser—and neither rose too early—nor sat up too late—but I could not help working against time for the five months [13]— Still—I did not do myself much harm, and came home in the spring very well— and set to write my book. But then came three months of society—and late hours: then—after a little useless trip in the autumn [14]—good hard work—and a great deal of worry with engravers [15]—writing *Stones of Venice*—all winter [16]—then society again in the spring— I did not notice much mischief however, till about a month before I came away— when my nights again became sleepless—and another symptom showed, which made me go to Dr Watson [17] as you know, myself.

This was numbness and sleepiness of the left foot: occurring for a minute or two at a time if I got it into a cramped position. This frightened me thoroughly, for I have always been nervous about two things,

7. A doctor at Leamington, Warwickshire, under whose care Ruskin had also been placed in 1841 when it was feared he had contracted tuberculosis.

8. In August and September 1847 Ruskin was in Scotland visiting his friend Macdonald Macdonald at the latter's Scottish seat. An account of the visit is given in *Praeterita* (*Works, 35,* 423 ff.).

9. Ruskin was in Folkestone, Kent, from mid-November until mid-December 1847.

10. In July 1848 Ruskin was at Salisbury with his bride Effie, studying the cathedral. They were joined there by his parents.

11. From early August until late October 1848 Ruskin was touring Normandy with his wife.

12. From April until September.

13. From November 1849 until March 1850 Ruskin was gathering material for *The Stones of Venice.*

14. In the autumn of 1851 Ruskin accompanied his wife on a brief trip to her home in Scotland.

15. Ruskin was proud of being one of the few authors to illustrate his own work; and with these illustrations he took much time and also worked the engravers very hard.

16. *The Stones of Venice I* was written in the winter of 1850–51.

17. Dr. Watson of Henrietta Street, London.

paralysis, and disease of heart. It was not however *altogether* a new symptom—for I recollect noticing as long ago as 1841, that the left foot went to sleep in the carriage much oftener and more totally than the right. I had noticed also in the winters of 1849 and 1850—that on some cold days when I was tired, the blood would leave some of the fingers of my hands perfectly white—and without feeling—for half a minute or so—they recovering gradually by friction and warmth: It was quite a different thing from common numbness with cold—affecting one finger more than another—chiefly I think the little finger of left hand— I have never felt this once all this winter—the last time I felt it was I think in May—last Spring—one day before dinner—Dr Grant [18] was dining with us—I was going to tell him—but you were so ill yourself that I was afraid of making you worse—so I went to Watson.

When I did so—I gave up all society—Effie knows that I refused positively to stir out—the last month I was in London—and I would not do anything but rest. This was the reason of my affairs being left in such disorder at Park St.

It almost always happens that the effect of any overwork shows most when you give in—and lie back in your chair— You don't feel how tired you are before. Accordingly—the effect of the London season did not tell upon me until I began to rest completely; and then I found that I must mind what I was about. I did not feel it entirely even while I was excited by having Mr Moore and Newton [19] with me: on the contrary I felt very strong in the Alps: Watson relieved my mind by telling me there was no disease—and I only wanted my Swiss journey; so I was in good spirits and it was not till I began my work *quietly* here that I found how much I needed caution.

I found first—that every hour of thought or work of any kind, but especially writing, was just so much acceleration of pulse—with slight flushing of cheeks and restless feeling all over— That I never was healthily sleepy at nights—and often could not sleep more than four or five hours, even if I went to sleep at a proper time. That any violent exercise would make me restless and excited for hours afterwards, instead of wholesomely fatigued—and that the slightest plague or disagreeable feeling in society would do the same— I got into a little dispute with Mr Cheney about some mosaics one day—and was quite nervous the whole day after—merely a question whether the colours were faded or not— Also—when I first came here, I had not been drawing for some time—and my hand shook so—this sort of way that I could not draw a straight line. You will see, even by the

18. Dr. Grant, physician to the Ruskin family. He is mentioned in *Praeterita* (*Works*, 35, 97–100, 246–7).

19. When Ruskin and his wife were en route to Venice in the late summer of 1851 both Newton and Moore accompanied them for part of the journey. For the complete itinerary of the Venetian trip see *Works*, 10, xxiv n. 1.

scrawls I have sent you that *this* symptom has disappeared. When I got
into this excited state, I found the pulse beating not only quickly and violently but irregularly—three long beats and a short one—three long and a
short, and so on—and the short one seemed to be a little freak of the
heart itself—and not answered by the pulse—but I could not make this
quite out. But it was not so much the quickening of pulse that annoyed
me, as its excessive feebleness when *not* quickened: When—in a healthy
state—I lay on my right side I could not feel the heart beat at all; and
could not feel it strongly whatever way I lay—but to jump—or run a
dozen paces, would make it set off at the gallop, still, never so hard as
in the old bad time—the morbid pulsation in the back and temples having entirely ceased. The sleepiness and numbness of the foot is also
gone—except that it still goes to sleep sooner than the other: at night
until within this last month, I used often to wake with one or both hands
perfectly dead; especially if they had been thrown back above my head
—this symptom has now nearly disappeared, and I have not once had
the white chill in the daytime—though my hands have been much
swelled and cut by the frost.

So much for the circulation—next for the stomach. I find that what
I like does not make much difference—except that I cannot eat pastry—
at least Italian pastry—creams—and such things—nor vegetables—all
being bad here— I eat roast and boiled—chiefly roast—meat and poultry
with bread—rice pudding—a fig or date after dinner, (this at 5
o' clock), some toast and tea at seven: The dessert is a winter indulgence
—I never used to take the fresh fruit— I find that—dessert or none
—pudding or none—tea or none—there is always a bad taste in the
mouth in the morning, and a tendency to acidity of stomach—if anything
puts me out of order, with headach [*sic*]—often a little headach when I
walk in the morning—going off as I dress—sometimes in the middle
of the day, fitfully off and on—whereas when I *used* to have headaches,
they began slightly in the morning and increased steadily till I went
to bed— I don't take medicine for them—but fast—sometimes if not
violent, they go away when I dine—so that if I feel hungry I don't
mind them. The bowels are exceedingly regular, the headaches being
generally the sign of looseness with burning rather than of confinement.
(I wrote *ir*regular above—I *meant* regular, observe). I am certainly
better than when I came to Venice—but of course—still obliged to
be watchful—avoiding all over labour and excitement, and I have
no doubt all will come right with time and peace, and no more
society. Of course you can ask any doctor about it—if you like—but
I believe there is no occasion—they can tell you nothing but that I must
rest which I already know. I think rising too early is a great mistake.
I always found it do [*sic*] me harm: I do not rise at present till near
eight o'clock; I wake about ½ past seven—and think a little about get-

ting up: then dress leisurely, generally having my Turners on the chair beside me: read a chapter, so to breakfast—coffee toast and butter—no meat, at nine exactly. I then write your letter—it is usually done by prayer time, 10: or afterwards—at ½ past 10 I am generally setting to my day's work—I write till ½ past twelve—or one—never more: then (no lunch) go out and draw or make notes till three. Then row gently till ½ past four—dress for dinner at five—read Galignani and hear Effie play till 7, tea—round of toast and butter—then read history or do any bit of easy work I have in hand if I feel all right; if tired—not, till 10; in bed always by eleven. I generally can work in the evening—giving me about 5 to six hours of good work each day: I had two before breakfast also when I first came—but found it too much. So you see why I write that I must be cautious—and that I want as much time here as possible. I think the climate to *me*—thoroughly healthy— It is near post time dearest love to my mother.

Ever my dearest Father
Your most aff^e. Son.
J Ruskin.

How Newton could be so ridiculous as to expect me to go to Greece after him I cannot imagine. You need not be afraid of my going on shipboard —I will promise you whatever you like—on that head.[20]

LETTER 139

9th February [1852]

My dearest Father,

I forgot to add to my yesterday's letter that my muscular strength was as great as ever. When my *writing* as well as drawing is to be done in the churches, as generally in describing these tombs, I go out to my work at 11 o'clock—and it is seldom that I am able to sit down while I am at it—often doing my drawings upon steps and my writing leaning on the nearest balustrade—so that I am not unfrequently on my feet for three or four hours, and then rowing—always standing, for an hour and a half more—but I am always surprised in the evening if I feel at all fatigued, and when I do—it is almost always when the work has required great attention which seems to tire body as well as mind.

I have been writing a line to Mr. Fawkes to ask how he is—so I must be short today. Dearest love to my mother.

Ever my dearest Father
Your most aff^e. Son
J Ruskin.

---

20. Ruskin had promised his parents never to travel by water save when it was impossible to do otherwise. This assurance, together with the whole tenor of the letter, is indicative of the firm grip the old couple had upon their son.

Did you get all Murano in good order? I sent *three* little coloured sketches—did they come safe? I might possibly send some more careful ones in the same way.

LETTER 140

10th February [1852]

My dearest Father,

In the enclosed sheet there are as usual—references to things not said and chapters undone—and various features are described as common and well known of which the reader has never heard before. But all will be consecutive when you see it together. When I go to a church and get my ladders into a chapel I am of course obliged to do all the tombs in it at once, though some are of the 13th and others of the 17th century—hence the epithets "well known" &c., mean little more at present than well known to myself. But I think you must have had enough of tombs for the present—I shall send you a little general talk.

February has begun very beautifully—the birds, sparrows, I suppose, chirping in a most spirited manner in the mornings, and though we have still fires—the weather is so mild that one does not much mind whether the windows are open or shut, and Venice is beginning to look something like the Venice I recollect in old times.

Dearest love to my mother.

Ever my dearest Father
Your most affec^e. Son
J Ruskin.

Do you know—you look so bellicose in England that I am quite afraid to come home—for fear I should be shot in "effecting a landing" by some of the gentlemen of the Stock Exchange.

LETTER 141

11th Feb [1852]

My dearest Father,

I had yesterday your nice letter from Cambridge—with enclosed leaves from Art Union [1]— That rascally Mr Hall [2] steals my arrangement of Turner's works out of *Pre-Raphaelitism* and never says where

1. Originally known as *The Art Union,* this monthly magazine changed its name to *The Art Journal* in 1849.

2. Samuel Carter Hall (1800–89), editor of the *Art Journal* from 1839 until his death. Turner's obituary appeared in that magazine in February 1852, pp. 46–7, and though unsigned was most probably written by Hall, for the classification alluded to by Ruskin is also made in the death notice.

he gets it from. I don't know who Edinburgh Dickson [3] is—Effie says a writer to Signet.

You don't read Longfellow with the proper Yankee accents— If you could read his verses with the accent always on the wrong syllables, you would find them very harmonious indeed— Where the Accent is to be is you know—a mere matter of taste—you should consider whom he writes for. I used to think it prettier to say gondóela than Góndola.

I assure you there is no fear of my accusing either you or my mother of taking too much care of me—I always take very good care of myself, and know it to be necessary. I sent you a report in full of my health the other day, but there is one thing I forgot which may be useful as a sign of the change in constitution of *stomach*—if you get a medical opinion. When I first went to Jephson in 1841, he ordered me to take an egg at breakfast—in 1847 he forbid me eggs altogether saying they would "make me bilious"—I find he was quite right—I now never take them without their disordering me.

It is noticeable also that the whisker on my right cheek grows strongly. I have always to cut it—that on the left hardly at all—when the head was oppressed—the veins on the left temple were those which swelled. Vice versa—I see far better and further with the left eye than the right—it has nearly all the work in drawing.

The enclosed—V. 1. begins abruptly—I got into the subject out of an account of the *mosaics* of St. Marks; then saw that all this had better be put separate—and cut it off—introductory sentence wanted.

Dearest love to my mother.

Ever my dearest Father
Your most aff[e]. Son
J Ruskin.

LETTER 142

12th Feb. [1852]

My dearest Father,

Please note that at the * in page V. 3. enclosed the following sentence should come in, which George has missed "and knows foreshortening—and perspective—and optics—and chromatics—and comparative anatomy, we do not think he can possibly be an artist. What is worse, we are very apt to think we can make him an artist by teaching him anatomy, and how to draw with French chalk. Whereas," &c.[1]

It is curious how people misunderstand and misquote authors, for

3. Henry Gordon Dickson, writer to the Signet.
1. This passage, quoted by Ruskin, is closely related to the second chapter of *The Stones of Venice III*. There, in discussing architecture, Ruskin expresses the belief that technical knowledge alone does not suffice to make a man a true artist.

want of quiet reading— How often one hears that line of Pope—"the proper study of mankind is man" used to show that we ought not to study stones and stars. Whereas, if the people had ever read the context they would see (Essay on Man. Epistle II) that Pope opposes the study of *man* to the prying into the *councils of God*—and that so far from intending to cast disparagement on the physical sciences, he adduces them as that which most displays the power of Human intellect—only thirty lines below.

> Superior beings, when of late they saw
> A mortal man *unfold all natures* law
> Admired *such wisdom* in an earthly shape,
> And showed a Newton—as *we* show an Ape.

It is very curious that when an author is misunderstood at all, he is almost always quoted as meaning the *exact* contrary of what he did mean.

Dearest love to my mother.

Ever my dearest Father
Your most aff^e. Son
J Ruskin.

LETTER 143

13th Feb. [1852]

My dearest Father,

I had yesterday your nice letter from unpleasant Leeds, whereat I pitied you very much, and thought it exceedingly wrong that I should be sitting in a luxurious drawingroom with a beautiful fire and two wax candles and a lamp, and an outlook on the Salute by Starlight, while you were "sitting with a penny tallow candle in a bedroom four feet long, at Leeds." These things Ought not so to be: why in the world did you not drive over to Otley and call on Mr Fawkes [1]—and refresh yourself with a look at Mont Cenis?

You say of railroads what I have always believed—and of manufactories also. The fact is that almost every power that mankind gets, in its present state, it will use for evil to itself. It is not so much a question whether a penknife be a good thing—as whether it is a good thing in a child's hand. And until we begin at the right end of things—and consider what is the end of life and how we shall best forward *that*—and understand more than we do at present of that in which real happiness consists, we shall every day get into greater agitation of spirit and suffer greater exhaustion of strength. To go quickly from place to place is no

1. Whose residence, Farnley Hall, was a mile and a half from the village of Otley in Yorkshire.

advantage unless you have first determined that you *ought* to be in a hurry. I have been thinking over these things a good deal. I believe I shall some day—if I live—write a great essay on Man's Work, which will be the work of my life. I don't see anything beyond it.

I am well pleased by Smith's Bill [2]— I feared a much heavier one. I shall certainly however publish no more numbers at present, and perhaps not at all. There still remain—as you will find on enquiry—the two patientest and best men to be paid—Armytage and Lupton— Armytage did two plates—which I suppose will be from 15 to 20 each—and Lupton three—two of which were 40 each. The last is richer—but I should hope 120 would pay the three. I offered to pay Lupton before leaving London —but he knew the book was not selling and was very costly to me and said he would rather wait. I sincerely trust the loss will not be so great as you calculate on—I assure you I don't *intend* to lose a farthing by the book, and if I lose on these three numbers, the public shall not have one more, by the bye have you asked Smith whether the expenses of *printing* the plates are in his account? We are then I hope—clear of all debts— The plates of this third volume may perhaps absorb all its profits—i.e. Smith and Elder will give me nothing for it—but undertake its plates— I am prepared for this—but I will not *lose* a farthing by it—and I hope to gain on a second edition. I have got it all into form. Four parts. 12 chapters in each of the three first—four in the last, but the chapters are some, terribly short—others terribly long. I shall perhaps be able to cut down to 7 chapters each—as I trim the edges, and fit in, giving 25 chapters in all: Of plates, I shall use the best I have—until I have gone as far as Smith and Elder think adviseable—perhaps in future editions adding one here and there if the sale pays it.

I saw here yesterday the only genuine bit of Paul Veronese that ever I have seen for sale—a sketch of a woman with two dogs—life size—50 Napoleons. I name it to you in case you yourself would like to have a bit of the great fellow—and because I never yet saw an unquestionable thing at a price that would even admit of one's thinking of it: Of course it is very slight, and a *mere* sketch—or it would fetch more money—but a grand thing—about a quarter of an hour of the man's handling, altogether—but the suggestion of a complete picture. There is with it a sketch of Tintoret's which once belonged to Rumohr, and which I believe also to be the right thing—but as you know—Tintoret on a *small scale* is never so thoroughly determinable as other men. I am going to look at it again. They both belong to the painter Nerly—Rumohr made him a

2. A bill from George Smith, the publisher, for plates of *The Examples of the Architecture of Venice*. The "three numbers" mentioned below in the same paragraph refer to three of the proposed twelve numbers of *The Examples*. The "plates of the third volume," however, refer to those for *The Stones of Venice, III* as, indeed, does the rest of the paragraph. It is evident that Ruskin senior had been grumbling a little about the cost of publishing his son's work.

present of the Tintoret— I believe he would take 80 Napoleons for both
—but I should not much like to beat him down as he lost all his money
with that bank of Holmes's, which failed two years ago, and I particularly wish you to understand that there is no fear of my taking to buy old
pictures—nor do I care about these—but I never saw a bit of good and
untouched work for sale before and so thought I might as well name
them to you. The Tintoret is a sketch for a picture in Ducal palace—the
Doge Grimani [3] kneeling before Christ.

    Dearest love to my mother.

Ever my dearest Father
Your most aff^e. Son
J Ruskin.

LETTER 144

14th Feb. [1852]

My dearest Father,

    I am glad you enjoyed what I was able to tell you about the ball—
Marshal Radetzky's— I was sure you would be pleased by the unison of
rationality and hospitality in it. You will also be glad to hear that he sent
us two verbal messages by two of his officers—to say how sorry he was
that we had not come to the ball last Monday and that he hoped we
would at any rate come on the last, the 23rd—this I think we cannot but
do. It is, as you say, a fine sight—the assemblage of noble soldiery—and
the more because all are evidently enjoying themselves and mean to be
kind to each other. At an English ball—I don't know if the people really
enjoy themselves or not, but they all look excessively miserable, here
they dance with spirit—and talk with ease.

    I overslept myself this morning, so must be short—by the bye you
speak of the "deliberately written" look of my Verona letter. In general
my letters are written *before* work, and therefore rather scrawled; that
was late at night, at least, after nine. General Reischach gave us his box
at the Opera. I took Effie there at 7 o'clock, not having been in a theatre
before, this winter. I soon tired of it however—came away a little before
nine and walked home round the Coliseum and the Scala Tombs—sat
down in my room—wrote your letter, and went to bed.

    Dearest love to my mother.

Ever my dearest Father
Your most aff^e. Son
J Ruskin.

3. Ruskin means the Doge Alvise Mocenigo.

LETTER 145

[15 February 1852]

My dearest Father,

Last Sunday I sent you an analysis of the mischief which I had done myself up to my 33rd birthday.[1] I think that ought to be followed by some statement of the advantages I have gained by so much over labour, which certainly cannot be represented by the four volumes [2] which are their present visible result.

When I look back to any of my former work, I am always dissatisfied and feel as if I had utterly lost my time. Thus, as I said to you a few letters ago—the sketches I made when here with you, in May, 1846, are now so worthless in my eyes that I would give them all for a single walk with you in the piazzetta. And so of nearly all that I have ever done.

But I forget when I feel in this way, and long for the time to come over again, that those sketches are *not* the result. The dissatisfaction with them is the result. It was necessary I should do them, before I could despise them. If I had not done them then, I should be doing the same kind of things now.

It is therefore the knowledge that I have gained to which I ought to look as the true result of these years' labour: and I am only apt to be discontented because I forget—in the feeling how little I know now, how much less I knew in 1842.

When I wrote the first volume of *Modern Painters* [3] I only understood about *one third* of my subject: and one third, especially of the merits of Turner. I divided my admiration with Stanfield [4]—Harding and Fielding. I knew *nothing* of the great Venetian colourists—nothing of the old religious painters—admired only, in my heart, Rubens, Rembrandt, and Turner's gaudiest effects: my admiration being rendered however right as far as it went—by my intense love of nature.

In 1843, I studied under Harding [5]—Studies now nearly forgotten, but useful in teaching me a little how to lay on colour, in 1844 I made some coloured studies of rocks which are still useful to me. But in 1845 came a total change: I had luckily tried to draw some of Raphael's fig-

1. Letter 138.
2. *Modern Painters I* and *II, The Seven Lamps of Architecture,* and *The Stones of Venice I.*
3. Which appeared in May 1843.
4. William Clarkson Stanfield (1794–1867), marine painter, with whose work Ruskin was familiar at an early age. Ruskin discusses Stanfield's work in *Modern Painters I* (*Works, 3,* 226 ff.).
5. Ruskin's memory is at fault here. In *Praeterita* (*Works, 35,* 308) we are informed that he took lessons from Harding in 1841. In *Letters to a College Friend* (*Works, 1,* 425) it is clear from what Ruskin says that he was taking lessons from Harding in 1840. The latter date is probably correct, for the letter was written immediately following the lessons.

ures and landscape, and read Rio [6] on the old religious painters: and
bought Turner's Liber Studiorum. I went into Italy with a new perception of the meaning of the words drawing and chiaroscuro. My first attempts with my new perception were those of the stone pines at Sestri [7]
now in your bedroom—the brown avenue [8] behind the door in the study
—the little wild one you liked so much that used to be in the anteroom
of the breakfast room—and my mother's study of trees at Isola Madre—
the mountain ones in the study, Conflans, &c.: and many others—all indeed that are framed about the house except St Michel [9] were done in
1845. They cost me great labour—but from that time—I understood
the meaning of the words "light and shade" and have never since had
any occasion to alter my views respecting them.

This course of study altered all my views about Turner's early works
—formerly despised. The value I have assigned to the Yorkshire drawings and the price I made you pay Lupton for his proofs—were all the
consequence of this year's work.

But meantime—I began to study the religious painters. Till 1845 I
had never seen an Angelico—did not know what a Giotto was like— In
about four months, I explored a whole half world of painting in Florence
—and was able to write second volume of *Modern Painters* when I came
home.

But farther. When I went to Venice with Harding,[10] I was introduced
for the first time to the Venetian colourists. The overwork mentioned in
my former letter was in studying Tintoret and architecture at once. But
I got an entirely new perception of the meaning of the word *colour:*
which altered all my views respecting Turner's *latest* drawings, as my
spring work of that year had altered them respecting his earliest: I came
home—to find that his last works were his greatest, and that he would
never do any more—for his mind failed in 1845.

Now observe—I say all my views were altered—altered that is—into
higher admiration—instead of as the public thought—into less. And they
were altered with respect to two thirds of his works—I having—as I
said above—understood only *one third* of my subject. Of his middle
drawings—I think what I always did— His early drawings I once despised, but last year you know I gave Lady Barnes [11] 100 for two in-

6. A.-F. Rio's *De la Poésie Chrétienne dans son principe, dans sa matière et dans ses
formes* (Paris, 1836).

7. See *Works, 4*, Plate XII, for a reproduction of this drawing.

8. Perhaps *Study of Trees at Sens*, reproduced in *Works, 35*, Plate XXXII. This study
is mentioned in *Works, 36*, 131 n. 4, where attention is drawn to the date 1846 rather
than 1845.

9. This may be *S. Michele: From the Monastery between Turin and Mt. Cenis*, a
water color briefly noted in *Works, 38*, 280. See also *Works, 35*, 637 and n.

10. In 1845.

11. Most probably Georgiana Catherine, daughter of the 7th Earl of Coventry, who in

jured ones, which I would not part with for 200 each. His late drawings I at first thought slovenly—now you see them named in my catalogue [12] as above *all* price.

This change, or advance, rather than change, in all my views was like being thrown into a great sea to me. I wrote 2nd volume of *Modern Painters* in the first astonishment of it. I then perceived a thousand things that I wanted to know before I could write any more and 1846 and 7 were passed in floundering about, and getting my new self *together*.

If in 1848, I had got abroad to Switzerland, the fruits of these years' work would have been seen sooner. But being driven into Normandy, my attention was turned in a new direction—and the *Seven Lamps* and *Stones of Venice* were the result.

The materials collected in 1849, in Switzerland, are of immense value to me—the fruit of 1846–7—and—9 is all, I hope, yet to come in second [13] volume of *Modern Painters*. The architectural works have been merely bye play—this *Stones of Venice* being a much more serious one than I anticipated.

So that my time has not really been lost, though I often feel as if it had been. But it is one somewhat unpleasant result of my work, that I have got to feel totally differently from the public on all subjects connected with art, and that the effect of what I believe to be my superior wisdom, is that nobody will attend to me. When I wrote about Stanfield and Harding, there was a large audience ready to hear what I had got to say, and confirm it: But now that I don't care for either of them and write about Millais [14]—nobody attends to me— And I see that this is very natural. It has cost me 7 years' labour to be able to enjoy Millais thoroughly. I am just those seven years' labour farther in advance of the mob than I was, and my voice cannot be heard back to them. And so in all things now—I see a hand they cannot see; and they cannot be expected to believe or follow me: And the more justly I judge, the less I shall be attended to.

It is a most heavenly day, and I am going out for a long walk.

Dearest love to my mother.

> Ever my dearest Father
> Your most affe. Son
> J Ruskin.

1807 married M. William Barnes of Reigate, Surrey. She died in 1858 at the age of 72.

12. In Letter 123.
13. Ruskin makes a slip here. *Modern Painters II* had appeared in 1846.
14. References to Millais's painting are frequent in Ruskin's work.

LETTER 146

16th Feb. [1852]

My dearest Father,

I have had to do the enclosed bit over again, so it does not matter if it is spoiled in coming, if it seems pretty clear when you get it, I may send the proper measurement of it to Boys and let him correct and begin upon it by way of experiment as to his power of doing delicate things. But would you be so kind as to ask Smith and Elder what is the expence of engraving as much text as would go at the bottom of the vignette page? I have several little vignettes which would look small on a whole page— and would be spoiled by being put in couples— They would look well at heads of chapters. I suppose it is only on the side of the page which has the plate that the text must be engraved, not on the reverse side also.

Yesterday afternoon the Riva di Schiavoni—before Danieli's and as far as the Arsenal was a wonderful sight—as thickly charged with people as the alleys of our Camberwell fair: It was a heavenly day, and every soul I suppose in Venice—whose body could walk, under a certain rank —(for there were few respectable people) had come out to sun itself in St Mark's place or on the Riva: It was the last Sunday but one of the Carnival, and there were a couple of troops of from 30 to 40 masquers, besides a long nose or two here and there in the crowd—but it was very tragical mirth—the crowd seemed sulky and against the masquers, and hustled them, and it was very woful—except only the sight of the long quay black with its multitudes. My Sunday walk is backwards and forwards on the low quay opposite Murano, looking over to the Alps. There is never anybody there and the sea air is fresh and pure, and free from cigar smoke, which on Sundays, it is nowhere else in Venice.

I wish there were some more definite means of ascertaining from the Bible how far the passages written of the Jewish sabbath are applicable to the Christian one. It must always be a difficult thing to press upon a man educated with opposite feelings.

Dearest love to my mother.

Ever my dearest Father
Your most aff^e. Son
J Ruskin.

LETTER 147

17th Feb. [1852]

My dearest Father,

This has indeed been a strangely unfortunate journey as far as home news are concerned—and I am beginning to wish I were out of Venice;

I shall I hope have done all that I want in about ten weeks more, and then we will come straight home—at all events I will settle myself quietly for the present to my work here, and we will talk more about tour, &c., in a month: As the first thing to enable me to work quietly I must beg you to get me out of the executorship; as the thing now stands, it would be mere madness in me to act and besides I should get no good by it: I see in Galignani that "the executors" hope to exhibit his pictures this season. I think one of them might have done me the honour to communicate their intentions to me before advertising them—I will have nothing to do with the matter. I am sorry I was out of England this year—as I might have had the rummage in his house [1] with Monro—but now that is over, I have no motive to remain executor. I shall think therefore as little as I can of the matter, even if sales come on, I shall not trouble myself, but trust to you to get me as many mountains as you can. It is tantalizing, too—this of Colnaghi's getting those proofs from Charles Turner [2]— The old lying rascal C. Turner, I mean told me he had not got one—only a book of etchings which "was bequeathed to his daughter" and now of course Colnaghi's customers have had the pick of them and what they don't take he makes a favour of keeping for me, but I must beg of you to secure all that are left—there will be things among them worth any thing to me—what I don't want I can always change—but I cannot give any particular directions, as I know nothing of the collection —only whatever the old scamp kept was sure to be worth keeping.

I am very glad you got the little Prout at Hewitt's and were able to show it him. Strange, in my dressing room, I have on the opposite sides—ever since I came here—six plates from Turner and three of Prout; all now by dead men. I carried nobody else with me on this journey except some Albert Durer, which Effie has mixed with Prout and Turner in the bedroom—as Durer is dead already it does not signify.

Apoplexy! [3]—hardly the kind of man one would have expected to go that way— Poor little fellow—it will be long ere England sees the like of him again—little as she thought of him compared with her R.A.'s and Sir this and thats.

Quaker very characteristic. I think it needs an answer, so enclose one. I enclose also, what I suppose is called a bill of lading of some property of mine on board the Mary Stewart. There are two boxes: which *ought* to contain 21 pieces of plaster. All that I am afraid of is that they will contain a great many more by the time they arrive: please tell McCracken if they are much broken, to take care to lose none of the *crumbs,* but send me all home. They could not receive anything which required more

1. For John James Ruskin's account of this "rummage" through Turner's house see *Works, 13,* xxvi–xxvii.
2. Charles Turner (1774–1857), no relation to the painter for whom he executed many engravings.
3. Prout died of apoplexy on February 8, 1852.

care in the unpacking. I believe the Mary Stewart is off—I saw her pluming her wings yesterday, and see nothing of her today. Dearest love to my mother.

Ever my dearest Father

Your most affec. Son

J Ruskin.

I have another bill of lading—should I send it? You can kindly put an envelope to enclosed scrap. John Copper. Upper Clapton.

LETTER 148

[18 February 1852]

My dearest Father,

I had yesterday your kind letter saying what you had done with Colnaghi. I am very much obliged to you indeed, as this way you have secured all that I *most* wanted—and my letter of yesterday did not, when it said secure all, contemplate anything beyond Liber Studiorum. I don't want any touched plates of engravings—large or small: when I see one that interests me particularly, as was the case with Lupton's set of black marines, I of course would make an effort to get it—but the touched proofs of common prints are endless, and I cannot indulge myself in them. The Liber Studiorum are very different—they are literally Turner's *own studies:* and I would always buy an impression which showed so much as a change in the roll of a cloud: You would see how many apparent duplicates of these I have already. If therefore Colnaghi have still any more touched proofs of any of the Liber Studiorum—or of the brown plates unpublished in it, pray get them all, but not any touched engravings. I wonder whether, among those you have got, there were the plates either of Scylla, or Sheepwashing at Windsor; [1] or the etchings of the Devil's Bridge (St Gothard) [2]—or of those two other outline subjects lent me by Mr ———— I forget his name, which I had at Malvern with me? I want those especially. In fact I have only *two etchings* and want all, if I could get them—but the mountain subjects especially.

I am sorry you are not at all interested in my antiquarianism—but I believe you will like the book better when you see it finished—at all events, it would be foolish to abandon the labour of two whole years, now that it is just approaching completion. [3] I cannot write anything but

1. A Turner drawing originally intended for the *Liber Studiorum*. Part of it is reproduced in *Works, 15,* Fig. 20, and discussed in the same volume on pp. 94–6.

2. Either *Swiss Bridge, Mount St. Gothard,* reproduced in *Works, 20,* as Plate B, or *The Old Devil's Bridge, Pass of St. Gothard,* reproduced in *Works, 13,* as Plate XIX.

3. From the drift of this sentence it seems not unlikely that Ruskin's father entertained some doubts about the popularity of the forthcoming volumes of *The Stones of Venice.*

what is *in* me and interests me. I never could write for the public—I never *have* written except under the conviction of a thing's being important, wholly irrespective of the public's thinking so too—and all my power, such as it is, would be lost the moment I tried to catch people by fine writing. You know I promised them no Romance—I promised them Stones. Not even bread. I do not *feel* any Romance in Venice. It is simply a heap of ruins, trodden under foot by such men as Ezekiel describes 21, 31 :[4] and *this* is the great fact which I want to teach : To give Turneresque descriptions of the thing would not have needed ten days' study—or residence. I believe that what I have done will be found useful —at last. You say Fergusson [5] and others can give details. Yes—but they can't put the details together, besides—they are not here to do it. If Fergusson and Cockerell [6] were both at work on Venice, I should not be, but the one works in India—the other in Greece. No one is inclined to work here, but I.

I think however you will find that the antiquarianism interests a good many more people than the construction—at all events, this volume will have the antiquarians *added* to the readers of the other. I fancy we have at present in England, more Oldbucks than architects—and that A.D.I.L. will still have its charms for them : But at all events, I must work out my purpose now it is gone so far.

Emma's sketch is *admirable*. The *architecture* rather too much of the Renaissance for me.

I don't know what to say about the Isaacs house— What is the rent, and what the state—furnished or not ? I wish we could get some place to put our heads in this next winter—because you may be running abroad *next* year if not this—and then Effie and I may be on a long tour in England in search of Turners. But I suppose it is impossible to get any place on Denmark Hill for a year, from beginning of June, 1852 ?

Dearest love to my mother.

Ever my dearest Father
Your most aff^e. Son
J Ruskin.

4. I.e. Ezekiel xxi.31.

5. James Fergusson (1808–86), an architectural writer who also started an indigo factory in India. He published many works, one of the most important being *Picturesque Illustrations of Ancient Architecture in Hindustan* (London, 1847).

6. Charles Robert Cockerell (1788–1863), R.A., was a professor of architecture from 1840 until 1857. Having studied in Greece in his earlier years, he maintained close contact with that country all his life. His publications were numerous and concerned both Grecian and British architecture.

LETTER 149

19th Feb [1852]

My dearest Father,

The Austrian officers gave their last carnival ball last night and as there were to be masquers and much festivity, I thought Effie might as well see it—so I took her there at nine—and left her—staying till ten myself to see what was going on. Although they are much earlier here than in London, there was however no masquing before I came away, but I saw something, worth going for, in the toilette of the grand duchess Constantine: Of course as the Russians have done so much for the Austrians lately, the Russian grand duke and duchess are infinitely feted —and as there is no person here at present superior to them in rank, the Austrians, whose guests they are—make them the centre of a kind of court, and invest them with a sort of vice imperial dignity. So the grand duchess who does not dance—is taken up to the top of the room—and set in a kind of throne chair—with her ladies behind her—and the circle of officers in front exactly as if she were our queen—or their empress. She is not exactly pretty—but very delicate and interesting—a face between Marie Antoinette and our Sir Peter Lely beauties—pale by day —but very brightly and sweetly flushed at night, her hair was dressed in the French way—in the small close clustered curls projecting out the side, like la belle Gabrielle—and the rest of her dress very rich and delicate at once—lace over rose brocade—with a row of six or seven emeralds clasping the dress from the neck to the waist—each about the length of a small walnut. Madame Palavicini was standing behind her, leaning forward to talk to her—and she—though anything but pretty, is exceedingly sweet and refined in feature and expression—dressed in white, all— with a crown of white roses: You never saw anything so courtly or pretty as the group of the two together. In our society, a duchess is generally a fat old woman, worse dressed than anybody else and highly painted—and with a whole jewellers shop of diamonds shaken over her till she looks like a chandelier, but here there was youth and refinement, and considerable beauty: and though there were at least £20,000, of stones on the front of that dress, they were not put so as to catch the eye.

Effie enjoyed herself very much, and came home at ½ past one which I thought very moderate.

Dearest love to my mother.

> Ever my dearest Father.
> Your most aff^e. Son
> J Ruskin.

LETTER 150

20th Feb. [1852]

My dearest Father,

I am getting quite into the world again—I took Effie to the opera last night as they said there would be a good many masques there. There were none however—or only three in a side box—but St Mark's place was worth seeing both before and after we went; it was lighted up with large temporary circlets of gas, and full of masques—some showing a good deal of spirit, and all making a very sufficient quantity of noise, which however mixed itself altogether into a great murmur, not harsh nor discordant—but soothing—lost amidst the great walls and wide sea air.

The opera was intensely disagreeable—bad singing—bad dancing and plot at once tragic and absurd. It is difficult to express the degree of degradation into which the operatic amusement is sinking the European mind— First you have every possible means of excitement—music— passion—acting of the coarsest and most violent kind—glaring scenery —everything that can excite in the highest degree—then, the people, who are rich and idle—take this excitement every night—till it ceases to be an excitement any [more?]. But they still go, because it is fashionable— and—not caring to look or to listen—open their boxes as drawingrooms —and receive their company in the theatre instead of at home. No conversation except of the lightest kind is possible in such a place of course —but every body talks—and nobody listens— Thus the tone of all conversation is rendered habitually frivolous—the *ear* loses its refinement from talking in the midst of an orchestra—the actors—unable to draw attention by just or quiet play—seek for it by rant—and only obtain it—momentarily—by shrieking or performing miracles of pirouettes—so the entire school of dramatic writing, music—and dancing, is degraded lower and lower—and—one evil reacting on another, the final result of the general corruption is still unseen—and to come.

Dearest love to my mother.

Ever my dearest Father
Your most aff^e. Son
J Ruskin.

LETTER 151

21st Feb. [1852]

My dearest Father,

I had yesterday your *two* kind letters of the 13 and 14th together, a most pleasant dispatch—every way—chiefly as relieving me from a feel-

ing which, do what I would—your last letter had left upon me of somewhat painful discouragement, and as conveying also Dr Grant's opinion
that there was nothing wrong with me.

I could not help feeling discouraged a little by your former letter—for
in the course of a long work like that which I am about, mere enthusiasm
will not last—a great deal of it has to be done by dogged insistance—
getting over the ground as one does the steep or dull parts of a long
day's walk. And in this kind of labour one hardly knows what one is
doing—whether it be well or ill—and there are times when one feels
tired and doubtful even of progress at all—times when one is especially
liable to be depressed by finding that what—from its constant weight
upon you—is losing some of its interest with yourself, has as little for
others: There is a fine paper, or passage, in one of Johnson's prefaces [1]
or conclusions—expressing this kind of languor in the course of a long
work, and the way one has to fight through it, so that I was much relieved by your yesterday's letter. I allowed, in the case of the first, for
all the despondency caused by poor Prout's death, and I must allow—in
this last—for your kind desire to obliterate the impression of the other—
but still I was depressed by the first—and am refreshed by the last, and
both to a degree which, if you could know it, would give you some pleasure as showing my respect for your opinion. Yet you must not think I am
flagging in my labour. I am—as far as it is possible to be in its present
stage satisfied with it myself—and have good hope of its being popular
too— I begin to see my way now to its concentration, and I hope that
now the long days are coming, I shall get some pieces of colour—description which will give you pleasure. But I cannot promise. If I was to say,
I will write this or that—in such and such a way—I should be instantly
cramped and incapable of writing. I have indeed some bits of the kind
done—but I don't like to send you them till they are in their places, and
properly finished, every word of them, and as I said in a former letter,
I cannot finish here with patience.

Your letters were also very delightful as assuring me of the acquisition
of 15 etchings which was more than I had any hope of—but you must
have been aghast when my letter came telling you to secure all—for I had
not thought of black prints—nor of the possible quantity of Libers. Of
black prints or engravings I want none—no Rogers [2] nor anything. I
would not give sixpence for any line engraving ever published, except for
reference: I must complete my collection for this purpose, and I left a
general order with Halstead [3] to get me cheap impressions of such plates
as I had not—and to pick up any curious ones with touches or alterations
if he could get them cheap—but this need not trouble you at all. If Scott

1. To the *Dictionary of the English Language.*
2. Turner's drawings for Samuel Rogers' *Italy.*
3. A Bond Street engraver patronized by Ruskin.

says there are any among the black plates thoroughly interesting and
with a good deal of Turner's work upon them, and not about 40/– or
50/– in price, I would take them perhaps at another time—but not now
—the thing is to get as many Liber as possible. Read first below line on
opposite page. First then; I see Scott says he is to give you a list of
proofs which he thinks I should like. I shall be glad to see this—but
can tell you thus far at once, that if he has any of the following plates,[4]

> Source of Arveron.
> Mer de Glace.
> Grand Chartreuse.
> Devil's Bridge.
> Aesacus and Hesperie.

never mind Rizpah.

One more, I forgot—a woodland scene with a wooden bridge—and a
castle on the right [5]—this kind of thing.

Of the other plates I am satisfied with the impressions I have and therefore would not at present buy anything but etchings or touched proofs.

The etchings I want, of all—one impression of course enough—you
have got 15. I had two before. Any others to be had I should be glad
of, at any price, though they are rather dear at 50/–.

I forget what plates Charles Turner engraved—and therefore cannot
say what his touched proofs are likely to be, but I know he had the
Devil's Bridge—and if you could get all the touched proofs he has of
that plate—it would be a great thing. It is always better to have the
entire series of touched proofs of one plate, than a broken one of two or
three.

I have just looked over the plates I had here—and I see that Charles
Turner engraved four which I want—i.e.

4. All the plates and drawings mentioned in this letter are from Turner's *Liber
Studiorum*. For a guide to Ruskin's references to specific plates see *Works, 39*, 636–8.
For reproductions of the various plates see *The Liber Studiorum of J. M. W. Turner*,
ed. Rev. Stopford Brooke, 3 vols. (London, 1882).

5. The drawing described and reproduced here is *Raglan Castle*.

Devil's Bridge—above named. ⎫ pray try and get all
Mont St Gothard.   ⎪ the touched proofs of
Lake of Thun.   ⎬ these plates, and never
Holy Island Cathedral.   ⎭ mind anything of mere

proofs at present, unless Charles Turner won't part with his proofs except in the mass—and then you can get what Colnaghi has of the six named on last page. I am confusing myself and you—it is embarras des richesses: Here is a clearer statement—below the line.

Please get at any reasonable price—

1. All etchings of Liber Studiorum, which I have not.

2. Charles Turner's touched proofs of
     Devil's Bridge.
     Mont St Gothard.
     Holy Island.
     Lake of Thun.

3. Any unpublished etchings or plates in his possession—the etchings being by Turner's own hand—the plates small mezzotint, like Liber Studiorum.

After these are secured, I am afraid we must not go much farther. But the best things to get are the touched proofs—always the entire series of single plates. You can look over Charles Turner's collection perhaps, and see any plates you would like the subjects of.

In case Charles Turner sells his entire collection elsewhere, deal with Scott as on last page.

Dearest love to my mother.

Ever my dearest Father. Your most aff^e. Son

J Ruskin

My head is so full of Turner, I have not spoken of Richmond's letter. What drawing was it of mine that poor Prout was looking at that last evening?

LETTER 152

22nd Feb. [1852]

My dearest Father,

I paid—yesterday—one of what are now the rarest of my payments—a morning call: Mme Esterhazy having invited me again and again to see her. I went yesterday with Effie for the first time—Marmont came in while we were sitting with her, and crossexamined me not unintelligently respecting the chief styles of the architecture I was examining at Venice:

the Countess's house is the prettiest thing I ever saw on a small scale—
only wanting some Turner pictures to complete its perfection. It is a
corner house with side windows looking up and down the grand canal—
every window having its balcony, be it long or short, roofed in, and
hung with silk, and filled with flowers; not inconveniently—as—begging
my mother's pardon—that corner in our anteroom is sometimes filled—
especially when I want to look at my Isola Madre drawing [1]—but a pot
here—and a pot there—not pots exactly—but nondescript vases of graceful forms, of glass, overrun with leaves—the one that struck me most was
in the form of a large star or flower—and of coral-red colour—hung from
the ceiling—with a fresh *green* climbing plant straggling over it—it
looked as if it were at once the support and the blossom— I found it was
only of common *smooth* earth painted a delicate red, but its effect was
exquisite. Then the inner rooms are an exact and most skilfully compounded harmony of French fancy and English comfort—the pretty
silken and golden and enamelled luxury of Paris, with a grave tone of
English quiet through it all—effected I believe—first by everything
being good and well furnished—fit for use—and not overcrowded—
secondly by a good deal of dark colouring in the decorative painting, one
room being painted with a deep bronze or mahogany colour, and the
lights touched upon it in silver-white so skilfully as to delight me merely
as a piece of artistical painting—the man who did it could have become
a real painter if he had liked, the handling just like Etty's.[2] The rooms
are very small—one as long or a little longer than our drawing room—
but much narrower—the rest like our library—so that they can be richly
furnished without making them look like an upholsterer's store, and if
their pictures had been good, they would have been perfect: for these,
however little could be said—except that their frames were pretty—and
their portrait-subjects interesting. One or two tables covered with trin-
kets, but these very precious and full of interest, and in the midst of all
this refinement a couple of courtly dogs, and a parrot. I have said nothing of the view, which is of the canal—and down the canal—from the
Pewterers, or Ca Foscari, to the Tallowchandlers—or Ducal Palace.

I have been resting a little during this carnival time—after—as I
wrote you some letters back, getting my work into its final form—subject only now to contraction—not to expansion. The reason that I have
added the fourth part [3] to it is chiefly because I see a very interesting
connection [4] between it and *Modern Painters:* The first part of this book
will give an account of the effect of Christianity in colouring and spir-

1. A Ruskin water color executed in 1845.
2. William Etty (1787–1849), who was elected R.A. in 1828. He specialized in the
female figure and is remembered for subjects of a voluptuous character.
3. Which, in the final arrangement, became *The Stones of Venice III.*
4. For amplification of this "connection" see *Works, 10, 207* n.

itualizing Roman or Heathen architecture. The second and third parts [5] will give an account of the Transition to Gothic, with a definition of the nature and essence of the Gothic style. The fourth part of the decline of all this back into Heathenism: and of the reactionary symptoms attending the course of the relapse of which the strongest has been the development of landscape painting: For as long as the Gothic and other fine architectures existed, the love of Nature, which was an essential and peculiar feature of Christianity, found expression and food enough in them; vide 7 *Lamps,* p. 182, to bottom. *Stones,* Vol. I, p. 42, § xiii. xiv— the whole of Chapter 20, and p. 343. § VI., but when the Heathen architecture came back, this love of nature, still happily existing in some minds, could find no more food there—it turned to landscape painting and has worked gradually up into Turner. The last part of this book therefore will be an introduction to the last of *Modern Painters.*

The chapters on the Nature of Gothic, Part III. Chap I. and on the effect of too much knowledge upon art in the Renaissance period—Part IV. Chap III. will I think turn out very interesting but I cannot send you any of them till quite done, and they will not be finished here, where I am obliged to do all the technical parts. I have had great difficulty in defining Gothic, the fact being that to define an architectural style is like defining a language—you have pure Latin—and impure latin in every form and stage—till it becomes Italian and not Latin at all— One can say Cicero writes Latin and Dante Italian. I can say that Giotto built Gothic and Michael Angelo Classic—but between the two there are all manner of shades—so that one cannot say, here one ends and the other begins. I shall show that the greatest distinctive character of Gothic is in the workman's heart and mind—but its outward distinctive test is the *trefoiled* arch,   *not* the mere point.   Gothic is pure

or impure according to the prominence and severity of this arch. If people say, can we build Gothic by covering our buildings with trefoils, I answer, no—any more than a child can write Latin by copying words at random out of Cicero, but the words he copies are nevertheless, the tests of a pure style. I have worked gradually up to this conclusion from the time I wrote the note "10. p. 87" at page 203 of *Seven Lamps,* and I shall show that this Distinctive test of Gothic architecture is so by a mysterious ordainment, being first a type of the Trinity in unity, Secondly of all the beauty of Vegetation upon the earth—which was what man was intended to express his love of, even when he built in stone—lastly because it is the perfect expression of the strongest possible way of building an arch—

5. These parts, together, became the second or Gothic Period of *The Stones of Venice II.*

which I, I believe, was the first to show, in the *Stones,* Vol. I. page 129. §
IV. V. VI. VII. (misprinted VIII). I think now you have the general idea
of what the book is to be, you will be more ready to pardon its details.

Dearest love to my mother.

Ever my dearest Father.

Your most aff^e. Son

J Ruskin.

I beg your pardon for any bad writing. I have not time to go back today
and mend it.

LETTER 153

Feb. 23rd [1852]

My dearest Father,

We are just starting for Verona, but I forgot to say that if you thought
it worthwhile—it might be as well to effect insurance to the value of
£20 on the two cases sent by Mary Stewart. They contain about 10
pounds' worth each.

I hope my Saturday's letter [1] will not miss fire—as it contained some
clear notes about Liber Studiorum—in case it should not come right—
here is the thing better digested still.[2]

1. Don't buy any plates whatever—touched or untouched—except
   Liber Studiorum and the brown unpublished mezzotint plates connected with it.

2. Please—get one impression of every etching that comes into the
   market, of Liber Studiorum or such other unpublished plates.

3. Please get if possible, all touched proofs in Charles Turner's possession of the four plates following:

> Mont St Gothard.
> Devil's Bridge.
> Lake of Thun.
> Holy Isle Cathedral.

In case he should have, or at any other time there should come into
the market, *touched proofs* of the following Turner plates please get them
all if possible—but especially the first:

> Grande Chartreuse.
> Blair Athol.
> Alps near Chambery.
> Bonneville, Savoy.
> Hindhead Hill.

1. Letter 151.
2. All drawings mentioned in this letter are from the *Liber Studiorum.*

Jason.
Cephalus and Procris.

There cannot be *touched* proofs of the plates which Turner himself engraved, but there may be some *experiments* upon them. I should think however these must have been destroyed. If however any proofs before letters turn up of the three:

Source of Arveron.
Mer de Glace.
Castle Bridge—sketched in my last letter.[3]

there may be experiments in them, and I should be thankful to have them. These are all I want. Dearest love to my mother.

Ever my dearest Father. Your most affec[e]. Son
J Ruskin.

LETTER 154

Verona. 23rd Feb. [1852]

My dearest Father,

I have just come back from the ball—and sit down in order to have this ready to slip into post office in morning, for I want to have all the morning light for a drawing I am at work upon. I have nothing to tell you of this ball more than of the others—it being managed exactly in the same way—except that the marshal [1] looked if possible even younger than he did a month ago—and by the bye there was a point in the teamaking, noticeable for mama—perhaps however one illustrative only of what you have so often complained of, the want of good cream in Italy: The teacups, as I think I told you, were very large—allowing for people's being thirsty—and at one end of the table there were jugs of cream as with us, but at the other, there was a *bowl* of cream, half a yard wide, beaten into a foam like snow—which was lifted with a silver ladle and a ladleful put into each cup of tea that came from that quarter of the Austrian dominions. It looked most tempting and pretty; but I thought the common cream, with which I began, tasted better. I always fancy it spoils cream to whip it—perhaps it was only done here that it might be more quickly handed—it was a far easier operation to fill the top of the cup with a foam-ball, than to pour the cream out of the jug, or it might be that the cream would not be got good enough or in quantity enough even by the Marshal—and his cook had beaten up some eggs with it.

We go back tomorrow for the last day of Carnival at Venice, which will be brilliant, they say: but I must have a couple of days or so here

3. Not his "last letter" but the one dated February 21.
1. Radetzky.

in coming home—and shall probably then see the marshal again. I will
not sit up later tonight, as every hour of daylight is precious in this
heavenly place. Dearest love to my mother.

Ever my dearest Father
Your most affe. Son
J Ruskin.

LETTER 155

Venice. 24ᵗʰ Feb. [1852]

My dearest Father,

I had today your kind and interesting letter of the 16ᵗʰ saying that you
had enjoyed the discussion on religious painting, and giving me long
accounts of various Turners. Touching the first, I hope there will be a
great deal in the book *at least* as interesting, but you can see at once that
it was not to write that kind of thing that I came here the second time,
or am staying here now. All that general discussion I can do near you—
and I grudge every moment unnecessarily spent here : When therefore I
come to a point where such an inquiry opens, I merely make notes of what
is to be said, and go on to the technical parts—on which the rest are
founded, and in which if a single link of evidence be wanting—I cannot
supply it, except on the spot. But I will send you a bill of fare of the whole
book, some day soon, when I have some paper to spare, and then you
will see what a wide range it takes, of which however my Sunday's letter [1]
gave you a sketch. I am very glad however you enjoyed the little bit of
discussion into which I was tempted—but I miscalculated your taste a
little in sending you so many tombstones.[2] I thought you had a great
liking for the kind of melancholy with which these objects affect one—I
don't mean common churchyards—but ancient tombs like those in question— At least I hope you will like a drawing [3] I am making, (more satisfactory than usual to myself) of that one at Verona—my most beloved
—at St Anastasia. I think you will see a considerable advance in my
drawing this year, though I have not drawn so much as usual.

Next about Turners : do not on any account annoy yourself about any,
go they cheap—or dear, except those named in my catalogue. Early
drawings of Girtin time I care nothing for—the one I bought from
Cheney, I bought on account of the pig in it, which I saw to be the original
of one in Liber Studiorum ; [4] but I don't want any more of the time : I
am sadly afraid that you need never be concerned at any drawings going

1. Letter 152.
2. A motif prominent in some of Ruskin's January and February letters to his father.
3. This may be *The Castelbarco Tomb* reproduced as Plate D in *Works*, Vol. 9.
4. Probably a first study for Turner's *Farmyard and Cock*. It is reproduced in Stopford Brooke's edition of the *Liber Studiorum*, Vol. 2, Plate XIII.

cheap; for I believe none that I want, ever will—unless those sketches in bundles—which it makes my mouth water to hear of— You know what sketches I want—and I leave it entirely to you to adopt any way of getting at them you think most adviseable. Of the other drawings that I named in my catalogue none are likely to come into the market at present —unless now and then a Yorkshire. I know Lupton's drawings very well—he promised to let me have the refusal, when he parted with them —but of course I would have nothing to do with them at such a price. The "Rye" [5] was once a most valuable drawing—but having three wormholes in it and being thoroughly smoked, is about the worth of Lady Barnes's. I thought he might in conscience have asked 50, but he will probably get something near his price. He has a little "Margate" [6] which could be valuable to me from its being on the original mount with its rough edge, as Turner left it—his first touches on the white paper seen at the edge. If he would give that—for 30 or 35 I think it would be well spent money—at least if you like the drawing itself. It is fresh and in good condition. All Lupton's drawings are of Turner's middle period— the time of our Nottingham: [7] but have been grievously abused.

Dumbarton [8] you will find in the study table to the right of my seat in a wooden frame. It is a subject like this, in brown. It belongs to

Lupton—so of course he must have it, but as I am to have the refusal of it at £10, when he has done with it, please have it so arranged that he can't hurt it—it is all touched over richly with Turner's lead pencil— and as this would rub out if taken out of frame, please have it thoroughly pasted in, and then sealed with my seal at the corners of the frame— and tell him he must not take it out. Never mind Hill [9] or Dawson [10]

5. A water color.

6. Perhaps the study of Margate done by Turner in 1822 and mentioned in *Works, 13,* 60 n. 1.

7. Executed in 1833 and briefly mentioned in *Works, 6,* 43.

8. Most probably a mezzotint of Dumbarton Castle made by Lupton from Turner's water color.

9. Perhaps David Octavius Hill (1802–70), landscape and portrait painter who was instrumental in founding the Art Union of Edinburgh.

10. Henry Dawson (1811–78), a painter who, although unsuccessful until late in life,

or anybody else—and let no Turners, once ours—out of the house.

I am very glad to hear of M[rs] Richardson's [11] good fortune at Sydney — But it is melancholy to think of my poor cousin Bridget dying there— almost of hunger—probably treading gold [12] under her feet at every step— How little the Society for the diffusion of useful knowledge [13] have done, as yet. I could not be in a gold country for a quarter of an hour without discovering it—nor anybody else who knew chalk from flint—or copper from iron, and was in the habit of looking to their feet. Dearest love to my mother.

Ever my dearest Father. Your most affec[e]. Son
J Ruskin.

We had a delightful journey from Verona. I never saw Italy look more lovely—the snowy mountains against soft blue sky—and the purple hills below them clear in the early sunshine of the spring. It is very stormy tonight however. I am afraid my casts are by no means at their ease in the hold of the Mary.

LETTER 156

Ash Wednesday [25 February 1852]

My dearest Father,

I think the change of air to Verona did—or does me good— I have been very hungry and sleepy ever since, and as I told you I got a nice piece of drawing done. I am better pleased with some bits I have done this journey than I have been for years, partly because I have not—in general, been in a hurry—and I am glad to say that I now see the way to the end of my work very well. Having the book once in form is a great thing : I have not however been sending you any bits lately—partly because George has been working for me in tracing inscriptions—and partly because I have not anything in complete form enough for sending. The chapter on the Ducal palace [1] which has cost me a great deal of reading— is still devoid of all adornment : some chapters, finished to within a certain point, contain rather more of the homely facts of Venice than I am afraid you would like : and in fact the whole book, even where it is quite put up—is a good deal like a house just built—full of dust and damp plaster —you could hardly see it at a worse time, and I must let it dry before I paint or paper it.

Carnival finished brilliantly last night—with a violent gale, which I

---

is praised by Ruskin in *Modern Painters I* (*Works, 3*, 391 n.). Dawson's later work is said to show a strong influence of Turner.

11. Doubtless the wife of one of Ruskin's cousins who had emigrated to Australia.

12. The postscript to Letter 68 is indicative of the gold rush of this time.

13. A society established in 1826 "for the purpose of promoting the composition, publication, and distribution of elementary works upon all branches of Useful Knowledge."

1. Chap. viii of *The Stones of Venice II*.

suppose a Scotch old wife would have said was the Devil flying away
from Venice. They don't calculate by hours; the last ball, masqued, in
the Fenice, only *began* at 12 o'clock last night: Effie having had a great
succès at the Marshal's, came home to Venice just in time to organize a
costume of the Moliere time—poudrée—for Mme Esterhazy—who had
invited all the ladies of her circle to take the old French dress for that
night: Effie looked excessively nice—very simply dressed—hair very
white indeed—and a scarlet riband round the neck and wrists—her court
dress with the ivy leaves tucked in some incomprehensible manner into
an ancient form. She went out—at 10—to Mme Esterhazy's—and I to
bed. All the ladies went to the opera in their powder—and made a sensation as you may suppose—for last year, none of the great ladies would
go at all—this time all the principal women in Venice taking a kind of
part in the masquerade, pleased everybody. I had been looking at the Alps
all the way from Verona and was tired, so would not go out, and I am
very sleepy to-night also—so goodnight and dearest love to you and my
mother.

> Ever my dearest Father. Your most aff^e. Son
> J Ruskin.

LETTER 157

26th Feb. [1852]

My dearest Father,

I have today your kind letter of the 19th and am only a little anxious
lest you should further annoy yourself as you say you are a little unwell
—either about Veroneses or Turners: I hope you will have seen by my
late letters which do not return to the subject, that I do not care a farthing
about the Veronese—and Effie also says she would not like me to have
it. I think you are quite right about old pictures—but very wrong in
fearing that I shall ever ruin myself in any kind of pictures— First—
did you ever know any man ruin himself in pictures—unless he merely
bought them in vanity—or was a speculator as well as a picture buyer?
Are not the picture buyers in general safe men who keep their houses
locked up—and rather save than spend much—Monro—Wells [1]—Allnutt—Windus—who lost—observe, by his *wines,* never by his pictures
—and is it really likely that I shall ever be ruined merely because I have
more frankness and honesty than most of these men? You must not,
really, be alarmed, as if I were taking a new fancy which might open into
another Turner passion— You may read my books for years back, and
you will see the old masters always rated at same value, and I never
cared to buy them and never shall, though always speaking of Veronese

1. William Wells of Penshurst, Kent, collector of paintings, especially those of Landseer.

and Tintoret and Titian as among the greatest of men—yet not in *my* way. And for the pieces of extravagance which I am begging you to commit about Turner, just now, I think they are surely justifiable when I am myself quite unable to be on the ground and when his death has just opened so many depositories, probably of the most interesting of his works, which I have never seen: I am now 33 years old—and am not likely to change my feelings—or seek for pleasures of other kinds; nor, when I am a little older, shall I much care to buy new drawings—I shall think them then too dear for the time I am likely to have them. But at all events—don't let us buy anything but Turners—my great mission is to interpret him.

Of the list sent by Colnaghi, re-enclosed I only want three—Clyde,[2] Devil's Bridge, and Lake of Thun. *They* are crossed, the rest scratched out—total sum £10.

You must not think Turner is slovenly: All men are a little careless in places, the greatest men the most so—but it is always a carelessness like a King's; not like an Idler's: What you think is slovenliness in Turner is either in parts of the picture which he wishes to foil something in the rest—or it is a hasty laying on of colour to get some quality in the *colour* only attainable by haste. My care—and Hunt's,[3] are both the result of a certain degree of feebleness, we are forced to copy slowly because we cannot invent— All the tree drawing in my brown studies put together is not worth Turner's *single etching*—Aesacus and Hesperie— nor worth, in real understanding of the characters of a tree, *one* of the trunks in the Bolton: All the practice I have had in tree drawing would not enable me even to copy the little jutting branch of the tree next the river on the right hand: His is a power essentially above mine; of a different and totally unattainable class.

I am however, I am happy to say, recovering some confidence in myself, as I get the whiphand of my book—I see so much of interest coming out of it that I have no doubt of its success. Colnaghi may say my plates won't sell. I will sell them at a couple of guineas each—and that before very long. They don't consider that there was never a writer before who could illustrate his own writings—and when the enmity of the architects is crushed—when they *dare* not say anything against me, and the mob *begin* to be told on authority the drawings are good—there is no fear but they will sell. As yet—in spite of all that has been complimentarily said of me and to me—people of most authority have looked upon me as enthusiastic—clever—and wrongheaded. When I have shown them that I was *right*—all the while—and when I get real *useful* authority—anything I write will sell. Did you read Arthur Acland's [4] note

2. *The Falls of Clyde,* which is highly praised in *Praeterita* (*Works, 35,* 549).
3. William Henry Hunt's lack of inventive power is noted in *Modern Painters III* (*Works, 5,* 332).
4. The brother of Sir Henry Wentworth Acland.

—an example of the kind of man I mean? You see he says the hard work
of the *Stones* has made him read *Seven Lamps*. This is the operation
which will take place on a grand scale, when my second volume comes
out.

I wrote 3rd for 2nd only, (volume) you must have seen this by my
latter letters.

Your remarks on Turner are very valuable—most truly does he "drop
the reins in drawing the chariot of the sun." But in comparing even my
best works to his in any respect you compare Collins or Gray with Shakespeare. You ought to delight in his negligence—it is Homeric— He is in
a word one of the Great of the earth—the first class men—Homer—
Phidias—Dante—Milton—Shakespeare—Tintoret—Michael Angelo—
Giotto—Turner—I am not sure that I could add another name to that
list—but if I did it would assuredly not be—in any form of comparison
or companionship whatever—my own.

Dearest love to my mother. Ever, my dearest Father,

Your most affectionate Son.
J Ruskin

LETTER 158

27th Feb [1852]

My dearest Father,

I have today your most interesting and kind letter of 21st: which
with yesterday's, relieves me from a good deal of anxiety. Yesterday's
says there can be no sale nor exhibition of Turner this year; today's
speaks without so much feeling of anxiety about the Veronese—I have
regretted sending that note about the Veronese [1] hundreds of times,
and I was sadly afraid it would make you ill, when you told me your
liver was wrong again; so that I am a good deal relieved when I find
you are not vexing yourself. I hope you will think no more about it.

But don't send me any more critiques. I did not use to be sensitive to criticism—I used to be very angry when I was taxed with
being so. But I am so now—partly from being nervous—partly because my works cost me more labour. I could sit down and write a
poem—with a good deal of nonsense in it—in a couple of hours—if a
reviewer said it was nonsense, I felt he had a right to his opinion and
did not care. But when I work over a volume for two years—and
weigh *every word* in it—and a dim brained rascal like this of the
Guardian [2] walks up to me and tells me "half of my statements are

1. In Letter 143.
2. A review of *The Stones of Venice I* and *The Examples of the Architecture of
Venice* appeared in the *Guardian*, February 18, 1852. Not only did the critic fail to
appreciate the logic of Ruskin's arguments but he also took issue with the plates in
these books.

diametrically opposite to the others," simply because the poor long eared brute cannot see that a thistleleaf has two sides, it *does* worry me considerably, and makes me very angry, and yet depresses me at the same time. Miss Edgeworth says nothing will *satisfy* an author but "large draughts of unqualified praise." I believe I am getting to be a good deal of this temper—at all events don't send me any more reviews. I have quite enough to spoil my temper in my work.

Now to answer the main points in your letter. First by the bye— I am quite delighted with Mr Gray on Bullfights—it is admirable— I think he has a lurking grudge at Blackwood for my sake, but any rate the letter is excellent and must do good.[3]

1st. then, I don't want Harding's Como [4]—nor anything else of anybody's but Turner.

2nd. Ask Willis to wait till Midsummer—they are very honest people—but disorderly and once before sent me a bill twice—and I believe I paid this one, but the receipt is probably among my packets where nobody can find it but myself.

3rd. Foord is right.

4th. I wish you would look again at the Yorkshire drawing [5] which Griffith showed you. In the engraving it is most beautiful—a complete epitome of the Border scenery of England—the Red Gauntlet scenery: there is a whole pastoral poem in the village on the left—a complete mass of its streets, and all the incidents of village life—and some castellated ruins on the hill above—and all the Cumberland mountains sweeping round the bay—and the rustic and wild character of the place more marked by the shepherd boy with a girl's *bonnet* on, standing on the great stone in front— If it is quite faded—of course I should not like it, but the Yorkshire drawings are never strong in colour and if it is as bright as our Richmond it is as much as I shall expect from it. You do not say what Griffith asked. I have never seen the drawing and cannot tell therefore if it be as delicate in execution as I suppose it to be—but if the chains of distant mountains are clear, it cannot be fatally destroyed—at another time, I should have asked you to secure it if not above 100—but at present I must leave it entirely in your hands—as I cannot in the least tell what I may find among those reams of treasure in Queen Anne St. But of the drawings that I *know*—this is one I have long set my mark on, as far as I could judge of it from engravings. I cannot refer you to the page—but by looking

3. Ruskin is doubtless expressing his appreciation of a letter written by his father-in-law in protest to a criticism in *Blackwood's Magazine* of *Tauromachia; or, The Bullfights of Spain* (London, 1852) and *Spain, As It Is* by G. A. Hoskins (London, 1851). The reviews of these books appeared in *Blackwood's Magazine* for February 1852.

4. *High Alps from Near Como,* which is mentioned in *Modern Painters II* (*Works, 4*, 340).

5. Turner's *Heysham and Cumberland Mountains,* which is reproduced in Whitaker's *History of Richmondshire, 2,* 317.

to the general chapter on all modern landscape in 1st Vol *Modern Painters,* you will see in the account of Turner's early works, the importance I have always attached to the Yorkshire series. But If the chain of distant mountains be quite indistinct, I would not have the drawing.

Touching the heaps of Liber Studiorum in Queen Anne St. Turner —as you know—told me he had *no* proof copies—and actually had a copper plate printer sent for—and fresh impressions taken from the plates to sell to me: Either he lied worse than Charles Turner—or the plates in such heaps cannot be proofs—but at all events, they cannot be *touched* proofs, for only *one* proof is touched at each stage of the plate, and these the engravers keep: there are no duplicates: I therefore still keep to my request that you would secure if possible the touched proofs of the four plates named in my letter of somedays back, of Liber Studiorum.

Many thanks for account of his house. The Windmill lock [6] *is* a magnificent picture—but I don't care a farthing for it. It is done merely to show his skill in tone—there is no thought in it—and very little sentiment—except one of foggy repose in autumnal sunset. Nothing can be finer than the mere painting, but it is Turner's brain I want, not his hand.

I have a good deal to do today, must continue this letter in the evening. Dearest love to my mother. Ever my dearest Father

Your most affect. Son
J Ruskin.

Who is the editor of this Guardian? I thought I knew him—and that he was a man of sense—please ask Smith. I am like Imogen, "sprited with a fool—frighted—and angered worse." [7] That a man should be able to spell—and not see the difference between religion bettering art —and art bettering religion—and then that the blockhead should give himself airs to *me*.

LETTER 159

Saturday Evening. 28th. [February 1852]

My dearest Father,

I stopped today just as I was coming to that part of your letter where you say we shall—or should have too much (10,000) in Turner, because I should not see my pictures if I went to the Alps. But do you count for nothing the times out of time you see me looking at them morning and evening—and when I take them up to sleep with? I have

6. *Canal, Lock, and Windmill,* which is included in the *Liber Studiorum.*
7. *Cymbeline* II.iii.159–60.

fifty pounds' worth of pleasure out of every picture in my possession *every week* that I have it. As long as you live, I shall not be so much abroad as in England—if I should outlive you, the pictures will be with me wherever I am. You count all I "would buy"—but I have named to you all I ever hope to get—supposing I live long—and out- live their present possessors—on which I have no business to calculate— I don't think that to have spent—by the time I am 50 or 60—10,000 —in Turners—sounds monstrous. People would not think it extrava- gant to buy a title or an estate at that price. I want neither. Some people would think it not too much at a contested election. But all de- pends on the view you take of me and of my work. I could not write as I do unless I felt myself a reformer, a man who knew what others did not know—and felt what they did not feel. Either I know this man Turner to be *the* man of this generation—or I know *nothing*— You cannot wonder that as long as I have any confidence or hope in myself, I should endeavor to possess myself of what at once gives me so great pleasure—and ministers to what I believe to be my whole mission and duty here. It is a pity that I cannot frankly express my feelings on this subject without giving you cause to dread the effects of enthusiasm—but it is just because I am enthusiastic that I am—*if* I am—powerful in any way: If you have any faith in my genius— you ought to have it in my judgment also. You may say, (probably all prudent fathers *would* say)—"if he wants to buy all these just now— what will he want to buy as he grows older—he began with one— and thought himself rich with two—now he has got 30, and wants thirty more: in ten years he will want 300." I feel the force of this rea- soning as much as you do, and I know this to be the natural course of human desire: if no bridle be set upon it: nor am I so foolish as ever to expect in this world—to have all my desires gratified—or to be even able to say there is nothing more than [*sic*] I wish for. That I believe, *ought* only to be said by a man when he is near death. But I can very firmly and honestly assure you that I *am much* more satisfied with my collection now—than when it was smaller and that if I now express more exorbitant desires, it is not because I want more—but because you are more indulgent to me. When I was a mere boy, I had not the impudence to ask you—or even to hope for—a present of more than 50 pounds once a year: Then it came to 160 pounds once a year—and my *expres- sion* of desire has always increased exactly in proportion to the degree in which I thought it might be expressed without giving you pain— The longings were always there—but I did not choose to utter them—know- ing that they would cause you suffering—perhaps also—knowing that their expression would be of no use—they would not be granted. Yet, you may remember, that when Griffith proposed to sell his whole collection— I *did* in a humble manner—lay his offer before you—of 15 drawings at

50 each. You gave me four, and I did not press the rest : but be assured, I longed for them just as much as I do now—though I did not then know half their value—else I should have permitted myself in more importunity. Again—when the offer of 20 drawings at 40 each was made to us—I laid it before you—in a timid hope that you might take them. I had exactly, myself, as much longing, and as large desires as I have now —nay, *greater,* by the smallness of my possessions, but I had not the face to express them. Now—that I am older and wiser, and you are more indulgent—I come out with all that I want—and it looks as if my desires had greatly increased—but they have not increased one whit. I am on the contrary, infinitely nearer contentment than I was, and if I had the drawings named in my first and second class, and a bundle or two of sketches, I certainly should never feel sickness of heart for a Turner drawing any more—as it is—I think that my going on quietly with my work here, while such things are going on in London, may show you that I am *tolerably* content with what I *have*—though in sober conscience, I think it right and wise to "ask for more." [1] I intended—when I began, that this should be a nice long letter on various topics, but having this morning—Sunday, 29th, opened at breakfast my *Stones of Venice* [2]—it led me on—and I did not lay it down till near prayer time —and now I must finish my letter for the post. *I* find it a most interesting book, not at all dull, and it gives me a great impression of reserved power, on coming to it with a fresh ear. I am quite sure it will sell eventually.

The emperor has come here to visit his Russian guests—and Radetsky came to meet him, and sent a most polite message to Effie by his aid de camp—saying that he was extremely sorry he could not call upon her himself—but that he was held entirely at the Emperor's service. This is of course, mere politeness—but it *is* politeness just like Sir R. Inglis's [3] —and I find that in reality—the Marshal was much pleased at our twice coming to Verona merely to go to his ball—and that while we esteemed it a favour to be asked—he did not less think it polite in us to come.

I am afraid poor Marmont will soon cease to be the source of ambiguities—he had an apoplectic stroke the night before last—and is still "neither better nor worse" certainly very ill—I am glad I saw him and had a little talk with him.

I am getting, I think, considerably stronger and better in health within the last week or two—especially I am getting into good spirits and conceit about my book. I like seeing my way to the end of it. I think the little depression I got from your letter about the tombs has been of use

1. An expression that occurs with some frequency in *Oliver Twist.*
2. Pt. I.
3. Sir Robert Harry Inglis (1786–1855), for many years M.P. for Oxford University. He was a prominent Tory, strong churchman, and held high office in the Royal Academy. George Richmond did a portrait of him.

to me like the cold water cure—this "wet band round the stomach"—
very disagreeable in its first application—but doing good in the reaction.
If only the weather would come warm—I shall be very happy—but now
we have biting northeast winds and I cannot stand or think even so well
as in the calm winter frosts. It seems to me as if no heat would ever
come again—and I have utterly lost all feeling of being in Italy, or the
south. I am among fine buildings—standing in dirty sea—in a climate
like that of Yarmouth.

Dearest love to my mother.

Ever my dearest Father.
Your most affec^e. Son
J Ruskin.

LETTER 160

Monday. 1st March [1852]

My dearest Father,

I have always forgotten to say that in one of the boxes which was
sent per Mary Stewart was a small pasteboard box containing some glass
bead manufacture, which one of our friends asked us to buy for them—
it may give trouble if McCracken are not aware of it.

Among the pieces sent home I should think you would be interested
by the very ancient symbolical Greek sculpture of six sheep under a palm
tree—part of a tablet of which I have cast the centre also which will
come in next box. The centre is a throne—with a cross and a Lamb: [1]
inscribed, ὁ ἀμνός "the lamb:" on each side there are six sheep and a
palm tree—inscribed οἱ ἅγιοι ἀπόστολοι "the Holy apostles"—the one
side with οἱ ἅγιοι is that sent home. The Byzantine cross,[2] with the doves
at its feet, is a beautiful example of quaint and early architectural sculpture, so also the peacock in the circle. The three groups of small figures
are signs of the zodiac from Ducal palace capitals.[3] Observe the man
holding the "Pisces," and the Sagittarius beside him, small, preparing
to draw the bow, which is on another piece of leafage. There are four of
the great lion's heads cut for distant effect—from ducal palace, and two
pieces of its magnificent flat foliage at the angles, which I Cannot enough
admire or praise.

I am not able to send you any more text at present—for I am at work
on the whole book putting a touch here and a touch there—and the
pieces I have finished are I am afraid still a little too much of the detail
species.

1. For a description of these see *St. Mark's Rest* (*Works*, *24*, 241–2).
2. This may have been used in preparation for Plate xi in *The Stones of Venice II*.
See *Works*, *10*, 166.
3. For a description of this see *The Stones of Venice II* (*Works*, *10*, 412–15).

I may as well send you a list of the several pieces in boxes in case any should be broken—vide opposite side.

Dearest love to my mother.

Ever my dearest Father
Your most affec^e. Son
J Ruskin

Mary Stewart

1. Arch with cross under it and two doves—four feet high.
2. Flat leaves—ducal palace—some two feet square.
3. Do. Do. ——— ———— ———— ———— ———— ————
4. Sheep and palm tree.
5.
6. } Three groups of small figures from ducal palace capital.
7.
8. A large rose, from the ducal palace.
9. A round bit of foliage from an angle of a capital.
10. A little bit of stalk and bottom of leaf—from the angle of a capital, (small and light).
11. A little bit of plaited ornament round a corner.
12.
13. } Three triangles with early leafage ornaments.
14.
15.
16.
} Four Lions' heads, (one sideways).
17.
18.
20. A peacock in a circle.
21. I find noted as a bird or birds—but I forget what it was.

LETTER 161

March 2nd [1852]

My dearest Father,

The emperor went away yesterday evening at ½ past six—being by no means so punctual as our queen, which considering that he is a young soldier, is very wrong. It was first announced he was going at five—then at seven—and he went at half past six—much disappointing Effie and doubtless many people more, who in obedience to the request of the podesta, had got themselves and their gondolas ready to accompany him to the station, and causing a very useless waste of colours in old carpets and tapestries—hung out of the windows along the grand canal in expectation of his leaving at 5—which waved only in darkness at ½ past six. It somewhat spoils people, even in the best disciplined institutions of men, to have all their own way. Here there are only three railroad trains running—and everybody's business must give way to the emperor's—so the post is kept waiting as long as he likes. This would not do between Slough and London.

By way of interlude among more serious business, I have been looking at Cooper's *Bravo* [1]— It is marvellous how ridiculous the common novel-sentiment about Venice appears to any one who really knows anything about it: but more marvellous still that a seaman like Cooper should never have found out that the lagoons were shallow—and should have represented the State inquisitors as drowning a criminal in the lagoons—a statement precisely as rational, as three hundred years hence, it would be for a novelist to represent our New Police executing a criminal by throwing him into the London Docks: nay, *less* rational, for a man might be drowned in the latter—but not in the former—except by holding his head under water. The republicanism and abuse of the Venetian government are also so absurd that it may be worth while taking notice of them in a short note, as I daresay this book is an authority with the Americans about Venice.

I have had great delight in examining Titian's Peter Martyr, lately, thanks to the Americans—a poor baby of a painter is trying to copy it to be sent to America—it is put on the floor therefore—and I can examine it as I would in my own room. It is truly almost a miracle of mighty painting. Titian stands to Tintoret very nearly as Raphael to Michael Angelo, but the mob understand neither of them.

Dearest love to my mother.

Ever my dearest Father.
Your most aff^e. Son.
J Ruskin.

LETTER 162

3rd March. [1852]

My dearest Father,

I must be short today for it is mild and beautiful and I want to make the most of it— Nothing can be more striking than the contrast between dark and sunny weather at Venice, the mere shining of the sun through the green of the water is such a blessing—compared to the dark leaden grey of the canals in winter.

Our Galignani subscription is over—but I get a look at it now and then—and I believe Mr Dawkins the English consul is going to send it

1. Fenimore Cooper's *The Bravo,* 3 vols. (London, 1831).

us after he has read it—it is not worth while now to open another subscription—especially as the postage is enormous: But I have been much
edified by the proceedings of Mr F. O'Connor [1]—and by his declining
any breakfast in his prison except "meat and brandy and water"—truly
the Roman Catholics are honourably represented in our Parliament—
and our Parliament is getting to be a very respectable place in general.
People may abuse any Venice government as much [as] they like—but it
would have been long before a member of the Council would have shaken
hands with a man fresh out of prison for assaulting an executive—much
more before such a man could again have taken his seat in the senate.

I like Sir Charles Napier's [2] letter in defence of the poor old musket,
and I don't like these American revolvers and Mimic shooting at people,
heaven knows where; I like all that Sir Charles Napier does and says
very much—it is upright and English—rather *simple* in a man to ask
for a situation for himself, openly—but infinitely better than plotting for
it by stealth—as other people do.

Dearest love to my mother.

Ever my dearest Father.
Your most affec^e. Son
J Ruskin.

I never read anything so *brutal* in my life—(except some of the docu-
ments of the French republicans) as Lord Grey's dispatch to Sir Harry.[3]

LETTER 163

3rd March [1852]

My dearest Father,

There is so much in your two letters just received that I must answer
in haste as things come into my head. First however inquiry shall be
made as to delay of letters—I suspect it rests partly with packets at
Boulogne. Whenever you do not get a letter each day—it is the post's
fault, not mine.

1. Feargus O'Connor (1794–1855), barrister, M.P., and Chartist leader. O'Connor's
liking for brandy was as well known as his eccentric behavior and abuse toward his
fellow members of Parliament. Ruskin is referring to O'Connor's imprisonment in 1840–
41 for seditious libel. His incarceration is mentioned briefly in G. D. H. Cole's *Chartist
Portraits* (London, Macmillan & Co. Ltd., 1941), p. 319.

2. Sir Charles James Napier (1782–1853), who had a distinguished career in the
British army, mostly in India. Ruskin is referring here to Napier's *Letter on the Defense
of England by Corps of Volunteers and Militia,* which appeared in February 1852.

3. Ruskin is writing of a dispatch sent by Viscount Howick and 3rd Earl Grey,
Secretary for War and the Colonies from 1846 until 1852, to Sir Henry George Wakelyn
Bt. (1787–1860), who was in command of British troops in the Kaffir war which broke
out in December 1850.

Touching what you say of Charles Turner, the great value which I attached to the Lupton collection was just on this account, that I was quite sure I could depend on Lupton—and that these were the last touched proofs on which I *could altogether* depend— I should not however hesitate in buying those from Charles Turner which I named to you [1]—many a man would tell a lie to conceal his having property (which he thought he had a *right* to *conceal the fact* of his possessing) —who would not forge the property itself. A pretended touched proof may of course be forged—and when they have been once through dealers' hands, I would never buy them except on close examination: Hence the importance of just and honest hands: Etchings and simple proofs cannot be forged, and are therefore of definite constant value—but a true touched proof is worth ten or twenty etchings or common proofs. Of etchings and common proofs, there *may* be in existence an indefinite number—every touched proof is of course unique. I would therefore buy the plates I named to you from Charles Turner—if they can be had. But not the collection.

One thing puzzles me very much. Scott says he bought two books from Charles Turner which he had intended for his daughter. One of these books I had seen; it was a series of about 20 or 25 etchings in excellent condition and all of which I wanted. You say Scott thinks I have *"all* the etchings but two." Now the fact is I had *none* but two—and one of your late letters mentions buying 16 or 15, at 50/– each, but you have now sent me the names of only eight—saying "those I bought were, 1, 2," &c. up to 8, and no more; Although I want all, yet of those that I want chiefly, and first, there is only among these eight, the Lake of Thun, and it seems to me that Mr Stokes must have had first choice— for of these eight etchings I know that he had before nearly all. I have, and can have—no objection to Scott's showing his old customer Mr Stokes—who has bought much more from him than I have—first choice —only I wish he would say so frankly—and also I think it a little unfair to be charged 50/– each for leavings: I have always gone on the plain principle of paying—if I could—any price for what I *wanted,* without grumbling—and never buying what I did not want because it was cheap, but I think 50/– an enormous price for etchings taken in this way, if I had my choice it would be another matter.

Charles Turner's prices are also preposterous— I thought—when he said 500 pounds—he had five or six impressions of each plate he had printed—but to ask at the rate of £8 each for these few is rascally: My own belief is that both he and Lake [2] have got plenty more—and are trying a few first—like Windus. There are named among them:

1. In Letter 151.
2. Perhaps Lake Price, a lithographer.

Thun (query—*Town* [3]—or *Lake*?) touched proof.	10	10	0
do. etching, touched.	5	5	0
do. proof touched.	8	8	0
	24	3	0

Holy Island. Etching (4 4/ 3 3/. I don't understand this statement.)	7	7
do. artist's proof. (price ridiculous)	6	6
Devils Bridge. 3 proofs touched.	31	10
St Gothard. proof touched.	10	10
	54[*sic*]	13 0

Total. 78[*sic*] 16   0 for 10 plates!!

Now, if the first 24 pounds' worth is *Town* of Thun—I don't want them at all— But if *lake*—I should like to have them at a reasonable price.

If you have in compliance with my former letter—secured these plates —I have only to thank you with all my heart. But if you are still in treaty—for the four last plates—Devils Bridge and St Gothard—I would give—whatever I must to get them, and for the three first, if of *lake* of Thun, 20 guineas. But I won't give more than two guineas for the etching of Holy Island, which is not stated to be touched—and the "artist's proof" as he calls it—which I suppose is not even before letters —I won't have at all. I think the whole transaction very rascally—and would advise Scott to have nothing to do with the plates at such prices. But he knows better than I what he can get for them.

I said I wanted all the etchings. So I do—but I won't give *more* than two guineas each for them as a lot. But for these following etchings, if at any time they come into the market—we must give what is asked— up to 10 guineas.

Valley of Chamouni (Source of Arveron).

Mer de Glace.

Grande Chartreuse.

Devil's Bridge.

Two unpublished etchings, one of St Gothard—the other of trees with woodmen—and brook in hollow.

And now to the most important part of your letter—which however may be much more shortly answered with best thanks for getting the Herne Hill house,[4] in which I hope to be very happy and to make you

3. *Ville de Thun,* a drawing from the *Liber Studiorum.*

4. The residence which John and Effie Ruskin occupied upon their return to England from Venice.

so. You seem to misunderstand my half objections to it—you seem to think I did not think it large enough—but I thought it *too large*— You know best however, and I shall leave furnishing in your hands, only let the bookcases have glass doors with handles like those of mine in the study: and keyholes—not for large keys—but which the key will go into in a *moment*—not like the library downstairs.

Dearest love to my mother, who I hope is happy at the thought of our coming to live near her.

Ever my dearest Father.

Your most affec^e. Son

J Ruskin.

In looking over Charles Turner's list, my eye did not catch the *Eton*— This if it is the sheepwashing—I have got no plate of—so I would take the etching and one of the proofs—or the whole of the proofs of this plate if there is any way of general arrangement. There are I see—four of Eton and four of *Fall of Clyde* [5]—in case the Devil's Bridge &c., cannot be had alone. I think £100 for the plates named on last page and these eight, would be a pretty fair bargain.

78	16
26	5
52	11

LETTER 164

5th March [1852]

My dearest Father,

It shows—among other things—how little people buy at present with any real intention of studying art, that Scott speaks as if the scattered character of Turner's (Charles) collection increased its value—whereas to any person who really cares about the working of the artist's mind— (and if they don't—I see no reason why they should buy touched proofs at all)—every addition to a series of a *single plate* adds to the value of all the rest: A touched proof is usually a dirty piece of paper—an impression carelessly taken—scratched over with a penknife and black pencil— The effect of it is not half so good as that of a common impression— The use of it is to see the course of the artist's invention—it is like the original MS of a poem—Not so pleasant to read as print— much more interesting to study. Now every link in the chain of thought is valuable just as you are able to show the links with which it joins— valueless otherwise, therefore I would always pay more for *two* proofs of *one* plate than for *three* of three separate plates. My object is if possi-

5. Included in the *Liber Studiorum*.

ble, to get together the touched proofs of Turner's *mountain* studies in the Liber Studiorum—I have got two most precious ones—the Ben Arthur and Solway Moss [1] and a wonderful series of *different states* of the Mer de Glace—there can be no touched proofs of this for Turner engraved it himself. Now—if I can get the Devils Bridge—Lake of Thun —and St Gothard, out of Charles Turner, there are only the Grande Chartreuse and Source of Arveron left of much importance. I named the Clyde in my last letter—but that is more of water and rocks than actual mountains so I don't care so much about it. The Source of Arveron I shall look out for at Turner's sale—he engraved it himself. I never heard of any touched proofs of the Grande Chartreuse—there must be some, somewhere—don't miss them if you hear of them—and then I shall have all I *want* of the Liber Studiorum: and should only buy examples of other plates at reasonable prices—nor many of those.

We have terribly windy weather at present. I hope my poor Mary Stewart will get home safe— Dearest love to my mother.

Ever my dearest Father. Your most aff^{e}. Son
J Ruskin.

I think I shall make a very nice place of the house at Herne Hill—between Liber Studiorum and casts from Venice. It is very lucky you have got it—I was seriously afraid of bringing the Denmark Hill floors down. I am very glad Mr Bicknell is going to stay in the neighbourhood.

Letter 165

6th March [1852]

My dearest Father,

These news from England are really too ridiculous and I can stand it no longer. I am going for three days to give the usual time I set aside for your letter to writing one to the Times—on Corn Laws—elections —and education.[1] George shall copy it—if you like to send it—you can —if not—you can consider it all as written to you—but you must have short letters for a day or two.

Dearest love to my mother.

Ever my dearest Father.
Your most aff^{e}. Son
J Ruskin.

1. *Ben Arthur* is singled out for praise in *The Elements of Drawing* (*Works, 15,* 99), and *Solway Moss* is considered one of the "more noble monuments of his art" (*Works, 35,* 549).

1. For a detailed account of the letters written to the *Times* see *Works, 12,* lxxviii–lxxxv. What was completed of them is to be found in *Works, 12,* 591–603. The correspondence between Ruskin and his father about the proposed letters shows the political cleavage which was developing between the two men.

LETTER 166

Sunday. March 7[th.] [1852]

My dearest Father,

I did not thank you in any of my former letters for your very interesting description of Turner's house [1]—in its likeness to *Pompeii*. It
must have been very grand—I am sorry I did not see it—on its first
excavation—but very thankful it is no worse—and that there are such
heaps of drawings in a decent state. I did not either reply to your most
just criticism on Wilson.[2] He would have made a true painter—had he
been born in a more fortunate period—he is worth a dozen of Gaspar
Poussin [3]—and some of his pictures in which he had been struck by
a natural scene—and painted it merely to please himself—and without
any special imitation of other landscapists—are full of power. I have an
engraving from a study by him of the crater of Cader Idris,[4] which I
value next to my Turner engravings—and M[r] Ford has a picture of a
single golden cloud, full of sunset, resting behind the [*text mutilated*]
hills, which I would rather have than any dozen of Claude's [5] I ever saw.
But his was not a first rate genius—he could not break through the nets
of the existing system—though he showed life under the restraint—
his mind appears also to have been of a coarse stamp, so that even had
he been better taught, he would never have gone into the details of Nature
with any affection—but painted always broadly and heavily. But he would
have produced some majestic pictures—very nearly, to Turner's, what
Reynolds' are to Raphael's; supposing Raphael to have had a little more
eye for colour—and Reynolds a little less.

I will write to Macdonald to congratulate him. I am getting desperately
lazy about writing letters—they seem so much work—and so little good.

One o'clock. I have just got your delightful letter of the 27th–28th
saying you so enjoyed the brown Liber, Stonehenge [6] &c. You are quite
right—there is nothing in the world like them— That Stonehenge with
the sunset and galloping mailcoach is a perfect poem—the mountain

1. An interesting account of Turner's Queen Anne Street residence is given in
Works, 13, xxvi–xxvii, where portions of descriptive letters written by Ruskin senior
on February 19 and 21 are reproduced.
2. Richard Wilson (1714–82), landscape painter, ranked by Ruskin with Reynolds,
Gainsborough, Hogarth, and Turner as one of the five great English painters.
3. Gaspar Poussin (1613–75), landscape painter and brother-in-law of Nicolas Poussin (1594–1664), whose surname he took. Both are not infrequently mentioned in
Ruskin's work.
4. Wilson's painting, *The Summit of Cader Idris*, was engraved by E. and M.
Rooker.
5. Claude Gelée (1600–82), called Lorraine, French landscape painter. His artistic
connection with Turner is given in Finberg's *Life of Turner*, pp. 128–30.
6. A Turner drawing in the *England and Wales* series; it is described in *Modern
Painters I* (*Works, 3*, 413).

scenes are my constant companions wherever I go— I must shut up for post. Dearest love to my mother.

> Ever my dearest Father.
> Your most aff^e. Son,
> J Ruskin.

LETTER 167

March 8th [1852]

My dearest Father,

I am so glad you have now some motive to make you interested in looking over my plates and Liber Studiorum—you will find so much to interest you in them when you examine them in this way— I never could understand how the Heysham, (which is the subject I supposed was Griffith's drawing) had got among the Yorkshire series—but I fancy there must be some outlying bit of Yorkshire in the middle of Lancashire, of which Turner has taken advantage to vary his subject. I am very sorry you miss the MS so much in these last few letters—but perhaps the sketches I sent of the plan of the book will interest you— I not only did not send more because I had none by me which I thought quite interesting enough, and was a little afraid of chilling both you and myself— but because I have been dictating lately to George some notes on the Tintorets which I had not before examined at Venice, and which I wish to be able to speak of in *Modern Painters,* besides which George is now daguerreotyping for me—so that his time is a good deal taken up. But I will make him copy some of the aforesaid notes on Tintoret, which I think will interest you—when my own letters are short. The enclosed sheet I see fits on to the one you had last and finishes Foscari,[1] but I will not send you any more tombs. Dearest love to my mother.

> Ever my dearest Father
> Your most aff^e. Son
> J Ruskin.

Poor Marmont is gone—I forgot to tell you on the day he died. For a few hours before his death he was constantly trying to rise and dress himself "to go to Paris." Effie is gone today to call on the Duchesse de Berri [2] —another of the old—or rather of the older, school, still left.

1. For Ruskin's description of the tomb of the Doge Francesco Foscari see *The Stones of Venice II* (*Works, 11,* 102–3).

2. A prominent Venetian social figure much liked by Effie Ruskin. The Duchesse de Berri's Venetian residence is mentioned in *The Stones of Venice II* (*Works, 10,* 144), where it is said to be one of the few palaces in Venice inhabited and well maintained.

LETTER 168

9th March [1852]

My dearest Father,

I had yesterday your delightful letter of the 3rd, saying you would not part with St Catherine's Hill for any money—and were enjoying the Liber Studiorum as much as I, also Mr Melvill's enclosed—which very pleasant—and that mama was pleased with account of dresses &c. There was not much to describe in Effie's dress at the last ball—it was very simple—but quaint, white, with little rosettes or bows or knots of divers coloured riband fastened over it, on the Gothic principle of no one colour being like the next to it. It was Carnival time, and she looked as if she had just sustained a shower of sugarplums. She received many compliments—and the old marshal [1] expressed to her in very touching terms his regret at being too old to dance with her.

You are quite right in thinking my present collection of Liber Studiorum quite *good* enough—I have chosen the impressions with great care—and do not want better than I have nor expect to find any—the only things I *do* want are the touched proofs. Do not buy anything of mere impressions from Colnaghi or anybody else at present, as there are so many in Turner's house it is quite possible that the "Source of the Arveron" series may be among them, and as this is a plate coveted by everybody, I may have to pay dear for them—but should be sorry to lose them. The Grande Chartreuse also may turn up some day, and I must not spend money on inferior plates. There is only one of my collection of which it is possible much to better the *impression,* the one I sketched with the wooden bridge in one of my late letters.[2] As Turner engraved this plate himself it is not likely any proofs of it should be in the market —but if any turn up, I should be thankful for them.

Newton's conduct is disgraceful [3]— A man cannot help having no heart—but that is no reason why he should have no manners.

Dearest love to my mother.

Ever my dearest Father
Your most affe. Son
J Ruskin.

I have only got a scrap of my Times letter ready, which I enclose— perhaps I shall be able to send tomorrow as much as it may be likely they will insert at once.

1. Radetzky.

2. The drawing is *Raglan Castle,* which is sketched by Ruskin in Letter 151.

3. Ruskin was angry with Newton because the latter, en route to Mytilene as British consul, asked Ruskin to meet him at Corfu. Ruskin was extremely annoyed that he should be asked to give up his work to embark upon such a journey. For Effie's spirited account of her husband's indignation see James, *John Ruskin and Effie Gray,* pp. 189–90.

LETTER 169

10th March [1852]

My dearest Father,

If Mr Ritchie kindly copies the back of this sheet, page 4, you will have pages 1, 2, 3, and 4, all ready for the first letter to the Times which please send if you see no objection—page 1. was sent last letter—pages 2. and 3. enclosed. Dearest love to my mother.

Ever my dearest Father. Your most aff^e. Son
J Ruskin.

LETTER 170

11th March [1852]

My dearest Father,

There are a great many mistakes in the first page of the enclosed leaf —so that I fear both will have to be copied, especially as it wants a prefatory sentence. Would Mr Ritchie be kind enough to begin it thus.

Sir.   Venice. 11th March

I pass to the second of the subjects named in my former letter, namely "Election."

If by a member of Parliament, &c.

I shall I hope be able to send you the conclusion of this section of the letter tomorrow, so that it may be then immediately sent to Times. Dearest love to my mother.

Ever my dearest Father
Your most affec^e. Son
J Ruskin.

LETTER 171

12th March [1852]

My dearest Father,

I had yesterday your delightful letter 6th March—apropos of my long delayed answer about Harding's picture, have you got *a letter* for *every* day I have been in Venice? If not—some are lost. If you have a letter for every day—it is of no use enquiring whether you have this or that one of importance, but I sent a sketch of the whole plan of my book and its connection with *Modern Painters*,[1] which I should be sorry that you lost, and an important letter also about Charles Turner's touched proofs. For those at present got from Colnaghi—many thanks—and tell Scott

1. See Letter 152.

on no account to keep the others for me as they were of subjects which I should never buy in an expensive state.

Lupton's Liber at 250 will not, I believe, be in my way either. If it is very fine and really worth the money—above all—if it has *all the etchings,* I might beg you to lend me 250 for a year, and buy it—and part with such of my own scattered plates—as I then did not want so as not to lose any money—my own collection being now worth much more than 250. But I certainly should not buy it in addition to mine.

I am very curious about those *spoiled* plates which Lupton was going to burn—and Colnaghi bought. If Scott would keep *those* for me to look at, I should be thankful to him.

Don't tell Mʳ Harrison—but the plates he has of Regulus,[2] &c. are to me quite worthless—they are line engravings. They may bear some value in the market. Don't give my name for Lord Yarborough's [3] picture—I hate all engravings—much more now that they must be done without Turner's help.

I am hindered more totally from my out of door work than I have been all the winter by the furious March Winds—I cannot draw even in the Gondola—much less out of it. You were in the right about Steamer.[4] We fear there is one gone down in the Adriatic, with 80 of the Emperor's suite on board— I am obliged to work in the house, chiefly, so the enclosed sheets lose little time. The leaf enclosed—p. 1. 2. fastens on as you will see to the one sent yesterday—and forms the second letter, which when copied, may if you approve, be sent to the Times. Dearest love to my mother.

Ever my dearest Father
Your most affecᵉ. Son
J Ruskin.

LETTER 172

March 13ᵗʰ [1852]

My dearest Father,

In Galignani, last night, I saw an extract from Bulwer's Caxtons out of Blackwood [1]—about Maclise's picture of the invention of Printing [2]

2. An engraving made from Turner's oil painting, *Regulus Leaving Rome.* Scored by Ruskin as one of Turner's "preposterous accumulations," this work, both in *Modern Painters I* (*Works, 3,* 241–2) and in *Notes on the Turner Gallery at Marlborough House, 1856* (*Works, 13,* 151), is most adversely criticized.

3. Charles Anderson Worsley (1809–62), 2nd Earl of Yarborough and a Turner enthusiast.

4. The *Marianna.* A brief account of the wreck of this ship is given in the *Times,* April 9, 1852.

1. *The Caxtons* ran serially in *Blackwood's Magazine* from April 1848 until October 1849.

2. The picture by Daniel Maclise (1806–70) is *Caxton Showing His Printing Press*

— There is I believe really no hope, now for the arts in Europe—when literary men are so utterly—inexcuseably—and basely ignorant. It is curious that the whole weight of the literary men of the day is thrown into the wrong scale—Wordsworth evidently knew no more about printing than one of his own mountain sheep, and writes sonnets all his life long to Sir George Beaumont! [3]—Frank Stone! [4]—and Haydon! [5]—and here is the whole mob of the admirers of Bulwer led away to the feet of the "great" Maclise. But that unlucky Blackwood—I never read such a magazine—it never touches on art without doing mischief—running down Millais—and running up Maclise.

During these cold March winds I have been looking at some of my old favourite Tintorets— Nothing in the world gives me so great an idea of human power— No writing, neither Homer's, nor Dante's—nor Shakespeare's, seems to me indicative of so colossal an intellect. Their work is only thought—Tintoret's is actual Creation, it seems one of the Powers of the Divine spirit granted to a creature— After being long before one of his uninjured—at least untouched works, I come away feeling very nearly as if I had seen an actual miracle—with the same kind of awe and wonder. None of the changes or phenomena of nature herself appear to me more marvellous than the production of one of his pictures—I should as soon think of teaching another to do like it—as of teaching lightning to strike—or flowers to grow. [6] It is pleasant to find that my course of hard and dry study has only increased my admiration of the higher powers of man.

Dearest love to my mother.

Ever my dearest Father
Your most aff^e. Son
J Ruskin.

LETTER 173

Sunday March 14th [1852]

My dearest Father,

I don't know whether you have found my Times letters worth sending —or whether the Times will put them in, but I rather hope so—not in

---

to *Edward IV in the Almonry at Westminster*. An oil, exhibited at the Royal Academy in 1851, it is considered by many critics to be one of Maclise's finest paintings.

3. Wordsworth wrote two epistles and some *Elegiac Stanzas* to Sir George Beaumont and several poems concerning that gentleman's country seat, Coleorton.

4. Ruskin has in mind Wordsworth's *Lines, Suggested by a Portrait from the Pencil of Frank Stone* commencing "Beguiled into forgetfulness of care" or lines on the same subject beginning "Among a grave fraternity of monks." Frank Stone (1800–59) was a painter who was elected A.R.A. in 1851; he exhibited at the Water-Colour Society and had considerable popularity in his own time.

5. Ruskin is doubtless thinking of the celebrated sonnet to Haydon commencing "High is our calling, Friend."

6. The foregoing passage is the genesis of the conclusion of chap. viii of *The Stones of Venice II* (*Works, 10*, 438–9).

any hope of their doing any good at present—but because I want to be able to refer to them in future. I was a mere boy when the present design for the houses of parliament was chosen [1]—but I saw in an instant it was vile— I did not say so in print—because I felt that no one would care for a boy's opinion but I heartily wish now that I had then written to the Times—and could now refer to my then stated opinion. In like manner, I hope the Times will put these letters in, for twenty years hence, if I live, I should like to be able to refer to them—and say, "I told you so, and now you are beginning to find it out." And that would give me some power, then, however little it may be possible to do at present. I have kept these letters as plain and simple as I could—I was tempted to go into the question of cheap wages as connected with that of cheap bread but found it would land me too far : in the same way, I should have liked to have gone into some further statements of the mode in which the increasing percentages of income tax were to be fitted to each other —so that a man who had 900 pounds a year, might not be forced to pay 81 pounds, and reduced to £819, while a man who had 899 pounds a year, paid only 71–18–4¾ and would have left therefore 827–1–7¼— but all this would have taken too much room—I only want to get at the principle.

Nothing heard yet of that unhappy ship—everybody is very sad about it—very nearly as bad as the Amazon.

I missed an hour this morning and sat down too late to write my letters—it is just post time. Dearest love to my mother.

Ever my dearest Father
Your most aff^e. Son
J Ruskin.

LETTER 174

Venice March 15th [1852]

My dearest Father,

I must be short today, too, for I want to finish my letter to the Times —and it is an intensely bright day, of which the brightest part I intend to give to Tintoret. In these March winds it is impossible to work out of doors—but one sees the pictures nobly. Now that Lord Lansdowne [1] is at leisure, I am going to write to him to ask him if there is no way of getting some of these pictures to England. It is a piteous thing to see the marks and channels made down them by the currents of rain, like those over a portmanteau after a wet journey of twelve hours—and to

1. The design by Sir Charles Barry (1795–1860) for the Houses of Parliament was selected in 1836. Ruskin's criticism of those buildings is in *Modern Painters II* (*Works, 4,* 307 n.).

1. One of the trustees of the National Gallery. Ruskin's desire to purchase paintings for the gallery, and the attendant confusion, are indicated in *Works, 12,* lx ff.

see the rents where the bombshells came through them—still unstopped
—indeed better so—for if they were to patch them up—they would
assuredly begin to retouch them—and so farewell Tintoret. I hope for
a letter today—it is the fourth day, I think, since I had one. Dearest love
to my mother.

Ever my dearest Father.
Your most affec. Son
J Ruskin.

LETTER 175

16th March [1852]

My dearest Father,

I have today your letters of the 8th–9th. I am much puzzled by the
irregularity of my letters. Pray remember always when you find them
irregular, that my letter is always written either over night—or before
breakfast, and that *every day* at ½ past 10, i.e. after prayers, George
takes it to post office. I have been also rather particular in my dates—so
that I think my letters ought when you at last get them—to be arranged
with little trouble. When you do not get answers to anything you want
to know—please observe if the dates are consecutive—and look out for
the missing letter. I hope you have by this time at any rate received my
letter about Charles Turner.

I am a little vexed at the enormous sum spent in furniture, and should
be more so—but that I consider the chance of your using this house with
my mother, when we may be travelling, and I know that neither my
mother nor you can be comfortable without Mr Snell's [1] furniture. For
my own part I am happier in a room with rushbottomed chairs that I can
knock about—and plank walls, than in the best furnished house in the
world—and have no ambition to have furniture as Good as the Queen.
The Queen buys expensive furniture, and £5 daubs at the watercolour
society—I had rather have deal tables and Turners. But surely the expense may be a little diminished by not furnishing all the house— The
only good of fully furnishing it will be that I shall have to pay for more
servants—and that my kind acquaintances—who will not subscribe a
guinea for my books—will invite themselves to pass a "week in the
country" with me— I shall very assuredly tell them they had better look
out for lodgings elsewhere—but it would be all the better that I could
say to them I had not rooms— If you and my mother wanted to come
into the house—you could always furnish at a month's notice. Effie and
I want a dining room and a drawing room—two rooms only—for daily
service—and I want a study—a room that is, with a bit of old carpet

1. Of the firm of William and Edward Snell, 27 Albemarle Street, Piccadilly; they
were upholsterers and house agents.

in it—and an easy chair—and a bookcase—and a writing table—and good light. I want also an empty room for plaster casts and stones, and we want a bedroom and dressing room—the latter with a bed in it in case either of us were ill. Surely all this is attainable for less than 2000 pounds. Dearest love to my mother.

Ever my dearest Father.
Your most affec^e. Son
J Ruskin.

LETTER 176

17th March [1852]

My dearest Father,
  I think I dated my yesterday's letter 15th instead of 16th. I must have doubled a date somewhere. I had yesterday your kind letter of the 10/11, with much that is pleasant—chiefly Mr Moore's dedication [1] most kind and gratifying. Cuff's experiment [2] most excellent : you rightly find fault with the want of the little refinements in distribution of shades—but these things can never be expected in a copy— If these refinements *were* perceived and followed—Cuff would cease to be Cuff—and become Ruskin— All that can be hoped for is the diligent *try* to follow, and the care in measurements and other such mechanical points, as well as delicacy in execution, all which this engraving has in a high degree. Then a touch or two on the missed parts would put it nearly right : although the difference between a thing done by the artist's own hand, and a copy, however able—is always the difference between gold and gilding. But Cuff has done this little bit excellently and with a degree of *pains* to copy accurately which only he and Armytage will take.
  Nevertheless, it will have to be done over again, for it *is* to go on a large plate with five other traceries, and there was a mistake in the measurements of this, if you refer to my letter—you will find I said *I* had to do it over again. I will therefore send another little drawing or two belonging to the plate and the measurement of this, and then Cuff can go on.
  I am very glad my mother is happy in the idea of our new house. I have no doubt I shall be very happy there ; peaceful—and in my old ways, and I have enough to do in the neighbourhood of London to employ me contentedly several years : and I trust Mama and you both will be happier than you have been for a long long time—and so I do not regret the two

  1. Of a devotional work.
  2. The "experiment" is connected with a plate for either the last two volumes of *The Stones of Venice* or the *Examples of the Architecture of Venice*. What follows illustrates the great pains Ruskin took with plates for his work.

thousand pounds' worth of furniture. As for poor Effie—I am rather afraid; her London Society will be out of her reach—and though we have worthy people in our neighbourhood—there is a wide difference between the society of the gentry of Camberwell—and the kind of companions she has had—more especially lately—who—however frivolous they might be—yet could hardly say anything even in its frivolity—was not interesting—owing to its large bearings. Last Sunday we had for instance—two generals and a commandant of a city—side by side on our sofa—and however the time might pass in badinage—things *come out of* the badinage of such men which are not to be had out of a decent teaparty in Camberwell; and after being made a pet of by Marmont—and able to run in in whenever she likes in the evening to the drawingrooms of women of the highest rank in Austria, I don't wonder at her beginning to look a little melancholy at the idea of the seclusions of Dulwich. For me, the being near you—and near Mr Bicknell's pictures and within a walk of a hedge and ditch, and quiet—makes the house as delightful as any house can be, not in sight of the Alps, which for some years to come, I don't care to be in sight of, as they won't spoil by keeping. But for Effie—who does not care for pictures—and dislikes quiet—and whose "beaux jours" are fast passing away, the trial is considerable. We must be as kind to her as we can.

I don't know anything that gave me much more pleasure in your letter than your being so much pleased with both Lupton and Humphreys. The only two men whom I have confidence in—nay—I forgot poor Armytage —whom you don't know—but who is just another Humphreys—in better health.

You ask if Frank Howard be a Catholic. I believe so, but am not sure. Thanks for leaving study for me to fit up at Herne Hill.

You mention "Flint Castle" [3] in Rucker's collection.[4] It ought to have been put in my list of "positive negatives"—of the drawings which I would not have at any price. Of course no Harding's nor anybody else's —except Prout and Hunt [5]—nor any of theirs at present. By the bye— there might be an exception if Prout's sketches were sold—have you heard anything of the Family? There *is a little thin book of slight sketches of Verona—with the Scala monuments, which—if they were sold, I should like to have—for love of the old man—and of Verona.*

Dearest love to my mother.

> Ever my dearest Father
> Your most aff^e. Son
> J Ruskin.

3. A Turner water color praised by Ruskin in *Works, 13,* 442–3; it was also engraved for the *England and Wales* series.

4. Sigismund Rucker, whose collection of water colors was sold in 1876.

5. William Henry Hunt, rather than William Holman Hunt, was associated in Ruskin's criticism with Prout as a perusal of *Works, 14,* 365–448, indicates.

LETTER 177

18 March [1852]

My dearest Father,

I enclose half of my final letter, of which the second page will have to be copied, being in a great mess—perhaps even the first may be too obscure for printers by the time it reaches you. I think this letter will amuse you—even if you do not send it to Times. I will send the rest of it tomorrow or next day. I am sorry to hear you are going out of town again—not because you cannot execute my commissions—but because I don't like those nasty railroads, nor mama's being alone. I won't be away any more in winter time at any rate. It destroys all one's impressions of Italy—it is still as cold as it was in January.

I am very glad to hear I may remain executor a little while—and run no risk. It is just as well I was out of the way at first. Dearest love to my mother.

> Ever my dearest Father.
> Your most affe. Son
> J Ruskin.

LETTER 178

19th March [1852]

My dearest Father,

I had yesterday your kind letter of 13th March, with very interesting and encouraging account of incident in British Institution which must have been grateful to you and my mother—and is a very nice counter-balance to newspapers—with respect to which, thank you for all your remarks—and nice extract from Foster [1]— I am sorry to hear you say that I "punish" you by not have [sic] lately sent MS. I will send some more directly, but I hope you will find the enclosed finish of the Times letters quite as interesting. I have taken some pains with it. I did not send any more MS at first, because I was a good deal down and out of spirits about my book and was really afraid of fancying—even if you did not say so—that you thought I was writing ill but now I am all right again, and will send more, only I cannot answer for every day—for George is much more occupied by my dictating to him and by daguerreotyping than he was.

That little bit in the leader of Times [2] about "objection being always

1. Perhaps Myles Birket Foster (1825–99), water colorist and much admired by Ruskin.
2. The main editorial in the *Times,* March 8, 1852, discussing a contemporary political question, commences, "Objection is always easy . . ."

easy"—excellent—and so the piece from *Punch* about smoking,[3] so also the arrangement about furniture with Mr Snell. I am looking forward with great pleasure to a Herne hill life.

Thank you for the "London Bridge," [4] but I think it will be safer on the whole to buy *no* engravings of the common kind, touched or not: the money may be better spent in sketches. I have been thinking over the Charles Turner proofs, and I believe I ought to add the *Clyde* ones to those which I named as desirable. I shall probably be sorry for it afterwards if I do not get them. I am exceedingly glad you have got an etching of this subject, and of Holy Island. The Thun—Morpeth [5]— Jason, and pigs [6] are also great acquisitions. I wish I could get Devil's Bridge. I have been laughing all last night at your announcement of Miss Potter's marriage, which we are very glad to hear of, only sorry to hear that she was met at Joseph Humes'.

Still the same invincible winds. I am getting a good study of Tintoret however and am going today to the Scuola di St Rocco to try if I can get the feeblest likeness of the most noble piece of animal painting ever produced by man—the Donkey's head in the Flight into Egypt. I like the madonna there better than any of Raphael, and I like the donkey *all but* as well as the Madonna. Dearest love to my mother.

Ever my dearest Father
Your most aff^e. Son
J Ruskin.

LETTER 179

20th March [1852]

My dearest Father,

I have given George a piece of MS to write out but I find he will not have it ready before post time, so I must send you another uninteresting letter, except so far as the enclosed slip which was sent me by McCracken, may be worth your reading, it is a very intelligent and close piece of criticism. I am ashamed to say I have not answered McCracken's letter so don't know how he likes the picture.

I am glad you like Frank Dillon.[1] I think he has a great deal of talent —but not intensified enough to come to anything, but if he works hard he may be a good average artist of the Harding stamp.

I am learning a great deal just now by some quiet study of Tintoret—

3. A cartoon that appeared in *Punch*, March 6, 1852.
4. This may refer to an engraving made from Turner's oil painting, *Old London Bridge*.
5. One of the drawings in the *Liber Studiorum*.
6. A Turner drawing briefly noted in *Works, 13, 272*.
1. Frank Dillon (1823–1909), landscape painter known in his day for his studies of the Far East.

and comparison of him with the men of his school: convincing me every day more of the great fact that between the average men and the mighty men, the gulph is immeasurable—there is no gradation to it, a man must be either great, or small: There are countless degrees of *smallness*, but among the great, they are like the stars, I cannot measure them—and though there are different degrees of glory among them—yet all are infinite; and the longer I gaze, the larger they grow.

Dearest love to my mother.

Ever my dearest Father
Your most aff^e. Son
J Ruskin.

LETTER 180

Sunday, 21st March. [1852]

My dearest Father,

I send you the opening of the 8th Chapter of the first part,[1] which I am surprised to see go into such small space— My hand must be getting straggly as well as illegible—for George always contrives to get a fools-cap page and a half of mine into a page of his—it was no use making him go on however as the text plunges into plans and figures—but it will be an interesting chapter, for out of this heap of unsightly ruin, I rebuild the old palace, bit by bit, until I set it again before the reader, with all its perfect pillars—an arcade of 200 feet in length—blazing with gold and with its marble sculptures of birds and foliage relieved on ground of blue—like a palace out of the Arabian nights—and I do this piece of "furnishing and repairs"—with a much less bill than Mr Snell's will be for my palace on Herne hill.

I see you describe the east winds at home as *black*. Here they are white —like the "Solway, White with foam—and sunshine—and sea mews" a line which, by the bye—is always to me like a week of change of air whenever I recollect it. But I believe the air on the Solway is never so bleak as these bitter mixtures of east and north—which cover the lagoons with foam, and drive all the seagulls to take sanctuary in the grand canal, and wreck the poor fishermen—who have found the Madonna of little use to them this year— I suppose the loss of the Marianna—of which not a stick has yet been found, is by this time in the English papers—but no one will hear of the vulgar calamity of the poor fisher population of Chioggia. Four hundred were drowned in that gale—wrecked on various points along the Lido—and down to Rimini. And the sun shines all the time—not a cloud from his rising to his setting—the storm in full fury— and the stars bright all night—and the sea merciless. I will assuredly never winter any more in any place on the Continent of which I wish to

1. The chapter on "The Ducal Palace" in *The Stones of Venice II*.

retain a pleasant impression. But it is just as well that I have been forced
to take a little to the pictures, as I may not see them again for a long time,
and I am very very glad to find that all my former impressions about the
men I love were true, only not strong enough.

Dearest love to my mother.

Ever my dearest Father
Your most aff^e. Son
J Ruskin.

Do you find my writing very difficult to read? I am always ashamed when
I read it over.

LETTER 181

21st [1] March [1852]

My dearest Father,

Yesterday being Sunday I have no text to send you today but hope to
have a sheet tomorrow.

On Saturday evening I went out—wonderful to relate—to an evening
party at our landlady's—Mme Wetzlar's, merely having to step across
the landing place of the stairs in order to hear Rubini [2] sing once more.
He is now living quietly in his native town of Bergamo, being some 50
or 55 years old—and having lost all the splendour of his voice—but I
was curious to hear its modulation again. He came to Venice to pay his
respects to the Grand duke Constantine, and then to Mme Wetzlar as an
old friend. I never was so surprised as when he came into the room—I
recollected him in grand tragic parts—in Lucrezia Borgia—and Lucia
di Lammermoor—scowling and striding in a very heroic manner indeed
—and there came in a little man in a brass buttoned coat—with the most
good humoured English farmer like look conceivable—how he ever got
himself to look like an opera hero I understand not. Every body is fond
of him, saying he is one of the most goodnatured of men, and I should
think they were right. He put me more in mind of Mr Severn [3] than anybody I recollect. He sang twice—but only in concerted pieces with Count
Nugent—and M. Cinq Mars—who both sing beautifully. Rubini's voice
appears quite gone—but his old taste and feeling—and quiet comic power,
are of course still delightful. I enjoyed my evening exceedingly, Mme
Wetzlar knowing how to make people comfortable—and the party being
very small—only, I think about twenty people altogether—a lady, Mme
Marini, sang magnificently, but too loud for me—or for the room—
everybody however declared it to be sublime. I should have liked to tone

1. This letter is misdated. It was written on March 22.
2. Rubini (1795–1854), one of the greatest operatic tenors of the century.
3. Joseph Severn (1793–1879). Ruskin's first meeting with Severn is described in
Praeterita (*Works*, 35, 274–5).

it down a little—or to have heard it from the other side of the Canal: The merit of a woman's singing seems, in modern musical science, to be measured by the pitch of her shriek; I really think, without any hyperbole, that I could have listened with great satisfaction to Mme Marini if she had been on one side of the Mer de Glace—and I on the other. Dearest love to my mother.

Ever my dearest Father.
Your most aff^e. Son
J Ruskin.

LETTER 182

23rd March [1852]

My dearest Father,

I had yesterday your nice letter of 16th, 17th, with mention of received first parts of letters,[1] and of your waiting before sending them [2]—in order to consider whether I should not be too sensitive about replies. Now, to replies or abuse to things of this kind, I should be utterly insensible. I write a letter in a few mornings—which any man, who has given a few mornings to the subject—has a right to say what he thinks of, and welcome. But when I give ten years' hard work, and that at the best of my life—to a subject—and a poor idiot—who not only has never worked an hour at it—but could not understand it if he worked a century—sits down deliberately to hinder me as far as in him lies—from doing any good—I *am* provoked—just as I am by the blackguard children who hinder me by their noise and filth and impudence when I am labouring in St Mark's. I don't think *less* of myself, but I am provoked and worried —and therefore I say not to send any more critiques— But you don't find me sitting down to answer those I have received—much less should I engage in a paper war in the Times. These three letters I want to be able to refer to twenty years hence—people may call them as futile as they like now. I know also how much is said on the subject. When every mouth out of (I know not how many millions of men there are in England) is talking on the same subject it is likely the truth will be occasionally said, and occasionally admitted: Everything true has been said millions of times, but as long as it is mixed up with falsehood, it will be the better of extrication. Whatever I read of public press shows me the *confusion* of men's heads on simple matters— Those three letters do not profess to say anything new—any more than an Eton grammar does. But they profess to give grammatical and common rules in a simple and clear form, and are likely to be useful, as far as they may be attended to, more than a library full of treatises on political economy. If people say they

1. To the *Times.*
2. An indication of John James Ruskin's conservatism.

are common truth—let them act upon them—if people suppose them all wrong—there is the more need of them.

I hear nothing of the Izio. I am afraid she is lost in the gales.

Anecdote of Senator and sacrament very interesting. I enclose beginning of fourth chapter of fourth part. Dearest love to my mother.

Ever my dearest Father

Your most aff^e. Son

J Ruskin.

LETTER 183

24th March. [1852]

My dearest Father,

I sent you a good long sheet yesterday—I must let my letter be blank today, George not having been able to get another ready. The passage which gives the conflicting testimonies that are of no use, in yesterday's sheet, is to go in a note, but I cannot always tell as I write what bits of information will look foreign to the matter in hand when the chapter is completed—so as to enable me to prune them off or put them into notes. A good many of the notes as you will see are rather my own marginal references than for public edification, and will either be expanded or expunged. This chapter is the last of the book—at least of chapters properly so called. There will be a general "Conclusion."

I was rather disgusted yesterday by a man's coming up to me as I was going to my work, to ask if I would buy any of the sculptured stones of the Church of the Servi.[1] It is a ruin of the year 1318, and would be exquisitely beautiful—were it not in one of the vilest suburbs of Venice—and used for every vile purpose by the population. The man says he wants the ground—and must throw it down some day soon—but is waiting to see if he can find anybody to buy the sculptures. I told him I would much rather pay to keep it up, than to throw it down. So it is—Our wise Europe has not yet discovered that a relic of past centuries—which millions on millions cannot recover—is worth at any rate, the ground it stands upon, nor that a fine picture is worth as much space as is necessary to show it.

1. Of this church and its environs Ruskin has remarked in his *Venetian Index* (*Works, 11*, 432): "Only two of its gates and some ruined walls are left, in one of the foulest districts of the city. It was one of the most interesting monuments of the early fourteenth century Gothic; and there is much beauty in the fragments yet remaining. How long they may stand I know not, the whole building having been offered me for sale, ground and all, or stone by stone, as I chose, by its present proprietor, when I was last in Venice. More real good might at present be effected by any wealthy person who would devote his resources to the preservation of such monuments wherever they exist, by freehold purchase of the entire ruin, and afterwards by taking proper charge of it, and forming a garden round it, than by any other mode of protecting or encouraging art. There is no school, no lecturer, like a ruin of the early ages."

I have no news for you today—Effie was out at the opera last night "taking charge" of a young lady some five years older than herself. But she is considered such a grave and well conducted person here that her chaperoneship is as much esteemed as if she were sixty. I have not yet heard what she saw—but nothing much worth. Their opera here is wretched. I only entered the house once the whole season—and was glad to get out of it.

Dearest love to my mother.

Ever my dearest Father
Your most aff^e. Son
J Ruskin.

LETTER 184

25th March. [1852]

My dearest Father,

No MS today either: George was packing a box of casts which is to sail on Saturday.

I did not answer your mention of people saying I had begun a work in numbers, and then stopped.[1] They would say this with effect if I did finally stop in my great work. I have no intention of doing so, though I may delay its continuance for years. But it is an immense point for *me* especially to show people that I will do what I say, and that I neither change my opinions nor my purposes. But I calculate in spite of all that the dealers say—on making my plates pay—if I do not, I will reconsider the matter.

I am in haste today, but Effie bids me beg of you to tell Mr Snell not to put a four poster—but a large French bed in the bedroom at Herne hill.

Dearest love to my mother.

Ever my dearest Father
Your most aff^e. Son
J Ruskin.

LETTER 185

Venice. 27th March [1852]

My dearest Father,

The bearer, Dr Gaetano Faccioli has I believe a very beautiful collection of Italian pictures. You may have pleasure in looking over them— and I should be obliged to you if you would kindly tell Dr Faccioli how

---

1. Ruskin is writing here of the *Examples of the Architecture of Venice* (*Works*, 11, 309–50), whose publication was suspended after three numbers had been issued. The *Examples* were expensive to publish, and the response to them was quite unsatisfactory.

to obviate any difficulty which he may happen to meet with in clearing
his pictures at the docks.

> Ever my dearest Father.
> Your most aff^e. Son
> J Ruskin.

LETTER 186

27th March [1852]

My dearest Father,

I wish you had seen the pretty letter my mother wrote me yesterday—
in the spare paper of yours from Leicester. I sent some messages to you
yesterday—in answering it—together with a sheet of MS. I have not been
able to get one today, but hope for tomorrow. Effie went yesterday to
pay her devoirs to Monseigneur: (Henri cinq) [1] who has within the last
few days arrived with the duchess.[2] She was very much pleased with her
reception—first of all, pleased by being *kept waiting,* for instead of there
being a servant at the head of the stairs to receive her, as usual in great
houses, when she got to the top of the first flight, there was no one to
be seen—till—on advancing a step she found behind a screen the two
laquais in waiting [so?] deep in a *game of chess* that they had heard
no call. They jumped up in great consternation, and ushered her forward
—but one doesn't find English footmen occupying their time so well.

She was much surprised by the excessively *quiet* look of the duchess
and her ladies—she says they had not the least appearance of French
women, no *paint* about them—no *putting on* of dress or coiffure so as
to produce an effect, nor any of the piquancy in manner either—but
exceeding quietness and simplicity—both of dress and *address*; like
English ladies in middle rank of life—but *vraiment grande dame*—nevertheless.

It shows what the French are made of. Last year, when they thought
there was a chance of these people coming to the throne again, there was
quite a little court about them here. This year, Louis Napoleon looks
firm in his seat—and there are—*two* legitimists in Venice.

Effie declares the duke [3] himself to be very handsome. I am rather

1. Henry Charles Frederick Marie Dieudonné of Artois (1820–83), who, as Henry v,
was the Bourbon claimant to the French throne. The son of Charles Ferdinand of
Artois (1778–1820), he was better known as the Count de Chambord. He was married
to the Archduchess Maria Theresa.

2. The Duchess de Berri (1798–1870), mother of the Count de Chambord. The
count, his wife, and his mother were all resident in Venice, his mother being the owner
of the Vendramin Calerghi, a Renaissance palace mentioned in *The Stones of Venice
II* (*Works, 10,* 144).

3. The Count de Chambord also held the title of Duke of Bordeaux.

doubtful on this head myself—having only seen him at a distance—when his effect was not striking. But everybody says he is very good. They made Effie sit beside them, and were much pleased by her recollecting having seen them, somewhere or other—on their visit to Scotland.

Dearest love to my mother.

Ever my dearest Father
Your most affe. Son
J Ruskin.

LETTER 187

Sunday. 28th March [1852]

My dearest Father,

I must send you a mere line today, for we have been out seeing a grand procession at the Scuola di St Rocco which has taken us all the morning and I shall only be in time for the Chiasso post by sending this off forthwith. There were some interesting and disgusting things in the procession as usual—some handsome gondoliers in fine dresses, and two children meant to represent St John and an angel, with wings tied on behind—and leading a real lamb—who baaed in a way sufficiently indicative of the sagacity of the whole ceremony. George has not got his sheet done either so I must send you a stupid letter altogether, but I hope at any rate it will be in time. Dearest love to my mother.

Ever my dearest Father
Your most affe. Son
J Ruskin.

LETTER 188

Monday. 29th· March [1852]

My dearest Father,

I had yesterday your nice long letter from Leeds—but was sorry to hear from my mother that you were annoying yourself because you did not agree with me, and I am sorry that in the midst of your labour in travelling I have caused you the additional work of these long letters.[1] Keep mine until I get home and then we will talk about them, but do not vex yourself because you think I am turning republican [2]—I am I believe, just what I was ten years ago in all respects but one, that I have not the Jacobite respect for the Stewarts which I had then: when I was at College I used to stand up for James the IInd—I have certainly changed

1. To the *Times*.
2. Ruskin senior was constantly troubled about his son's lapses from traditional Toryism.

no opinion since I wrote that passage in the *Seven Lamps* about loyalty.[3]
I meant the word to signify what it really *does* in the long run signify
loy—alty—respect for loy or law: for the King as long as he observes
and represents law: and a love—not merely of established laws at a
particular time; but of the principles of law and obedience in general. As
for the universal suffrage in my letter, if you look over it carefully you
will see that I am just as far from universal suffrage as you are—and
that by my measure, one man of parts and rank would outweigh in voting
a whole school of the mob, so that the mob would no more be worth
canvassing—and the whole system of bribery would go to the ground
at least in its 5 pound note form. Cabal would take its place, but might
be in various ways prevented—into which I do not enter, for my three
letters are merely statements of great *theses,* not endeavours to support
them. I have purposely not made any specification as to number of votes
to be given by property or education—because—in order to do that it
would be necessary for me to study the average distribution of property
and education in order to give it a proper preponderance over the mob.
But I hold it a gratuitous and useless insult to make any man incapable
of *giving* an opinion. Only let the proper weight be attached to his opinion. In the same way I entered into no discussion of the way in which
land might keep up or increase its value. I said only that *if any* harm was
done, that would be *the* harm. As for d'Israeli, you will see by my day
before yesterday's letter that I have no animosity against him. I know
nothing about Wood [4]—D'Israeli's works gave me the idea of his being
a coxcomb—but clever—only the last person fit to make a Chancellor
of— Perhaps Wood was worse—I think it is very likely there may go as
much brains to write a bad novel as to make a very good politician—in
the modern sense of the term. Lord John [5] is evidently nothing but a dirty
knave. But on no account vex yourself—I believe when you have read the
letters once or twice more, you will see there are no very serious points
of disagreement between us—and as for publishing them at present, I
daresay you are very right, that it would draw down useless ridicule.
So keep them till I come home.

I did not like to set George to copying yesterday—so I cannot send
MS till tomorrow. Dearest love to my mother, and thank her for *two
more* letters—received yesterday in yours.

Ever my dearest Father
Your most aff[e]. Son
J Ruskin.

3. "The noblest word in the catalogue of social virtue is 'Loyalty.'" (*Works, 8*, 250.)
4. Sir Charles Wood (1800–85), Chancellor of the Exchequer from 1846 until 1852.
5. Lord John Russell (1792–1878), whose ministry, having been weakened by Palmerston's dismissal from the post of Foreign Secretary, had fallen in February 1852.

My head is now full of other things, so that I answer your kind long letter hastily—I cannot let myself get into the discussion again—or I should get off my present work.

LETTER 189

30th March [1852]

My dearest Father,

I had yesterday your nice letter from Darlington—and am very glad indeed to hear that you respect the present ministry.[1] I should be exceedingly sorry, if any letters of mine were to do any harm to people whom you respected—and who were doing as well as they could, and I shall be excessively so if anything said in the letters you are just now receiving induces you to publish what may *at present* do harm—though I believe it would in the long run do good. I have thought for three years back over all the points to which you allude respecting election.[2] I should be very glad if it were possible to keep the common people from thinking about government—but since the invention of printing it is not—of all impracticabilities that is now the most so—the only question is how to make them of exactly the proper weight in the state and no more. At *present* the electing body of England is the lower and easily bribable middle class—I want to add to this, the mob whom it would be too troublesome to bribe at 2/6 each—and the upper classes, in a mass of weight proportioned to their rank, sense and wealth— You and I have both our vote—and so has, I suppose, our radical coachman. *I* don't think it worth my while to give in my one vote— *He* does, and the coachmen carry it. According to my system—he would have being now 70 fifty votes—and I four or five hundred—I should take the trouble to vote—and swamp him and a good many more radicals. As for the difficulty of counting—I believe it is to an accountant easy to add in 1000's as in 10's: for verification, every man should have his name and number of votes graven on a seal which should be verified on certain days called Verification days—every five years: At an election he should walk into the registering room—show his seal—write its number opposite his candidate's name—his own name being taken at same time under its letter, and walk out again. Not much confusion in this. And there should be no *talking* at elections.

1. A Conservative ministry headed by the Earl of Derby had been formed a few weeks before, in February.

2. Ruskin's second letter to the *Times* was to deal with the problem of elections. It was not completed, but there is every reason to suppose that this communication to his father represents what might have been added had the letter to the paper been finished.

I have made the limit of age 70—for I believe many men in very active life have hardly *time* to *think* till they are past 50. I have myself never yet seen any decline in powers of mind—but always increase—in men under 70.* Turner was exactly at his zenith at 70, and not till then. I believe the mind is never meant to fail under the Seven Weeks,[3] appointed for man's proper life—and that all its best and most useful powers will remain—if it be properly treated—as long as the body holds together. I am scrawling today shamefully, for it is mild and sweet and I must go to my work as soon as may be.

Dearest love to my mother.

Ever my dearest Father
Your most aff^e. Son
J Ruskin.

* Unless such a decline as might as well have taken place at 16, from idleness or dissipation.

LETTER 190

Tuesday [1] 31st [March 1852]

My dearest Father,

I dispatched on Monday, by the Mystery, the case of casts specified in enclosed: it contains 23 pieces, small and large, and is worth about seven pounds—I don't know if you insure so small values: In unpacking, would you tell Messrs MacCracken that I believe the cross pieces of timber which hold the casts should be *sawed* across carefully—the casts are sure to be broken by any attempt to take the box to pieces. This box contains nothing but casts.

I forgot to say that I had given a line of introduction to you to an Italian gentlemen—*Dr Gaetano* Faccioli, for whom my bookseller asked it. I * don't know the Doctor, but he is reported to have a good collection of pictures which he has brought to England to get rid of—in case of any difficulty in getting them through docks or customhouse I gave him the line to you: as he knows no one in England. The pictures may also be worth a glance, if only to know what sort of rubbish is sent to the English market, and to compare with our French friend's importations. My bookseller has been very obliging to me in lending books for indefinite periods, so I could not but do him thus much kindness in return.

I am in hopes the weather is coming right at last—I am quite wearied with waiting— Six whole months of Winter! and two of cold spring and autumn—and four of summer—seem to form the Venetian year.

3. Perhaps a reference to Daniel ix.24, 25.
1. March 31, 1852 fell on a Wednesday.

I have no slip today, but hope tomorrow. Dearest love to my mother.

> Ever my dearest Father
> Your most aff^e. Son
> J Ruskin.

* He doesn't speak English.

LETTER 191

1st April [1852]

My dearest Father,

I had yesterday your kind letter from Sunderland, and a line from Mama upon it— My mother seems to write at present, counting her letters to you, a good deal more than I do, and a great deal better.

I am obliged to Lupton for waiting till you get my answer, but I cannot take the Liber. My own impressions are as good as I want, and I can spend the money better. Please send him a polite note of thanks: but at the same time, ask him why when he knew I was so much interested in the *fragmentary* plates—he parted with these "spoiled ones" —Stonehenge and others unpublished—to Scott—when I had begged him week after week, when I was in London, to show me all he had— And he pretended he couldn't find any more— They are all alike, I believe.

Do not plague yourself any more about these matters. I don't like the tone of this last letter of Scott's. Let them all alone till I come back— break off altogether and don't have any more dealings with him for anything.

I am surprised that my letter about Flint Castle has not reached you— I think it must have been lost—it is surely more than a fortnight since I wrote it: But you cannot have done wrong in offering 75 for it, as a Turner will always be changeable at that price, and many thanks.

You say you "write too often." I only wish you could write to me twice a day; I feel the days when I get no letter just as blank as you do; only I am not anxious as well, as you and my mother are, except only a little when you are travelling. I don't like these railroads at all.

I have been reading over Scott's letter again and I don't like it at all— Give up all dealings with him: I have got touched proofs enough to show me Turner's manner of working, and I want to spend forty or fifty pounds here in casting the Ducal palace, which it will be wiser in me to save than to buy touched proofs which I can see elsewhere. I find the casts I have taken so valuable—and so true—and so much better than any drawing that I should like to get the whole series of the small figures in the capitals, which are just going to decay, and which it will be a public benefit to save. I believe I can do them all for fifty pounds; and I can get my whole beautiful Gothic St Anastasia tomb at

Verona done—figure and all for about twenty more. I hope you will not
think me very extravagant if I do this. And this will be better than
touched proofs.

Dearest love to my mother.

Ever my dearest Father
Your most aff⁰. Son
J Ruskin.

Just write to Scott that I asked Charles Turner a year ago if he had
any touched proofs—that he lied to me—and that I will have nothing
more to do with the matter; and that however enthusiastic I may be
about Turner, I am not inclined to pay 100 pounds to any one for
bringing a book from Southampton St to Pall mall.

LETTER 192

2ⁿᵈ April [1852]

My dearest Father,

I don't think we can much complain of the posts, now. I had yesterday
your letter by second post, 26ᵗʰ March from Whitehaven—only six days
including Whitehaven to London. I am very glad indeed the education
essay [1] gave you pleasure—and I quite concur in all you say of hitting
slightly in order to do the work—not too hard at first: One gets
this practical lesson every time one drives a nail into a deal board. At
first the great thing is to hit lightly—in the right direction—and to take
care of *one's own fingers*— The least to one side or the other—or the
least too hard, and the nail will never go in— But once well entered—
one may hit harder every minute—get one's fingers out of the way,
and at last clinch the matter with all the swing of one's arm. I consider the public may be very fitly represented by a deal board, and all
men who make anything of them may be considered as clever carpenters: It is likely there will be more typical lessons in carpentering
than in any other trade, as it was appointed to be St Joseph's. So keep
the letters till we can look them over.

I do not know when I have been more pleased, in a small way, than
the other night, when I was indulging myself with a laugh at this
French theatre, where there has been a very good company giving little
one act Vaudevilles for some time back. The piece was *Le poisson
d'Avril,* in which the principle character is an English Baronet, "Sir
Georges." I was surprised in the first place by the real truth and
vraisemblance of the caricature—the English dress and way of walking
and sitting got in perfection, but much more pleased because "Sir
Georges"—though very stiff, and rather stupid, and made in various

1. A draft of the proposed third letter to the *Times.*

ways the Poisson d'Avril, was represented as the honestest—kindest—best natured—most openhanded fellow that ever I saw on the stage: If the French often give such caricatures of us, there cannot be much bitter feeling towards us, however they may talk in journals.

I am very sorry I have no text for you today, but George has been in great confusion and discomfiture with his daguerreotype.

Dearest love to my mother.

Ever my dearest Father
Your most aff^e. Son
J Ruskin.

LETTER 193

April 3rd [1852]

My dearest Father,

The enclosed sheet is sent rather to have a copy of references which it has cost me trouble to get together, than with any expectation of your wading through it. I have written the Italian references partly in the original words, meaning to explain in the outset to my readers in general, that there are many sentences which in the original, are interesting—but are not of importance enough to have translations given as well, and That these are given in Italian—for the sake of those who can read them—but that they may be missed without detriment to the general meaning by readers ignorant of the language.

I have been a good deal plagued for a week or two by a kind of cold in the head. I caught a little cold for the first time this winter, in those nasty March winds, which for that matter, are I find dreaded by everyone in Venice: The cold is gone—but it has left a kind of relaxation of the membrane, (I suppose) between the nose and throat, which obliges me to make sometimes disagreeable noises like those which you may recollect poor old Mr Rowbotham [1] used to make—I hear people doing the same here—but they always seem to spit afterwards, and get rid of what annoys them—and I cannot: the affection remaining the same, more or less, all day, but with no symptom of cold otherwise. The thing is not altogether temporary—I felt it first last summer, after a cold I had in London—it left the same feeling of phlegm at the back of the throat, but in a much less degree than I have it now—still, it staid a little all the summer—and, oddly enough, went entirely away when the cold weather began, and I forgot it—but this cold in my head has brought it back to a very disagreeable extent. I don't like to ask any of the doctors here about it—but something should be done for it, as I have now no cold and am in other respects perfectly

---

1. An early tutor of Ruskin's. An account of this dismal man is given in *Praeterita* (*Works*, *35*, 83–4).

well—free from the nervousness which annoyed me in the winter—and yet—now for a fortnight, I have had this disagreeable feeling—a constant desire to make an effort like snoring, and yet without being able to clear the throat.

Dearest love to my mother.

Ever my dearest Father
Your most aff^e. Son
J Ruskin.

LETTER 194

Sunday. 4th April [1852]

My dearest Father,

I have many times in my life sat down to read Milton all through—but never *got* through. I suppose few people have : I am now reading a few lines every day, and I don't think I shall miss any. I came upon a great deal I had never read, and more that I had never noticed or understood : but I am most struck with his dextrous use of language—he is the very master of Verbiage in its best sense : just as Paul Veronese is a master of costume. It is true that dress does not make a man, neither do words make a thought, but as Veronese and Tintoret bring highest dignity out of—or rather put it into—furs—tissues—and brocades, so Milton puts a play of colour into his wordy tissue which is as majestic as most men's ideas : For instance—in order to exalt the idea of the dignity of Satan, he exhausts the *terms* of monarchy : First "The Uplifted spear; Of their great *Sultan* waving to direct" [1]— Then presently,

> Who first—who last,
> At their great *Emperor's* call. Then presently,
> Thus far, these beyond
> Their dread *Commander;* he, above the rest. Then again,
> "In order came the grand infernal peers,
> "Midst came their mighty *Paramount,*" [2] and just before
> "Thus saying rose,

"The *Monarch,* and prevented all reply"; while Prince and Archangel are used in general. All this is nothing more than magnificent State of words; but it is very grand of its kind. There needs an essay on noble and ignoble verbiage. There is exactly the difference between them that there is between Titian's velvet or Vandyck's point lace, and Chalon's.[3] What a delicious sound of splintering of lances there is in

1. *Paradise Lost* 1.347–8.
2. *Ibid.* II.507–8.
3. John James Chalon (1778–1854), a painter whose *Sketches of Parisian Manners* (London, 1820) contained designs of clothing and dresses.

the single line, "Jousted in Aspramont—or Mont Alban;" [4] dying
away into pensiveness as he goes on,

> "When Charlemain with all his peerage fell,
>   By *Fontarabia*."

Tennyson is a great master in this kind of verbiage, also, but more fine-
drawn and affected. I must manage to put a little more of it into the
pages enclosed, or they will hardly go down.

Dearest love to my mother.

Ever my dearest Father
Your most affec^e. Son.
J Ruskin.

Letter 195

Monday 5th [April 1852]

My dearest Father,

I must be short today; for it is very mild and sweet, and I must make
the most of it, and I have no MS for you either yesterday being Sunday: There was much piping and droning in all the churches—Palm
Sunday: the priests seem to make a grand harvest out of Lent. Enormous quantities of copper money are given away even by the poorest
people: Even my barber was expressing his surprise at it the other day—
he says "he doesn't know what they give it for, for they—the gondoliers—do nothing but blaspheme all day; but they have always a half-
penny to put into the priests' box at night."

The affection of the throat of which I wrote to you seems diminish-
ing. I hope it will go quite away as the weather gets warmer.

Dearest love to my mother.

Ever my dearest Father.
Your most aff^e. Son
J Ruskin.

Letter 196

Tuesday 6th April [1852]

My dearest Father,

I had yesterday your delightful letter from Kendal and Lancaster
of 29th and 30th giving account of your room and sojourn at Bowness
and of meeting with poor Hungarian, which is most interesting and
touching. I am glad to hear something from that side as we hear only
the other in Venice: but it is a grievous thing that in all the disputes

4. *Paradise Lost* 1.583.

which are agitating Europe at present, both sides are partly right and partly wrong. The protestants have got themselves mixed with the republicans, and the Conservatives with the Roman Catholics: and according to the temper of the man who is in command at a particular place or time, you have the bad or the good element prevailing on each side. One cannot plead for the Hungarians as long as they have men like Kossuth among them—one cannot act with the Austrians because they are everywhere maintaining Roman Catholicism, which on both sides, the bad division of the party being incomparably more noisy and talkative than the good, nearly all that is told one is false; and the opposite lies merely neutralize one another, without helping one to guess at the truth.

I am quite alarmed for my mother's eyes—almost every letter I have had for the last fortnight has had some of her writing upon it—all careful and clear; yesterday a kind note to Effie, besides what she writes to you.

I am very glad you think my hand is improving. I am trying to make it more round and even: but the hasty writing of notes with no support for the book, and on bits of paper, is very ruinous to it. What you tell me of Windus on Scott's report, is at once curious and probable. He is a totally uneducated man, with a mind naturally meagre and shrunk: no possibility of expansion in it: curiously alloyed with a certain natural taste. I never met with so anomalous a man: when nature made him, somebody had misplaced her pots of ingredients; and when she intended to take her commonest clay—got hold of a handful of opal porcelain—and left it glittering in the middle of the hard brick—after she had pied it.

I am very sorry to hear what a high price the Flint Castle brought—it is the worst sign of rise in prices we have had yet, for it was not a drawing likely to be very popular with any one, very heavy and clumsy both in sky, architecture and shipping.

I hope you will get my late letters in time to prevent you annoying yourself about those to Times or thinking of sending them. I am quite as well pleased that you have not.

Dearest love to my mother. Ever my dearest Father.

Your most affectionate Son J Ruskin.

Windus is exactly the reverse of Pope's flies in amber. There are things in him both rich and rare—and one "wonders how the devil they got there." [1] He has a most true instinct in painting—never buys a bad thing—yet does not know why it is good.

1. See *Epistle to Dr. Arbuthnot*, ll. 169–72.

LETTER 197

7th April [1852]

My dearest Father,

I am only able at present to send you little bits as George writes now chiefly from my dictation, when he has time. I am rather glad to hear that the north east winds have been so bitter in England as it is some apology for Venice—but I am getting very fidgetty about it now. I thought when I came here in September I should at least have had time to get one or two drawings done in the open air before the cold weather began: but not so—I had only begun one, when it got too damp to work—and at present, I cannot so much as stand for ten minutes to look at anything. It appears to me that the climate of Venice may be briefly described as "nine months winter, and three months mosquitoes."

I see the Flint Castle described in the papers as an *"early* drawing." If it was a *large* early one, of which I think I have heard, the price is not so frightfully exorbitant: I see now, however, how the trade of a picture dealer must make people dishonest or greedy: for the habit of changing prices according to demand—or as Scott says, make the most of their purchases: What would your buyers of sherry think if they were charged a profit of 25 per cent on a transfer, yet Scott seems to think this quite a matter of course?

Dearest love to my mother.

Ever my dearest Father
Your most affec^e. Son.
J Ruskin.

LETTER 198

8th April [1852]

My dearest Father,

At last the winds have lulled—and the afternoon yesterday was delicious—so is this morning—and I hope to get some nice work done. I am already better pleased with my drawings than I ever was before, but I have got great good from being forced to look more at Tintoret— and hope to do better still. I was getting too careful and nervous; he has put some hotter spirit into me—and I feel as if I could go to work properly, and my "properly" implies a good deal: The relaxation of the throat too is better and I have no doubt will go away, like the nervousness, in its own good time. I am very thankful to be so well.

I have no text for you, for I was dictating to George all last night, and his day is completely taken up.

I see in Galignani an impudent letter from Scott Murray,[1] but he has the best of it. I have no doubt the letters are done for him: The "Monsignor" of the levee seems to be making a "case" for himself too. Both our law and our lords are too indulgent with these gentlemen. I see also among the articles stolen from a young Englishman the other day in London a "locket" with the hair of—"Flying Dutchman"[2] in it. By what Mr Kossuth would doubtless call a remarkable coincidence, I read today Deuteronomy 17th, where the things forbidden to the King are *first Horses*—then women, in numbers; and lastly gold and silver in quantity: If I ever amplify my letter on education I shall touch upon all these things.

Dearest love to my mother.

> Ever my dearest Father
> Your most affec^e. Son
> J Ruskin.

LETTER 199

Good Friday [9 April 1852]

My dearest Father,

I have written you a long letter today, so long that I cannot finish it to my satisfaction before post time—it being on religious matters—so I shall merely send you this line to say I am exceedingly well and very thankful you approve of my intention of going on with my work, as I originally planned it, and that I trust you and my mother will both be spared to see, in good health and happiness, all my promised works completed—and something more besides. I think I have taken one of those old jumps that I used to make in my youthful days for I am painting with more spirit than I ever did before and feel as if I could do what I want, and I see my literary work before me as if it were done; which I never yet did, to the same extent, but used to flounder through it, and come to the end when I could. I don't think *Modern Painters* will take me very long and it will certainly as you expect, put people right as to my *expectations of legacy*.[1]

Dearest love to my mother, from whom I have a nice little pencil line round the edge of yours from—Liverpool—with excellent account of

---

1. Charles Robert Scott Murray (d. 1882), an Oxford friend of Ruskin's and member of Parliament from 1841 until 1845.

2. A race horse.

1. Ruskin is evidently replying to his father's wish that *Modern Painters* be concluded. The old gentleman, remembering that the first volume had brought distinction to his son, believed that fame would be most firmly secured by completion of the work. He constantly exhorted the younger man to finish it; but not until 1860 did the fifth and final volume appear.

steeplechase and drunken man. I cannot say delightful the things being not so in themselves.

> Ever my dearest Father
> Your most aff^e. Son
> J Ruskin.

Don't buy *any* line engravings—on *any* account—in *any* state—or at *any* price.

LETTER 200

Good Friday [9 April 1852]

My dearest Father,

I had yesterday your delightful letter from Liverpool: [1] with account of Mr Bunsen [2] of steeplechase, and drunken man; (curiously enough the steeplechase and your expression of disgust at it coming just on the day when I sent off a letter with some disparaging accounts of horses [3] —by the bye—I must make this a long parenthesis, so wait patiently for the fence on the other side of it—Tintoret seems never to have liked horses; the Ass in the Flight into Egypt [4] is painted with as much respect as if he had been a senator—but the horses are always neglected and as far as it is possible for Tintoret to draw ill, even ill-drawn—fence—) and terminating with the very clever and agreeable criticism of the young lady on *Stones of Venice*. I think she could write a very good book herself: But I must pray leave to dissent from you respecting the exquisiteness of the England and Wales engravings: I never look at one without wishing to throw the inkbottle at the engraver's head: You will find most of them in my stores—just put the Llanthony torrent beside the drawing, and see how it looks. I never look at them except for mere reference: to know how many figures there are in a drawing—or how many trees—and I don't always find them safe guides even for that. Please don't let anyone tempt you to buy any line engravings—in any state whatsoever.

I am very glad also that you approve of my not giving up any of my plans. I trust that both you and my mother will be spared to see, and see in great comfort and good health, the fulfilment of them all, and I think this the more because I am now pursuing them in a better spirit than I ever did before. A great light seemed to open upon me a few days ago: I have been as I have several times told you—though I did not tell you to the full extent, often very despondent in working this winter—

1. Known as a steeplechasing center.
2. Baron Christian Bunsen (1791–1860), German ambassador in London from 1846 until 1854. Ruskin speaks of the Bunsen family in *Praeterita* (*Works, 35,* 502).
3. In Letter 198.
4. Ruskin analyzes this picture in the *Venetian Index* (*Works, 11,* 405–6).

partly from the sense of diminished strength and increased nervousness; partly from increased appreciation of beauty in my subject, and incapability in myself, partly from a feeling that no one would listen to me or believe me—increased by the criticisms I saw, as I told you: and more than all this, because I was studying the Bible very carefully and every hour that I read and studied it—more and more doubts of it suggested themselves to me, until I felt myself on the very edge of total infidelity —and utterly incapable of writing in the religious temper in which I used to do, and exactly in the degree in which this infidelity increased upon me, came a diminution in my *enjoyment* of even what I most admired more especially of natural things; together with a terrible sense of the shortness and darkness of life—and dread of death—and feeling that all the happiest days of my life were already passed, these feelings of course giving tenfold weight to any little expectation of illness—or any bad news like deaths of Turner and Prout: One day last week I was getting very nervous about the *continual* feeling of relaxation in the throat, though in itself such a trifle: more especially because I thought it might be connected in Mr Rowbotham with his asthma and because my friend Mr Kingsley [5] had suddenly been attacked with asthma just at my age: and I felt as if I had caught fresh cold, and had a good deal of all-overness besides, and towards evening I could not stand it any more and went to bed—but not to sleep: I began thinking all over my past life, and what fruit I had Had of the joy of it, which had passed away, and of the hard work of it; and I felt nothing but discomfort in looking back; for I saw that I had always been working—for *myself* in one way or another: Either for myself—in doing things that I enjoyed, i.e. climbing mountains—looking at pictures &c. or for my own aggrandizement and satisfaction of ambition, or else to gratify my affections in pleasing you and my mother: but that I had never really done anything for God's service: Then I thought of my investigations of the Bible and found no comfort in that either—for there seemed to me nothing but darkness and doubt in it: and as I was thinking of these things the illness increased upon me—and my chest got sore, and I began coughing, just as I did at Salisbury [6]—and I thought I was going to have another violent attack like that one—and that all my work at Venice must be given up. This was about two in the morning: So I considered that I had now neither pleasure in looking to my past life—nor any hope such as would be any comfort to me on a sick bed, of a future one. And I made up my mind that this would never do.

So after thinking a little more about it, I resolved that at any rate I would act as if the Bible *were* true; that if it were not, at all events I should be no worse off than I was before: that I would believe in Christ, and take Him for my Master; in whatever I did; that assuredly to dis-

5. Rev. William Kingsley (b. 1814), sometime Rector of South Kelvington.
6. In the summer of 1848.

believe the Bible was quite as difficult as to believe it—that there were mysteries either way : and that the best mystery was that which gave me Christ for a master. And when I had done this, I fell asleep directly. When I rose in the morning the cold and cough were gone, and though I was still unwell, I felt a peace and spirit in me I had never known be- fore, at least to the same extent : and the next day I was quite well, and everything has seemed to go right with me ever since—all discourage- ments and difficulties vanishing, even in the smallest things. The relaxa- tion of the throat is still there—but I don't care about it, and have no doubt it will go in its time.

Now there is one curious thing connected with this, the excessive reluctance I feel to talk about it, even to you, and which I make a great effort to overcome, because I think it may be useful to you, it is a difficult thing for a son to write to a father respecting that father's religious opinions : and as I think I told you before—nothing costs so much as to approach these subjects—I cannot understand the feeling—I suppose a kind of shame is at the bottom of it. It is like stripping the soul naked. But it is not a wholesome shame—it is Eve's taking to fig leaves. I will not say more at present—because I wish to see if these feelings will stay ; or rather, I wish *you* to see that they *will* stay—for I have no doubt of it myself, and that the more—because this crisis is it seems to me the natural result of the course of thought and action I have been pursuing for years : I *must* have turned either one way or the other, for, I have come to the place where the two ways meet. But you must know also that such a change of feeling has in *part* occurred to me twice before— once coming home from my solitary Italian journey, at Nyon [7] on the lake of Geneva, and once at Cormayeur ; in both cases the impression gradually wearing off : and yet not so as to leave me *exactly* what I was before.

Effie advises me not to send this letter : I yield to her so far that I do not send it today ; as if I did, it must be sent off before I read it over, and I should not like it to be sent inconsiderately. *Sh*e thinks it will make you very uncomfortable, and that you will merely think my stomach was out of order, and that I am getting ill and fanciful. I assure you it is not—and if you could see the kind of work I am doing, you would be sure it was not—it was of course out of order when I felt all-overness, but that has nothing to do with the matter more than that it set me to thinking. My stomach has been out of order many a time : and I have had many a sharp fit of illness in my life—and lain awake many a night— all night long—but without coming to any similar conclusion.

Dearest love to my mother.

Ever my dearest Father
Your most aff^e. Son
J Ruskin.

7. Ruskin was at Nyon in October 1845.

Saturday. 10th April. A fine sunny day but cold again : could infinitely better get on with work out of doors in England than I can here, at this season. But then I have my delightful Tintorets. Quite well—only still the relaxation in throat.

LETTER 201

Easter day [11 April 1852]

My dearest Father,

I have begun another rather long letter this morning but it is not finished and it is post time so I merely send off this with an Easter salutation to you and my mother. Dearest love to her. I am quite well and very happy.

Ever my dearest Father
Your most affectionate Son
J Ruskin.

What a heavenly account of the Resurrection that is of St John's. The first words that Christ speaks after his arising are, "Why weepest thou ?" [1] And I think the whole scene—the *blindness* of Mary at first, in her tears and agony—"she supposing him to be the gardener" and then Christ changing the tone of his voice—and uttering only her name, "Mary." I suppose that was the greatest joy ever given to a human heart on earth.

LETTER 202

Easter day. [11 April 1852]

My dearest Father,

I did not in my Good Friday's letter [1] explain enough what I meant by saying I had come to the place where the "two ways met." I did not mean the division between religion and no religion; but between Christianity and philosophy: I should never, I trust, have become utterly reckless or immoral, but I might very possibly have become what most of the scientific men of the present day are : They all of them, who are sensible—believe in God—in *a* God, that is : and have I believe most of them very honourable notions of their duty to God and to man : But not finding the Bible arranged in a scientific manner, or capable of being tried by scientific tests, they give that up—and are fortified in their infidelity by the weaknesses and hypocrisies of so called religious men, (who either hold to what they have been taught because they have never thought about it—or pretend to believe it when they do not). The higher

1. John xx.13 ff.
1. Letter 200.

class of thinkers therefore, for the most part, have given up the peculiarly Christian doctrines, and indeed nearly all thought of a future life. They philosophize upon this life, reason about death till they look upon it as no evil: and set themselves actively to improve this world and do as much good in it as they can. This is the kind of person that I must have become, if God had not appointed me to take the *other* turning: which having taken, I do not intend, with His help, ever to look back: For I have chosen to believe under as strong and overwhelming a sense of the difficulties of believing as it is, I think, possible ever to occur to me again. No scientific difficulty can ever be cast in my teeth greater than at this moment. I feel the geological difficulty; no moral difficulty greater than that which I now feel in the case of prophecies so obscure that they may mean *anything*, like the oracles of old. But I have found that the other road will not do for me—that there is no happiness—and no strength in it; I cannot understand the make of the minds that can do without a hope of the future: Carlyle for instance is continually enforcing the necessity of being virtuous and enduring all pain and self denial, without any hope of reward. I do not find myself in the least able to do this: I am too mean—or too selfish; and I find that vexations and labours would break me down, unless I could look forward to a "crown of rejoicing." [2] My poor friend Mr George used to talk of death in exactly the same tone that he did of going to bed, as no evil at all, though expressing no hope whatever of rising from that bed. I cannot do this: so far from it that I could no longer look upon the Alps, or the heavens, or the sea, with any pleasure—because I felt that every breath brought the hour nearer when I must leave them all. To believe in a future life is for me, the only way in which I can enjoy this one, and that not with a semi belief which would still allow me to be vexed at what occurred to me here—but with such a thorough belief as will no more allow me to be annoyed by earthly misfortune than I am by grazing my knee when I am climbing an Alp. Of course it is not in any human nature—and assuredly not in mine—which is a very illtempered and weak one—to conquer the sense of vexation or of pain—that is not intended: mental pain is—and must be, as definite as bodily pain—as the aching of the flesh after it is torn, so must the aching of the heart be, after that is hurt; and if you were to write me word that all my Turners were burned, I don't mean that my heart would not ache about it, but that I could now bear the heartache as a thing which in time would pass away—as if it had not been—and not as an additional bitter in a cup of life which when I had drank out— no more was to be had: So far (Monday morning) from being able to bear great misfortunes as if they were nothing, I find it very sufficiently difficult to bear patiently, at this moment, the return of the bitter March wind—with a temperature nearly down to freezing—to the utter cessa-

2. I Thessalonians ii.19.

tion of all out of doors work—and the still greater destruction of all ideal of an Italian spring. But it makes *all* the difference whether one regards a vexation as a temporary thing out of which good is to come in future, or a *dead loss* out of a short life.

The March wind came back in its bitterest form on Saturday morning and all Sunday blew mercilessly: this morning it seems relaxing and I may perhaps get something done.

I don't mean by what I said above of Mr George that he *had* no hope, beyond this world—but he never *expressed* any—it was not his way. He seemed to have made up his mind to work as well as he could here: and to leave the hereafter in God's hands. His sister said his mind passed through many struggles and changes before his death. Scientific men are less likely to feel the slightness of this world, because their labours are handed down from one man to another, and though the men die, the work accumulates, and the bit of it that *each* man does, is done forever: But in my field of labour, it is otherwise. The work goes, like the man: "All his *thoughts* perish." [3] Perish by time—at latest—or by violence— earlier: A fool may abuse Newton's *Principia*. He cannot overthrow them. But the Venetian Academy repaints [4] a Paul Veronese—and it is as if the painter had not been born.

Dearest love to my mother.

Ever my dearest Father
Your most aff^e. Son
J Ruskin.

LETTER 203

14th April [1852]

My dearest Father,

I had yesterday your delightful letter of 5th-6th from Chester and Crewe, with account of your train of misfortunes—ending with your often *dreamed* of misfortune par excellence of "losing a train"— I congratulate you however on the security of the point of honour, on which I think you stand very strictly—of not being *too late* for it, and on the consequent accession of the Derby correspondent: I pity you in your Sundays at Bowness and Harrogate much more from my heart. Bowness I avoided when I was last among the lakes, just because I had the same feeling of regret for the happy days passed there. In fact this sense of loss has been as I have said in my late letters, increasing upon me for years, and I cannot understand how people of a somewhat quiet or despondent temperament, can bear it without some hope of better days

3. Psalms cxlvi.4: "His breath goeth forth, he retaineth to his earth; in that very day his thoughts perish."
4. A practice abhorrent to Ruskin.

still in store for them. The fact is one's days must be either a laying up of treasure, or a loss of it: life is either an ebbing or a flowing tide; and every night, one must either say, here is so much of my fortune gone— irrecoverably—with nothing to restore it or to be given in exchange for it, or here is another day of good service done and interest got—good vineyard digging, for which very assuredly, "Whatsoever is right, that I shall receive."

There are a certain class of people, with warm affections, who can realize heaven and look forward to it—and there are certain passages in the Bible meant for them. But for you and me—(whose affections—I beg your pardon—but is it not so—are of rather a contracted character and do not at all embrace humanity in general)—I believe those other parables of the servants in the vineyard—and the Talents—are intended, and we are meant to be content with the general promise, "Whatsoever is right, that thou shalt receive." [1]

I am certainly a little vexed at what you tell me of Prout's "dispositions"—he was a sort of man whom I expected to leave *no* directions at all, but, since he did—and considering the way he used to phrase, I think he ought to have left me a single memorial sketch: Turner never phrased—and only *once* in the years I knew him said, "Thank you, Mr Ruskin." Prout made all manner of speeches: [2] I quite agree with you as to not buying anything at Sotheby's; [3] I would not on any account: But do not let us be *spiteful* to the family. If they are in distress, [4] let us help them just as we would any other persons of our acquaintance in distress, without any consideration of what Prout did—or did not.

I cannot write more today though there is much more in your letter to be answered. Dearest love to my mother.

> Ever my dearest Father. Your most aff[e]. Son
> J Ruskin.

LETTER 204

15th Wednesday [April 1852]

My dearest Father,

I must send you a short line today, but hope to enclose you a sheet more of ducal palace, if it is not inside it will come tomorrow. I see you are afflicted with the North east wind in England as we are here— It is black and bitter in England—bright and keen here—there it is like a

1. Cf. Matthew xx.7.
2. A remark of Effie Ruskin's on Prout is revealing: "The letters that man Prout used to write John were quite disgusting with flattery," James, *John Ruskin and Effie Gray*, p. 183.
3. On February 8, 1852, a sale of Prout's work took place at Sotheby's.
4. Prout was never affluent, and as his life came to an end he was less able than ever to command good prices for his work.

rusty knife—and here like a polished razor : but I think the razor cuts deepest. It has just the character of the Bize of Provence : not the same violence—but the same gusty—whirling, uncharitable impatience and *searching* character—and is most abominable. Set in steadily again to-day, we can *just* do without fires and no more.

My Calendar of a Venetian year will run thus.

September }
October } Damp and cold—with occasional rain and great risk of fever : and the Sea coming upstairs.

November }
December } Perpetual rain and storm.

January }
February } Hard frost.

March }
April } North east wind and blight : with coughs and colds.

May }
June } Said to be pleasant by the inhabitants.

July }
August } Mosquitoes. Venice uninhabitable.

Dearest love to my mother.

Ever my dearest Father
Your most aff^e. Son
J Ruskin.

LETTER 205

16th Thursday [April 1852]

My dearest Father,

I hope the enclosed pieces of MS will be rather more interesting to you than those you have had lately. They are so to me as finally settling a question which has cost me much trouble to investigate : more perhaps as a victory over difficulties than for the actual value of the results. But it is curious, among the other coincidences which offer themselves as I work the thing more completely out, that the first hammer should have been lifted against the *old* palace, in the very year, from which I have dated the *Visible* commencement of the Fall of Venice, 1424.

However patriotic and fine the conduct of the Doge, I intend to show that he was mistaken in his patriotism, and that old palaces should *not* be thrown down to build new ones. There is another curious thing re-specting this epoch—that at the accession of Foscari, "si festeggia la citta un anno intero" the city made feast for a *whole year,* "Woe unto you that laugh now, for ye shall mourn and weep." [1]

It all comes together very wonderfully. [2]

Dearest love to my mother.

Ever my dearest Father
Your most affectionate Son
J Ruskin.

LETTER 206

17th April [1852]

My dearest Father,

I am beginning to weary for my letter—here are four days without one. I suppose I shall have two at once, as the post favours me very often with that arrangement.

No wonder you are nervous about steamers. I think this last African wreck is the most terrible I ever read of—excepting always cases of ships foundering like the President. But I do not recollect any *wreck* of so large a vessel in which so little time was given—and all resolution and discipline so powerless, surely these steamers must be ill put together to break in two like a tobaccopipe in 10 minutes.

The weather is a little better but still most inclement. I think the climate of Europe must be altogether changing: however I find mention in various old writers of great cold at Venice, and in all things of small importance, I am an unlucky person—and if it is cold to any one it is sure to be cold to me, just when I want it to be hot. It is one of the most curious phenomena in the Divine government of small things— but one of which I have no more doubt than of one man's being brown and another fair—that there *is* such a thing as that *Irish* false deity—so much attacked by Miss Edgeworth called *Luck:* and that—wholly irrespective of prudence or imprudence, one man has in the little things of this world a tide against him; and another, for him: It is a great sin to think of—or to trust to such fortunate tendencies—or to complain of the unfortunate ones—but the *fact* is self evident. One man is upset every other time he gets into a stage coach—another travels all his life without a serious accident—one man wins at dice—another always loses— Monro and I engage Turner to do us three drawings each—his are all good—mine all bad—and I go to spend a winter in Venice just when I should most have liked to be in London, and when Autumn—winter— and spring—are all to be unfit for work here. This is what I mean by ill fortune. But the use a man makes whether of good or evil fortune

1. Luke vi.25.

2. For the close connection between this letter and *The Stones of Venice II*, see *Works, 10,* 352.

is everything—and by that, the evil may be made good, or the good evil.
I am quite well—all but the slight relaxation in throat which still continues—and very happy in such work as I can do: I do not expect the
throat to get quite well until the north east winds cease definitely—we
have at present one warmish day between two bitter cold ones—the most
trying arrangement possible.

Dearest love to my mother.

Ever my dearest Father
Your most aff^e. Son
J Ruskin.

LETTER 207

18th April [1852]

My dearest Father,

I had yesterday your kind letter of the 10th with enclosed notes from
Dr Watson, &c. I shall try the hot water vapour, and if that does not
do I will speak to a nice quiet Dr Walshman-like [1] doctor here—but I
believe the thing is one that will stay and go at its own liking and time
—like the nervousness and sleepiness of hands &c. which has now quite
left me—though I believe no medicine would have removed it previously.
I cannot expect to get rid of it as long as these terrible winds continue—
Every one says that *usually* they terminate in the Middle of March—this
year they hold on a whole month later and today it is worse than ever—
exactly like January with a black sky. But though this weather may
make the thing worse, I believe it is in reality some slight change of the
locality of the irritation of the mucous membrane which has always
annoyed me— I have not now the same sneezing and *morning* colds
which I used to have—nor the roughness of chest after reading, and I
rather hope that after this endeavour to fix itself in a new place—the
affection will leave me altogether. My eyes are thank God better than
they have been for a long time, and I hope I am getting generally right.
And though I have nothing to say for Venice, which has treated me
shamefully, yet it ought to be remembered that the affection began in
England, and that it continued even at Chamouni, for I recollect being
troubled with it a little as I went up the Montanvert with Mr Moore.[2] I
believe there is nothing for it but patience, and care of the general health.

The piece of newspaper which you enclosed with prices of Mr Rucker's
sale, is very curious. Evidently there is a stupid fashion for modern pictures at present—but this cannot be *my* doing for the man I most dis-

---

1. Dr. Walshman was one of the physicians to the Ruskin family; his medical
prowess is noted in *Praeterita* (*Works, 35*, 151–2).

2. Ruskin and Moore were together at Montanvert on August 18, 1851, when the
former was en route to Venice.

paraged—Lee—sells highest—and yet is thought to have gone cheaply, while Turner is—considering the other prices—rather at a low mark. Perhaps "Modern Painters" may have acted a little in this way—the people who were formerly buyers of bad *old* pictures which they did *not* like for fashion's sake, may have been induced to judge for themselves, and now buy bad *new* pictures instead, which they *do* like: There is at least a chance of their learning something, in this latter case: there was none before.

Dearest love to my mother.

Ever my dearest Father
Your most aff^e. Son
J Ruskin.

LETTER 208

Sunday. 19th April [1852]

My dearest Father,

The relaxation of throat has been much better these two or three days, so I thought it best to let it alone and not steam it—for fear of the after exposure to North East wind.

Do what I would, I could not help feeling a little annoyed yesterday at the weather—exactly the feeling of one of our black November days, with all the Keeness of a March wind added to it. I could do nothing and all the work I had laid out for this time is at a dead stand. Who could have calculated on an eight months' winter, in Italy? I wish indeed that it were as good as winter—in the calm frosty days I could draw for half an hour or an hour without getting any harm; except my fingers pinched —now I cannot stand for half a minute— I don't so much care about the drawing that I miss—but I cannot get any *thinking:* I cannot look long enough at anything to fix it in my mind—not even read an inscription of the front of Sta M. Formosa, for want of which that chapter is broken off where you have it. I believe, for another thing, that the north east wind has an effect both on the body and mind—and dries up one's good resolutions as it dries one's skin. How true that is of Pope, "Perhaps the Wind just shifted from the East" [1] of a man's sudden amiability. But there is all the difference in the world between feeling oneself chilled and wrong, fighting against it; and yielding to every petulant feeling that comes into one's heart.

I don't see, for one thing, why I should write badly today because the North east wind is blowing.

When I spoke, the other day, of the moral difficulties of believing,[2] I meant for instance in such a passage as Hosea, XI. 1. "I called my son

1. *Moral Essays in Four Epistles to Several Persons, Epistle* 1, 112.
2. In Letter 202.

out of Egypt." Now this is a perfectly natural expression as applied to the Exodus: but when St Matthew (2nd 15) applies it to the coming up of Christ out of Egypt, it is enough to make any *merely scientific* reader of the Bible throw up both Hosea and St Matthew: For if the same forced application were made in any other book—and a passage was called a "prophecy" because it *could* by a severe wrench, be applied to a future event as well as to a past one, it would be to any candid person, very strong evidence of an attempt at imposture. So again, in Hosea IX. 3. we have, "Ephraim shall return to Egypt" and in XI. 3, and 5. "I taught Ephraim to go— He shall *not* return into Egypt." Now whether Ephraim ever returns to Egypt or not—it is evident that the Prophet is perfectly safe— No Heathen oracle, that ever I read of, was more doubtful, or more explicable according to events.

But this is assuredly not the way in which God intended Scripture to be proved: He never intended men to be saved by mathematics—or by syllogisms—but by fair trial of the Presence and Power of God, by throwing themselves upon Him, and trusting Him in all their acts and ways: and then Scripture will be made their food—and the Inspiration of it will be felt by them though they cannot, a priori, prove to themselves it is inspired.

But I do not think the full difficulty of Belief is half enough confessed by Divines. They all seem to me to shirk it—and try to keep people from finding out the real state of the case, by reading bits of Scripture at a time, and dwelling upon detached words and phrases: and thus people go on in a semi-belief, of which the deadness and uselessness is never probed to the quick—there is something the matter with it—and they don't know what—and dare not look and see.

It is indeed very *strange* that Scripture *has* been permitted to be written in this way—but everything in the world is strange—and the fact being, that God intended a world so full of vice and folly to exist—the fact of his giving only a mysterious and questionable Revelation to that world, such as only can be of use to men whom God predisposes to read it in a certain way—is a necessary accompaniment of it. And the only question now is, how we may make the most of such revelation as we have—trusting God with its fitness or unfitness: But I don't think the way to make the most of it is to conceal its real character—or to close our eyes to its difficulties and I believe that faith is always to be a literal victory 1st John. v.4. (epistle for today)—and not the result of a reasoning process. You will perhaps remember some notes on this point in a letter written from Lisieux [3] in 1848.

Dearest love to my mother.

Ever my dearest Father
Your most affectionate Son.
J Ruskin.

3. The letter from Lisieux is in *Works, 36,* 90–2.

LETTER 209

Sunday. 19th April [1852]

My dearest Father,

Looking over some letters which ought to be answered, I find one from D[r] Close [1] of Cheltenham, dated October 16th '51, but which beginning "Dear Sir" and ending "most truly yours" must be I think to you and not to me. It asks for money for training students for some work which I, or you, are to learn by "the enclosed" but what the enclosed was I know not. I find with it but perhaps by accident a report of the Lay association for supporting the missions of the Church of Scotland. Do you recollect anything of this letter?

I have now found "the enclosed"; it is the Cheltenham Church of England training institution. I wonder whether the letter was to you or me.

I have been reading the occasional paper of the Scripture readers society. That seems a thing necessary to be supported. I have been too much taken up with my own concerns; but unless one is nearly all given to one thing, very little can be done.

Monday morning. It seems a little milder, but black and raw. I must be content to do what I can—if I could only recover a little feeling of old Venice I should not mind—but it seems to me at present a species of Greenland or Spitzbergen. I might nearly as well be on the arctic expedition—and get presents from the ladies of embroidered comforters.

I shall have some more MS I hope, for you, tomorrow. Dearest love to my mother. Ever my dearest Father.

Your most aff[e]. Son
J Ruskin.

LETTER 210

21st April [1852]

My dearest Father,

Weather worse and worse— I was obliged to give up my work yesterday a quarter of an hour after beginning it, today I do not think of stirring out—except to call on M[r] Brown whom you enquire after.

He is as *kind* as ever, but we see little of him, for he is as jealous as he is irritable—he has quarrelled with everybody who lives in Venice and does not come to see us lest he should meet them in our drawing room. He did meet a lady once—to whom he was so rude that we were made all very uncomfortable—and he himself the most so—and he did

1. Dr. Francis Close (1797–1882), Evangelical divine who had a living at Cheltenham from 1826 to 1856. He assisted many church societies often including those not in accord with the Established church.

not call again for six weeks— Whenever he comes, we are obliged to tell the servants to let no one else in: He never dines out—neither do we, but if anything is to be *done* he is always ready, and so are we. We were able to do him a considerable kindness the other day, by getting the brother of one of his servants who had been drawn for a conscript— allowed to stay in Venice on condition of his working at the arsenal. This we did through an officer whom Mr Brown *wouldn't* know. But the other day he asked some information from me for an Italian friend about the Ducal palace. I gave it him, saying at the same time that I had worked rather hard to get it, and that if his friend printed it, he ought in justice to say from whom he received it. Mr Brown went and translated my whole letter into Italian himself—had it copied by the public librarian; and inscribed with the date of sending—in order that there might be no possible mistake as to the real origin of whatever may be found useful in it: Many men would do an ordinary kindness who would not spend a whole forenoon in translating a letter.

I had yesterday your letter of 13th and 14th with nice account of house. I wish I were in it—instead of shut up here in a storm of two months long, but I am grieved to hear of influenza—nothing else is to be expected, however, in this weather.

If the Sheideck will bring 150 or more, I would sell. Otherwise not. Turner's pictures will take sudden rises—but I have never yet known them *fall* in value, and I believe they never will.

I shall be glad to see M^r and Mrs Charles Woodd.[1]

Dearest love to my mother.

> Ever my dearest Father.
> Your most affec^e. Son
> J Ruskin.

LETTER 211

22nd April [1852]

My dearest Father,

Still bitter cold—and as I can do nothing out of doors, I am actually —what should you think? Packing up! Not that I am coming away just yet, but I have so many things to pack that the sooner I begin the better, and it is bright today so I shall get a little study of Tintoret, but I am in despair about my final studies of the outside of St Mark's which I expected to have had all April clear for, and I cannot stand and look at it for five minutes. I hope I shall have a letter today saying my mother and you are better: I don't like influenza for my mother, it always seems to tell upon her and weaken her. My throat is decidedly better. I think

1. Charles H. Woodd of Skipton, Yorkshire, was associated with Ruskin in several of the enterprises of the St. George's Guild.

going away, but I have allowed myself to be annoyed by this East wind and that is very wrong of me—and so the throat is not quite well yet—merely to show me that I am wrong.

I am a little surprised at finding no notice in your letter of mine about casts in lieu of Studiorum, my mother thought you would be pleased but I was by no means so sure of that, for I have a notion you do not like casts: neither do I, of fine work—but of rough outside work they are really as good as the originals—only do not suppose that I want casts here, and then shall beg for Liber Studiorum when I get home— My admiration of Turner is brightened by imagination—and I am at present literally *disgusted* with Venice, so my choice between the two is quite deliberate.

Dearest love to my mother.

Ever my dearest Father.
Your most affec. Son,
J Ruskin.

My mother and you will be perhaps sickening in doubt of my stay. Though it should rain—hail and blow—every day henceforward, with East wind to boot—yet, with God's permission, I will be at Denmark Hill at latest on the 1st of July, unless that day be a Sunday, and in that case on the last day of June.

LETTER 212

23rd April [1852]

My dearest Father,

The wind has changed at last, but it is still very cold, however, I daresay I may get something done towards the afternoon. I quite agree with you in your fondness for Milton's pieces of *softer* verse—still I think both Dante [1] and Shakespeare beat him far in true tenderness: the passage you quote from Dante, and many others like it, are the most truly noble pieces of tenderness that the world possesses. I think it is Byron who says—and it is one of the truest things that he ever said—that there is *no* tenderness like Dante's. [2] It owes a peculiar charm to its *short*ness—it is always as if the words had been stopped by tears: Shakespeare comes near him sometimes—but never quite touches him: I think in the setting forth of a sublime vision by the best possible words

1. The comparison here stated between Dante and Milton is echoed in *The Stones of Venice II* (*Works, 10,* 307–8).

2. In *The Works of Lord Byron, Letters and Journals,* ed. Rowland E. Prothero (London, J. Murray, 1901), 5, 194, Byron says in his diary, "Why, there is gentleness in Dante beyond all gentleness, when he is tender. It is true that, treating of the Christian Hades, or Hell, there is not much scope or site for gentleness—but who but Dante could have introduced any 'gentleness' at all into Hell? Is there any in Milton's? No—and Dante's Heaven is all love, or glory or majesty."

and metaphors, Milton beats them both. I know nothing in Shakespeare or Dante so grandly *painted* as the two scenes of preparation for battle; between Satan and Death [3]—and Satan and Gabriel.[4] The Death Scene every one knows—but I don't so much care for the first mysterious sketch of the Shadow, as for the opposition of the Dark and light—in their most appalling forms—when they prepare for battle—like the two clouds "over the Caspian" [5]—Satan burning like a comet—Death wrapped in darkness. The other passage is in the end of the fourth book, when the angelic squadron *"Turned fiery red*—sharpening in mooned horns." [6] That change of colour is very *like* Dante, and the rest of it is finer than Dante—in its kind—as a piece of painting.

I would infinitely rather have written the passage where the Angel opens hell gates to Dante,[7] the evil spirits leaping out of his way *like frogs*—than either of these—the best in Milton—but still in *their way* —they are finer than anything in anybody else. Dante *thinks* immeasurably finer things than Milton, but draws them more hastily: in this respect he is a good deal like Tintoret beside Titian.

Dearest love to my mother.

> Ever my dearest Father.
> Your most affect. Son
> J Ruskin.

When I say that Dante paints more hastily, I don't mean less *distinctly.* Far more so: Dante would never write a piece of rank nonsense—like the expression "Sat horror, plumed." [8] He would have either told you nothing—or told you that the crest was of such and such a shape. But for this very reason he often does not excite the imagination to help him out—as Milton does.

LETTER 213

24th April [1852]

My dearest Father,

I had yesterday your letter of the 16th–17th (with enclosed review) for which letter I was very thankful; as I was a little afraid of the effect of mine respecting religious impressions, and am much relieved by finding that it has not made you anxious about my health, so that I may speak of the thing further. Two days after that lie-awake night, of which I told you,[1] I was drawing, in the morning, from a high subject at St

3. *Paradise Lost,* II, 704 ff.
4. *Ibid.,* IV, 977 ff.
5. *Ibid.,* II, 716.
6. *Ibid.,* IV, 978.
7. *Inferno,* IX, 75 ff.
8. *Paradise Lost,* IV, 989.
1. In Letter 200.

Marks which made me raise my eyes and let them fall very often—and the black specks tormented me excessively, and I fancied there were more of them coming and was getting despondent about them. But I thought presently that it was now God's affair, not mine, and that if He thought I could serve Him better with specks in my eyes than without them—or chose that I should not draw any more—but only write, and read a little, that it was none of *my* business. So I put the matter into His hands—and went on with my work very merrily. That very afternoon the eyes were better—and they have been better ever since than for these ten years: so much so that I am not without hopes of the black specks disappearing altogether—not that I look for such a sign as this would be, as a thing to be asked for more especially to be asked for in any way for my own sake: But it seems to me that it would be very useful to other people if it did happen: and so I pray for it—only taking care that I am not disappointed if it should be refused, for I have indeed no business to ask for such a thing, for it would be something very close upon a miracle. I was doubtful whether I should tell you this, lest—if the eyes got bad again, your doubts should be rendered stronger. But that also I must leave in God's hands—only praying you to consider the thing just as I do myself—as one which we have hardly any business to ask for, much less to be doubtful or disappointed—if instead of getting well—the eyes should get much worse—or fail me altogether—which would be God's shortest way of showing me that I was not to draw.

I wonder, by the bye, why Bunyan, in describing the Slough of Despond, did not tell us: "And there was in that place also a gust of that old Egyptian *East wind:* which brought the Locusts upon Pharaoh?" [2]

Many thanks for the review of Lord Holland,[3] admirably written—and very nobly eulogistic of Burke. I have no doubt I shall like him—for as you say—I have come round gradually to all *your* old likings: But you know I have not read *any* of him, yet—except the essay on the sublime and beautiful, which was a mere piece of bye work, but is better than other people's.

I am very glad you enjoy Jeffrey so much, and that the life is so nicely done by Lord Cockburn [4]—how quickly done, too! But as for Jeffrey—I find that it ordered me that I am to forgive my *own* enemies—(which I will with all my heart) but I don't find it ordered

2. Cf. Exodus x.13.

3. A review of the first volume of *Memories of the Whig Party during my time* by Henry Richard, Lord Holland, ed. by his son Henry Edward, Lord Holland, 2 vols. (London, 1852–54).

4. *The Life of Lord Jeffrey* by Lord Cockburn, 2 vols. (Edinburgh, 1852). Francis Jeffrey (1773–1850) was editor of the *Edinburgh Review* for over twenty-five years and severed his connection with it in 1829.

me that I am to forgive *other people's*. I don't think I shall ever forgive him the attack on Keats.[5] However honest—it was so *stupid* a thing not to see the boy's power.

Dearest love to my mother.

> Ever my dearest Father.
> Your most affecᵉ. Son,
> J Ruskin.

LETTER 214

25ᵗʰ April [1852]

My dearest Father,

I must only send you a line today, for I am in disorder packing up the memoranda I don't want: and must get out of it as soon as possible. Today is bright—and wind south—but still by no means warm. Throat decidedly better.

I hardly know what there is in the enclosed—George is daguerreotyping very busily and writing from dictation—so that I can hardly ever get a sheet out of him for you.

Dearest love to my mother.

> Ever my dearest Father
> Your most affecᵉ. Son,
> J Ruskin.

LETTER 215

Monday, 26ᵗʰ April [1852]

My dearest Father,

I must have been misdating my letters by a day. I have got a day more than I expected—much need—North East still. I cannot at present conceive the possibility of a warm day, any where. High wind appears the normal condition of the world. But throat much better—otherwise quite well.

I can only send you this line today as I am obliged to go out the moment breakfast is over— Dearest love to my mother.

> Ever my dearest Father
> Your most affecᵉ. Son
> J Ruskin.

5. If Ruskin is thinking of Jeffrey's review of the *Endymion* and *Lamia* volumes which appeared in the *Edinburgh Review,* August 1820, he is hardly justified in terming it an "attack."

LETTER 216

26th April [1852]

My dearest Father,

The wind is back in north east, but yesterday, when the weather-cocks all agreed that it was south, it was not a bit warmer. I went out with my portfolio under my arm—but nothing was to be done—the streets felt all alike so many passages from a back door to a front one. Meantime—so long as the Sun shines, I get some study of Tintoret every day—which is a blessing to me, as I may not be in Venice again for a long while—and I daresay the east wind was partly sent to turn me from my studies of mouldings and cornices to my great master again, for a little while, for had the weather been fine just now, I should only have glanced at my favourite pictures to bid them good-bye—but as it is, I have got a study from one which I think will beat my old charcoal crucifixion, it is not quite done yet, but most of it, and goes on a little bit every day, more and more prosperously: And I am getting my chapters and drawings all packed up, so as to have my last days here quite free. And the turning of my mind to another subject is very useful for a day or two—for in working on the de-tails of my book, I was beginning to lose sight of its general plan and pursuing stray game too far, here and there—the leaving it off a little is like going back to see the effect of a picture: and I see what I ought to leave out, or slur over: The fact is the whole book will be a kind of great "moral of the Ducal palace of Venice," [1] and all its minor information will concentrate itself on the Ducal palace and its mean-ing, as the History of Herodotus concentrates itself on the Battle of Salamis: He rambles all over the world, and gives the History of Egypt—and of Babylon—and of Persia—and of Scythia—and of Phenecia—and of old Greece—and to a careless student the book ap-pears a farrago of unconnected matter—but a careful one soon dis-covers that all in the eight first books are mere prefaces to the ninth—and that whatever is told, or investigated, is to show what the men were, who brought their ships beak to beak in the straits of Salamis. And so I shall give many a scattered description of a moulding here and an arch there—but they will all be mere notes to the account of the Rise and fall of the Ducal palace, and that account itself will be subservient to the showing of the causes and consequences of the rise and fall of Art in Europe.

1. This statement is the basis of Ruskin's observation in *The Stones of Venice II* (*Works, 10, 327*): "And it remains for us, therefore, at present, only to review the history, fix the date, and note the most important particulars in the structure of the building which at once consummates and embodies the entire system of the Gothic architecture of Venice—the DUCAL PALACE."

I have now done all the hard dry work: and I see my superstructure in progress—a noble subject. *Why it is* that we have now no great art—except in landscape—and what the consequences will be—if we continue in this state: while the "except in landscape" forms as I told you, the subject of the third volume of *Modern Painters*— All "Modern Painters" together, will be the explanation of a *parenthesis* in the *Stones of Venice*.[2] A propos of *cutting out;* I found the other day by accident a bit of MS of the letter which you would not let me send about the Pre-Raffaelites—the *second* to the Times, which I re-wrote at your request, cancelling the original draught of it.[3] I am amazed to find how *ill* it now reads to myself, and how right you were in refusing to let it go, so that I am quite ready to trust in your disapproval of the others to the Times [4]—indeed I am very thankful already— since I saw Lord Derby's appeal to the country [5]—that the attack on the ministry did not appear. It is rather painful to me however to find how unequal I am, at times and how little I can judge of what I write, as I write it.

I have not any more notice—in any of your letters, of the last on education, which you seem at first to have been much pleased with. I liked that, myself—and some time or other I must recast it in some way, for I want to *have at* our present system—I don't know any thing which seems to me so much to require mending. I was a little glad this morning to see it stated in Milton's life, that though one of our best Latin scholars, "he conceived a rooted antipathy to the University." For I am always partly prevented from saying what I should like to say about Oxford, by the sense of being a bad scholar, and of not having taken all the advantage of it which I might have done. But no one has a better right to quarrel with it than Milton.

I see however that I must be very much on my guard in reading Milton's prose works—for he is decidedly an Arian. There can be no question respecting this—the expression "of all creation first" about the 400th line of the 3rd book of *Paradise Lost,* is conclusive, even without the numerous objectionable passages in *Paradise Regained.* I think this is enough to account for all the Falls of Milton—for his occasional bathos—hardness, and coarseness. He who would humanize Christ—will at all events succeed in blighting something of what

2. For informative comment on this statement see *Works, 10,* xlvii ff.

3. The final draft of Ruskin's second letter to the *Times,* published on May 31, 1851, is reproduced in *Works, 12,* 324–7. It is one of several defending the Pre-Raphaelite movement.

4. This is a graceful "reconciliation" between Ruskin and his father after the latter's antipathy to sending certain letters of social significance to the *Times.*

5. Edward George Geoffrey Smith Stanley, 14th Earl of Derby (1799–1869), who succeeded to the earldom in 1851. Derby became Prime Minister for the first time in February 1852. His stand on Protection made him suspect in the minds of many people.

is divine in himself. I always begin my letters with an intention of writing like print—and break down.

Dearest love to my mother.

Ever my dearest Father
Your most aff^e. Son
J Ruskin.

LETTER 217

Scuola di San Rocco, 27th April [1852]

My dearest Father,

I came here to work in the early morning—and brought my paper with me to write to you. I must be shorter than I intended, or shall be late for post.

I am aghast at William's [1] proceedings, chiefly because I dread the effect on his own mind. He will be so mortified and chagrined—and so injured by the effect of the dullness of the country—his being evidently and eminently a *town* mind, that is quite enough to throw him into a consumption. It is very sad indeed—but the best thing any one can do, and especially you, is to *soothe* him as far as possible. You cannot *praise*—but encourage as much as you possibly can. Praise such good qualities as his wife has—do not appear more annoyed than you can help—above all, praise his talents to him. They are in *their way,* of no mean order—(though as you say, of a very *remarkable* order.) Everything now depends on his not losing confidence in himself.

You say Effie and I seem happier within the last few weeks. *I* am happier, just as in my first letters, you will find I said I should be, as the effect of London society worked off, which I was sure it would take six months to do. I feel as if my mind had *double* the power, just now, that it had when I came here in the Autumn. I am also happier because the nervousness, thank God, is gone—but most of all as being now settled in my mind as to what is right for me to do, and having made up my mind to do it, so that I look forward with as much pleasure to the house at Herne hill as if it was at Chamouni, as regards myself, and with much more, as it may enable me to make you and my mother happy.

For Effie, I believe she is in better health than she was, but I cannot say she is quite as happy as I am. She looks forward regretfully to leaving Venice—and with considerable dislike to Herne hill, and for the present avoids the subject as much as possible—to which I

1. Ruskin is apparently railing against the decision of his "Perth" cousin, Dr. William Richardson, to set up his medical practice in Tunbridge Wells, Kent. An interesting account of this doctor is given in *Praeterita* (*Works, 35,* 411–12).

make no objection—for if she cannot or will not make herself happy there, it is no reason why she should not be happy here.

We are aghast as you report of Miss de Sali's box. There ought to have been fifty shells in it, instead of one—but I cannot make out from Effie's account exactly what sort of shells. The address to Cavendish sq. should have been *M*orlay,[2] not Harley. I hope it will find him.

I am rejoiced to hear good accounts of poor Mungo. His installation as Moderator to the Dogs of Dulwich is delightful.

Dearest love to my mother.

> Ever my dearest Father
> Your most affec[e]. Son,
> J Ruskin.

LETTER 218

Scuola di San Rocco, 27th April [1852]

My dearest Father,

Only a line today, to say very well, and getting on nicely with my work. Weather milder, affection of the throat nearly gone, and eyes continuing better, thank God.

I have been led on to paint longer than I intended today, but I have not anything particular to tell you, and I think I answered everything in your last that needed answer. Dearest love to my mother.

> Ever my dearest Father. Your most affec[e]. Son
> J Ruskin

I am thinking of returning over the Splugen by Schaffhausen and Strasburg—have you any objection to our doing so? I am rather tired of the Geneva line when I don't stay on the lake: and it would show me the Via Mala and Constance, which since Turner painted it I have longed to see. I do not know if there is any straight railroad from Strasburg to Paris, or what would be the shortest way from Schaffhausen home.

LETTER 219

29th April, (Thursday) [1852]

My dearest Father,

Yesterday I had for the first time, these eight months, a *thoroughly* pleasant walk in Venice—no wind nor chill to disturb me—and it was very beautiful—and I think I could soon recover the feeling of the place, if it would only stay so—today the wind is back again in the north east, and as bad as ever. It cannot however, in the nature of

---

2. Perhaps a connection of the Lady Morley mentioned by Effie as one "who is distinguished by her loud talking and incessant wit . . . ," James, *John Ruskin and Effie Gray,* p. 108.

things hold much longer now, but the probability is that it will rain for three weeks without stopping. I can however in rainy weather work in cafes or under arcades: but in this windy weather, nowhere except at San Rocco—every open door producing a current of air in which it is impossible to sit for ten seconds.

I have got—in consequence of this weather—first—a good deal of rest, which I doubt not was good for me—secondly a study of Tintoret, which I have still less doubt, is good for me—and finally a lesson as to the characters of continental climate which is probably best for me of all.

Meantime your letters are sadly short—for the light in San Rocco is best in the early morning—and in the evening I have always something to dictate to George or notes to make for myself—and I do not like to write much in the evening at present, because the work from Tintoret is in a dark place and the eyes are of course the better for resting after that kind of exertion. They continue better. Dearest love to my mother.

Ever my dearest Father
Your most aff^e. Son
J Ruskin.

LETTER 220

30th April [1852]

My dearest Father,

I had yesterday your kind letter of 23rd with further bad accounts of W^{m.} and the Boldings [1]—I cannot answer it today, having been writing another long letter to Lord Lansdowne in answer to the enclosed—which I think will please you— There was one inside it to Effie,[2] so prettily expressed that I shall ask her to copy it for you, as I think she is too proud of it to part with it.

Milder weather at last, but inclining to rain. Throat affection all but gone—and eyes very well. You will see by some of my late letters that I am preparing to come away at last. You will find by referring to former ones that I never proposed leaving Venice till the Spring—and have only allowed 10 days more in consequence of all this miserable weather, and of the comparative incapability of work which affected me during great part of the Autumn. Dearest love to my mother.

Ever my dearest Father
Your most aff^e. Son
J Ruskin.

1. Ruskin's cousin, Dr. William Richardson, married, secondly, a Miss Bolding, and William's sister Mary married her brother-in-law, a Mr. P. Bolding.
2. Part of which is reproduced in James, *John Ruskin and Effie Gray*, p. 192.

LETTER 221

30th April [1852]

My dearest Father,

I am very sorry they are at the wine duties again, and very glad you have been writing about them. I am glad to hear also that W[m] Richardson of Sidney [1] was dining with you and that you like Bridget's [2] singing and manner so much. How is my uncle Richardson? [3] I have nothing in your letters about Croydon.

I see you have not disturbed the casts. Would you be so good as to order them to be put in a thoroughly dry place—even a bake in the kitchen would do them no harm. I am afraid of their getting mildewed.

You say in one of your former letters that you suppose they are necessary. They are not *necessary*—only great helps and great possessions. Almost every time I *look* at these things, I get a new idea, but I don't get a new idea every time I look at my own drawings. I have also spared myself a great deal of labour for the present, in making drawings, for which my eyes are all the better. A cast of a piece of detail is better than the best sketch, for information—though the sketch is usually more delightful. Effie says she will copy Lord Lansdowne's letter for you, tomorrow.

Dearest love to my mother. I am very sleepy tonight.

Ever my dearest Father
Your most aff[e]. Son
J Ruskin.

LETTER 222

Sunday 2nd May [1852]

My dearest Father,

There is not any passage which I oftener repeat to myself, of profane literature than that of Young.

A soul immortal, ruptured, or alarmed,
At aught this scene can threaten—or indulge,
Resembles ocean into tempest wrought
To waft a feather—or to drown a fly.[1]

And yet I find it utterly impossible, at present, to prevent myself from being in great exultation if I get on with a drawing—and very

1. One of the six children of Ruskin's "Croydon" aunt.
2. Another of Ruskin's "Croydon" cousins. Ruskin has an interesting note on Bridget in *Praeterita* (*Works*, 35, 88).
3. A Croydon baker who married Ruskin's aunt, Bridget Cox.
1. *Night Thoughts*, I, 154-7.

uncomfortable—if my black lead pencil does not do exactly the thing I want. It blackleads my mind for the whole day.

I believe this is a kind of trial to which I am more exposed than most men, owing to my pleasure in my work being entirely dependent on my satisfying *myself*. When a man is drawing or working in anyway, for other people, he has always a hope that if he is not pleased, they may be—or perhaps he works without much hope of particularly pleasing anybody—but for a certain sum of very definite cash. There is great satisfaction in that same steady—quiet, *profitable* work. I don't wonder that a good many men sink into it. But for me, who am always doing things for love of them, if I can't do them, I feel like a lover who has lost his mistress—and a quantity of labour besides, and it is difficult to retain one's equanimity under such circumstances. I fancy also, I have more intense pleasure than others, in succeeding, and in obtaining something of what I want—and great light always implies great shadow—somewhere. A colour that is to be very brilliant, cannot be very broad. It is so difficult too, to find out the real state of one's own mind. One minute, I suppose myself perfectly resigned to God's will in everything—and the next, I find myself in a great fret because I have not painted a pillar purple enough. Truly the Cares of this world choke the word.

My mother often speaks—and I fully recollect—that time at Croydon when you were in so very weak and nervous a state—and making Indian ink drawings— Did it put you out when you did not get on, or were you then annoyed about other and more important things?

Not that I am weak or nervous now, except perhaps as I shall be all my life, unless I can steadily strengthen my constitution. That is another plague. I am terribly self indulgent—and it puts me out to go without a cup of tea, or a bunch of raisins. I believe I could live upon bread and water—if I were in a cell where nothing else came in my way, very well—but one is always (here is a letter just come in, but I will finish my sentence before I open it) taking things when one sees them.

It is your nice one of 26ᵗʰ-27ᵗʰ which relieves my mind about the casts, and saying John Lewis is coming—but I have been reading it till just post time. I wish I had been at home to show Mʳ Lewis the pictures— If he has not come—would it be possible to send him a line to ask him if he could defer his visit till after 1st July? Dearest love to my mother.

Ever my dearest Father
Your most affecᵉ. Son,
J Ruskin.

LETTER 223

4th May [1852]

My dearest Father,

If there be any honesty or truth in postmen, this letter, sent off to-morrow, ought to arrive on your birthday morning, but whatever time it arrives, let it neither be too early nor too late to wish you length of days, and long life—and peace. There is a double meaning I think—not a repetition, in that verse, Life may be long—and yet its days short. Days only are long when every moment of them is enjoyed, and yet peacefully enjoyed, not dreading their departure. Therefore the days seem so long to children—and ought to be to us. I am sorry I am not at home to make your birthday happier and longer—but I will now leave you no more, for any protracted period—a little run here or there is good for us, only making us the gladder to be with each other again. I may go for a week to Mr Fawkes—or a fortnight into Wales—next year, if you persist in not going abroad, but I will not go anywhere, for any long time, away from you.

I have today your kind letter announcing to me the purchase of a new Turner. I am very thankful for it indeed—and for everything of Turner's that you have bought for me— I do not know the drawing, and therefore cannot tell you in the least *how* much obliged I am. I said to buy none of the southern coast because I have no *sympathies* with it —all my affections go to the north—Cumberland—Scotland, York-shire—Wales, but some of the southern coast drawings were very beau-tiful and I cannot but suppose that there is something very striking in this or you would not have bought it. At all events keep it till 1st July. The fault of the Southern coast drawings was in most instances tameness—without beauty enough of subject to make quiet truth: all that one wanted—as in my mind—is the case with such a drawing as Bolton Abbey: But they were for the most part exquisitely finished, and are often of great value.

Respecting the Liber Studiorum, I leave it entirely to your judgment —except only that I should not for a moment hesitate between Col-naghi's even at 400 and Lupton's book. The corrections *quadruple* the value of the finest plate: and I am quite content with the *impressions* I have—but should certainly be glad to add the touched proofs to my collection— This I say only because you seem hesitating between Lup-ton and Colnaghi—for I have long ago given up all thoughts of either, not because I did not covet the proofs—but because I can do very well without them and thought it improper at present to go to greater expenses. Neither Lupton nor Colnaghi deserve any consideration—the former ought to have told me of this book long ago—and still more of the spoiled plates he let Colnaghi have.

Your letter contained also your excellent one to the Times on wine which I think is as neatly put as any that you ever wrote on this subject. The Times answer is absurd in another point than that which you mention. It says "It is contrary to experience to assume that an increased use of one article of luxury will necessarily lead to a diminution in analagous articles." This not only, as you say, overthrows their last sentence about intoxicating drinks but it is itself an absurdity— A man *can* absorb but a certain quantity of liquid in the day—without killing himself. The limit is at present fixed—in some by sheer bodily capacity—in others by expense—and in others by prudence— The man who drinks as much as he *can*—if he takes more wine—must take less beer— The man who drinks as much as he can pay for, if he now pays for wine—be it as cheap as you choose—cannot pay for so much beer, and the persons whose limit is prudence, will be still more definite in their choice of *one* or *other* stimulant.

I wish you had given a detail or two in support of your assertion. There is no cheap wine in Europe worth the trouble of exportation, and I think you might also have made something of this broad fact, that, taking a map of Europe—and laying your finger on the districts where bad wine is grown—sold cheap—and drunk by the common people, you will also lay your finger on the centres of revolution—of ignorance—and of incapability of all good in the population: Observe—The Rhine wines are of *value*—and much exported—and there the peasantry are in better state. But look at the President's reports of the population of the south of France—Burgundy and the Rhone—and look at the whole of Italy—and compare these countries with Holland, Flanders—England—North Germany—Russia—as far as regards the industry and availability of the population. You have hinted at this in your sentence about the Furies of 1789 &c. but you have half allowed before that where wine is produced—it may be a wholesome and cheering beverage— It may be cheering—but it cheers to idleness.

If anything nice comes out of Garden, I would send it to Lady D, without the smallest compunction on the score of etiquette—but also— I should like anything fresh or nice in flowers sent now and then to Lady Eastlake [1]—just send the enclosed line with the first basket.

Ever my dearest Father—with constant wishes for your happiness and health and well being, and dearest love to my mother.

Your most aff[e]. Son
J Ruskin.

1. Born in 1809, she was the wife of Sir Charles Eastlake. She reviewed books (her most notorious criticism was of *Vanity Fair* and *Jane Eyre*), kept a gossipy journal, and wrote reasonably scandalous letters. Lady Eastlake played an important role as confidante to Effie Ruskin during the annulment proceedings. Much regarding her various talents can be gleaned from George Paston's (pseudonym for Emily M. Symonds) book, *At John Murray's* (London, J. Murray, 1932).

LETTER 224

May 4th [1852]

My dearest Father,

I was much surprised—though pleased for your sake, that you spoke so contentedly of the east winds and blue skies. The Skies are blue and clear also here—but I cannot stand to look at them. You will see by Lord Lansdowne's letter that they are felt also severely in some cases at home, and I see a paragraph in Galignani from Dublin, mentioning colds and catarrhs and bronchitis brought on by two months' east wind. It continues here as steadily as ever—a little less bitter, but not one whit more fit for work.

I am sorry to hear of M[r] Monro's death. What is to be done for the family? Are they at Carnarvon? they could not do better. I should think—if any place is cheap—Wales was.

I am glad you are pleased by my beginning to pack up. I am sending for carpenters and making boxes and dismantling in a very comfortless way—a little put out at present by the feeling that I must leave Venice in this state of disgust—and yet I shall be glad to get away. Dearest love to my mother.

Ever my dearest Father
Your most affec[e]. Son,
J Ruskin.

LETTER 225

5th May [1852]

My dearest Father,

Yesterday happened a wonderful event. The box arrived per Izio: all safe—though the poor ship lost her masts in protecting my property. I am much pleased with the three numbers [1]—but I see Lupton and Richmond were right in thinking I made my things too black— A fresh eye is a great thing, when one has laboured a drawing long one cannot see it as other people see it.

The books are very interesting—Miss Mitford delightful.[2] I think she writes better than ever, and I am quite sure this judgment is unbiassed by anything she has so kindly said of me.

Collins, not ill written,[3] is a gross imitation of Dickens— He can-

---

1. Of the *Examples of the Architecture of Venice.*

2. Ruskin had just received Mary Russell Mitford's *Recollections of a Literary Life; or Books, Places, and People,* 3 vols. (London, 1852). In this publication Miss Mitford pays graceful tributes to Ruskin.

3. *Mr. Wray's Cash-box* (London, 1852) by Wilkie Collins.

not be a man of genius—or he would not have done such a thing—
Every bit of the book is not merely imitated—but stolen. The carpenter
from the awkward man in the "Battle of Life"—the old man and his
daughter from the "Curiosity Shop." The church scenes at Stratford
from *do*—the burglary scenes from "Oliver Twist." It is a mere stew
of old cooked meat—Jeremiah's cast clouts. Millais has made a great
mistake in doing such a thing as the frontispiece, wholly out of his
line—yet showing all his faults.

Mrs Colvin's [4] little book very lady like. Take the word in its best
and worst sense, at once.

Account of city interesting, but does not define its terms before setting out. I am lost in the second page.

I am sorry to hear of the differences between various Turner trustees.
I like the impudence of the gentleman who "asked for" the water-
colours; I don't know what Pictures, may mean in a court of law, but
I know that Turner would as soon have thought of calling a water-
colour drawing a "Sculpture" as a "Picture."

You will I am sure get me out of the thing as soon as there is
any danger. I cannot suppose there is any at present as I have received
not a single official communication from any person on the subject.

Dearest love to my mother.

Ever my dearest Father
Your most aff^e. Son
J Ruskin.

LETTER 226

Thursday Evening. 6th May [1852]

My dearest Father,

I had today your kind letter, (with Gordon's,[1] which I will answer)
inquiring what sum is left at my credit at Blumenthal's— Alas I fear
you will think that there are other persons besides my poor cousins to
whom you cannot trust money without its melting, like snow off
a dyke. I was on the point of writing to you for another credit, and
should have done so several days ago—but I was afraid the begging
letter might arrive on your birthday: and I should not have liked

4. Perhaps the mother of Sir Sidney Colvin. Her admiration for Ruskin and the
closeness of the two families are mentioned in the opening chapters of her son's book,
Memories and Notes of Persons and Places (London, E. Arnold & Co., 1921).

1. Rev. Osborne Gordon (1813–83), tutor to Ruskin in his youth. Gordon was
censor at Christ Church College and later had the living at Berkhampstead, Berkshire.
He was a close friend to Ruskin all his life. An account of this man is given in
Praeterita (*Works, 35*, 252).

that, for it must be accompanied with a sad confession, that I gave thirty pounds the other day for the—*not* Paul Veronese—but Tintoret —as I afterwards discovered it to be by accident: It was put into a frame too small for it: in talking over it one day, moving it into a light, it slipped and came out, and behold, behind the frame, a piece of foliage and landscape which only one man's hand in the world could have painted. I wrote most truly to you that I did not care about the "Paul Veronese" but a genuine sketch of Tintoret's was another matter— not a thing likely to be offered me twice in my life—more especially a sketch containing a careful piece of foliage. I thought over it a good while and then determined to offer thirty pounds for it, believing that you would not be alarmed at the price of a common watercolour draw- ing for a piece of canvas which had been touched by the one man of old time at whose feet I should have longed to sit. I was almost sur- prised when, after a week's consideration, the offer was accepted— about a fortnight ago. I was afraid to tell you—and thought of bring- ing the picture home that you might see it before you heard of it— but I must tell you now—because you are buying for me at home per- haps on *the strength* of my supposed abandonment of this picture— *I* bought this picture on the other hand—on the strength of abandon- ing the Liber Studiorum for the present—but as you are still thinking of that—it is time you should know what I have been guilty of here. The rest of the money has gone—as you will see by accounts in legitimate ways— Effie did without half of her allowance the first quar- ter of this year—but on her marriage day I gave her her full quarters', 25; and 12, before, make 37: 30 have been paid for our lodgings from March 9th to May 17th; 97 in all, exclusion of current expenses. I have already paid about 40 for casts, a considerable sum in charity, and something in books, leaving about 130 pounds of the last credit for current house expences since I received it—together with certain stray purchases of Venetian glass and porcelain, in which I have allowed Effie now and then to indulge herself with a view to the Herne hill house—having this advantage also, that being now well known from our long residence here, people who have things to sell bring them to us, and by now and then laying out a small sum, we get sight of many curious pieces of old Venice work. Our most naughty expence of this kind has been for a tabernacle carved in the 14th century—in ivory—(about 1360)—Christ and the twelve apostles—a work of Venetian Gothic—St Mark principal among the four evangelists over the centre— I never saw such a thing before except in Cathedral treasurehouses: and as it has the Venetian mouldings in perfection, I thought it a very precious thing for *me*—for this and some Greek sculp- tures in ivory of still earlier date—and as much of the 16th century Venetian Glass as will very well furnish our dessert table on grand occasions, we have paid about twenty pounds. They are all things unattainable in England; and I do not expect again to have an opportunity of buying such in Italy for many a year to come.

I daresay you are tired of hearing me say that I am *going* to be economical while I continue to be extravagant—so I will not say anything for myself at present—only not to suppose that I buy everything that I have a fancy for. I assure you I have denied myself much more than I have given myself—and I do think when we come home to you—that you will not think we have spent anything unwisely.

Dearest love to my mother.

> Ever my dearest Father
> Your most affec^e. Son
> J Ruskin.

LETTER 227

Saturday [8 May 1852]

My dearest Father,

I will enclose a line for Gordon tomorrow. I was interrupted last night at letter writing time. I must write a letter very carefully to Miss Mitford, for I cannot easily express to her how much I am delighted with her book: and with its overflowing love. It brings in so much example of what persons are in places where I know and hear nothing of them—I think its greatest achievement however has been the making me take pleasure in the account of a baby. I think the lines

> Hands all wants—looks all wonder
> At all things the heavens under
> Pullings off of all thats able
> To be caught from tray or table,
> Silences—small meditations
> Deep as thoughts of care for nations
> Breaking into wisest speeches
> In a tongue that nothing teaches.[1] &c.—quite inimita-

ble in their truth and affection. I find Miss Mitford the best adversary to North east wind, and alas, I still want one.

Dearest love to my mother.

> Ever my dearest Father
> Your most aff^e. Son
> J Ruskin.

Indian corn they say has risen a penny a pound—the year looks as if it would cause actual famine.

1. From W. C. Bennett's "Baby May," which poem is reproduced in Mary Russell Mitford's *Recollections of a Literary Life*, *3*, 103–5.

LETTER 228

Sunday. 9th May. [1852]

My dearest Father,

I got such a nice letter from Gordon yesterday that I must send him more than a mere line in answer—so I cannot write with this—as there is English service today for the first time these six months, and I must have this to the post first. I am overflowing with delight at the pieces of *Andrew Marvel* in Miss Mitford's book—the most heavenly—simple—and natural poetry I ever read—beating Wordsworth at his own weapons; If I did not know how completely one man of like mind might tread in another's steps—and unconscious of his predecessor, I should say that the finest passage in the *White Doe of Rylstone* had been *altogether* borrowed from Marvel. But I know how uncharitable such an idea is—Wordsworth never could have seen Marvel—or he would not have dared to follow so closely. You may not be able to refer to Marvel—so I copy the lines; This first stanza is exactly in the tone, and expresses the entire moral of the beautiful *Hartleap Well*. The other separated from it by other exquisite lines is as follows:

The nymph complaining for death of her fawn.

1st

The wanton troopers riding by
Have shot my fawn—and it will die,
Ungentle men—they cannot thrive
Who killed thee—thou neer didst —alive,
Them any harm—alas—nor could
Thy death to them do any good.
But if my simple prayer may yet
Prevail with heaven to forget
Thy murder, I will join my tears
Rather than fail. But oh, my fears,
It cannot die so. Heaven's King
Keeps register of every thing,
And nothing may we use in vain
Even beasts must be with justice slain.

I have a garden of my own
But so with roses overgrown
And lilies that you would it guess
To be a little wilderness,
And all the springtime of the year
It only loved to be there.
Among the beds of lilies, I,
Have sought it oft, where it should lie,
But could not, till itself would rise
Find it, although before mine eyes.
For in the flaxen lilies shade,
It, like a bank of lilies laid;
Upon the roses it would feed
Until its lips een seemed to bleed,
And then to me it would boldly trip
And print those roses on my lip.

It is very odd—I thought Wordsworth was exactly like this—but on referring to the beginning of the *White Doe of Rylstone,* I find it not at all so like as to justify any suspicion of plagiarism. I think I am in a humour for poetry this morning—for Wordsworth reads exquisitely beautiful, too.

I have some difficulty in getting this letter sealed without some damage to Andrew Marvel. My writing does him injustice to [*sic*]— there is a little stiffness in some of the lines, and they do not read well unless they come easily to the eye.

Dearest love to my mother.

Ever my dearest Father. Your most aff^e. Son

J Ruskin.

LETTER 229

9th May [1852]

My dearest Father,

I have today your nice account of exhibition,[1] of 3rd May, with enclosed— 1. Speeches at dinner—very pleasant—and very kind of Sir Charles [2]— 2. Mrs Tyrrwhitt's letter [3]—she is very—or pretty well —and speaks enthusiastically of our Emma— 3. Seddon's [4] milk and water Art union letter. I wonder we did not see him here—he must have been here in the autumn. 4. Letter from Macdonald—which I will enclose, with my answer to it, tomorrow—i.e. the day after to-morrow, as I shall only keep this letter open to wish you many happy returns, tomorrow morning.

I am *very* glad you like the Ophelia [5]— We will make the Times [6] change its note, yet. But thanks for the nice and true account of all the pictures, but I cannot write more tonight—wishing at present to reserve my sight as much as possible—as the weather is getting milder and I want to take advantage of the last few days I have here. Dearest love to my mother.

10th May. All blessing and happiness be with you—my dearest Father now and ever, prays always Your most affectionate Son

J Ruskin.

1. At the Royal Academy.

2. In the *Times*, May 3, 1852, there is an account of the annual dinner of the Royal Academy at which Sir Charles Eastlake mentioned Ruskin favorably.

3. The first wife of Richard St. John Tyrrwhitt (1827–95), art critic and devotee of Ruskin.

4. Thomas Seddon (1821–56), landscape painter. He is mentioned in *Works, 14,* 464–70.

5. The Millais oil painting which was first exhibited at the Royal Academy in 1852. Elizabeth Siddal was the model for Ophelia.

6. In the *Times*, May 1, 1852, there is a detailed account of the Royal Academy exhibition. Of Millais' *Ophelia* the critic wrote, "There must be something strangely perverse in an imagination which souses Ophelia in a weedy ditch, and robs the drowning struggle of that lovelorn maiden of all pathos and beauty, while it studies every petal of the darnel and anemone floating on the eddy, and picks out a robin on the pollard from which Ophelia fell."

May you see many years—and be able to look back to them with delight. Please enclose the enclosed to Gordon. There is not much in it to interest you, but you would be disappointed perhaps if you had it not to look over.

LETTER 230

10th May. Evening [1852]

My dearest Father,

We drank your health after dinner, and I had a most successful day of daguerreotyping and drawing and a lovely row after dinner and fine sunset. Your birthday has been the happiest day I have yet spent in Venice— I enclose Macdonald's letter, and my answer: I do not know where he is—will you find him out—and arrange the matter for me as you think right.

I beg your pardon for sending such short letters, but I am drawing a little more each day now than I have been doing lately, and do not want to try my eyes by any thing, more than I can help.

Effie is getting up a little party of pleasure with two Venetian ladies —Madame Palavicini and Mad^{me} Arco; all the three are going together to Treviso to visit a gentleman there!—Count Falkenheim—one of the plainest men in Venice—but one of the best, and the ladies are all so fond of him that now he has been sent away to command at Treviso, they must needs go and see him there. It was he who got Mr Brown's servant put into the Arsenal, for Effie.

Mr Brown was as much delighted yesterday as I should have been with a Turner, by Effie's gathering three wild strawberries—and sending him them in a bit of Venice glass. He likes to be *thought* of—in little things or great.

Dearest love to my mother.

Ever my dearest Father
Your most aff^e. Son
J Ruskin.

LETTER 231

12th May [1852]

My dearest Father,

You need not be afraid of my putting off packing up, for my agreement for the Casa Wetzler expires on the 17th and I am moving into St Mark's place for the last fortnight—to try if I can recover a little of the sentiment which this winter has destroyed. I could soon get it again, one fine afternoon did a great deal for me last week—but actually today the wind is N.E. again, and so cold and black that it was just a question whether I could draw or not, with my greatcoat on.

Meantime I have a great deal to do in packing up, and must be brief. You have better direct Post office, now: till the 25th and then post office, Verona. My German map 1851 says the Strasburg and Paris railroad is not quite finished—would you be so kind as to ascertain for me accurately whether it breaks, or not—between Nancy and Bar le Duc, as on that it depends whether I can pass Sunday the 27th June at Strasburg or must push on to Reims, or Paris. I know the railroad does not touch Reims—but if I had to pass Strasburg I would go off the road the little bit for the Sunday there. But I rather hope I can get from Strasburg to Paris on Monday. I have planned to leave Verona—at the earliest, on the 10th—at the latest on the 14th—in the first case I should have time to see the Lake of Wallenstadt—in either case I have allowed a whole day for Schaffhausen to see Turner's view of it, and the falls—and the Alps. I am very glad you do not mind my coming by Splugen. I will take care of malaria. Dearest love to my mother.

> Ever my dearest Father
> Your most aff^e. Son
> J Ruskin.

LETTER 232

13th May [1852]

My dearest Father,

Only one of my shabby lines today again—of which the chief purpose must be to thank my mother for the beautiful extract she wrote out for me from Gregory's letters [1]—very nice. There is something of the same kind in that essay on Baptism [2] of mine that lies on your drawers' head.

There was an extract in Galignani from the Times on the Militia bill,[3] which I saw yesterday—very clever and amusing—but how *is* it that the *time* of the country is wasted in this way—and that a bill is brought forward before people know whether they have got 90 or 19—thousand men at their disposal?

Dearest love to my mother.

> Ever my dearest Father
> Your most affec^e. Son
> J Ruskin.

1. Ruskin's interest in Pope Gregory 1 was of long standing. And in his projected work, *Our Fathers Have Told Us*, a life of that prelate was to have been included.

2. This essay, written in 1850–51, was not published until it appeared in *Works, 12*, 573–89.

3. A series of leading articles on the militia bill appeared in the *Times* in April and

It is very nice your having Galignani and seeing what we see. I wonder at the enormous collection of unheard of crimes which it assembles. Do the English in Paris like breakfasting on horrors?

LETTER 233

[14 May 1852]

My dearest Father,

I had yesterday your nice letter of 6ᵗʰ–7ᵗʰ May, with kind message to Effie, for all which best thanks. The way I have got better in Venice is merely by being quiet and keeping out of every body's way. Every hour of talking to people is like so much shortening of my life— I have had regular exercise—plenty of fresh air, interesting work, and not too much of it.

Pardon my scrawl, but I have a great deal to see to at present, which will save me further trouble in going away 14 days hence.

The Galignani I spoke of was that for 7ᵗʰ May. In its first page— second column, at end of quotation from Chronicle who is the sordid *pamphleteer* who boasts that *Mills would turn*—&c. I should like to be able to quote this passage in its original purity.

Dearest love to my mother.

Ever my dearest Father
Your most affᵉ. Son
J Ruskin.

LETTER 234

15ᵗʰ May [1852]

My dearest Father,

We are just bidding goodbye to our lodgings—I have been so disgusted with the weather here that I do not care—I am only sorry to leave—or shall be—in a fortnight more sorry to leave St Mark's— I am even disgusted with the Ducal palace—from having tried some 50 times to stop in the upper loggia—were it but for five minutes, and never having been able—*perpetual wind*. But St Marks has always been good to me—warm inside in the wildest days—no draughts nor chill —it is now the only spot in Venice with which I have a pleasant association.

I think I must be much stronger than I was when I came here for I am so much better able to see what I ought to do and where time will

May 1852. The specific article to which Ruskin refers here was that published on May 5, 1852; it concerns the wide discrepancy in the count of men available in the British army.

be best spent, and I look with great scorn upon a good deal of the
drivelling and small work I did at first. I suppose however it was just
the small work that gave me the large views. Dearest love to my mother.

Ever my dearest Father
Your most aff^e. Son
J Ruskin.

LETTER 235

St Mark's Place. 16th May [1852]

My dearest Father,

We are in our new house—rooms I should say—and feel as if
we had a new lease of Venice, and as if it were Venice itself again—
we have had the band playing under our windows for the last hour
—and though the weather is not warm—it is still come to that point
that the said windows are pleasanter open than shut, so that I am getting a little into the feeling of the place—but now too late—as all the
pleasure of it is destroyed, nearly—by the preparation for going away,
or will be—in the course of a day or two—for as I said above, for the
present we feel as if we had just come. It is very delicious looking
down upon the place—as Turner found out long ago—when he painted
the first picture I defended—Juliet and her nurse.[1]

I have a letter from Sir Charles Eastlake today, mentioning with much
delight your *beautiful* flowers and cucumbers—and note to himself respecting Academy dinner—with a good deal more chitchat—and some
important report of progress respecting National Gallery and Tintoret,
which I will enclose you his letter on Tuesday—but must show it to
some people tomorrow. I fear nothing can be done—they are too slow,
but I am glad to find that I *have some* power—even with such immove-
able people as Trustees for National Gallery.

There will [be?] something for me to do tomorrow in consequence—
besides my own work, tomorrow—so I have written this overnight. I
have left my proper writing paper in our other lodgings—but think this
will fit the rest of your sheets—if you still keep my present scrawls.

Dearest love to my mother.

Ever my dearest Father
Your most aff^e. Son
J Ruskin.

1. Ruskin's defense of this oil painting is in *Works, 12,* 635–40. Some interest is
attached to the MS of this "defense," which was sent first to Turner and then, by the
artist, to Munro of Novar. It was lost, but a copy was found after Ruskin's death
among his MSS at Brantwood. A succinct account of this document, which was directed against *Blackwood's Magazine,* is presented in Collingwood's *The Life and
Work of John Ruskin, 1,* 76–9.

I had nearly forgotten poor Lady S.[2] I enclose a statement which she copied out of some paper. I hope, as the name is *European,* that this life office can do what she wants. A certificate of age and health can be given by the physician here, and Lady S would give an order to the office to receive so much annually out of her jointure, which is paid on houses in London, belonging to her children after her decease. If this cannot be managed I thought she might select property—plate or jewellery—out of what is insured here, and send it to London, as security for a loan from any banker—to be paid in instalments of £50 a year.

LETTER 236

Sunday, 16th May. [1852]

My dearest Father,

What a quantity of unnecessary suffering is caused in this world by people's "keeping up their position." The enclosed letter is from our friend Lady Sorel, not very explicit, as she says in the beginning—but still enough so for you to make out—however I may as well make a short abstract of it—or rather of the main points to which it alludes.

Lady S. is a woman of more birth than rank—of the old French. I forget her maiden name—it was a high French family—her husband a Sorel—and has a great deal of ancien regime about her—a great deal of heart, and not *very* much sense—but she is regular and well conducted in all her affairs—and got into this scrape at the Revolution—by being turned out of her house here by force—and compelled to keep another at Trieste, during the siege, she and the *regime* being little agreeable to the Republican gentlemen. Her only pleasures in life are in knowing everybody—that *ought* to be known—more especially the Duchess de Berri and such other people—she has never been a dashing person—but holds —as I do to my Turners—to the "position" of the late Sir Thomas, and to her own present respectability as his widow: So for the sake of respectabilities and delicacies—and points of honour—and tender recollections—and so on—she is as you will see, making herself more miserable than any beggar that sweeps a crossing—unless perhaps—and for aught I know, it is very likely—there are "delicacies"—and "positions" in that line of life also, and respectable sweepers who lie awake at nights for fear of descending from a crossing in Hanover Square to one in Bloomsbury.

However, she is one of the kindest people in the world, and I should be very much obliged to you if you would make the necessary enquiries for her—or tell me—as you doubtless can, by return of post—what she must do.

It may save you a little trouble if I digest the unconnected letter for you.

2. Lady Sorrel.

At the revolution she incurred a debt of £200.

She has paid to her banker in these four years, 40.

He charges her six per cent—and Lady Sorel states her present debt at 350. How this can be I don't understand—as if she had never paid anything, her debt at 6 per cent ought not to have reached 300. She must have written 2 for 3 or 3 for 2, in one or the other case.

She wants 350, at the worst.

She has a jointure of £570, and can save 50 of it.

And property insured here to the value of £1800.

What is the best way in which she can obtain the present necessary sum—without getting into Jew's hands?

I shall see her today, and make her tell me on what terms her jointure stands—and why she must lose half upon the plate—which she ought of course to sell. But is it not scandalous that a banker should charge six per cent to a woman who cannot pay him, when if she did pay him he could not get 2½ for it?

It is just church time—English service today.

Dearest love to my mother.

> Ever my dearest Father
> Your most aff^e. Son
> J Ruskin.

LETTER 237

17th May [1852]

My dearest Father,

I had today your kind letter of 10th–12th May. You say you have *all* mine, including, I hope, one sent to be with you on your birthday. I am very glad you have not bought the Libers. I should have been quite ashamed of my expences here if you had—I have the letter of credit. Blumenthal offered me anything I wanted but I do not like irregularities of this kind, and have done very well.

The picture people are as you say, sad deceivers— It must be a wretched trade in which the real value of nothing is known—or even if known—not to be had without puffing. So much depends on humour and fashion. The Libers will be shown and pawed about all day—and I never yet met or saw any man who knew how to handle a print— Their value will be a third gone by this time.

Your definition of William's opinion of himself is quite delicious. Yet I think there is a little appearance of depression in the letter—you say you need change of air—have you been overworking yourself—or have you been vexed by my buying the Tintoret and yet not liked to tell me so? I enclose Sir C. Eastlake's letter—which has given me a good deal to do in talking over Mr Cheney [1] so as not to make him jealous. A word

1. While Ruskin was trying to persuade the trustees of the National Gallery to buy

that piqued him might have spoiled all—however it is all right—only they ought to have told me this a fortnight ago. I fear it is now too late —I shall be at Verona when the Trustees give me their final answer— and can only set the thing in train—if *any*thing can be done at all.

Meantime I must be short—for it is late. I have to go and look at a picture which *is* for sale, positively—and is said to be a Tintoret of importance—price 1000—this at any rate I hope to be able to get for National gallery—if no larger game. Dearest love to my mother.

Ever my dearest Father
Your most affec^e. Son
J Ruskin.

LETTER 238

[19 May 1852]

My dearest Father,

We are really enjoying our sojourn in St Mark's place—I am only sorry I did not live here all the winter. I like the small rooms much better than the large—and there is all the difference in the world between looking out on the Madonna della Salute, or on St Mark's. The weather is pleasant too—though far from hot. I was again obliged by the wind to leave the Ducal palace arcade yesterday, though I had on my greatcoat. The mornings and evenings are however calm.

Who is the Duke of Buccleugh,[1] and why should he lend me his Turner studies—if he buys them—does he like my books—or what grounds has Scott for saying this?

I hope I shall have a letter soon saying you are better and are at Tunbridge Wells—but do you stay there and rest, or come up often by railroad? I never should look upon a day as one of rest, if it had any railroad travelling in it.

Have you heard anything more about the executorship? I am a little anxious now that I am leaving Venice and my head is turned towards home, to know if I shall be in time to look over the things in the gallery.

I have had a long letter to write, with Mr Cheney's, to Sir C. Eastlake—so I can send you only a line today.

Dearest love to my mother.

Ever my dearest Father
Your most aff^e. Son.
J Ruskin

---

two Tintorets, they were negotiating with Mr. Cheney. It was Ruskin's opinion that Cheney later "put a spoke in the wheel for pure spite" and prevented the purchase of the pictures. The matter is mentioned in *Praeterita* (*Works, 35,* 503–4).

1. Walter Francis Montagu-Douglas-Scott (1806–84), 5th Duke of Buccleuch.

LETTER 239

Thursday, 20th May [1852]

My dearest Father,

Only a line today, for now that the weather does at last admit of my standing to look about me, I see so many things that I want to take some note of that I must spare my eyes as much as possible— It was a great mistake to come here in the winter at all. All that I have done except writing which would have been done at home—might have been better done in three months of summer.

But I am very well—and now enjoying myself exceedingly.

Dearest love to my mother.

Ever my dearest Father
Your most aff^e Son
J Ruskin.

LETTER 240

Friday, 21st May [1852]

My dearest Father,

I am ashamed to treat you so shabbily—but the Woodds are here, and what little time I have to spare must be spent in doing them what service I can. Mr Tite [1]—of exchange is here also, and in better health, he seems not bigoted—and impossible, and I am going to show him something. Quite well, but I find myself the better always for a glass of your sherry at dinner—I went without for a day or two when I came here first, and found I felt languid—recommenced with good result.

Dearest love to my mother.

Ever my dearest Father,
Your most affec^e. Son
J Ruskin.

LETTER 241

Saturday. 22nd May [1852]

My dearest Father,

I was much delighted by your nice letter from Tunbridge written in so much better health and spirits—though in rain and wind (13th May) but expressing your feeling of the difference between Tunbridge and

---

1. William Tite (1798–1873), architect, who designed the Royal Exchange. He also drew up plans for several London railway stations, a task which has by no means endeared him to posterity.

Geneva— Cannot you still come and meet us—if you can, I don't care
about Turners or anything else—and will come directly wherever you
would like best—we cannot even call it late—for the spring has only just
begun: and my book will not be kept back in the least. It is more likely
to be kept back at home by my looking at Turners— Pray think if it
can be managed.

I had a pleasant afternoon with M[r] Tite who is a droll—clever commonplace person—highly "practical" and very fit to build railroad stations—and crystal palaces. He was polite enough to tell Effie that he
met an American on the Lake of Como—who was going over the
Splugen [*text mutilated*]—but who—finding M[r] Tite an architect—inquired instantly if "M[r] Ruskin was at Venice"—for—said he—if I
could [be?] sure he was there—I would turn back directly— M[r] Tite
was not sure—and the American went on over the Splugen—saying
that there were only two men in Europe he wanted to see—M[r] R. and
another whom M[r] Tite, I suppose because he thought the association
might not be flattering, said he had forgotten.

Pray offer the presentation at Christs [1] to M[r] Snow—or anyone
whom you think best.

The Birthday [2] must have been illustrious, with flowers—and teapot
—which I well remember, for I admired it exceedingly. The money is
not wasted which admits of making a festive occasion— We make our
pleasures commonplace by frequency. I highly approve of the monastic
seclusion of teapot until 10th May.

I hope the lumbago will soon leave you—or that you will leave *it,*
and come to the Alps. Dearest love to my mother, who, I am sorry to
hear, does not partake your sentiments in this respect.

Ever my dearest Father. Your most aff[e]. Son

J Ruskin.

LETTER 242

Sunday, 23rd May. [1852]

My dearest Father,

I never recollect in time to tell you when to alter your post office
direction— You may now at any rate write to Verona—I may be kept
a week later than I intended in Venice by the reply from Sir Charles
Eastlake [1]—and if they [2] give me any money to spend, I must of course
spend all the time I had set aside for Verona here—if any thing can be

1. John James Ruskin presented £5,000 to Christ Church College in tribute to
Osborne Gordon.
2. Of Ruskin senior, on May 10.
1. Concerning the purchase of Tintorets.
2. The trustees of the National Gallery.

done—but I shall at all events get your letters to Verona a day or two after they arrive, as I pass. I am very glad you think my late letters have no east wind in them, though I fear my lines lately have been less satisfactory. I have given up a little time these two last days to the Woodds —whom I find intelligent—and much interested in all I have to show them, so that it is not *wasted* time by any means. Mrs Charles Woodd is a very agreeable—wise—and serious young lady—marvellous grave, for a young bride, his sisters seem nice girls and are rather pretty.

Venice is now looking like itself—but I have been so soured by its illtreatment of me that I can no more regard it with any patience— Still the warm days are soothing me down a little—it is very pleasant—nothing to call warm—but nice open window weather and perpetual sunshine.

I have seen a good deal of Russell and we have long arguments together. But when once people have taken that leap—it is like trying to pull them out of a well with a cobweb, to argue with them. They break line, and tumble back, the moment you pull.

I hope you will think about coming to Switzerland—more than think about it— There is English service this morning which cuts my letter short— Dearest love to my mother. Ever my dearest Father

Your most aff^e. Son
J Ruskin.

LETTER 243

Monday, 24th May [1852]

My dearest Father,

I have been laying the foundations of a letter to Miss Mitford which I will enclose to you tomorrow—and then forthwith proceed with one for Mr Rogers.[1] I could not write to him, before, I was in so prosaic a humour with Venice. But these letters take up all my spare time—so I can merely say quite well today—and dearest love to you both. You have despatched Miss M's book,[2] I see, without reading it quite through. There are many allusions to me besides the principal one—scattered through it.

Ever my dearest Father.
Your most aff^e. Son
J Ruskin.

1. This long and interesting letter, dated June 23, 1852, is reproduced in P. W. Clayden's *Rogers and His Contemporaries*, 2 vols. (London, 1889), *2*, 303–9.
2. *Recollections of a Literary Life.*

LETTER 244

Monday Evening 24th [May 1852]

My dearest Father,

I have not yet got Miss Mitford's letter finished—having been again to Torcello [1]—it is so beautiful now—there never was a place on which season made so much difference. The fields and vineyards in winter are lost among the marshy land—all trampled into mud—but now, they are separated from the canals which encircle the little island by hedges of briar and honeysuckle and hawthorn—and the vineyards are in young leaf—and in the little piazza of the ancient city—round its flagstaff—they are mowing their hay—and it lies in fragrant heaps about the bases of the pillars of the cathedral—and all the peasantry look happy—and even healthy, the spring sunshine making their faces ruddy—they sing everywhere as they go— I am very glad I have seen it at this season—it will at least give me *one* pleasant picture for the opening of my book— I daresay I shall go there once more—leaving here at three o'clock we get there at ½ past four—can see the long sunshine fading over the narrow field—and gilding the marble vineleaves of the old shafts—and be back in Venice by twilight, much to enjoy one's tea after the long row. I forget whether you ever were at Torcello—I think I was afraid to take you for fear of the marsh air—but you would enjoy it at this season.

I am sorry by the bye to hear of the fate of the old carriage—the more because it alarms me for my Tintoret—which I am forced to send by sea—it being too large to take charge of over the Alps, about four and a half feet each way—and it is an unreplaceable thing, if lost. But I must not let the accumulation of treasures be an accumulation of *cares* also. If I get it home it will be a great delight to me—if it goes to the bottom I can do without it. Dearest love to my mother.

Ever my dearest Father
Your most aff^e. Son
J Ruskin.

LETTER 245

Tuesday, 25th May. [1852]

My dearest Father,

I had this afternoon your delightful letter of 15th–17th–18th with accounts of exhibition [1] &c. You say my letters have not been quite so

1. Which became the subject of the second chapter of *The Stones of Venice II*.
1. At the Royal Academy.

cheerful—I believe this is merely because I have been packing and some-what disquieted and though glad to come home—still a *little* feeling the leaving Italy just as I find myself able to work out of doors. But I have got a great deal and am well satisfied; as far as I shall ever be satisfied with what I can do—or have done. I should like for a moment, to feel—just for the sake of knowing the feeling—what a man's joy is in being able to do what he wants—like any of the great ones. Not that *they* absolutely do what they want, but one is sure that they have done it up to a certain point, for one so often sees them stop short—do less than they could have done. I always do my best—and find it too little. The first flitting was quite my own choice—I wanted to live a little in St Mark's Place—and I should always come here in future visits to Venice —it is so delightful being able to get at the Church in a moment.

I shall send to Blumenthal for the accounts as you desire: but—within a day or two. The following list of my drafts is accurate. I say within a day or two because I sometimes did not put down the receipt from Blumenthal till I got to the bottom of a page of my account book; and so might make a mistake in the day, and I have made out this list hastily and rather asleep, and so missed out Jan. 17th and put Decem-

Drawn.				
September	1st	100	} 1st letter.	200
——	15th	100		
October	25th	50		
November	17th	50	} 2nd letter.	300
December	6th	100		
January	17th	50		
February	7th	50		
December	29th	50		
March	6th	50	} 3rd letter.	300
——	23rd	50		
April	10th	75		
——	20th	75		
May	18th	50	} 4th letter.	200
——	26th	50		

ber 29th out of its place. I have put down a draft of 50 for tomorrow, which I shall take, as I write to Blumenthal for list, and so leave 100 still of the last letter. I have been living exactly at the rate of 100 a month. I enclose Miss Mitford [2] at last—I do not know her present address. Infinite thanks for all your kind letters.

Dearest love to my mother.

Ever my dearest Father.
Your most affec⁰. Son.
J Ruskin.

2. Miss Mitford, in a letter to John James Ruskin dated July 1, 1852, mentions having received a letter from his son "dated Venice." The letter from the authoress to Ruskin senior is reproduced in Elizabeth Lee's edition of *Mary Russell Mitford's Correspondence with Charles Boner and John Ruskin* (London, T. F. Unwin, 1914), pp. 214–17.

LETTER 246

26th May. [1852]

My dearest Father,

I have just been reading in Galignani the report of the first day of Marshal Soult's [1] sale. Tintorets at 500 francs are, I suppose, like Turners at £2–10; of doubtful parentage. Murillo still fetches his price.

I have a great deal to do, before I shall lower him—but I hope to bring him down, some day.

I am glad to hear that Griffith has so high a reputation as a salesman. As for honesty, I fancy they are all alike. I had only faith in Lupton—certainly not in Halsted. The business which sets long chance profits against numerous chance hopes, always makes rogues.

I merely enclosed my list of drafts to Blumenthal today, asking them to correct the dates. I now copy it with their corrections.

September	3	100	I am very glad you can enjoy your walks at
———	21	100	Tunbridge with my mother. She is indeed a
October	25	50	happy companion for a walk, for she enjoys
November	17	50	it so—except when there are *flies,* and is
December	6	100	never tired. I wish I had you both here—
———	29	50	though perhaps, now, it would be a little too
January	17	50	hot for you. It is very decidedly warm, quite
February	6	50	delightful. Effie went to Lido to bathe today,
March	6	50	and came back in high spirits—the water so
———	23	50	soft and warm compared to what she has
April	7	75	felt of Northern seas. Probably there is in-
———	19	75	deed more difference between the tempera-
May	18	50	ture of the Mediterranean and German ocean
———	26th	50	than there exists between Italian and English
	29	100	air.

Dearest love to my mother.

Ever my dearest Father
Your most affec^e. Son
J Ruskin.

LETTER 247

27th May [1852]

My dearest Father,

I have today your nice letter from Tunbridge, with enclosed 100, in 25 notes for which many thanks: and account of many Turners for

1. Nicolas Jean de Dieu Soult (1769–1851).

sale—you speak of exchanging Tamar [1] for Cumberland Heysham. Do not do this; the Heysham at 160 is now exorbitant—the Tamar I have never seen, and at 80 is likely to be much better worth the money, more especially as you must have liked it before you bought it. You have never told me the least of what it consists—or what it is like. The other drawings you speak of I do not know—but do not buy any on tinted paper. I only have seen one Stirling Castle [2]—that was in the Scottish novel series—not likely to occur separate. Many thanks for trouble taken for Mr Dillon.

The word which you could not read in the Countess Maison's [3] letter, is, I believe racines—roots—the letter is very interesting. It is [*text mutilated*] a little ridiculous of Macdonald to ask me to give my name in this way to a man picked up by the roadside: It is a great pity that religious people are so continually wanting in judgment—for after all—it is want of judgment that sets the other party wrong—Gladstone and Co—as well as the evangelicals—But I fear that not much is to be done with Gladstone. All these Puseyites are obstinate—wrongheaded—uncomeatable.

We have just been at a grand procession on the grand canal—in honour of the new Patriarch [4] who arrived in Venice today; all the houses hung with tape and the whole thing very pretty—but the best of it all was seeing the boats preparing for the procession in the morning at the post office (*Turner's* palace as you know) with red draperies, hung over their sides exactly as the yellow one is in our picture, and the whole scene as like as possible—except that the gay drapes of the figures were wanting. I enjoy the long days here very much—for I can work pretty well from an eight o'clock breakfast to 5 o'clock dinner with incidental rests—and then I leave myself quite free in the evening, and row or otherwise enjoy myself— But it is late tonight, and I must to bed. Dearest love to my mother.

Ever my dearest Father.
Your most aff^e. Son
J Ruskin.

1. *Sunshine on the Tamar,* discussed by Ruskin in *Works, 13,* 433–5.

2. Ruskin is perhaps referring to one of the sixty-five vignettes executed by Turner for Cadell's edition of Scott's prose and poetical works in 1834.

3. Countess Diane de Maison, one of the daughters of M. Domecq, a business associate of Ruskin senior.

4. Petrus-Aurelius Mutti occupied this position in the Catholic Church in Venice until 1857.

LETTER 248

29th May. [1852]

My dearest Father,

I am in haste this morning—at least in as much haste as I ever allow myself to be—for I do everything deliberately—only, with deliberation I have not time to write more than a line. I find the warm weather agree[s] with me much better than the cold, and Effie was never so well in her life. Mr Brown has given her a tent, and she goes bathing every day on the lido beach, the water as warm as if it had been boiled— But the wind, though now warm, is still obstinate, and troubles me by blowing my sketches about—if I don't tie all tight.

I must however really run away this morning. Dearest love to my mother. Ever my dearest father

Your most aff^e. Son
J Ruskin.

LETTER 249

Sunday, 30th May. [1852]

My dearest Father,

I have been obliged to give up my fortnight at Verona. I shall only take a couple of days there to finish my drawing— I found my study of Tintoret came out so much better than I hoped, that I thought it was a pity to leave it incomplete, and I cannot work long each day in the Scuola di S. Rocco, it is so dark except for a couple of hours in the morning. The ten days would not have done much on Veronese architecture, and they will enable [me] to complete my study of this picture thoroughly: and to see the great festival of the Corpus Domini which is in Venice what Easter is in Rome. I shall have the letters you have sent to Verona sent here, but *now* you may send one more to Verona— to catch me there, D.V. on Sunday the 13th: and after that one to Como: I have been looking at maps and enquiring and I am a little nervous about the road over the Splugen which I don't know the distances of— lest it should delay me—especially as the Strasburg rail will at any rate take two days. So if you have no objection I will take the road I know —over the St Gothard thus.

Monday 14th.	Brescia.
Tuesday.	Bergamo.
Wednesday.	Como.
Thursday.	Bellinzona.
Friday.	Faido, or Airolo.
Saturday.	Fluelen.

Monday 21st.	Lucerne, by Schwytz and Aart [1] to see Goldau &c.
Tuesday.	Rest at Lucerne—allow in case of bad weather on Monday.
Wednesday	} Get to Basle.
Thursday	
Friday.	Strasburg.
Saturday.	Nancy or Bar le duc.
Monday 28th.	Paris.
Tuesday 29th.	Boulogne.

I hope this way I shall keep to my day, D.V. without any fatigue—or trouble with more than the French customhouse—a great point with me. I have been out to see the Patriarch installed, and have not seen it, but have been kept till near post time. Dearest love to my mother.

Ever my dearest Father
Your most aff^e. Son
J Ruskin.

LETTER 250

Monday, 31st May. [1852]

My dearest Father,

I had a curious instance yesterday of what was comparatively new to me—*unsophisticated* bad taste. A Captⁿ Robertson [1]—just come from India—wrote to ask leave to call on me to ask my opinion of a translation of Tasso. I answered I could give none—had never read Tasso, but if he wished to call on me I would see him. He came yesterday evening—fresh in Venice—fresh in Italy—had read some of my books—and was interested in architecture and art. He thought the Ducal palace a "very ugly building." So did all his friends. Thought Paris very grand—especially the Madeleine— Thought St Mark's grotesque and paltry. Thought the only striking thing he had seen in Venice was the inside of la Salute. Thought Tasso very grand—but Dante great stuff—except little bits. Thought in Virgil and Milton there were only a few bits worth reading. Thought—&c. It was quite a study for me—for these were not engrafted or affected notions—but the natural feelings of a weak mind. I never saw them in such purity. I forgot to say he had sent me a specimen of his translation—of which here is a specimen for *you*.

Armida smiled—but did not cease, for that,
Her graceful task, nor while he spoke, neglected

1. Ruskin means Arth on Lake Zug.
1. Perhaps Captain Alexander Cuningham Robertson (b. 1816) of the 8th (King's) Regiment of Foot, who published *A Historical Record of the King's Liverpool Regiment of Foot* (London, 1883).

> Her toilette. Her hair she braided, and what
> Locks wanton strayed, in order fair collected
> Twisted the golden ringlets in a plat.
> And with bright flowers like an enamel decked it.

He seems not quite clear of the quantity of the second syllable in Armida, for a stanza a little farther on begins

> Then answers; On you, Armida, tis sad,
> Enough, to think.

I hope he does not *admire* my books, though he may have read them.
Dearest love to my mother.

> Ever my dearest Father
> Your most aff^e. Son
> J Ruskin.

LETTER 251

Verona. 1st June. [1852]

My dearest Father,

I am here after all on the day I intended—but must go back to Venice for a day or two. The weather grew suddenly windy and cold again—and as I had my subject to finish here from the window—I thought it would be better to get it done in the bad weather, it was hanging on my mind and plaguing me. Now after a violent thunderstorm, the weather seems settled again. I got just before leaving Venice your letter about Lady Sorel &c. which is all very true—but alas—in the present case quite in vain. You might just as well recommend her to seek peace by a leap into the lagoons—as by breaking up her "establishment."

I hope your next letter may contain Harrison's [1] answer—as all that can be done for her is merely to let her embarrass herself in her own way—or rather—at present she has borrowed the money from a man who is cheating her and tormenting her—all that I want to know is whether she cannot be rather in the hands of a public office than of a private and dishonest banker.

The Brunig [2] must not be sold at anything less than 150, it is valuable as Turner's last watercolour drawing, and done for me. I would rather for the present keep it. I am glad Mr Scott's 90, drawing went for 32, it will give us some hold on him. These prices are not so monstrous—any of them, as those we have heard of lately.

I am very glad that Mama thinks her walk like that of Castell'a mare

---

1. W. H. Harrison, whose experiences in the financial world would doubtless be of assistance to Lady Sorrel.

2. This water color is mentioned briefly in Finberg's *Life of J. M. W. Turner*, p. 420.

—still more so that you long to have another look at Calais, as I hope I shall get you there next year: I shall be contented wherever I am—but I do not love the Continent less—at least when it treats me kindly. The inexpressible beauty of this place makes me a little sad at quitting it so soon.

Dearest love to my mother.

> Ever my dearest Father
> Your most affec. Son
> J Ruskin.

LETTER 252

Verona 2nd June. [1852]

My dearest Father,

I begin to think that the real characteristic of men of genius—be they large or small—is that they are more instinctive and less reasonable than other people—that your true genius fights as Falstaff ran away, upon instinct. Miss Edgeworth may abuse the word "genius"—but there is such a thing—and it consists mainly in a man's doing things because he cannot help it, intellectual things, I mean: I don't think myself a great genius—but I believe I have genius—something different from mere cleverness, for I am *not* clever—in the sense that millions of people are —lawyers—physicians—and others: But there is the strong instinct in me which I cannot analyse—to draw and describe the things I love— not for reputation—nor for the good of others—nor for my own advantage—but a sort of instinct like that for eating or drinking. I should like to draw all St Mark's—and all this Verona—stone by stone—to eat it all up into my mind—touch by touch. More and more lovely I find it every time—and am every year dissatisfied with what I did the last. But I think you will like the drawing which I have come here to finish.

Dearest love to my mother.

> Ever my dearest Father
> Your most aff^{e}. Son
> J Ruskin.

LETTER 253

Verona. 4th June [1852]

My dearest Father,

I have today your letters of the 22nd and 25th—from Tunbridge—and am very glad you were not annoyed by my taking the Tintoret—it was not the sum spent, but the inconsistency which I thought might annoy you—that after saying I did not care for it in the least, I should go and buy it. But it takes me always a good while before I quite see what a picture is—and it was only the piece of landscape hidden behind the frame which settled the thing to be Tintoret's— The work of Veronese is of course to be known from his, at once—in a finished picture, but all great masters *sketch* well—and the features of the woman's face are so much more Veronese's type—(none the *worse* for that,) than Tintoret's, that I did not for a long time suspect it to be by the greater man.

It is not so much a proof of character as of my knowing something about the matter that I do not buy old pictures. Good old pictures are never to be had cheap, and the pleasure I have from them is not enough to make me desire to buy them dear. What would be a moderate price for a good old picture, would still buy me two or three Turners, and I would rather have one Turner than any old picture I ever saw—except the very noble ones whose prices are in tens of thousands, and which I of course could never think [of]. People who buy old pictures, now, in quantities are always ignorant. I have, at different leisure times, rummaged over every picture dealer's in Venice—and in the year 1845 I hunted over all Florence to see if I could find a cheap bit of Giotto. I did not find a single genuine bit; and this year, out of cartloads and shiploads of simple rubbish—or clever cheats, of which there are a good many; and clumsy cheats, of which all showrooms are full, I have only succeeded in finding this single picture worth having—for I can hardly count as worth having —though I would not willingly part with it, the Shadow of a head by Bonifazio for which I gave a napoleon, having pulled it out from some torn canvasses which the dealer had not so much as thought of showing me. He had cut the head out of a picture which had been scrubbed away down to the canvas in the time of the French—and thought himself marvellously fortunate to get sixteen and fourpence for head—picture— and all. It grows upon me as I keep it by me—and if my Tintoret—which I must send by sea—should go to the bottom—will always be a little reminiscence of Venetian colour for me.

Miss Mitford's letter is very nice. Poor thing, that rheumatism [1] must be terrible in such a house. I hope my letter will give her pleasure—as the extracts from the one to you seem to have done.

We are excessively petted here—Marshal Radetsky sent Effie his picture yesterday with his own signature—I wish I could write as well —as dashing and firm as if it had been written at thirty instead of 86, and his chief of staff who is not now in Verona—left his carriage for us—with all manner of insists on our using it when we wanted—and the Marshal's two aid de camps—and another young officer—came to escort us in our drive in the evening. It was pleasant—after being so long in Venice—to see the young men's riding—the nice—loose—cavalry bal-

---

1. Mary Russell Mitford was crippled with rheumatism during the closing years of her life; in addition, she was far from affluent. Despite loyal friendships her last years were spent in pain and discomfort.

anced swinging seat, and the horses as happy as their masters—but keeping their place beside the carriage to a hair's breadth—we went to an old Veronese castle on one of the first slopes of the Alpine spurs above the plain—and it was delightful to have one's foot again upon the rocks —and see the shadows of the cypresses on the long summer grass. I stay here today and tomorrow—back to Venice on Saturday—return here finally D.V. on Saturday next. Dearest love to my mother.

Ever my dearest Father
Your most aff^e. Son
J Ruskin.

LETTER 254

Verona Friday 4th June. [1852]

My dearest Father,

We had the most delightful drive last night conceivable—going out by the gate towards the mountains, where I never was before—and up a little into the hills, till we came to a farm on a sloping bank of grass set with mulberries—with such a view as I never recollect seeing before even in Italy— The Adige takes a sweep below just like the head of the river at Richmond hill—and putting olives and mulberries in place of elms and oaks—and an unbroken sweep of meadow land instead of the rugged slope of Richmond—the front part of the view was precisely like—but beyond the plains came the mountains of the Lago di Garda, some of the grandest forms of the southern Alps—all purple—like Highland heather, Robson's [1] old colour, against the golden twilight—one of the most perfect landscapes that ever summer twilight faded from. We are promised *better* things this evening—but I expect nothing half so good. If I can put any of my impressions of Verona into good language—they will be worth reading.[2] But it is curious after being long in Venice, how terrible —at least how tiresome—the noise of waggons and carts is and the rattle even of one's own carriage over the stones. One might habituate oneself to silence till a grasshopper's chirp became pain.

Dearest love to my mother.

Ever my dearest Father
Your most aff^e. Son
J Ruskin.

1. George Fennel Robson (1790-1833), a water-color painter. *Lecture VI* of *The Art of England* (*Works, 33*, 371-93), "The Hill-Side," is devoted to a discussion of Robson and Fielding. But Robson's predilection for purple is directly reflected in *Works, 3*, 193.

2. Ruskin recorded his impressions of Verona many times. Not the least successful of his attempts is *Verona and Its Rivers* (*Works, 19*, 425-48).

LETTER 255

Verona Saturday 5th June [1852]

My dearest Father,

I am ashamed to say that I kept your yesterday's letter in my pocket until too late for the post—and crushed it sadly besides; this Verona makes me lose my wits: it is so beautiful: I find all I want to do here in the way of casts will not cost above 15 pounds—in fact the limit is rather fixed by the supposed capacity of Herne hill stables for boxes than by the cost of the things here. We had a long drive last night—but—as I supposed, the great view was not the tenth part so good as the little one—but we saw a fine Italian garden and avenue of cypresses, which was new to Effie—one of the grand dark avenues with fountains and statues, like the Vignettes in Rogers' Italy, and we were lighted all the way home by sheet lightning and fireflies. I am pleased with the young men; they are so highbred—so lighthearted—and so fond of each other, as well as desirous in every way to oblige us. Effie is a great catch for them, as they have no ladies' society here except one or two of the wives of the generals, who are very kind—but are forced to be always en grande dame. It is pleasant to hear the way that his young aides de camp speak of Radetzky—they say it is exactly the same for them as if they were living in their fathers' houses; and their fathers in the Marshal's position —that he is as watchful over them, and as kind to them, as any father could be, whose time was as much taken up.

I have just got your letter of the 28th—asking where to address—and enclosing the delightful Punch on Millais.[1] I don't know when I have got anything that gave me so much pleasure—the worst of it is, it is a little overdone—makes one suspect a friend's hand—and will make all the R.A.s terribly angry. But a great gain nevertheless.

My route is now—I hope, quite fixed for St Gothard—it is the shortest line to Basle, and I can agree with the postmaster for horses all the way. A *voiturier* offers to take me from here to Basle in six days so it cannot be very heavy work.

I shall leave this line behind me here, and write tomorrow D.V. from Venice. Dearest love to my mother.

Ever my dearest Father
Your most aff^e. Son
J Ruskin.

1. An article praising Millais entitled "Our Critic among the Pictures," which appeared in *Punch* on May 22, 1852.

LETTER 256

Venice. Sunday. [6 June 1852]

My dearest Father,

I was more sorry to leave Verona yesterday than glad to get back to Venice. I think the Gothic of Verona more and more superb every time I examine it—and it is curious how many new things I find out every time. I wonder if there ever will come a time when I shall be pleased with the work I did last year. I fancy I have examined a thing accurately—when I go back to it a year afterwards, I always find I have missed something—or made some mistake which I am glad to correct.

I suppose the fact is that in the transition from my old Proutish ways of drawing to my present, that is to say, from drawing a capital this way, to drawing it this way—or with much greater accuracy than this, every step that I have taken has been so much an in-crease of accuracy upon the last, that by contrast, it appeared *perfectly* right—and now I have got to such a pitch of fastidiousness that no drawing will satisfy me at all as regards its expression of mere facts—but I must have a daguerreotype or a cast—and even grumble at those, at the one for exaggerating the shadows—at the other for losing the sharpness of the hollows.

But yet, I am happy to say that a fine drawing, made with feeling—is always worth a great many casts or daguerreotypes—and a first rate one—a Lewis or Turner—(I put Lewis in this sentence before Turner because I am thinking of truth of architecture, and for detail—Lewis is as much superior to Turner as he is inferior in imagination)—is worth any quantity of them. There is something in it besides the facts—a greater fact than any of them—a human soul.

I wish Lewis would take up St Mark's. He could do it—and he only: and none of the Byzantine architecture he brought from the east is equal to it.

I will take care and not overwork myself this week. I have not over much packing—all my MS and drawings except those in hand, are packed, and I have only my Tintoret and some casts and glass—and so on—to look after.

You ask what we are to do about Servants—I will think of that as I come home. I am living from hand to mouth at present.

Dearest love to my mother.

Ever my dearest Father
Your most aff^e. Son
J Ruskin.

LETTER 257

Venice. Sunday Evening. 6ᵗʰ June [1852]

My dearest Father,

I never had time, when I was writing from Verona, to tell you what an interesting investigation we had of the Marshal's Secretaire: He gave Cᵗ Thun his private keys, that he might show us all the pretty things that had been sent to him by crowned heads—towns—municipalities—&c.: and his orders. Of these last there was a chest full—as much as a man could carry, divided into five tiers or sliding drawers, each filled with some two dozen or two dozen and a half of Orders—generally two of each—the usual one—to be worn commonly, and another in diamonds or otherwise enriched—in compliment to him—an enormous value in mere jewellery: and I suppose no man in Europe except our own Duke, could show such a box full of honour in its Scutcheon form.[1] But on the whole, the more interesting things were the various freedoms of towns —or other complimentary papers, addresses &c.—bound in velvet with chasings of silver—black, or gilt—wrought out into the more perfect form of German fancy—and with drawings on their title pages in water-colours, exquisitely laboured, and many of them full of genius—in fact [all?] the genius of this country goes into things of this kind. Some of these books were two or three feet long—and so heavy with silver that they were as much as could be lifted—one at a time. It is pleasant to hear that the marshal enjoys these gifts—and really values them—and keeps his keys very jealously—as I do of my Turners. He has conquered, by consistent kindness, even the sulkiness of the Italians—as far as regards himself. None of them now speak ill of him, however furious against Austrians in general.

And indeed—of both Italians and Austrians, we have reason to speak well—for I do not think that either have ever refused us anything in their power that could oblige us. And there is one point in the Italian character which is very pleasing, though the result perhaps of reprehensible ones: the entire freedom with which they throw open their pleasure grounds to any one who likes to use them. You see a garden gate open—you walk in as if it were your own—stare about you—touch your hat to the proprietor if he happens to be there—explore all his grounds at your leisure —and find at the gate his gardener waiting with a bouquet for you.

Fancy what Emily would have said—to the bare idea of such a thing! Dearest love to my mother.

Ever my dearest Father
Your most affᵉ. Son
J Ruskin.

1. Cf. *I Henry IV*, v.i. end of scene.

LETTER 258

7th June. Evening. [1852]

My dearest Father,

All is very lovely at Venice now—though I got so thoroughly sick of the cold that nothing is too warm for me. I am getting my things as well finished as I ever do—there is always something one would do better if one had time—but I am well satisfied on the whole.

I want to be up early tomorrow—for the mornings are lovely—so only write this bulletin. The letters of Gordon and Colquhoun [1] are interesting—but Gordon is quite a Gladstone man himself, now. I mean very high church, and not knowing exactly what he would be at.

Dearest love to my mother.

Ever my dearest Father
Your most affe. Son
J Ruskin.

LETTER 259

Wednesday. 9th June [1852]

My dearest Father,

I am ashamed to say that I forgot your letter altogether till too late: I have been in the habit of writing it overnight lately—and going out immediately after breakfast. I could not write last night and went out this morning hastily—and never stirred from my work till too late for post. It will not however, I trust, be a Saturday's letter that you will miss. I am well on with all packing—&c., but things which one hoped to do—and still could not do conveniently, at last crowd themselves together inconveniently—though every hour I throw something or other overboard. I wonder whether I shall ever be able to measure time and possibilities accurately. However, I have, with many small or imperfect drawings, three which if they do [not] *deserve* frames, will at least be much improved by them, and for which therefore I shall ask you to let Mr Foord have frames ready. By the bye—before you receive this, I shall, D.V. be within ten days of home, so that he will hardly have time to get them ready, but must do his best.

		ft.	in.		ft.	in.
The first drawing is	▭	3	6¼	long by	2	6 high.
The second is upright.	▯	1	11½	broad by	3	1½ high.
The third long.		1	8	long by	1	1 high.

1. Possibly Macdonald Macdonald, one of whose Christian names was Colquhoun.

The first will bear a rich deep frame. The second should have a light one, it being a pale drawing—the third will do with an average frame of any kind.

God willing, I shall have much pleasure when I get home to you—but I don't quite like the pinch of leaving Venice. Dearest love to my mother.

Ever my dearest Father

Your most aff^e. Son.

J Ruskin.

LETTER 260

Thursday evening [10 June 1852]

My dearest Father,

Tomorrow I am to be at work by what is—I am sorry to say, now an unusually early hour for me, eight o'clock. I have been paying some goodbye visits—and have reserved tomorrow for a last touching up of my study of Tintoret, which I hope you will like—it is the one for which I want the largest frame mentioned in my last letter. I have not been looking at it for a good while—and now I like it very well, always when it is not beside the picture itself.

I am not so much sorry to quit Venice as sorry to find how little can be done in so large a fraction of human life as I have spent here. I am a poor little animal—and nine months of me is soon spent.

I work tomorrow and Saturday, and one day more at Verona, Monday—then D.V. shut up shop, and rest all the way home.

Dearest love to my mother.

Ever my dearest Father.

Your most aff^e. Son.

J Ruskin.

LETTER 261

Venice 13th June [1852]

My dearest Father,

I am unluckily detained here for a couple of days by a robbery [1] committed on Effie's jewellery as she was packing—a very strange one—requiring me to make declarations in order to free several of the servants

---

1. The details of this robbery are confused, although some of Ruskin's biographers, among them Amabel Williams-Ellis, hint that the thief was a friend of Ruskin. In Cook's *Life, 1, 280*, it is stated that "Ruskin had his suspicions, and at one stage of the affair it looked as if he might have to accept a challenge to fight a duel." Cook and Wedderburn in the *Works* pass over the whole affair as rapidly as they do his unfortunate marriage. Suspicion fell on a Captain Foster, who was subsequently cleared of the charge.

of the inn from suspicion, but I will not be after my time, D.V. at home—
We are quite well—though of course somewhat annoyed—more at my
being forced to date this from Venice still for you and my mother will
be quite sick about it.

Dearest love to her.

> Ever my dearest Father
> Your most aff^e. Son.
> J Ruskin.

LETTER 262

Sunday evening. [13 June 1852]

My dearest Father,

My letters lately have been very unsatisfactory—and I am afraid this
morning's would be the climax—tonight however we have news of the
jewels, though as yet very doubtful—and the more so because they appear to implicate a person whom we have known at Venice and whose
name I do not yet wish to write—though I may perhaps be able to give
it tomorrow morning before I seal this letter. I have been pulled about
all day to this and that police office—but I am not at all tired, though
very sleepy. I was much interested in the thing—and it seemed to be a
good stretch for my mind after it had been set so long on *Stones*. But I
hope to be able to tell you more tomorrow. For one thing, having all my
drawings and MS [finally] packed up and sealed by the police to pass the
customhouse without being examined, is a great relief to me.

We have just at the eleventh hour made the acquaintance of a Venetian
lady whom I am really glad to have known—bearing two of the greatest
of ancient names—born, a Morosini [1]—married, a Venier: now, Con-
tessa Morosini-Venier and who does not disgrace her name—domestic
—quiet—industrious—fond of her children and her brother—if not of
her husband, it must be his fault. She is eight or nine and twenty—and
never goes out usually—but was brought by her brother to see *us* as
being out of the way people— Effie returned her visit yesterday—and I
today—and it is a great pleasure to me to have been received by *one*
noble Venetian lady, whom I could respect.

I leave room for a P.S. tomorrow morning, if I put none, you will
understand there were no distinct news yet to be had.

Dearest love to my mother.

> Ever my dearest Father
> Your most affec^e. Son
> J Ruskin.

1. A descendant of Doge Michele Morosini, who is mentioned in *The Stones of
Venice III* (*Works*, 9, 99–100).

LETTER 263

Venice Tuesday morning [15 June 1852]

My dearest Father,

I do not know when I have been more puzzled as to what it would be best to do, than I am just now. On the one hand, I recollect you did not like losing jewels without some attempt to recover them—on the other, you and my mother will be thinking that you will never get us out of Venice. The jewels lost are to the value of about £100: the diamond dove and emerald being the chief—and I really do not know—at this moment, whether you would say to me, you would rather lose 100 pounds than we should stay any longer in Venice—or whether you would say that I ought not to come away and leave all this behind.

But I believe after today, the chance of recovery will be exceedingly small, and unless I hear something this morning, I shall assuredly leave for Verona tomorrow at 10 o'clock and get on beyond it if I can—and so push home as fast as may be. The circumstances of the robbery were curious: Effie had taken all her jewels out of her drawer at eleven o'clock in order to pack them up: and was about to do so—they lying on her dressing table *in their cases,* when a gentleman came in to bid us goodbye, with whom we have been on terms of considerable familiarity: He did so—and *I* went out on various business in the town—but the gentleman remained talking to Effie for twenty minutes more—until she also, having an appointment at 12—was obliged to tell him to go away—and they went downstairs together—Effie locking up the room, and giving the key to Mary:[1] Five minutes afterwards—they having parted at the bottom of the stairs—the "gentleman?" returns—tells Mary he wants to write a letter to me—is let into the room—stays there a quarter of an hour—and calls Mary—gives her the letter, and goes away. Mary locks up the room again, and, this time—gives the key to the waiter. About five minutes afterwards, I came in—the waiter took the key from its usual place and let me into the room—Mary came in—and gave me the gentleman's letter, which was to ask me to send him some razors! from England. I neither knew—nor noticed, that the jewel cases were exposed—but was very angry at the trunks not being packed up—and being in a great hurry myself, went out to my study, and left the key *in* the door—where it remained for twenty minutes—when Effie came in and found the jewels gone, and *cases left—all neatly shut*—so that if she had not felt them light as she put them into the trunk, the thing would not have been discovered. But for this last twenty minutes, the thing might have been brought home at once—but twenty minutes open door in an hotel leaves all quite vague. It is sufficiently disagreeable that unless the jewels

1. Effie's personal maid.

are found, suspicion attaches in equal degree to the people of an hotel where I have been well treated and to a person with whom I have been on familiar terms. But I must certainly get away tomorrow. Dearest love to my mother.

> Ever my dearest Father.
> Your most aff^e. Son.
> J Ruskin.

Letter 264

Venice. 16th June [1852]

My dearest Father,

Off at last—I will write from Verona D.V. this evening—dearest love to my mother.

> Ever your most aff^e. Son.
> J Ruskin.

Letter 265

[17 June 1852]

My dearest Father,

My yesterday's letter was premature. Just as we had our last trunk packed and the gondola waiting—comes an order from the governor that we were not to leave Venice. I went immediately to the police—and they explained to me that the thing was likely to be brought home to the person of whom I spoke, in my last letter but one, and that the governor would not let us go for a day or two—when if it appeared that the matter could not be decided, we should leave—and if it *were* decided, of course, also. I rather expect to get back the jewels, now—but am much vexed for you and my mother, who will both be anxious and heartsick. There is however no occasion for your being anxious: The person in question *must* be sent out of Venice in very safe keeping—so that there is no chance of his coming in our way: and as all my books and drawings are now locked up in our trunks or under customhouse seals, I am taking some rest which I daresay is very good for me. I have had to draw £50 beyond my credit with Blumenthal—of which I leave 25 in his hands for some sculpture work still undone, and for which I do not wish to pay before hand and 25 I have taken (that I may keep [the] Coutts' notes unbroken for travelling)—in order to meet the extra hotel bills here—and to pay for a copy which G. Richmond asked me to get for him of a picture in the Manfrini palace—for which I shall allow him to pay when I get home—otherwise he would not give me any commissions again—But don't tell him anything about it. I want to surprise him. Will you advise Glynn of the extra draft upon them for £50?

Mme Palavicini—who being the highest Austrian lady here—is nearly as good an authority as a general officer, says that she *thinks:* (which means that she is very nearly certain), we shall get away on Saturday. I don't think I shall be much behind my time, even now—and I have got a great deal of curious experience in many ways—worth some loss—not quite worth £100, but I think very well worth the inconvenience, and extra hotel bill, if I can recover the jewels. In the first place Effie has got a lesson about leaving her jewels about, which she used to do very carelessly. In the second, our servants have got a lesson about opening doors to people who come back to "write notes." In the third, I have seen something of Italian police system and policemen—worth seeing— though I suppose not *much* differing from ours, in the last place I have got a lesson upon character. For the person in question—having in his general character or appearance of character much that I liked—was continually attacking the clergy; never went to church, and in other ways showed a degree of irreligion which I have till now, supposed compatible with an ill taught honesty: but which I shall henceforth be apt to think as inconsistent with the character of a man of honour, as of a man of sense.

Today is Thursday—and I have great confidence in Mme Palavicini's opinion that I shall be able to leave on Saturday: I shall not again alter my route as various letters of yours will be lying for me at Lucerne, Basle, &c. but I don't think your answer to this could meet me before Paris.

Dearest love to my mother.

Ever my dearest Father
Your most aff^e. Son
J Ruskin.

LETTER 266

Venice. Friday, 18th June [1852]

My dearest Father,

I would not have missed, for a great deal, seeing the various little points of character and ways of managing business, which have come out in this affair—but I am tormented by my fears for my mother and you, who I know will be in a terrible state of anxiety— I cannot *yet* tell you when I shall get away—positively—but I trust soon—all my things are packed—and I am off by first train after I get leave— Mr Brown and Mr Cheney, both men of the world, are my advisors in anything requiring advice—and all is going on perfectly well. Dearest love to my mother.

Ever my dearest Father
Your most affectionate Son
J Ruskin.

I cannot write more today, for I am just likely to be called out and must have my letter folded and ready.

LETTER 267

Venice. Saturday, 19th June [1852]

My dearest Father,

Still nothing certain, I am sorry to say—everybody is very kind and sympathetic—but the jewels do not appear—and we cannot yet be allowed to go away. I called on the governor with the English consul—no one could have been more kind or polite—or have expressed more regret at the whole affair—but he could not let me leave Venice. This must be a terrible trial to you and my mother, the more so as you have no means of communication with me—for every hour I may receive permission to go—and therefore it is no use sending for any letter which may be lying at Verona—nor of course can any letters relating to this affair, reach me at all. I am not the least annoyed myself—except for you—but am much interested, and a good deal amused. Mr Brown [and] Mr Cheney are very indignant—and as they both have rich powers [of] satire, their comments on the police are delightful. But they are very important aids also in the management of the affair.

Pray be assured that there is nothing to disquiet yourself about and I trust I shall get away on Monday: and not be long after my time after all. Dearest love to my mother.

> Ever my dearest Father
> Your most aff^e. Son
> J Ruskin.

LETTER 268

Sunday, 20th June [1852]

My dearest Father,

At last we are coming to something definite. I believe the final depositions required will be received tomorrow—and that on Tuesday we shall get away. What an odd thing human nature is: I don't enjoy Venice half so much when I am kept there against my will—it seems to give a different colour to everything—but this is chiefly, I believe because I am afraid of the effect upon you. Pray do not allow yourself to get anxious—there is nothing whatever to be anxious about—and you will soon, I hope, be getting my letters in double quick time as I near you, in coming home.

I set to work yesterday upon my book very seriously so that *that* at any rate may not be delayed, and it is not in the least too hot, so that you need not fear for my health. So far from being too hot, if I wanted to begin any new drawing, I could not, there is so much wind, at nearly all times of the day—not indeed cold, but yet, by opposition to the heat of the sun—so searching that it would be quite impossible to sit in it. In fact everything, this journey, has combined together to disgust me as far as possible with Italy and everything therein—and to make me in future, content at home—all perhaps has been sent as a warning—and yet it seems so strange to me that this should be so—when all which I fancy *most* my function to examine or describe, is *here*—or in Switzerland.

But I shall be very glad—this time—to find myself comfortably established at Herne Hill.

It is certainly most curious to look back on the contretemps of this journey. First setting out in a nervous state—joined by friends to whom I was most anxious to show every thing to advantage. Rain all the way from Dijon to Champagnole. No *view whatever* from the Jura, bad weather at Chamouni—Coutet gone away—Cold at Aosta—Cold in Venice—Cold—from September to May—without intermission—my friends lost at home—my opportunities missed—all in a season in which I could do but half work here, and then this catastrophe of uncomfortableness and considerable pecuniary loss at last.

Dearest love to my mother.

> Ever my dearest Father
> Your most aff^e. Son
> J Ruskin.

Letter 269

Monday 21st June [1852]

My dearest Father,

We are again sent for to the police today—but whether this will be the final examination I cannot tell—and I am obliged to send you this line before I go—lest I should be kept too late for post time. I post all your letters at present myself—that, such as they are, you may be as sure as *I* can make you of receiving them.

Dearest love to my mother.

> Ever my dearest Father
> Your most aff^e. Son
> J Ruskin.

LETTER 270

Tuesday, 22nd June [1852]

My dearest Father,

Things are really getting on at last—and I *hope* to be off the day after tomorrow, but I don't want to tantalize *you* as I am tantalized myself—if it is possible for you to make up your minds not to expect me on any fixed day, it will be better—all I know is that things are being pressed on as fast as possible—and that—if they are not brought soon to a conclusion—I shall be permitted to leave before that conclusion arrives. You will receive a bill of lading from Messrs Blumenthal of 21 boxes sent by a ship which either has left, or is leaving, Venice. I think the entire value of these boxes must be about £200, and I think they had better be insured for that sum.

I am again obliged to send off my letter early, because Lord and Lady Fielding [1] [are] here—and as all my MS and drawings are locked up and I don't [feel] much inclined for work I have promised to cicerone them a little. Very nice people, but Roman Catholics, of whose doings you must have heard at Rome. Dearest love to my mother.

Ever my dearest Father
Your most aff^e. Son.
J Ruskin.

LETTER 271

23rd June [1852]

My dearest Father,

It will be most provoking for you and my mother to be receiving letters from Venice just on the day when you hoped to have me home again but at all events, by the time you receive this, D.V. I shall be on my way to you and perhaps far upon it. If you can keep yourselves tolerably comfortable it seems to me not a thing to be regarded as altogether disadvantageous, for if I had not been put to considerable inconvenience, their way of managing things here would not have made so much impression upon me, and it is very useful to me that I should both find out—and feel the results of—their methods of doing business. Perhaps it was just as well for me to rest a little from my work before beginning my journey—and I have seen and done one or two things here which I had forgotten; and might have afterwards been inconvenienced by having missed. Still the affair is a very disagreeable contretemps—and will serve together with the weather, still more to reconcile me to living in my own country.

I think I should have a run of good fortune, after this "losing hand,"

1. Rudolph William Basil Feilding, later 8th Earl of Denbigh, and his wife.

at all [events] I hope you and my mother will have much pleasure in having me near [you] after so long a separation. Dearest love to her.

Ever my dearest Father
Your most aff^e. Son
J Ruskin.

LETTER 272

24th June. [1852]

My dearest Father,

We shall *certainly* not be much longer kept now. We should have had our passport tomorrow—but for a "misunderstanding" between two sections of examiners—and I have hardly any doubt of obtaining it on Saturday. I should not say this if I thought there was much risk of your being again disappointed. I believe the worst to be looked for is, that I get my passport on Saturday, and reach Verona that evening, but either on Monday or Tuesday—Effie will not be able to travel, and so we lose another day. Allowing for every mischance therefore— whether we be detained at Verona—Brescia—or Como—you may I trust now *calculate* upon us as (even supposing passport not got till Monday) leaving Verona on Wednesday morning and thence home without stopping except to sleep— The best that *could* happen would be [our] reaching Verona on Saturday, and Effie's day of necessary rest being [Sunday], so on Monday morning we should be finally off—but we have been throughout so unlucky that I do not hope this.

I am writing to Mr Rogers, and will enclose you the letter for him tomorrow. Lord Fielding is much interested by what I have shown him—and tells me a great deal which partly amuses me and partly interests me—of modern Romanist tradition. Every body pities us exceedingly—but nobody can help us—except by advice. One thing I am very glad of among the other good consequences of a misfortune, it has brought out Mr Cheney's character; I believed him to be a man like Mr Beckford. I have found him active—kind—and rightminded, in the highest degree, and he has been my chief adviser and support in this affair in which not only single words—but *tones* of words, were of great importance—for, as you must instantly have seen by my account of its circumstances, it required excessive caution in order to prevent the possibility of my having *hereafter* to refuse a challenge. All danger of that, however—which (though of course I should have done it unhesitatingly,) would have been not a little disagreeable in a country where respectability is measured by swordlengths just as silk is by yardlengths—is entirely over. Dearest love to my mother.

Ever my dearest Father.
Your most aff [*rest of letter missing*]

LETTER 273

Friday morning [25 June 1852]

My dearest Father,

I enclose the first sheet of Mr Rogers' letter—the second which I hope will be a more agreeable one I have not finished, but will send it to-morrow, with envelope for both, when you can seal and send them. I hope the postage of my letters will soon not be so heavy. I have not got anything new to tell you. I was very sorry—at dessert yesterday to see apricots put on the table—the idea of autumn, or something like it—being upon us, before we could leave Venice. I don't think I shall want to come here again in a hurry. It is odd that both at the beginning and end of my stay here, I should have been so long cut off from communication with you—this is of course to *me* the most immediately disagreeable part of the affair—as I know not what matters requiring answer may be in your letters at Lucerne &c. However, how much better is it than if I had been kept by illness, or accident. When I left Venice in 1845 and was kept those two days at Padua,[1] I assure you I thought myself in a much worse scrape—and I don't know if I have yet mentioned, among collateral benefits, that I have been taking some saltwater luke warm baths every day—which seem very good for me and have kept me from any return of nervousness, which under the circumstances —appeared not unlikely—and have made me as sleepy at night as if I was a child again— Effie bathes every day in the sea itself—and is better in health than I have ever known her. Dearest love to my mother.

Ever my dearest Father.
Your most affect. Son
J Ruskin.

In case my yesterday's letter should miss fire—I repeat the main information it contained, that, allowing for *every possible* adverse circumstance, you may D.V. calculate on our finally leaving Verona on Wednesday morning next—and coming home without a stop except to sleep.

LETTER 274

Saturday [26 June 1852]

My dearest Father,

I am happy to say I think there is now really no chance of our being detained beyond Monday. I have no doubt, D.V. of leaving on Monday morning, and Verona on Tuesday morning early, and then nothing I

1. Ruskin was detained at Padua by an attack of nervous fever from October 14–17, 1845.

trust will occur to delay us. The enclosed letter I am afraid is very
stupid, but I could not do better— Dearest love to my mother.

> Ever my dearest Father
> Your most affec^e. Son
> J Ruskin.

LETTER 275

Sunday, 27th June [1852]

My dearest Father,

I do not know that among the advantages of this very disagreeable,
contretemps—of which I try to discover as many as I can—(and may
perhaps have still a day or two for the practice of such philosophy for
I do not yet hear of my passport) I have yet enumerated the knowing
something of the feeling that people have when they are unjustly injured—by *formal* procedure for before this—nothing had ever happened to me but kindness from all quarters—and although nothing has
been done in the present case that is discourteous—still I consider the
liberty of the subject more encroached upon than is obliging. But I don't
know the forms of law in England and so ought not to complain of them
here—only it seems to me a little like one of the adventures in Gil Blas
which begin with a disagreeable rencontre with gentlemen of the light
finger—and close with complicated embarrassments produced by the
police. I cannot say that I am not worried—but it is on account of my
mother and you, chiefly—though I am now not a little impatient to get
home myself—but still I could check my own impatience, if I were not
anxious about you.

Do not however increase your anxiety by thinking about mine, for I
assure you in all *these* cases I never let it hurt my health. It hurt me
when I thought you and my mother were ill, because I got no letters—
but in mere cases of vexation like the present, I turn my mind to other
things: and am in excellent health. I shall probably send you some newly
written pieces of book, to show what I am about.

Dearest love to my mother.

> Ever my dearest Father
> Your most aff^e. Son
> J Ruskin.

LETTER 276

Monday. 28th June [1852]

My dearest Father,

I am really getting provoked beyond measure—another requisition
from the police came in yesterday for our attendance today—the Eng-

lish consul thinks it rather too much, himself—and called to tell me that he thought I should send in a formal note to demand my passport—which I therefore allowed him to do. I don't want to make another Mr Mather affair out of it—but I must really use every means in my power to get away.

It is really warm at last—but I cannot enjoy the place—I could not have believed that mere disagreeable accidents and associations could have so altered its aspect. I cannot feel interest in anything but Tintoret but I am always diverted from all disagreeable thought the moment [I come] before one of his pictures. Happily I have only to walk across the square—and the Ducal palace is as open to me as my own house—I can walk about all the rooms and stay wherever I choose—all day long.

Dearest love to my mother.

Ever my dearest Father
Your most affe. Son
J Ruskin.

LETTER 277

Tuesday. [29 June 1852]

My dearest Father,

I have your two letters to Venice—which have much relieved me. I hope it will relieve you to know that the Governor has officially promised me my passport this morning and that D.V. I shall get to Verona today and leave it tomorrow morning as I said you might calculate. I have no time for more.

Dearest love to my mother.

Ever my dearest Father
Your most affe. Son
J Ruskin.

LETTER 278

Verona, Tuesday Evening [29 June 1852]

My dearest Father,

As you may imagine I have enough to do tonight getting carriage and everything. I hope there is no fear of farther delay—and that I shall get off by six tomorrow morning—as the post is not then open—stay, the letter box will be always—so—if you receive this—you will understand that we are off for Bergamo— I have *all* your nice letters here with accounts of walks to Tunbridge, &c. and of your having the Heysham in your room, &c. I am very glad that you like it a little better—but I am sure it would be dear at such a price. God willing I shall soon

be home now—and you will see books in a hurry yet not done in a hurry
—*Modern Painters* [1] and all.

Dearest love to my mother.

> Ever my dearest Father
> Your most aff^e. Son
> J Ruskin.

1. The last three volumes of which had not as yet been published.

APPENDIX

PUBLISHING HISTORY OF THE LETTERS

PUBLISHING HISTORY OF THE LETTERS

Letter
Number

31. Complete in *Works, 10,* xxxv, except for the first sentence.
32. Hitherto unpublished.
33. Second sentence of the first paragraph is in *Works, 9,* xliv.
34. Part of the first paragraph and all the second, third, and fourth paragraphs are in *Works, 10,* 15 n. One sentence from the first paragraph is in Cook, *Life, 1,* 264; and *Works, 10,* xxvii.
35. Most of the second paragraph is in *Works, 12,* xlii.
36. Half of the first paragraph is in *Works, 10,* 353 n.
37. First half of this letter in in *Works, 9,* xxxix–xl. Another sentence is in *Works, 10,* xliv.
38. Half the third paragraph and all the fourth paragraph are in *Works, 10,* lxii–lxiii.
39. Hitherto unpublished.
40. Hitherto unpublished.
41. Complete in *Works, 14,* 167 n., except for the concluding sentence.
42. Hitherto unpublished.
43. Hitherto unpublished.
44. Hitherto unpublished.
45. A sentence from the first paragraph is in *Works, 11,* 259 n.
46. First half of the first paragraph is in *Works, 10,* xxxvi. The second and third paragraphs are in *Works, 12,* 105 n. The last paragraph is in *Works, 10,* xxxiv.
47. Hitherto unpublished.
48. Hitherto unpublished.
49. Hitherto unpublished.
50. Hitherto unpublished.
51. Hitherto unpublished.
52. A few sentences from the second and third paragraphs are in *Works, 10,* xxxiii, xxxvi; and Cook, *Life, 1,* 269.
53. Hitherto unpublished.
54. A few fragments are in Cook, *Life, 1,* 273; Wilenski, *John Ruskin,* pp. 57–8; *Works, 9,* xlvii n.; and *Works, 10,* xl.
55. Hitherto unpublished.
56. The first half of the first paragraph is in *Works, 10,* 5 n.
57. The first paragraph and part of the fourth are in *Works, 12,* lxxviii–lxxix. Parts of the first and fourth paragraphs are in Cook, *Life, 1,* 273–4. Passages from the fourth paragraph are also in Leon, *John Ruskin: The Great Victorian,* p. 157; and *Works, 10,* 422 n.
58. The last two paragraphs are in *Works, 11,* 77 n.
59. First sentence of the second paragraph is in *Works, 11,* 259 n.
60. Hitherto unpublished.
61. Various passages from this letter are in Williams-Ellis, *John Ruskin,* p. 150; Cook, *Life, 1,* 266; and *Works, 36,* 121–2. In the latter, however, it is printed almost completely.
62. Hitherto unpublished.

Letter
Number

63. Half the second paragraph is in *Works, 10,* 16 n.
64. First paragraph is in *Works, 10,* 447 n.
65. The third paragraph is in *Works, 10,* 62 n.
66. Part of the first paragraph is in *Works, 10,* xxix n.
67. Two sentences are in *Works, 10,* 5 n.
68. Hitherto unpublished.
69. Hitherto unpublished.
70. Hitherto unpublished.
71. Hitherto unpublished.
72. Hitherto unpublished.
73. Hitherto unpublished.
74. Hitherto unpublished.
75. The first half of the second paragraph is in *Works, 9,* xxxix.
76. Hitherto unpublished.
77. A fragment from the first paragraph is in *Works, 11,* 340 n. The final paragraph is in *Works, 14,* 68 n.
78. The first paragraph is in *Works, 11,* xxvi. The fifth paragraph is in *Works, 36,* 122.
79. Hitherto unpublished.
80. Hitherto unpublished.
81. Hitherto unpublished.
82. Hitherto unpublished.
83. Hitherto unpublished.
84. Hitherto unpublished.
85. Hitherto unpublished.
86. Hitherto unpublished.
87. Hitherto unpublished.
88. Hitherto unpublished.
89. Part of the last paragraph is in *Works, 9,* xxxix.
90. Hitherto unpublished.
91. Last sentence is in *Works, 10,* xxxi.
92. Part of the third paragraph is in *Works, 10,* 38 n.
93. Two sentences are in *Works, 12,* 421 n.
94. Hitherto unpublished.
95. Second and third paragraphs are in *Works, 11,* 149 n.
96. Passages from the fifth, sixth, and seventh paragraphs are in Leon, *John Ruskin: The Great Victorian,* pp. 161–2.
97. Complete, except for the first paragraph in Leon, *John Ruskin: The Great Victorian,* pp. 162–4.
98. Excerpts from this letter are in Cook, *Life, 1,* 409; Leon, *John Ruskin: The Great Victorian,* p. 154; *Works, 10,* 38 n.; and *Works, 13,* xxii–xxiii.
99. Hitherto unpublished.
100. Last two paragraphs and postscript are in *Works, 13,* xxv.
101. Hitherto unpublished.
102. Paragraphs four and five are in *Works, 13,* xxviii–xxix. Most of the fourth

      paragraph is in Cook, *Life, 1,* 413. A brief passage from the third paragraph is in *Works, 5,* xvi. And a paraphrase of part of the fourth paragraph is in Wilenski, *John Ruskin,* p. 373.

103. Hitherto unpublished.

104. The final paragraph, except for the first sentence, is in *Works, 13,* 478 n.

105. Parts of the second and third paragraphs are in *Works, 13,* xxviii, 164 n.; and Cook, *Life, 1,* 412–13.

106. Last sentence is in *Works, 13,* xxvii.

107. Hitherto unpublished.

108. First two sentences of the second paragraph are in *Works, 10,* 466. The third and fourth sentences of the same paragraph are in *Works, 10,* 436 n.

109. Excerpts, amounting to approximately half the letter, are in Leon, *John Ruskin: The Great Victorian,* p. 156; *Works, 10,* 436 n.; and *Works, 36,* 125–6.

110. First three sentences of the opening paragraph are in *Works, 14,* 444 n. The second paragraph is in *Works, 13,* 376 n.

111. The paragraph about *Paradise Regained* is in *Works, 10,* 112 n.

112. Hitherto unpublished.

113. Hitherto unpublished.

114. Most of the second paragraph is in *Works, 10,* xxxvi.

115. The second paragraph is in Leon, *John Ruskin; The Great Victorian,* pp. 164–5.

116. Hitherto unpublished.

117. Excerpts from this letter are in *Works, 10,* xl, 466; *Works, 9,* xxxix; and *Works, 11,* xxiv.

118. Hitherto unpublished.

119. Approximately the first half is in *Works, 10,* xxxvii; the second half in *Works, 9,* xxxv–xxxvi.

120. Beginning of this letter is in *Works, 12,* xlvii.

121. Hitherto unpublished.

122. Hitherto unpublished.

123. This letter, except for the first paragraph, is in *Works, 13,* xlvii.

124. Complete in *Works, 36,* 126–129. Most of the second paragraph is in Wilenski, *John Ruskin,* p. 336.

125. Hitherto unpublished.

126. Most of this letter is in *Works, 10,* xxxi. A fragment is in Cook, *Life, 1,* 267.

127. Complete in *Works, 10,* xxxi–xxxii. There are also excerpts in Cook, *Life, 1,* 267–8; and Wilenski, *John Ruskin,* p. 56.

128. Hitherto unpublished.

129. The postscript, except for the first sentence, is in *Works, 11,* xvi.

130. Most of the first paragraph is in *Works, 10,* xxxvii. A fragment from the first paragraph is in Wilenski, *John Ruskin,* p. 359.

131. Excerpts from the second paragraph are in *Works, 10,* 346 n.

132. Hitherto unpublished.

133. Hitherto unpublished.

134. A very brief fragment is in *Works, 10,* xxxiv.

135. Hitherto unpublished.
136. Hitherto unpublished.
137. The second and third paragraphs are in *Works, 36,* 129–30.
138. A short passage is in *Works, 9,* xxxii.
139. Hitherto unpublished.
140. Hitherto unpublished.
141. Hitherto unpublished.
142. Hitherto unpublished.
143. Last paragraph is in *Works, 11,* 375 n.
144. Hitherto unpublished.
145. All, except first and last paragraphs, is in *Works, 36,* 130–2.
146. Hitherto unpublished.
147. Brief excerpts are in *Works, 10,* 301 n.; Cook, *Life, 1,* 415–16; and *Works, 13,* xxx.
148. Second paragraph is in *Works, 9,* xxxvi–xxxvii.
149. Complete in *Works, 36, 133.* Excerpts are in Wilenski, *John Ruskin,* p. 56.
150. Hitherto unpublished.
151. Hitherto unpublished.
152. Excerpts from this letter, amounting approximately to two thirds of the whole, are in *Works, 10,* xxx, 180 n., 207 n. Part of the first paragraph is in Cook, *Life, 1,* 265–6.
153. Hitherto unpublished.
154. Hitherto unpublished.
155. A fragment of a sentence in the first paragraph is in *Works, 9,* li.
156. The last half of the first paragraph is in *Works, 10,* xxxvii–xxxviii. Brief fragments from the first paragraph are in Wilenski, *John Ruskin,* p. 359.
157. Hitherto unpublished.
158. The second paragraph and the postscript are in *Works, 9,* xlii.
159. The first two paragraphs are in *Works, 36,* 134–6. Brief excerpts are in *Works, 9,* xxxvii; and Wilenski, *John Ruskin,* p. 57.
160. Second paragraph is in *Works, 10,* 466.
161. Hitherto unpublished.
162. Hitherto unpublished.
163. Hitherto unpublished.
164. Hitherto unpublished.
165. Complete in *Works, 12,* lxxx.
166. Hitherto unpublished.
167. Hitherto unpublished.
168. Hitherto unpublished.
169. Hitherto unpublished.
170. Hitherto unpublished.
171. Hitherto unpublished.
172. The second paragraph, except for the last sentence, is in *Works, 10,* 439 n. Excerpts from the same paragraph are also in Wilenski, *John Ruskin,* p. 244.
173. Complete, except for the last two paragraphs, in *Works, 12,* lxxx–lxxxi. Excerpts from the first paragraph are in Williams-Ellis, *John Ruskin,* p. 156;

Letter
Number

Leon, *John Ruskin: The Great Victorian*, p. 158; *Works, 10*, xli; and Cook, *Life, 1*, 275–6.

174. The latter half of the first paragraph is in *Works, 12*, lx.

175. Hitherto unpublished.

176. Part of the first paragraph and all the second are in *Works, 11*, l–li. The third paragraph is in Leon, *John Ruskin: The Great Victorian*, p. 165.

177. Hitherto unpublished.

178. Most of the last paragraph is in *Works, 11*, 407 n.

179. Hitherto unpublished.

180. Complete in *Works, 36*, 136–7.

181. Hitherto unpublished.

182. Second half of the first paragraph is in *Works, 12*, lxxxi.

183. Second paragraph is in *Works, 11*, 432 n.

184. Hitherto unpublished.

185. Hitherto unpublished.

186. Hitherto unpublished.

187. Hitherto unpublished.

188. Excerpts from the first paragraph are in *Works, 12*, lxxxii–lxxxiii; and Cook, *Life, 1*, 276.

189. Complete in *Works, 12*, lxxxiii–lxxxiv, except for the last sentence.

190. Hitherto unpublished.

191. Hitherto unpublished.

192. First paragraph, except for the first two sentences, is in *Works, 12*, lxxxiv.

193. Hitherto unpublished.

194. Complete in *Works, 10*, 86 n. Last sentence is in Wilenski, *John Ruskin*, p. 359.

195. Hitherto unpublished.

196. Hitherto unpublished.

197. Hitherto unpublished.

198. Hitherto unpublished.

199. Hitherto unpublished.

200. A fragment from the first paragraph is in *Works, 11*, 407 n. Half the second and most of the third paragraphs are in *Works, 10*, xxxviii–xxxix; and Cook, *Life, 1*, 270–1. Fragments from the second paragraph are in Wilenski, *John Ruskin*, p. 337.

201. Hitherto unpublished.

202. Complete in *Works, 36*, 137–9. Fragments from the first paragraph are in Wilenski, *John Ruskin*, p. 337.

203. Last sentence of the first paragraph is in *Works, 10*, xxxix; and Cook, *Life, 1*, 271–2.

204. Hitherto unpublished.

205. Complete in *Works, 10*, 352 n.

206. Hitherto unpublished.

207. Hitherto unpublished.

208. Hitherto unpublished.

209. Hitherto unpublished.

Letter
Number

210. Hitherto unpublished.
211. Hitherto unpublished.
212. Complete in *Works, 10,* 307 n., except for the first sentence.
213. Hitherto unpublished.
214. Hitherto unpublished.
215. Hitherto unpublished.
216. Excerpts from this letter are in *Works, 10,* xlvii, 327 n ; *Works, 11,* lxxxv ; and Cook, *Life, 1,* 300.
217. The fourth paragraph is in Leon, *John Ruskin: The Great Victorian,* p. 166.
218. Hitherto unpublished.
219. Hitherto unpublished.
220. Hitherto unpublished.
221. The third paragraph, except for the final sentence, is in *Works, 10,* 467.
222. Opening sentence and quatrain are in *Works, 10,* 405 n.
223. Hitherto unpublished.
224. Hitherto unpublished.
225. Hitherto unpublished.
226. Approximately one quarter of the first paragraph is in *Works, 11,* 376 n.
227. Hitherto unpublished.
228. Hitherto unpublished.
229. Hitherto unpublished.
230. Complete in *Works, 36,* 139.
231. Hitherto unpublished.
232. Hitherto unpublished.
233. Hitherto unpublished.
234. Hitherto unpublished.
235. Last sentence of the first paragraph and a fragment from the last sentence of the second paragraph are in *Works, 10,* xli, and *Works, 11,* lx, respectively. There is also a fragment from the second paragraph in Wilenski, *John Ruskin,* p. 373.
236. Hitherto unpublished.
237. The last half of the third paragraph is in *Works, 12,* lxi.
238. Hitherto unpublished.
239. Hitherto unpublished.
240. Hitherto unpublished.
241. Hitherto unpublished.
242. Hitherto unpublished.
243. First half is in *Works, 11,* xxv.
244. The first paragraph, except for the final sentence and a fragment of the first sentence, is in *Works, 10,* 19 n.
245. Hitherto unpublished.
246. Hitherto unpublished.
247. Hitherto unpublished.
248. Hitherto unpublished.
249. Hitherto unpublished.
250. Hitherto unpublished.

Letter
Number

251. Hitherto unpublished.
252. Various fragments, amounting to most of the letter, are in Williams-Ellis, *John Ruskin*, p. 149; *Works, 10,* xxv–xxvi; *Works, 12,* 15 n; and Cook, *Life, 1, 263.*
253. Excerpts from the last paragraph are in *Works, 10,* xxxii–xxxiii; Cook, *Life, 1, 268;* and Wilenski, *John Ruskin,* p. 56.
254. One sentence is in *Works, 12,* 15.
255. One sentence is in Leon, *John Ruskin: The Great Victorian,* p. 153.
256. Hitherto unpublished.
257. Complete in *Works, 36,* 140.
258. Hitherto unpublished.
259. Hitherto unpublished.
260. Hitherto unpublished.
261. Hitherto unpublished.
262. Hitherto unpublished.
263. Second paragraph is in Leon, *John Ruskin: The Great Victorian,* p. 168.
264. Hitherto unpublished.
265. Part of the second paragraph is in Leon, *John Ruskin: The Great Victorian,* p. 168.
266. Hitherto unpublished.
267. One sentence from the first paragraph is in Leon, *John Ruskin: The Great Victorian,* p. 168.
268. Hitherto unpublished.
269. Hitherto unpublished.
270. Hitherto unpublished.
271. Hitherto unpublished.
272. Most of the final paragraph is in Leon, *John Ruskin: The Great Victorian,* p. 168.
273. Hitherto unpublished.
274. Hitherto unpublished.
275. Hitherto unpublished.
276. Hitherto unpublished.
277. Hitherto unpublished.
278. Hitherto unpublished.

INDEX

Acland, Lady, 99
Acland, Arthur, 199
Acland, Sir Henry Wentworth, 82, 99, 100, 169, 199
Albert, Archduke, 65
Alexander, Mrs., xvi
Alexander, Francesca, xvi
Alison, William Pulteney, 166
Allen, Mr., 89
Allingham, William, 142
Allnutt, Abel, 126, 198
Amazon, 219
American Art Union, 24, 40
Archaeological and Architectural Society, 55
Arco, Mme., 276
Armstrong, Sir Walter, 107, 117, 126
Armytage, J. C., 1, 2, 177, 221, 222
Arnold, Matthew, 1
Art Journal, 16, 174
Art Union of Edinburgh, 196
Artemisia, 13
Athenaeum, 6, 7
Atlantic Monthly, 1
Atlay, J. B., 99

Barker, Rev. W. Gibbs, 93
Barnes, Lady, 180, 196
Barry, Sir Charles, 219
Beaumont, Sir George, 120, 218
Beckford, William, 35, 308
Beever, Mary, xiv
Beever, Susan, xiv
Bellini, Giovanni, 162
Bennett, W. C., 273
Beppo (gondolier of the Ruskins), 29, 70, 73
Bible, 18, 123, 132, 182, 244, 245, 246, 249; *I Corinthians,* 152; *Daniel,* 150, 234; *Deuteronomy,* 242; *Ecclesiastes,* 37; *Exodus,* 259; *Ezekiel,* 149, 150, 162, 185; *Hebrews,* 149; *Hosea,* 253; *Isaiah,* 125, 149; *Job,* 18, 21, 30, 49, 60, 68, 80, 102; *John,* 119, 149, 246, 254; *Joshua,* 93; *Luke,* 153, 251; *Matthew,* 102, 249, 254; *Proverbs,* 30, 60, 130, 164; *Psalms,* 18, 26, 30, 31, 59, 119, 248; *Revelations,* 150; *II Samuel,* 59; *I Thessalonians,* 247

Bicknell, E., 118, 126, 146, 148, 212, 222
Binney, Mr., 83
Bishop, M. C., 43
Blackwood's Magazine, 3, 63, 66, 68, 75, 82, 83, 88, 201, 217, 218, 279
Blagden, Isa, xvii
Block, Mr., 5
Blumenthal, Carlo, 9, 21, 45, 81, 93, 94, 100, 271, 281, 287, 288, 303, 307
Bolding, Miss, 265
Bolding, P., 265
Bonifazio, 294
Boucher, Mr., 135
Bowerswell Papers, xviii, 86, 105, 108
Boxall, William, 82
Boys, T. S., 3, 78, 91, 182
Brayley, Edward, 91
Bronte, Charlotte, 1
Brooke, Stopford, 189, 195
Brougham, Lord, 21
Brown, Mr., 87
Brown, Dr. John, 5, 45
Brown, Rawdon, 1, 6, 33, 35, 39, 54, 70, 88, 123, 255–6, 276, 290, 304, 305
Browning, Robert, xvii
Buccleuch, Duke of (Walter Francis Montagu-Douglas-Scott), 282
Buchanan, J., 25
Buckland, Mrs. William, 129
Builder, 41, 43, 44, 50, 63, 66, 67
Bulwer-Lytton, Edward, 68, 217, 218
Bunsen, Baron Christian, 243
Bunyan, John, 259
Burke, Edmund, 259
Butler, Mr., 55
Byron, Lord, xi, 86, 257

Cadorin, Giuseppi, 153
Caracci, Annibale, 56
Caracci, Lodovico, 56
Carlyle, Thomas, 55, 247
Caxton, Pisistratus, pseudonym, *see* Bulwer-Lytton
Cervantes, 79
Chalon, John James, 238
Chantrey, Francis, 86
Charles, Archduke, 65, 154
Charles Ferdinand, Archduke, 154, 230

323